DUBLIN: PRINTED BY M'GLASHAN AND GILL, 50, UPPER SACKVILLE-STREET.

PREFACE.

Tuille feasa ar Eirinn óiġ— AN ADDITION OF KNOWLEDGE ON HOLY IRELAND:—These were the first words of Gilla-na-Neeve O'Heeren, when he undertook to complete the description of Ireland, which his predecessor, John O'Dugan, had left unfinished; and they form a very suitable motto for the book I now offer to the notice of the public. For this book completes the work that was only half accomplished by the first series of "The Origin and History of Irish Names of Places."

When I first took in hand to write a book on Irish Local Names, I thought I could grasp the whole subject in a single volume; and in the attempt to do so, I compressed as much matter into the First Series as any readable book of the size could conveniently hold. I found, however, after it was written, that I had used little more than half my materials, and that there were many things requiring elucidation, which I had not been able so much as to glance at.

The first book was received favourably, much more so, indeed, than I had ever dared to anticipate; and this encouraged me to continue the work. The result is the present volume; and I earnestly hope it may be found as worthy of public favour as its predecessor.

These two volumes comprise what I have to say concerning Irish Local Names; for I have noticed all the principal circumstances that were taken advantage of by the people of this country to designate places; and have explained and illustrated, as far as lay in my power, the various laws of name-formation, and all the important root-words used in building up the structure.

I have employed throughout this volume the methods of investigation described in the first chapter of the First Series, rendered, I may be permitted to hope, less liable to error by stricter precautions, closer investigation, and more experience. In that chapter I enumerated my principal sources of information, and I need not repeat them here. Only I think I ought to mention once more that chief among them are the works of O'Donovan, especially his magnificent edition of "The Annals of the Four

Masters," which no one can do without who wishes to study Irish literature, history, or topography; and those of the Rev. Dr. Reeves, which seem to exhaust every subject they touch on. I have re-read every page of these, with what profit the reader may judge by the number of references to them in this book. I have also derived much information from the recently published Lectures of O'Curry on the manners and customs of the ancient Irish, edited by W. K. Sullivan, Ph. D.

It would have been extremely interesting to compare our place-names with those of other countries, and to point out curious parallels and instances of striking similarity of laws. Opportunities for doing so occurred in almost every page of this book; but I thought it better to adhere to the plan pursued in the First Series—viz., to confine myself to what I understood best, the local names of my own country, leaving to other hands the work of comparison and generalisation.

I have now to perform the pleasant duty of acknowledging the help of my literary friends. The Rev. William Reeves, D.D.; the Rev. Thaddeus O'Mahony, D. D.; and William M. Hennessy, Esq., M.R.I.A., three men profoundly skilled in the subject here treated of, read my proof-sheets; not a mere superficial glance, but a close and critical perusal, that made it very hard for an incorrect statement or any error of consequence to pass unnoticed. They were, moreover, always ready to assist and advise whenever I found it necessary to ask for their opinions on special points. It is almost needless to add that though I often ventured to dissent from their views, yet in numerous cases their criticisms led to important modifications.

DUBLIN, *March*, 1875.

CONTENTS.

IRISH NAMES OF PLACES.

CHAPTER I.

THE GROWTH OF WORDS.

THERE are many terminations or suffixes, in the Irish, as in other languages, by which various new words are formed from one root, growing out like the branches of a tree from the same stem. It is not necessary in this place to enter on an examination of all these terminations; I intend to notice merely those that are found in our local names, to explain their meanings as far as I can, and to illustrate their use by examples. By a careful study of their laws, their combinations, and their various changes of form, we are often enabled to explain the formation of names which would otherwise be puzzling or unintelligible.

An attentive examination of the terminations of the Irish language would have saved many etymologists, ancient as well as modern, from error: for they have in numerous cases mistaken mere postfixes for separate roots; and have made compounds of words that are in reality simple, by slightly altering the old authentic forms to suit their own theories. One of the best examples of this deceptive process is Clogher, already examined (see First Series). Flann of the Monastery resolves the name of the ancient palace of *Aileach* (see Ellagh, 1st Ser.) into *ail*, a stone, and *uch*, a sigh; and Michael O'Clery, one of the Four Masters, derives the same name (which is applied to a circular stone fortress) from *ail*, a stone, and *teach*, a house—*ail-theach*, stone house—a conjecture which looks plausible enough. But they are both undoubtedly in error; for the *each*, as O'Curry remarks (Lectures, II., 153), is nothing more than the suffix *ach:—aileach*, stony, a stony edifice. *Erin* has been resolved into *Iar-in*, western land; but the *n* is a mere grammatical termination; and the most ancient written form of the name is *Eriu*, of which the genitive is *Erenn*, dative *Erinn*.

Several of the following postfixes have not been noticed before; but I take them as I find them in names, and it is our business to show how they pervade the language, and if possible to account for them. How far some of them may be compounds, or how far some of the letters composing them may be the result of mere phonetic change rather than of etymological descent, may admit of question. The whole subject would repay a further examination, and it would be interesting to compare the Irish suffixes with their cognates in other Indo-European languages; but what I have said in this chapter will, I hope, be considered quite sufficient for the purpose I have in hands.

Before proceeding further it is necessary to notice a peculiarity of Irish pronunciation, which often modifies words by the addition of letters having no signification. There are certain consonants which in the Irish language do not coalesce in sound when they come together in a word, so that when they are pronounced, a short vowel is heard between them—a sort of phonetic buffer—to prevent the disagreeable clash of two incompatible consonantal sounds. When for instance *sean* [shan] old, is joined to *caiseal* [cashel], a circular stone fort, a short vowel sound is uttered between the *n* and the *c*, and the compound—*Sean-chaiseal*, old stone fort—is pronounced in four syllables, Shanacashel, the name of some places in Cork and Kerry. Sometimes this vowel does not appear in anglicised names, as in Shancashlaun, old castle, in the parish of Kilmaganny, in Kilkenny. It is unnecessary to illustrate this principle any further here, as numerous examples of its operation will be found in the names occurring in this and the next chapter. (See also O'Donovan's Irish Grammar, p. 57.)

Ach, *lach*, *nach*, *rach*, *tach*, *trach*, *seach*. All these postfixes have a collective signification when placed after nouns, and generally convey the sense of "full of," "abounding in," much the same as the English postfixes *ful*, *y*, and *ous*. In Irish writings, especially if they be ancient, these terminations are often written *ech*, *lech*, &c.; and sometimes, in compliance with a grammatical custom, they are changed to *each*, *leach*, &c.; but these changes do not influence the anglicised forms.

Ach. This is the most common of all Irish terminations, and its most usual form in anglicised names is *agh*, which is sounded with a strong guttural by the people, but pronounced *ăh* by those who cannot sound the guttural. *Scart* means a brake or scrubby place; and Scartagh, the name of a place near Clonakilty in Cork, signifies a place covered with brakes—a bushy spot. From *draighen* [dreen] the blackthorn or sloe bush, we have *draighnech*, a place abounding in blackthorns; and this again compounded with *cill*, church, gives *Cill-draighnech* (so written in the Irish Calendars), the church of the sloe-bushes. It was one of the churches of St. *Ernin* or *Mernoc* (died, A.D. 635) who is mentioned by Adamnan in his Life of St. Columba, and who gave name to Inchmarnock and to the two Kilmarnocks in Scotland. This church has left its name on a townland, now called Kildreenagh, in the parish of Dunleckny in Carlow, near Bagenalstown.

In the parish of Kilrossanty in Waterford, there is a valley into which several glens converge, each carrying a stream from the surrounding mountains. The word *comar* or *cummer*, in one of its significations, is applied to the meeting of streams or glens; and this valley has got the very appropriate name of Comeragh, a place of *comars* or confluences. Moreover it was in former days an important place, and as such, gave name to the Comeragh mountains by which it is surrounded. The river that flows from Lough Derriana to Lough Currane, near Ballynaskelligs bay in Kerry, is called Cummeragh, the river of the glens or confluences.

In accordance with the principle examined in the First Series (Part I. Chap. II., sect. vii.), this termination very often appears in the Irish oblique form, *aigh*, which is pronounced like the English postfix *y*, and is often changed to it in anglicised names. *Abhal* [oul] is an apple, or an apple tree; Ouley (Irish *Abhalaigh*) a place full of apple trees, the name of a townland near Ballyhaise in Cavan, and of two others in Down, one near Saintfield, and the other three miles from Rathfriland.

The termination *ach* is often added on to a word for no apparent reason except to form "a sort of finish," without in any way changing the meaning of the word; but it is probable that this is a remnant of an old formation, whose proper use has been lost in the course of ages. Thus *smól*, a thrush, is in the spoken language more generally called *smólach; stór* (treasure) is often made *stórach*, as in the common term of endearment, *astórach*. *Lios* [lis] a fort, is occasionally lengthened to *liosach*, as we see it in Lissaghmore (great fort) in the parish of Agivey in Derry; and in Lissaghanedan near Ardagh in Longford, the fort of the face or hill-brow. *Dun* is similarly augmented in Doonaghboy near Kilkee in Clare, the yellow *dun* or fort—yellow probably from furze blossoms.

Lach. This has still the same general meaning—"abounding in;" but some of the following examples will show that like *ach*, it is occasionally affixed to words without adding much, or anything, to the meaning. Its most correct anglicised form is *lagh*, and we find this in such names as Muclagh, a place of *mucs* or pigs, Broclagh, a place frequented by *brocs* or badgers (See 1st Ser. Part II., c. VII.). Near Edgeworthstown in the county Longford, there is a townland called Cranalagh; here the short *a* is inserted in accordance with the principle explained at page 3; and the name signifies a place full of *cranns* or trees. Garravlagh, the name of a place in the parish of Tagheen in Mayo, signifies rough or coarse land, from *garbh* [garrav], rough.

This affix more commonly appears in an oblique

form (*laigh*, pron. lee); as in Garrifly in Fermanagh and Monaghan, which is the same as the name last mentioned; Cranally in the parish of Abbeylara in Longford, the same as Cranalagh. Brackly in Armagh and Monaghan is the same as Bracklagh in other counties, and signifies a speckled place (*breac*, speckled); Edentrumly in the parish of Clonallan in Down, south-east of Newry (*edan*, a brow, *trom*, the elder), is the hill brow of the elder trees.

Nach: usual anglicised forms, *nagh*, *ney* and *ny*. This postfix is well exhibited in Lougharnagh, a townland near Galway bay in the north-west of the barony of Kiltartan, anciently one of the seats of the family of O'Heyne: for the Irish form we have the authority of Mac Firbis (Hy F. p. 68), who writes it *Luacharnach*, meaning rushy land, from *luachair*, rushes. Another very good illustration is Sawnagh, the name of a place near Portumna in Galway; *Samhnach*, a place abounding in *samh* [saw] or sorrel. Bracknagh, Brackenagh (vowel sound inserted—page 3), and Brackney, the names of many places in various counties, same meaning as Bracklagh—a speckled place (from *breac*). In the parishes of Lackagh and Rathangan in Kildare, there are two townlands called Mynagh; and in Meath, Tyrone, and Cavan, there are several places called Moynagh; all meaning a level place, from *magh*, a plain; while with the diminutive, the name becomes Moynaghan (small level spot) near Irvinestown in Fermanagh. From *mothar* [moher] a thicket or a ruin of a building, comes Mohernagh near Shanagolden in Limerick, a place of thickets or ruins. In the parish of Moynoe in Clare, four miles north of the village of Scarriff, there is a mountain called Turkenagh, the name of which is derived from *torc*, a boar, and signifies a resort of wild boars; like Muckenagh, from *muc*, a pig, Brockenagh, from *broc*, a badger (see these in 1st Ser.). Exactly in the same way is formed the name of Ushnagh Hill, in the parish of Conry in Westmeath, celebrated in ancient Irish history—the point where the provinces met, and where King *Tuathal* the Acceptable built a palace and established a fair in the first century. In the oldest authorities the name is spelled *Uisnech*, which comes from *os*, a fawn (inflected to *uis* by a well known orthographical rule, just as it is in the proper name *Oisin*) and signifies a place of fawns. The *Dinn-seanchas* indeed accounts for the name differently (see O'Curry—Lectures, I. 191), but the story there told is quite worthless as an authority, so far as the etymology of the name is concerned. There is another place with this name, now called Usnagh, in the parish of Clogherny in Tyrone.

Rach: anglicised forms *ragh* and *ry*. Numerous examples might be cited of its use in the Irish language: but it will be sufficient to quote the term *maighrech*, used by O'Heeren (page 96, verse 6) to signify level land, from *magh*, a plain.

South of Millstreet in Cork, is the well-known range called the Boggeragh hills (vowel sound inserted between *g* and *r*—page 3), whose name is sufficiently descriptive, signifying a soft or boggy place. Those who visit Lough Gill near Sligo cannot fail to notice the demesne of Cleaveragh near the lake, about a mile from the town, whose name indicates, either that basket makers lived and grew osiers for their trade there at some former time, or that people used hurdles or rude wickerwork bridges to cross the river or the marshy spots near it: *cliabh* [cleeve] a basket or hurdle. Cleavry in the parish of Kilmacallen in the same county, and Clievragh near Listowel in Kerry, have the same origin; Drumcleavry in Roscommon, near the village of Drumsna, the ridge of the baskets or hurdles. Foydragh in the parish of Aghavea, Fermanagh, signifies literally a place of sods (*fód*, a sod), i. e. a spot whose surface is smooth and grassy.

Tach. This Irish postfix is not as common as the preceding, but it occurs often enough to assert its place as a distinct termination. In that part of the parish of Taghboy lying in the county Galway, there is a townland called Clytagh, a name which means a place of dykes or fences—*cladh* [cly], a dyke. A little stream called Oiltiagh runs down the slope of Table Mountain into the Glen of Imaile in Wicklow, and joins the Slaney near its source: the name signifies cliffy, from *aill*, a cliff. Reatagh in the parish of Fenoagh in Waterford, a little below Carrick-on-Suir, means plain, open, or cleared land, from *reidh* [rea], a plain or open place. The oblique form appears in Kilrossanty, a parish in Waterford, the name of which grew up in this way:—*ros*, a wood; *rossan* (dimin.), little wood or brushwood; *rossantach*, a place overgrown with underwood; Kilrossanty, the church of the woody or shrubby place.

Trach. This termination occurs very often in the forms *tragh* and *tra*, and in the oblique form *try*. *Cuileanntrach* is a name frequently used in the Irish annals, signifying a place of *cuilenn* or holly (see Cullentra, 1st Ser.). Fostragh in Longford and Roscommon, a wilderness (from *fás*—see 1st Ser.), the same as Fastry, the name of two townlands in Monaghan. From *lis*, a fort, we have *liostrach* (like *liosach*, p. 5), and this again goes to form Listraghee in the parish of Clonbroney in Longford, the fort of *Aedh* [Ay] or Hugh; as well as Listraheagny near the town of Monaghan, *Egnach's* or Eagny's fort. The oblique form is seen in Coultry near Santry in Dublin, a place of *colls* or hazels.

Seach [shagh]. This is not very common in local names, but it is often used as a kind of feminine termination. Thus from *Gall*, a foreigner, we have *Gaillseach*, which is constantly used in Irish writings to signify an Englishwoman; and this again is reproduced in Ballynagalshy (*Baile-na-Gaillsighe*) the name of a townland in the parish of Castlejordan in Meath, the town of the Englishwoman. But *seach* is in many cases used in much the same manner as the preceding terminations. *Bán* signifies a green field; and *Báinseach* means a level spot covered with grass, which gives name to all those places now called Bansha and Banshy; Derrynabaunshy in the parish of Attymass, Mayo, and Coolnabanch (shortened from Coolnabanshy) near Clonaslee in Queen's County, the oak-wood, and the hill-back, of the grassy plain. Kelsha near Baltinglass in Wicklow is the anglicised form of *Coillseach*, underwood or brushwood, from *coill*, a wood.

I have classed all the preceding terminations together, because they correspond generally in meaning, and because the first of them, *ach*, forms the ending of all the rest. But there are some others, differing entirely in formation, and somewhat different in meaning, which I will now examine.

Char or *chor*. This postfix conveys a cumulative sense, which is well seen in *Bennchor*, a collection of peaks or gables, from *beann*, a peak (see Banagher, 1st Ser.). Exactly similar in formation to this, is Cranagher, in the parish of Clooney in Clare, which is anglicised from *Crannchar*, as Banagher from *Bennchar*, and signifies a place of *cranns* or trees.

So also from *grean* [gran] gravel, we have *granagher*, a gravelly place, which forms again Gortnagranagher in Mayo and Limerick, the gravelly field (*gort*). There is a small river in the county Leitrim, flowing from Belhavel lake into the north-west corner of Lough Allen; it was formerly called the Duff, but it is now known by the equivalent name, Diffagher, which very well represents the sound of *Duibheachair* (*ea*, vowel sound, inserted), black river, from *dubh*, black. The celebrated plague called the yellow sickness, which swept over the British Islands and the Continent in the seventh century, is sometimes called *buidheachair* in the Irish annals. This word is reproduced in the name of Cloonboygher near Carrigallen in Leitrim; but here it is probable that the term was applied to the yellow colour of the water or of the mud; and that the name means the meadow of the yellowish water (*buidhe*, yellow).

Bhar, *bhre*. These two terminations, one of which appears to be only a varied form of the other, have much the same meaning as the last, that is, they convey a cumulative sense. The second form appears in *Dairbhre*, a place of oaks (*dair*, an oak), which has been already discussed (see Darrery, 1st Ser.).

From the first, *bhar*, is formed Darver (*Darbhar*), the name of a parish in Louth, which also means a place producing oaks. *Duille* [dullia] signifies the leaf of a tree; *duilleabhar* [dillaver, dillure], an Irish word in constant use, foliage: Lisdillure in the parish of Drum in Roscommon, south-west from Athlone, must have received its name from an old fort covered with leafy trees—*Lios-duilleabhair*, the *lis* of the foliage. The word itself gives name to the river Delour joining the Nore west of Mountrath, which, judging from the name, must have formerly flowed through a well-wooded district. In the north, the word is usually shortened to *dillur:* Tattendillur near Maguire's Bridge in Fermanagh, signifies the *tate* or field of the foliage; Corradillar in the parish of Aghalurcher in the same county, leafy little hill (*cor*). *Duille* is also used to signify leafiness, in Knockadilly in the parish of Killincooly in Wexford, the hill of the foliage; while the adjective form *duilleach* (formed by adding the termination *ach*, for which see page 3), signifying leafy, a leafy place, gives name to the lake and townland of Dillagh, situated about two miles south of the village of Bellananagh in Cavan.

Re, *aire*. By an inspection of some of the following examples, it will appear that the second of these is derived from the first merely by the insertion of the phonetic vowel (p. 3): both convey a cumulative sense, which is seen very clearly in the word *belre*, speech, from *bel*, the mouth. There is a townland called Fodry on the Atlantic coast within two miles of Loop Head in Clare, the name of which is pronounced *Fóidre* by the people, and signifies a place with a smooth green surface, literally a place of *fōds* or sods. Craggera in the parish of Kilgarvan in Mayo, is a mispronunciation for *Cnagaire* [Knaggera: *k* sounded] a hard little hill; and this is derived from *Cnag*, a knob, which gives name to the hill of Knag over the north shore of Lough Currane in Kerry: Mira near Athenry in Galway, *Maighre*, a level place, from *magh*, a plain. Crory, the name of some places in Wexford, and Cruary near Clonakilty in Cork, are both anglicised from *Cruaidhre*, signifying hard land, which itself is derived from *cruadh* [croo], hard. While St. Patrick sojourned among the tribe of *Hy-Tuirtre* on the west side of Lough Neagh, we are told in the Tripartite Life, that he founded seven churches in the neighbourhood, one of which is called in the old records *Domhnach-fhainre*. The latter part means sloping land, from *fán*, a slope; and the whole name signifies the church of the slope. In anglicising it, the aspirated *f* has disappeared, and the church is now called Donaghenry, and has given name to a parish in the east of Tyrone, near Lough Neagh.

R. The letter *r* (preceded by a vowel if necessary for pronunciation—p. 3) is often added to nouns to give a collective or cumulative signification, as in *clochar*, a stony place, from *cloch*, a stone (see Clogher in First Series). From *bo*, a cow, comes *buar*, kine, "cattle of the cow kind," a word in constant use; and from this again, we have Drumbure in the parish of Currin, south of Clones in Monaghan, the *drum* or hill-ridge of the cows; which by the addition of *aigh* (gen. of *ach*—page 4) gives Drumboory, having the same meaning, the name of places in Cavan, Fermanagh, and Monaghan. From *tul*, a little hill, we have Tullerboy, yellow hills, in the parish of Athlacca in Limerick; *bruach*, a border, gives us Brougher (i. e. limits or borders) in Mayo, Fermanagh, and Sligo. From *cnoc*, a hill, is derived *knocker*, which we find in Knockergrana in the parish of Clonca, Donegal, ugly hilly place (*grana*, ugly); and in Knockersally in the parish of Ballyboggan in Meath, the hill or hilly place of sallows.

In some of the preceding names, and others of this class, the letter *r* appears, like *ach*, to add little or nothing to the meaning.

S. This is a usual termination for abstract nouns; as for instance in *aeibhneas* [eevnas], delight, from *aeibhinn* [eevin], delightful; *maitheas* [mahas], goodness, from *maith* [mah], good. It occurs sufficiently often in local names (with a vowel sound preceding when necessary—p. 3) to deserve rank as a distinct termination; but in the greater number of those names in which I have found it, I am unable to perceive that it indicates abstract quality. Often it seems to have something of a collective meaning like *r*; but in many cases it appears to have been used for no definite purpose at all. *Bearna* is the usual word for a gap; but we have the authority of Irish MSS. for another form of the word, namely *bearnas*, which appears to differ in nowise from the first; and the two words *corcach* and *corcas*, both of which are in constant use to signify a marsh, are equally identical in meaning. Here, however, the conclusion we ought to draw is, that this letter as a termination had once a meaning which it has lost.

Pullis is the name of a townland in the parish of Donagh, county Monaghan, near Glasslough; and it means a place full of holes, from *poll*, a hole. *Leamh* [lav] is the elm tree; and Cloonlavis in the parish of Knock in Mayo, is the *cloon* or meadow of the elms. Magherascouse is the name of a place near Comber in Down, which very well conveys the sound of *Machaire-sceamhais*, the field of the polypody or wall fern, the Irish name for this herb being *sceamh* [scav, scow]. *Ragam* is the Irish word for horse-radish; and Ragamus, the name of a place near Knocklong in Limerick, signifies, according to the old people, a place abounding in horse-radish.

On the coast of Kerry, west of Tralee, just at the base of Brandon hill, there is a remarkable basin-shaped hollow, shut in by precipices on all sides except the north, where it looks out on the sea; and it is universally known by the name of Sauce. A plentiful crop of sorrel grows at the bottom of the basin as well as on the high land over it, and this evidently gave origin to the name, which is formed exactly like the two last:—*samh* [sauv or saw], sorrel: *samhas* [sauce], a place abounding in sorrel. This word is not given in O'Reilly, but there is one approaching it very nearly, namely *samhsa* [saussa], which is explained as meaning sorrel. I find *samhas* in one other name, though much disguised, viz. Lubitavish on the river Dall, a mile from Cushendall in Antrim; a name which exactly represents the sound of *Lub-a'-tsamhais*, the *loop* or winding of the sorrel, so called from a remarkable winding of the little river. In this name, the *s* is eclipsed by *t*, and the *mh* is represented by *v*, as is usual in the north. It is worthy of remark that at the distance of a mile and a half from this townland, there is another called Savagh—a place producing sorrel.

Many other names are formed in a similar way, of which the following will be a sufficient illustration. *Cruadh* [croo] means hard; and *cruadhas*, signifying hardness or hard land, is represented in pronunciation by Croase in the parish of Ballyconnick in Wexford. In like manner, Garroose (near Bruree in Limerick) signifies rough land, from *garbh* [garrav], rough; and similar to both is the formation of the common townland named Brittas, which means speckled land, from *brit*, speckled.

D. This letter is often added on to the end of words, sometimes with a collective meaning, sometimes with scarcely any meaning at all; and in anglicised names it is often replaced by *t*. The Irish word *cael* signifies narrow, and in the anglicised form *keal*, it is applied to a narrow stream or a narrow stripe; but in Kerry, between Listowel and Athea, it is modified to Kealid, which is now the name of a townland. Croagh is a common term denoting a stack-like hill; but there is a hill in the parish of Moyrus in Galway, called Croaghat, which is the same word with the addition of *t*.

In like manner is formed the name of the Bonet river in Leitrim, flowing into Lough Gill through Drumahaire and Manorhamilton, which is called in Irish *Buanaid*, signifying the lasting river. For the Irish seem to have been fond of applying the word *buan*, lasting, to rivers. In the Vision of Cahirmore for example, in the Book of Leinster, the Slaney is called *Sír-buan Sláne*, the ever-lasting Slaney. In exactly the same way, from *dian*, strong, vehement, or swift, we have *Dianaid*, the strong or swift stream, the name of a river in Tyrone, flowing into the Foyle below Strabane, which is now called Burn Dennet. There is a lake near Lough Shindilla on the road from Clifden to Oughterard in Galway, called Lough Oorid, which signifies the lake of the cold or moist land, from *uar*, cold.

It is hard to see that this termination carries any modification of meaning in the following names. The word *tearmann* [pron. tarramon in some places] signifies church land; but in the parish of Stradbally in Galway, south-east of Oranmore, *d* takes the place of *n* in the townland of Tarramud; and the same change takes place in Corrantarramud, in the parish of Monivea, same county, the round hill (*cor*) of the *termon*. It may be suspected indeed that in these names the *d* is a remnant of the old spelling, *tearmand*. *Fán* signifies a slope, and probably from this we have Fanad, the name of a district west of Lough Swilly in Donegal, written by the Irish authorities, *Fanad*, and signifying sloping ground; the same name as Fanit, in the parish of Kilvellane near Newport in

Tipperary. It seems certain that the *d* in these names is a termination, whether they be derived from *fán*, a slope, or not. In some parts of Ireland the people interpret *tap* as meaning a round mass or lump; from which the hill of Topped near Enniskillen derives its name, signifying a round hill. From the same root comes *Tapachán* by the addition of the diminutive termination *chán* (see next chapter), with the vowel sound inserted before it (see p. 3); which, in the anglicised form Tappaghan, is the name of another hill about eight miles north of Kesh in the same county, with the same general meaning as Topped. With the diminutive *an*, we have Toppan, a little islet in the eastern end of Lough Nilly in Fermanagh, near where the river Arney enters the lake. We must no doubt refer to the same root Taplagh, which is formed by adding *lach* (see p. 5), the name of a townland and small lake in the parish of Donaghmoyne in Monaghan, about five miles north of Carrickmacross, a place of lumps or masses, or as the natives interpret it, a place of rubbish.

Compound Terminations. The postfixes *nach*, *lach*, and *tach*, are often found combined with *r*, forming the compound terminations *rnach*, *rlach*, and *rtach*, of which the first occurs oftener than the others. *Smut* is a log or tree-stump; and Smutternagh near Boyle in Roscommon, signifies a place where there are many old trunks of trees—the remains of the wood which once clothed the place, the branches having withered, or having been lopped off for firing. *Clog*, a bell, a skull or head; Cloggernagh, the name of two townlands in Roscommon, and Claggarnagh in Mayo and Galway, both signify either a round bell-like or skull-like hill, or a place full of round hills. One of these townlands (in the parish of

Lisonuffy in Roscommon) is otherwise called Bellmount, which is not a bad attempt at translation, though calculated to convey a false impression as to the origin of the name. Brackernagh near Ballycanew in Wexford, speckled land, from *breac* [brack], speckled; Tullyskeherny, the name of two townlands in the north of Leitrim, the hill (*tully*) of the *sceaghs* or bushes.

Char and *nach* are combined so far as I know only in one particular compound, *sailchearnach*, which means a place growing sallows (*sail*); and for the correct form of this we have the authority of the Four Masters, when they mention a place called *Cluain-sailchearnaigh* (the *cloon* or meadow of the osier plantation), which is now a townland with the modernised name Cloonselherny, in the parish of Kilkeedy, county Clare. The same word is found in Annaghselherny in Leitrim, a little north-east of Carrick-on-Shannon, the *annagh* or marsh of the sallows.

Besides the preceding there are many other postfixes in the Irish language: but they do not occur sufficiently often in local names to require examination here. There is another class of terminations, viz., diminutives, which are so important that I think it necessary to treat of them in a separate chapter.

CHAPTER II.

DIMINUTIVES.

A DIMINUTIVE termination is a syllable that indicates smallness. The syllables *let* and *kin* for instance, are English diminutives:—streamlet, a little stream; mannikin, a little man. So in Irish the terminations *een* and *oge* are diminutives: *gort*, a field; Ballygorteen in Kilkenny and Tipperary, the town of the little field; *cullen*, holly; Cullenoge near Tara hill, north-east of Gorey in Wexford, little holly, or a place of holly trees.

Before proceeding to enumerate the Irish diminutives, it is necessary to make a few observations regarding certain changes and extensions of their meaning and application. While smallness was the idea originally expressed—an idea that many of the diminutives still retain—the greater number became in the course of ages widened in their application, and were used to convey other and very different notions. The signification of littleness was in many cases quite forgotten, and the diminutives came ultimately to be applied without any reference to absolute or comparative size. O'Donovan remarks "that some nouns ending in [the diminutive syllables] *án* and *óg* do not always express diminutive ideas;" and he instances *copóg*, a dock or any large leaf growing on the earth; *mórán*, a great quantity; and *oileán*, an island (Ir. Gram. 333). There is a remarkable mountain in Mayo, lying a little to the west of Nephin, called from its shape, Birreencarragh: *bior* [bir] means a spit or pin—diminutive *birreen; carrach* is rugged or rough; and Birreencarragh signifies the rugged little pin, whereas it is one of the highest and largest mountains in the whole county. Numerous instances of this change of application might be adduced. It is probable, however, that in many cases like this last, the diminutive was applied by "antiphrasis or contrariety of speech"—for the Irish were much given to this manner of speaking—in the present instance a kind of playful or ironical application of a term expressing littleness to an object remarkably large; just as Robin Hood's gigantic comrade came to be called Little John.

The diminutives of personal names passed through a somewhat similar transition: from littleness they were used to express affection or endearment, a very natural extension of meaning; and now the greater number have lost all distinctive signification, though they still form a part of thousands of personal and family names.

In local names, diminutives are often added to the names of certain animals, vegetables, or minerals, and the whole word is used to designate a place abounding in one of these several objects. This usage is of old standing in the language, for we find the word *lemnat*, a diminutive of *lem*, marsh mallows, given in the St. Gall MS. (Zeuss, p. 274), as the equivalent of *malvaceus*, i. e. a place producing marsh mallows. *Dealg* [dalg, dallag] signifies a thorn, and hence a thorn bush; the diminutive *dealgan*, a thorny brake, a place producing thorns; from which are derived the names of Dalgan Demesne near Shrule in Mayo, Dalgan near Geashill in King's County, and the Dalgan river in the north of the county Galway, with the townland of Dalgin on its banks. With a vowel sound inserted (page 3), it is reproduced in the name of the little river Dalligan in Waterford, flowing into the sea a little to the east of Dungarvan—the thorn-producing river—which itself gives name to Glendalligan in the parish of Kilrossanty.

Zeuss enumerates seven diminutive particles used in the ancient Irish language, all of which he found occurring in the St. Gall manuscript, a document of the eighth century. They are:—for the masculine and neuter genders, *án*, *én*, *tat*; for the feminine, *éne*, *ne*, *nat*, *net*. Most of these have long since dropped out of use as living terminations, but we find them still forming part of innumerable words; they retain their old places, but they are lifeless and fossilised; some retaining their primitive forms unchanged, some crushed and contorted, and difficult of recognition.

I will now proceed to enumerate the diminutives given by Zeuss, and examine how far they are represented in our present names.

An. This diminutive was anciently more common than any other, especially in the formation of personal names; and it has continued in use down to the present day. The investigations of Dr. Ferguson and Dr. Graves have rendered it probable that it is the same as the termination *agni* in Ogham inscriptions: but whether *agni* is the original form, or a mere artificial extension of *án* (for the old Ogham writers often lengthened words in this way) it is impossible, in the present state of knowledge, to determine. (See Proc. R. I. A., vol. I. ser. II., p. 54). *An* is pronounced long [awn] in the south, and short in the north; and this distinction is generally, but not always, reflected in modern forms. From *cnoc*, a hill, is formed *cnocán*; and this again appears in

Knockaunbrack in Kerry and Galway, and in Knockanbrack in Tyrone, speckled little hill. There is a small lake three miles west of Downpatrick, containing a little island which has given name to the parish of Loughinisland: this name is half English, and signifies the island of the *loughan* or small lake. Loughan-Island is the present name of a little islet in the Bann, a short distance south of Coleraine, on which the Mac Quillans had formerly a fortress to command the fishery of the Lower Bann; the name is a translation of *Inis-an-lochain* (Four Masters) the island of the small lake—for the river expands here into a sort of lake; and no doubt Loughinisland in Down is a translation of the same Irish name.

In numerous cases the local name in which this diminutive occurs is formed from a personal name, to which the diminutive properly belongs. The word *bolg* was occasionally used as a personal name: thus we find the name *Bolgodhar* [Bolgower—*Bolg*, the pale-faced], and also the family name *O'Bolg*, in the Four Masters. The diminutive *Bolgan* or *Bolcan* is used much oftener than the original. St. Olcan, founder and bishop of Armoy in Antrim, who was ordained by St. Patrick, is also called Bolcan; and the townland of Bovolcan near Stonyford in the parish of Derryaghy in Antrim, which Colgan writes *Both-Bolcain* (*Bolcan's* tent or booth), was probably so called from him, the *b* being aspirated to *v* (1st Ser. Part I., c. II.). Near the church of Rasharkin in Antrim, there is a ridge of rock called Drumbulcan (*Bolcan's* ridge) which also took its name from this saint (Reeves: Eccl. Ant., p. 90). There are two townlands in Fermanagh called Drumbulcan, one near Tuam in Galway called Drumbulcaun, and with *g* used instead of *c* we have Drumbulgan in the parish of Ballyclog, Tyrone; all of which received their names from different persons called Bolcan. Another *Bolcan* left his name on Trabolgan (*Bolcan's* strand) near the mouth of Cork harbour: this place is called in the Book of Rights *Mur-Bolcan* (*Bolcan's* sea), showing that the change from *c* to *g* is modern.

On the margin of Lough Owel in Westmeath, there is a parish taking its name from a townland called Portloman, the *port* or landing place of St. Loman. This saint, whose name is a diminutive of *lom*, bare, is commemorated in O'Clery's Calendar at the 7th February, and he is said to have built a small house on an island in Lough Owel near Portloman. The ruins of the monastery which arose on the site of St. Loman's original church are still to be seen within the demesne of Portloman.

Three miles above the village of Tallaght in Dublin, on the side of Glenasmole, looking down on the river Dodder, there is a picturesque little graveyard and ruin called Kill St. Ann, or "Saint Ann's Church;" near it is "Saint Ann's Well;" and an adjacent residence has borrowed from the church the name of "Ann Mount." The whole place has been in fact quietly given over to St. Ann, who has not the least claim to it; and an old Irish saint has been dispossessed of his rightful inheritance by a slight change of name. Dalton, in his history of Dublin—apparently quoting from the Inquisitions—writes the name Killnasantan, which he absurdly translates "the church of Saint Anne." But in the *Repertorium Viride* of Archbishop Alan, we find it written Killmesantan; from which it is obvious that the *na* in Dalton's Killnasantan, which he thought was the Irish article, is really corrupted from the particle *mo*, my, so commonly prefixed as a mark of respect to the names of Irish saints (see 1st Ser. 3rd ed., p. 141). The Four Masters give us the original form of the name at A. D. 952, when they record the death of *Caenchomhrac*, abbot of the place, viz., *Cill-Easpuig-Sanctáin*, i.e. the church of Bishop Sanctan. So that the founder of this lonely church was one of the early saints—of whom several are commemorated in the calendars—called *Sanctan* or *Santan*, who no doubt fought hard in his day to clear away the pagan mists from the valley. He attained the rank of bishop; and the establishment he founded continued to flourish long after his time. The name is a diminutive on the Latin root *sanct* (holy) borrowed into the Irish. Killsantan or Killmosanctan was naturally and correctly translated in the first instance, Santan's church, which the English-speaking people, knowing nothing of Bishop Sanctan and his spiritual labours, soon converted into Saint Ann's church, the form also adopted by Dalton: and it is to be regretted that the error is perpetuated in the maps of the Ordnance Survey.

The *án* belongs to a family name in Cloonygormican, the name of a parish in Roscommon, which is written *Cluain-O' Cormacain* in the Registry of Clonmacnoise, and signifies O'Cormacan's meadow.

In the sense of "abounding in," this diminutive appears in the name of Gowran in Kilkenny. This name is written *Gabhran* in ancient Irish authorities; and in old Anglo-Irish records the place is called (with some unimportant variations of spelling) Ballygaveran. In very early times it was a residence of the kings of Ossory; and it retained its importance long after the English invasion. The word *gabhar* [gower], as I have already explained in the First Series, signifies either a steed or a goat, and it is a question which signification it bears here; but on account of the early celebrity of the place, and as it must have been constantly the scene of royal and military gatherings, we may fairly conclude that it received its name from horses rather than from goats:—*Gabhran*, a place of steeds. The same word is seen in composition in Knocknagoran near Carlingford, which by the old people of the locality is understood to mean the hill of the goats. With the termination *ach* we have other names of a like signification. One of these is Goragh near Newry, which gives the name "Goragh Wood" to a station on the northern line of railway—a place of goats (formed like Brockagh from *broc*, a badger: see this in 1st Ser.). Gorey in Wexford is the same name, only with the oblique form of the postfix, as also is Gouree near Glengarriff in Cork; and the name of the place celebrated in the Scotch song "The Lass o' Gourie," has a similar origin and meaning.

The herb coltsfoot is called *spunc* in Irish: and from this we have the name Spunkane, a townland in the parish of Dromod near Waterville lake in Kerry—a place producing coltsfoot. In the north of the county Roscommon is a little village called Ballyfarnan, the Irish name of which is *Bel-atha-fearnain* [Bellafarnan], the ford-mouth of the *fearnán* or alder plantation—a name which was originally applied to a ford, where there is now a bridge, on the little river Feorish. The correct interpretation is preserved in the name of the adjoining residence of Alderford.

En, tat, éne. These do not exist as diminutives in the modern language. It is probable that *én* and *éne* have become in many cases confounded with either *án*, or with another diminutive *ín*, of which I shall presently speak—that the former have in fact merged into one or the other of the latter. We know that the *én* of *caislén* (a castle) has been changed to *án*, for while the word is *caislén* in all old documents, it is now always written and pronounced *caisleán*. There are a few examples of the preservation of this diminutive in its purity, one of which is Slieve Rushen, now more commonly called Slieve Russell (change of *n* to *l*—1st Ser. Part I., c. II.) a mountain on the borders of Fermanagh and Cavan, near the village of Ballyconnell. The correct form of the name is *Sliabh Ruisen* (Four Masters), which means the mountain of the little wood. Of *tat* I have not been able to discover any trace in anglicised local names.

Ne. Though this has been long forgotten as a diminutive, it was formerly in very common use, and it still holds its place in many local names. The parish of Ardcavan, which occupies the extremity of a peninsula jutting into Wexford haven, opposite the town of Wexford, is called in Irish records *Airdne-Caemhain* [Ardnakevan]—Kevan's little *ard* or height; and it was so called from a monastery founded there by a St. Kevan, or dedicated to him. According to O'Clery's Calendar (pp. 143, 169), he was a brother of St. Kevin of Glendalough; their mother was named *Caemell;* and she had two other sons, *Caemhog* and *Natchaeimhe*, who are commemorated in the calendars. The place still contains the ruins of an old church. Adjoining this parish is another called Ardcolm, taking its name from an old ruined church, which is called in the Annals *Airdne-Coluim*, Colum's little height. In both these cases the diminutive particle has been lost in the process of anglicising. There is an Ardcolum in Leitrim, and an Ardcollum in the parish of Kilronan, Roscommon; but the people interpret this last name as meaning the hill of the pigeons (*colum*, a pigeon).

The original name of Delgany in Wicklow is *Dergne*, which ought to have been anglicised Dergany in accordance with the original pronunciation; but it was made Delgany by the usual change of *r* to *l* (see 1st. Ser. Part I., c. III). The full name, as we find it written in Irish authorities, is *Dergne-Mochorog;* the latter part of which was derived from *St. Mochorog*, a Briton by birth, who, like many of his countrymen, settled in Ireland in the primitive ages of the Church. He lived in the beginning of the seventh century; and it was he who attended St. Kevin of Glendalough in his last illness in the year A. D. 618. The old churchyard of Delgany (which is at the lower end of the village) marks the spot where the saint built his little church twelve hundred years ago; and a slight examination of the place will clear up the name *Dergne*. Under the surface is a reddish coloured rock covered with only a thin layer of clay, which is hardly deep enough for a grave in the churchyard. The colour is very perceptible after rain on the road outside the churchyard wall; and it is still more so when the rock is laid bare in the burial ground. This rock in fact underlies the whole of the village and the adjacent fields, and the water that trickles through it leaves a reddish deposit. So the name, which *St. Mochorog* adopted as he found it before him, accurately described the place:—*derg*, red; *Dergne*, red little spot. There are places called Dergany, Dergenagh, and Derganagh in Tyrone and Derry, all signifying red places; but the terminations are scarcely the diminutive *ne*. From *leac*, a flag-stone, we have *leicne* [leckna], a little flag—a place full of flag-stones (page 19), which gives name to Lickny in the parish of Mayne in Westmeath, not far from Castlepollard;

which also appears in Dunleckny, the name of a parish in Carlow—the fort of the flag-stones; and in Drumleckney (*Drum*, a hill-ridge) in the parish of Racavan in Antrim. Just outside the little bay of Kilkee in Clare, there is a low reef of rocks called in maps and guide books, Duggerna, but which the people pronounce, according to the Irish spelling, *Dogairne*. In this word the *g* represents a more ancient *c*; and there can be little doubt that it is derived from *docair*, difficult or obstructive (the opposite to a better known word, *socair*); *Docairne*, or Duggerna signifying a hindrance or obstruction—a very appropriate name.

In some cases this diminutive is changed to *na*, as in the proper names *Fergna*, from *ferg*, anger, and *Fiachna*, from *fiach*, a raven. This change is also seen in the name of Blarney near Cork, which is pronounced and written in Irish, *Blárna*, signifying "little field," from *blár*, a field. I have never met this word *blár* in actual use in the language, but it is given in O'Reilly, and in the Scotch Gaelic dictionaries, as meaning a field; and it is very common in the local nomenclature of Scotland in the form *blair*.

Nat or *net*. There is a pretty example of the use of this diminutive, as a term of endearment, in *Leabhar na hUidhre*. In a conversation between queen Meave and her daughter Finnabar, the latter, when addressing the former, several times calls her *máthair* or mother; but on one occasion she says:—"*Atchiusa cairptech issamag a* MATHARNAIT"—"I see a chariotman on the plain, my little-mother" (page 105 b.—lines 29, 30). It was anciently very often used in the formation of women's names; for example, St. Brendan's mother was called *Neamhnat*

[Navnat], which may be rendered *Celestilla*, little heavenly one. Through the names of women it appears in a few local names. The parish of Killasnet in Leitrim preserves the memory of the virgin saint *Osnat*, mentioned by Colgan (A. SS. p. 337), whose name signifies "little fawn" (*os*, a fawn): *Cill-Osnata*, Osnat's church. About the year A. D. 1200, Cahal O'Conor of the Red Hand, king of Connaught, founded a nunnery at a place called *Kilcreunata*, which is situated about three miles north-west of Tuam; it is now called Kilcreevanty, and there are still remaining extensive ruins of the old nunnery. The Irish form of the name, as we find it preserved in the Four Masters, is *Cill-Craebhnatt* [Kilcreevnat], Creevnat's church. *Craebhnatt* was a saint, whose name signifies little branch (*craebh*); but I do not know her history. In the north-east of Galway, there is a parish called Kilbegnet; and in the south of the same county, near Gort, is another called Kilbeacanty. The Irish form of the latter name is *Cill-Becnata*, which was anglicised like Kilcreevanty, and the place was so called from a saint *Becnat* (*bec*, small; *Becnat*, extremely little body). The patron saint of Kilbegnet bore the same name; but I am not able to say whether or no she was the same as the founder of Kilbeacanty.

Except through the medium of the names of women, I have not found this diminutive termination in local names.

So far regarding the diminutives enumerated by Zeuss. But there are several others, some of them occurring—at least in later times—quite as often as any of the preceding; and these I will now proceed to examine.

Og, *óc*, or *óc*. This was certainly used as a diminutive as early as the oldest of the manuscripts quoted by Zeuss; indeed much earlier, for we find it forming part of the names of saints who lived immediately after the time of St. Patrick—*Mochonnog*, *Dabheog*, *Dachiarog*, *Maedhog*, *Mochaemhog*, &c. *Og* also signifies young; and it was no doubt from this that it acquired its force as a diminutive; for such an extension of meaning was very natural. It is exceedingly common at the present day both in personal and local names; and is easily recognised. It is variously anglicised *og*, *oge*, *ogue*, and sometimes by the almost identical English termination *ock*. Monog in the parish of Creggan, Armagh, little *moin* or bog; Sharavogue in King's County, between Roscrea and Parsonstown, Sharvoge in the parish of Killashee in Longford; and Sharvogues, three miles from Randalstown in Antrim—all these names signify dandelion, or (p. 19) land producing dandelion (*searbh*, *searbhog*); and there are places in the counties of Meath and Louth, and one near Santry in Dublin, called Silloge, from *sail*, ozier:—ozier or sallow-bearing land.

This diminutive also often appears in the names of places through the medium of personal names. The Irish personal name represented in sound by Mogue, which is still pretty common as a man's name in Wexford and the adjoining counties, is *Maedhog*, which again is contracted from *Mo-Aedh-óg*, in which *Mo* is the equivalent of "my," *og* is the diminutive termination, while the original meaning of *Aedh* is fire (see 1st Ser. 3rd ed., p. 141: see also chap. VIII. *infra*). There is a place near Fiddown in Kilkenny, called Kilmogue, i.e. *Cill-Maedhog*, St. Mogue's Church. Kilmeague, the name of a parish and village in Kildare, is another anglicised form of *Cill-Maedhog;* for in Rawson's Statistical Survey (1807) we find it written Kilmooge, and in an Education Report of 1825, Kilmoage. The same personal name appears in Timogue, now a townland and parish in Queen's County, in which the first syllable represents *teach*, a house. There were several saints named *Maedhog*, of whom the most celebrated was *Maedhog*, first bishop of Ferns in Wexford, who died in A. D. 625; and it is not unlikely that one or all of the fore-mentioned places took their names from churches dedicated to him.

Each of the preceding names consists of only two syllables; but when fully unfolded they become much longer than one would expect. Taking the last as the type, it is *Teach-Mo-Aedh-og;* and though its proper interpretation is "Mogue's house," yet if we go back to the primary signification of the words, and make allowance for the genitive, it includes in its signification this combination:—[the]-house-of-my-little-fire. And this is an excellent illustration of the manner in which language incorporates and assimilates its materials; and smoothes down the compounds so as to form pronounceable words—something like the way in which shells, gravel, and all sorts of stony fragments, are pressed together and cemented into marble; which again is carved into various forms, and polished by the hand of man, though to the last the several materials show faintly through the surface.

In [een]. This is also an old diminutive, though sparingly used in ancient manuscripts. But it is exceedingly common in modern times; and indeed it may be said to be almost the only one that still retains its full force as a living diminutive, which it does even among the English-speaking people of every part of Ireland. Every one has heard such words as *cruiskeen*, a little *croosk* or pitcher, *Jackeen*, little Jack (a nickname for a certain class of Dublin citizens), *bohereen*, a little *boher* or road, &c. In the south it is usually pronounced long (carrig*een*); in the north short (carrig*in*).

There is a place on the west bank of the Foyle, five miles north of Lifford, called Mongavlin; but it should have been called Moygavlin, for the Irish name, as the Four Masters write it, is *Magh-gaibhlin*, the plain of the little (river) fork; from *gabhal* [*gaval*], a fork, diminutive *gaibhlin*. Gowlin, another modern form of *gaibhlin*, is the name of a place near Dingle in Kerry, and of another in the parish of St. Mullins, Carlow, near Graiguenamanagh. From *maghera*, a plain, is formed Maghereen, little plain, near Macroom in Cork; Boggeen, little soft spot, is the name of a place on the hill of Howth; Luggacurren in Queen's County, well known for its great moat or fort, is in Irish, *Lug-a'-chuirrin*, the hollow of the little *curragh* or marsh. We have this diminutive also introduced very often with personal names:— Ballydaheen is a well-known suburb of Mallow, whose name means the town of little *Dau* or David, and there are several other townlands of this name in the same county and in Limerick. Ballyfaudeen, and Ballypadeen, are the names of some places in Clare and Tipperary, the Irish form of which is found in the Four Masters—*Baile-Phaidin*, little Patrick's town.

Cán or *gán*. This diminutive is very common, especially in ancient personal names, such as *Flanducan* (now Flanagan), little Flann; *Dubucan*, little black-complexioned man (now Dugan), &c. The more ancient form is *cán*: which, in the modern language, has quite given place to *gán*; and this forms the final syllable of many of our family names, such as Mulligan—*Maelagan*, little bald man (*mael*, bald); Finigan, little fair-haired man (*finn*, white), &c.

We have it in its original form in Briencan near Ballymore-Eustace in Kildare, little *bruighean* [brien], or fairy fort. Lucan near Dublin (from which Sarsfield took the title of earl of Lucan) is written in Alan's *Repertorium Viride*, *Livecan*, and in an Inquisition of Charles I., *Leivcan;* I have not found any authority for the original Irish form; but these, no doubt, represent *Leamhcán* [Lavcan—Lucan]. The first syllable might mean either elm or the herb marsh mallows (see chap. XIX. *infra*); but the forms of the name quoted above give more nearly the Irish sound of the latter; and we have, moreover, the precedent of the old word *lemnat*, another diminutive, meaning *malvaceus* (see p. 19); so that Lucan signifies "land producing marsh mallows."

The more modern form of this diminutive is seen in Colligan, the name of a little river flowing by Dungarvan in Waterford, from *coll*, hazel—the hazel growing river; and in Whinnigan, in the parish of Cleenish, Fermanagh, not far from Enniskillen—whitish little spot of land, from *finn*, white.

In the following cases and others like them, it may be doubted whether the termination is the diminutive *cán* with the *c* aspirated, or a combination of *ach* and *án*. From *fearn*, the alder tree, is formed *fearnachán*, from which again we have Mullafernaghan, in the parish of Magherally in Down, near Banbridge, the hill of the alder plantation; and similarly Carrowfarnaghan near Ballyconnell in Cavan, the quarter-land of the alders. *Tulachán* (from *tul* or *tulach*) signifies a little hill, and is usually anglicised Tullaghan: Tullaghanbaun in Mayo, signifies white little hill; while in Tullaghobegly in Donegal, the word is cut short, for the Irish name is *Tulachan-Bigli*, Begly's little hill. From *dubh*, black, we have *Dubhachan*, anglicised Dooghan in Donegal and Roscommon, black land.

Nán. In Cormac's Glossary, it is stated that the name *Adamnan* is a diminutive of *Adam;* and this is the only direct notice I have found of the diminutive termination *nán*. Dr. Stokes, in his commentary on this part of Cormac's Glossary (*voce*, *Adomnán*) instances the personal names *Lomnanus*, *Sescnanus* (Latinised forms of the Irish *Lomnán* and *Sescnán*), *Flaithnán*, *Lachtnán ;* but he doubts whether *nán* be not a double diminutive (*án* + *án*), or the old adjective *nán*, little.

It is found, though not very often, in local names; and the manner in which it is used tends, I think, to the conclusion that it is a simple diminutive. The townland of Clynan in the parish of Forgney, near Ballymahon in Longford, must have taken its name from a small dyke or rampart of earth:—*cladh* [cly] a dyke, diminutive *cladhnán*. Licknaun in the parish of Templemaley in Clare, is little flag-stone (*lec*), or flag surfaced land; Keernaun near Ennis in the same county, black surfaced land, from *ciar*, black; Gortlownan, south of Lough Gill in Sligo, the *gort* or field of the elm plantation—*leamh* [lav, lou], elm.

There is an old adjective *dúr* [doore] which signifies, among other meanings, stupid and obstinate; it is still a living word in this sense wherever Irish is spoken; and in the north of Ireland it survives, and is in constant use among the English speaking people. In Munster, a stupid, dronish, stubborn fellow is called a *dúradán* [dooradaun], a diminutive form (see p. 35), as familiar in the south as *doore* is in the north. With the diminutive termination at present under consideration is formed the word *durnán* [doornaun], which is well-known as a nickname given to the people of the barony of Iverk, in the south of Kilkenny. The peasantry of this and the surrounding districts have a legend to account for the name. They say that when St. Patrick, in his progress through the country, came to Iverk, the people treated him very rudely and unkindly; and when he called late one evening at the monastery of St. Kieran, the inmates gave him a most inhospitable reception—no reception at all indeed, for they shut the gates and kept him out all night. But what was worse than all, a woman who lived in the neighbouring village of Ballincrea, cooked up an old yellow hound, threw poison on it, and sent it to him on a dish for his dinner; but he detected the plot and shewed his followers in a most unmistakable way what sort of an animal it really was. The general conduct of the inhabitants, crowned by this last indignity offered to him by the unfortunate woman from Ballincrea, highly incensed the saint; and he uttered a bitter speech, in which he predicted that the inhabitants should be known to the end of the world by the name of *Durnauns*—that is, a churlish, boorish, plebeian people. It is believed that the little village of Doornane in the same barony took its name from the people. The inhabitants of Iverk are a silent and reserved race—" dark people," as they would be called in Ireland; and it is to be suspected that this story grew up among the people of the adjacent districts of Waterford and Tipperary, who have an ancient cause of dislike—not less indeed than fourteen hundred years old—for their neighbours of Iverk. The legend is not wholly without use, however, if it has helped to perpetuate in the word *dúrnán*, an interesting example of a long disused diminutive.

Tán or *dán*. There is an example of the use of this diminutive, in the sense of "abounding in" (see p. 19), in the St. Gall manuscript quoted by Zeuss (8th century), namely, the word *rostan*, which is given as the equivalent of the Latin *rosetum* (a rose plot), and is derived from the Irish *rós*, a rose (Gram. Celt., p. 180). It is to some extent used as a diminutive at the present day, but always in the modern form *dán*, and it forms part of several words used even by the English speaking peasantry. *Geosán* is understood in some places to mean a stalk of any kind; and the other diminutive, *geosadán*, is known in some of the Munster counties, as one of the names for the *boliaun*, *booghalaun-bwee*, or ragweed. There is a small red berry growing in heathery places, which is called *mónadán*, i. e., little bog-berry, from *móin*, a bog ("Have you seen the ripe monadan glisten in Kerry."—Edward Walsh, in the ballad of "O'Donovan's daughter"). The word *bolgadán* [bullogadaun]—a formation from *bolg*, a belly—is universally used in the south of Ireland to designate a little man with a big belly; and we have also *dúradán*, already quoted at page 33, from the root *dúr*.

The old form of this termination is exhibited in the ancient personal name *Fintan*, which has the same signification as *Finan* and *Finigan*, viz., little fair-haired man; all three being diminutives from *finn*, white. This name was common both in pagan and Christian times; and there were many saints called Fintan, one of whom gave name to Kilfintan (Fintan's church) in the parish of Street in Longford—another to Kilfountain in the parish of Kildrum near Ventry in Kerry, which exhibits the Munster way of pronouncing the name (see 1st Ser. Part I., c. II.). There is also a place called Ardfintan—Fintan's height—in the parish of Killursa, near Headford in Galway.

The bardic annals record that Lough Sallagh, near Dunboyne in Meath, burst forth in the time of *Aengus Ollmuca*, one of the pre-Christian kings. The Four Masters call it *Loch Saileach*, and Keating, *Loch Sailcheadáin* (the same name with the addition of the diminutive); both epithets signify the lake of the sallows; and the modern name is derived from the former. Funshadaun in the parish of Killeenadeema in Galway, signifying ash-producing land, is derived from *fuinnse*, the ash tree, exactly as *rostan* from *rós* (p. 35). Near the village of Clare in Mayo is the townland of Leedaun—a grey spot of land—from *liath* [leea], grey. Lyradane is the name of a place in the parish of Grenagh in Cork; there are some townlands in Derry and Tyrone called Learden; and a little stream called Lyardane joins the Shournagh river, three miles from Blarney in Cork: all these signify a little fork or river-fork, from *ladhar* [lyre], a fork. *Gabhal* [gowl], another word having the same meaning, gives name to Gouladane (little fork), a hill in the peninsula between the bays of Dunmanus and Bantry. From *scrath* [scrah], a sward, is formed the name of Ardscradaun near the city of Kilkenny, the height of the little grassy sward.

L or *ll.* It appears to me highly probable that this—either by itself or with a vowel preceding—is an ancient Irish diminutive termination, though I have nowhere seen it noticed as such. In one respect indeed it is more general than most of those already enumerated, for it exists in many languages; as for instance in Latin, in such words as *scutulum*, a little shield, from *scutum*; *homulus*, a dwarf, from *homo*, a man, &c. The Old High German abounded with diminutives in *l*; and we know that this letter forms one of the commonest of English diminutive terminations, giving rise to the numerous class of words ending in *le*, such as *thimble* from *thumb*; *nipple*, from *nib*; *girdle*, from *gird*, &c. It is also quite common in Greek, French, Spanish, Italian, &c.; and what is still more to the point, in Ebel's Zeuss it is recognised as a diminutive in a certain class of Gaulish names (Gram. Celt., 767).

The fact of its existence as an acknowledged diminutive in so many other languages, would of itself afford a strong presumption that it had originally a diminutive signification in Irish; and one can hardly avoid coming to this conclusion after examining the manner in which the termination is used in the following names.

It may be questioned whether the *ail* or *all* which ends so many Irish personal names, was not originally used in a diminutive sense:—as in *Cathal* (now Cahill), from *cath*, a battle (*Cathal*, a warrior); *Domnall* (now Donnell in the names O'Donnell and Macdonnell), from the same root as the Latin *dominus*; *Breasal* (now Brassil and Brazil) from *Breas*, which was itself a common personal name. (See on this suffix, Gram. Celt., 766-9).

This termination is found in a considerable number of local names, whose formation is precisely similar to that of many already mentioned as formed from other diminutives. From *cruadh* [croo], hard, is derived *cruadhail* [cruel], hard land, which takes the modern form Cruell in the parish of Aghaboe in Queen's County: and this name is derived exactly like Cruan, (Irish *Cruadhán*, same meaning), in the parish of Coolaghmore near Callan in Kilkenny, which comes from the same root, with the diminutive termination *án*.

There is a root *stur*, not found in the published dictionaries, though they give the derivatives, *sturric* and *sturrog*, both as signifying a hill-summit or pinnacle. From this root are derived the following names, with different diminutives, all signifying the same thing—a peak or hill top:—Sturgan near the northern base of Slieve Gullion in Armagh; Sturrin, the name of two hills north-east of Lough Derg in Donegal; Sturrakeen in Omey Island off the coast of Galway; and Mullaghasturrakeen, the name of a high hill on the boundary between Tyrone and Derry—the summit of the pinnacle. Lastly, with the diminutive at present under consideration, we have "The Sturrel," a remarkable peak-shaped rock on the coast of Donegal, near Glen Columkille, rising from the sea to the height of 850 feet; and this is also the name of a hill at the head of Mulroy Bay in the same county, two miles from Millford.

I have on other occasions observed how happily the old name-formers generally succeeded in designating places by their most obvious characteristics—every name striking straight for the feature that most strongly attracted attention; so that to this day, a person moderately skilled in such matters may often predict the physical peculiarities or the aspect of a place as soon as he hears the name. Nothing could be more appropriate in this respect than "The Dargle," which every one will recognise as the name of a beautiful glen near Bray in Wicklow. The prevailing rock in the glen is very soft and of a reddish colour, sometimes with a yellowish tinge, but in several places deepening into a dark purplish red. The visitor can hardly fail to observe this almost as soon as he enters the lower gate, where the red stones come to the surface of the path under his feet. The reddish colour also pervades the clay, which is merely the rock worn down; and is very striking in several spots along the sides of the glen, where the clay and rock are exposed, especially after rain, which brings out the prevailing hue very vividly. The name "Dargle" is similar in formation to "Delgany," (see p. 26), but with a different diminutive syllable:—*dearg*, red; *Deargail*, a red little spot. Still another name of the same kind, with the diminutive *án*, is Dargan in the county Donegal. But we have other parallels to the "Dargle" still more complete—in fact the very same name—in Darrigil in the parish of Kilgeever, Mayo, and Darrigal near Kilmeadan in Waterford, which is quite as remarkable for the redness of its surface stones as the Dargle. The "Dargle" is also pronounced in three syllables (*Darrigil*) by the old people of Wicklow.

This diminutive is also introduced through the medium of personal names. *Cet* [Keth] was the name of some of the most renowned warriors celebrated in ancient Irish story. Some old chief who lived beyond the view of history, gave name to the famous Drumcett, (properly *Druim Ceta*), translated by Adamnan, *Dorsum Cete*, Keth's ridge or hill, where the great convention was held in the year A. D. 574; but the name has been long forgotten, and the hill, which is a long mound in Roe Park near Newtownlimavady, is now called The Mullagh, and sometimes Daisy Hill (see Reeves's Adamnan, page 37). The name *Cet* still holds its place in Dunkitt in Kilkenny, Keth's fortress. The diminutive appears in Carrickittle, a remarkable rock giving name to a townland near Kilteely in Limerick, which the Four Masters, when recording the erection of a castle on it in 1510, by Garrett, earl of Kildare, call *Carraig-Cital*, Cital's rock (though the absence of the genitive inflection here might raise some doubt: *Cital*, gen. Citail?); and also in Dunkettle, near Glanmire, a little below Cork, which is the same as Dunkitt, only with the difference of the diminutive in the personal name.

Besides the preceding diminutives, there are others of a mixed character, which may be classed together. Words ending in *l* and *n* often take the letter *t* before suffixes or inflections, which is perhaps to be regarded rather as a euphonic insertion than as part of the termination. For instance, Coolteen in Sligo and Wexford is derived from *cuil*, a corner—*Cuiltín*, little corner—where the real diminutive termination appears to be *ín*, not *tín*. To the same category may be referred Seltan, the name of several places in Leitrim, written by the Four Masters, *Sailtean*, a place of sallows (*sail*); Keeltane in the parish of Tullylease in Cork, little wood, or underwood, from *coill*, a wood; and Fantane near Borrisoleigh in Tipperary, little *fán* or slope: in these, the diminutive affix is probably *án*, not *tán*.

Murhaun near Drumshambo in Leitrim, seems a genuine instance of a diminutive in *thán*, for the Irish name is *Múrthán*, little *múr* or wall. So also in the following names it would appear that the termination is *thín*, for no reason can be assigned for the presence of the *th* otherwise than as a part of the diminutive:—Bellaheen in the parish of Kilrossanty in Waterford, *Beilithín*, little *beile* or tree; Barheen in the parish of Annagh, near Ballyhaunis in Mayo, little *barr* or hill-top; Keenheen in the parish of Drumreilly in Leitrim, a beautiful surfaced spot of land, from *caein* [keen], beautiful. In the year 1581, Dermod O'Donovan headed a predatory excursion into the territory of Donal O'Sullivan, prince of Bear, and drove off a *creaght* of cattle; but O'Sullivan overtook the party, took O'Donovan prisoner, and hanged him from the branch of an oak tree. This event is vividly remembered in tradition; and the tree, whose trunk is still to be seen about four miles north-east of Castletown Bearhaven in Cork, is known by the name of *Dariheen Diarmada*, Dermod's little oak. This same diminutive (Irish *dairithín*, from *dair*, an oak) has given name to Derriheen near Cappoquin in Waterford.

In a numerous class of cases, the diminutives are preceded by some of the terminations noticed in chapter I. We have *r* combined with *án* in Lavaran near the village of Kesh in Fermanagh, and in Lowran near Borris-in-Ossory in Queen's County, both anglicised from *Leamhrán*, elm land, from *leamh* [lav], elm. *R* is joined to *nán* in Sellernaun in the parish of Inishcaltra in Galway, near the shore of Lough Derg--*Sailearnán*, sallow wood, from *sail*, a sallow; and the same letter combines with *óg* in Dooroge near Ballyboghil in Dublin, black land (*dubh*, black); which is also the name of a rivulet ("black little stream") flowing into the sea two miles north-east of Tara Hill in Wexford.

The diminutive *ín* is very often joined with *r*, of which Cloghereen near Killarney, from *cloch*, a stone, is a very apt example (First Series). Cranareen, the name of places in Wicklow and Mayo, signifies a place full of small trees, or a small plantation, from *crann*, a tree; and there is a little lake a mile from Clifden in Galway, called Lough Acrannereen, the lake of the small trees. Flugherine—a wet little spot of land, from *fliuch*, wet—is the name of a pool from which flows a stream, in the townland of Ballycormick, parish of Clonenagh, Queen's County; Cuingareen, in the parish of Columkille, Longford, a rabbit warren, from *cuinín*, a rabbit. Similar in formation to those is the well-known name of Skibbereen in Cork. It is situated at the mouth of the river Ilen, on a little creek much frequented by small vessels, formerly—and still in some places—called *scibs* (Eng. skiff); and *Scibirín*, as the place is called in Irish, means a place frequented by *skibs* or boats. It exactly corresponds in meaning with Cotteenagh, the name of a little island in the river Shannon, near Shannon Bridge, below Clonmacnoise, which signifies a place frequented by little *cots* or boats. It is to be observed, however, that the word *skib* is not now at least applied to a boat in the neighbourhood of Skibbereen; and this fact may lead some to doubt the correctness of the etymology.

In Fetherneen (parish of Kilvarnet, Sligo) we have a union of both *n* and *r* with the diminutive, the name signifying a little *fead* or streamlet; and it corresponds in formation with Fethernagh in Armagh, near Pointzpass, which means a place abounding in little brooks.

Observe the rich growth of terminations—branch on branch—in Sillahertane, which is the name of two townlands, one near Dunmanway in Cork, and the other in the parish of Kilgarvan in Kerry, on the road from Kenmare to Macroom. The Irish form, which the English very well represents in sound, is *Saileachartán*, all from the simple trunk, *sail*, a sallow; we have in succession *each* or *ach*, *r*, *t*, and the diminutive *án;* and the whole signifies a spot producing ozier or sallow trees. It appears probable that in this name the combination *rt*—whether compounded of *r* and *t*, each in its separate sense, or forming one indivisible termination—has a collective signification; just as it has in the word *conairt*, which is applied in the south to a pack of hounds (*cu*, gen. *con*, a hound); from which is derived Coolnaconarty, the corner (*cúil*) of the pack of hounds, a place in the parish of Kilmeen, five or six miles south-east of Dunmanway, which the inhabitants say was formerly a usual place of meeting on hunting days. The combination is also found in a name preserved in the Annals of Lough Key at A. D. 1192, viz. *Rath-cuanartaigh* (the fort of the hounds), the second part of which is derived from *cuan* (a litter of whelps), by the addition of the two postfixes *art* and *ach*.

Exactly similar in formation to this last is the name of Mangerton mountain near Killarney. The correct form is *Mangartach*, for so we find it written in several old Irish documents; which has been recently corrupted by changing *ach* to the diminutive *án*. The signification of the name depends on the meaning of the root *mang*, and this is doubtful. In Cormac's Glossary and other authorities, *mang* is explained a fawn; and if this be its meaning here, *Mangartach* would mean the mountain of the fawns. I am inclined to think, however, that *mang* is only another form of *mong*, signifying literally the hair of the head, but often applied in a secondary sense to long grass; just as *gort*, a field, was anciently often written *gart; folt*, hair, *falt; mór*, great, *már;* &c. If this be correct the name will mean a mountain covered with long hair-like grass. There are three circumstances that support this interpretation:—first, in the ancient historical tale called the "Battle of Moylena," this very term *mong* is applied to the mountain; for it is designated *Mangartha mhong-ruadh*—Mangerton of the red *mong* or hair (Battle of Moylena, p. 25); secondly, the flat moory summit of the mountain is actually covered with a growth of long coarse grass—the very kind of grass that *mong* is usually applied to; thirdly, whereas *mang*, a fawn, as far as I am aware, is not found in any other name in all Ireland, *mong*, as applied to long grass, and its derivatives *mongach* and *mongan*, are common in names all over the country, of which many examples will be found in chapter XIX.

CHAPTER III.

BORROWED WORDS.

WHENEVER two nations speaking different languages have intimate intercourse with each other for any considerable time, there is sure to be a mutual interchange of words; for each race borrows from the other certain terms which in course of time become incorporated with the language that adopts them. In this manner every language becomes mixed with foreign words; different languages exhibiting different powers and degrees of assimilation.

During the long intercourse of the English and Irish populations in Ireland, there has been a good deal of interchange of this kind, though not I think so much as we find in other countries under similar circumstances. I propose to examine a few such words, some borrowed from Irish into English, some from English into Irish; but I will limit the inquiry to those that find their way into local nomenclature.

Moreover I do not intend to go back to very early times; I will illustrate only such words as have recently passed from one language into the other, or are now in process of transfer, and of naturalisation. A good many of the Irish words retained by the English speaking people are only used locally; but though they are still circumscribed, they are holding their place among the people, and are gaining ground in point of extent; for the very good reason that they express exactly ideas not so well expressed by any synonymous English words known to the people. And every one acquainted with the history of the English language, or indeed of any other language, knows well how a word of this kind—provided it is a good word, and hits the idea straight on the head—though it may be at first spoken perhaps only in a single valley, spreads slowly and gradually over a larger and larger surface, till at length it becomes recognised by the whole nation, and has its citizenship acknowledged by being placed in the columns of dictionaries. Occasionally too, from some accidental circumstance, a word borrowed from a strange language, or not borrowed at all, but invented, springs at once into sudden and universal use. Some of the terms here illustrated are used only in a part of Ireland; others are known nearly over the whole country; a few again of the anglicised Irish words have found their way across the channel, and these are sure of a permanent place. To this last class belongs the five first words in my list.

Bog. The word *bog* has long been used by English writers who have treated of Ireland; and it had found its way into the literary language of England at least as early as the time of Elizabeth, for it is used in its proper sense by Shakespeare, as well as by Milton and Bunyan. It is now an acknowledged word in the English language, and is beginning to be understood in England almost as well as the English equivalent, peat or peat moss. *Bog* as it stands is Irish; it signifies soft; and it is still a living word, and in constant use, by Irish speakers. In this original sense it is found in several local names; such as Meenbog in Donegal and Tyrone, soft mountain meadow or *meen;* Aghabog, a parish in Monaghan, *Achadh-bog*, soft field; Maynebog in the parish of Aghmacart in Queen's County, soft field (*maighin*).

The original word *bog* is not now used in the native Irish to signify a bog or peat moss; it has been quite supplanted by the derivative *bogach*, which is in very general use in this sense, just as *smólach* has taken the place of *smól* (see p. 5). This word gives names to many places now called Boggagh, Bogagh, and Boggy; Boggyheary near Swords in Dublin, *Bogach-aedhaire*, the shepherd's bog. In the end of names it forms some such terminations as *boggy*, *voggy*, or *vogy* (*b* aspirated to *v* in the two last); as in Clonavogy in Monaghan, the meadow of the bog; Portavogie in the Ards in Down, the port or landing place of the bog. From the diminutive *bogán* (little bog or soft place) are derived the names of many places now called Boggan and Boggaun.

Bother. It appears to me obvious that *bother* is merely the Irish *bodhar*, deaf, although I know very well that a different origin has been assigned to it. For, first, it is in universal use—it is literally in every one's mouth—in Ireland. Secondly, what is more to the purpose, while it is used, as it is in England, to signify annoyance or trouble, it has another meaning in Ireland which is not known in England, namely, deaf, the same as the original word *bodhar;* and this is obviously its primary meaning. A person who is either partly or wholly deaf is said to be *bothered;* and this usage is perfectly familiar in every part of Ireland, from Dublin to the remotest districts—among the educated as well as among the illiterate. The word indeed in this sense, is the foundation of a proverb:—you are said to "turn the *bothered* ear" to a person when you do not wish to hear what he says, or grant his request. Moreover, so well are the two words *bother* and *bodhar* understood to be identical, that in the colloquial language of the peasantry they are always used to translate each other.

As to the English pronunciation, it is merely a case of what is so familiar in Irish names—the restoration of an aspirated consonant, which I have already fully explained and illustrated (1st Ser. Part I., c. 2). *Bodhar*, pronounced in Irish, bower, is called in English, *bother*, exactly as *Odhar* [ower] is made Odder (see this in index); as the river *Dothra* [Dohra] near Dublin, is called the Dodder; and as the word *bóthar* [boher], a road, is often sounded *bothyr* or *batter*. I do not see how any one, with these evidences before him, can hesitate to acknowledge that *bother* is an Irish word.

The word *bodhar* is used in local names, and in a very singular way too. What did our ancestors mean when they called a glen deaf? It is very hard to answer this question satisfactorily; but it is certain that there are several glens in different parts of the country called Glenbower, deaf glen. There is one in Kilkenny, three miles north of Piltown; one—a fine glen two miles long—at the base of Slievenamon in Tipperary, two miles east of Kilcash; a third in the parish of Kilbarron in Tipperary, near Lough Derg; a fourth in the parish of Offerlane in Queen's County, west of Mountrath; a fifth which gives name to a small lake at the base of Slieve Beagh mountain, south of Clogher in Tyrone; and a sixth—a pretty wooded glen—near the village of Killeagh, west of Youghal in Cork. In this last there is a peculiarity, which perhaps gives the key to the explanation of the names of all:—viz., it has a fine echo, "affording," as Smith remarks (Hist. Cork, I., 156), "seven or eight repercussions from the same sound." If this be the origin of the name, perhaps the glen was so called because you have to speak loudly to it, and you get a loud-voiced reply, exactly as happens when you speak to a deaf person.

But will this explanation apply to other places designated by *bodhar*. There is a "Drehidbower Bridge," (*droichead*, a bridge) over a small river in Clare, four miles north of Killaloe; which the people say was so called because it was built by a deaf man in 1799—but I confess I have not much faith in the explanation. Illaunbower—deaf island—is the name of a little islet in Lough Mask; and we have Cartronbower (*cartron*, a quarter of land) in the parish of Ballintober in Mayo. In Lenabower, near the village of Barna, west of Galway, and Curraghbower, a little south of the Blackwater, five miles west of Mallow, *lena*, signifies a marshy meadow, and *curragh*, a marsh; but whether the marshiness of these places had anything to do with the names, I must leave the reader to conjecture.

In the parish of Kilgarvan in Mayo, there is a little river taking its name from an old mill, called Mullenbower; and if one mill is found to be deaf, there seems no good reason why another should not be blind, which is the case with Mullenkeagh (*caech*, blind) near the village of Cloghjordan in the north of Tipperary. We may conjecture that these two names were given to old mills that had ceased to be used, and had fallen into ruin.

Tory. The two terms *Whig* and *Tory*, like many other class names, were originally applied in an opprobrious sense; they were nicknames, which gradually lost their offensive flavour when their origin was forgotten. The word *whig* is another form of *whey*, and it is used to this day in Scotland, and in the north of Ireland, to denote thick sour milk or sour whey; but as the word does not come within the scope of this book, it is not necessary to trace its history further here. *Tory* is an Irish word, anglicised phonetically like most other Irish terms; and the original form is *tóruidhe*, the pronunciation of which is very well preserved in the modern spelling, *tory*. Its root is *tóir* [tore], pursuit; and *tóruidhe* is literally a pursuer—one who hunts or chases. There is still another derivative, *tóruidheacht*, an abstract noun signifying the act of pursuing; and all three terms are in common use in the Irish language. We have, for instance, a well-known Irish romantic tale called "*Tóruidheacht Dhiarmada agus Ghrainne*," the pursuit of Dermod and Grainè.

In the time of the Irish plantations of the sixteenth and seventeenth centuries, great numbers of the native Irish who were dispossessed of their lands, took to the hills, woods, and bogs, and formed themselves into bands under the leadership of their principal men. From their wild retreats they made descents at every opportunity on the open country, drove off the cattle of the settlers, and seized on all sorts of movable property that they could lay their hands on. These men were called *tories*—hunters or pursuers; for they chased everything—the wild animals on which they partly subsisted, the herds of the settlers, and the settlers themselves if they chanced to come in their way. The settlers on their part combined for mutual protection, and vigorously retaliated; and this social war was carried on without intermission, in some districts, for a long series of years. Many traditionary stories of those disturbed and exciting times are still current among the peasantry. In course of time the tories became mere freebooters, and stringent laws were made for their suppression; so that at length the word *tory* lost its original signification among the English speaking people, and came to signify an outlaw—the first step in its singular change of meaning.

It is believed, according to a statement of Defoe, to have been first introduced into England by Titus Oates; for a story went round that certain tories were to be brought over from Ireland to assassinate Oates and some of his supporters; and after this he was in the habit of calling every man who opposed him, even in conversation, a tory; "till at last the word *tory* became popular." The two terms, whig and tory, came into general use as political designations about the year 1680; but they had previously, as Swift expresses it, been "pressed into the service of many successions of parties, with very different ideas attached to them."

The word *tory* is still retained among the peasantry of every part of Ireland in the sense of an outlaw or a miscreant of any kind; and it is quite usual to hear a nurse call a naughty child a "young tory." They have a nursery rhyme which preserves this sense very vividly; it is heard, with some variations, in all parts of the country; and Crofton Croker has given a version of it in his "Researches in the South of Ireland."

> "I'll tell you a story about Johnny M'Gory,
> Who went to the wood and killed a tory;
> Brought him home and ate his supper;
> Went to the wood and killed another."

In the sense of a hunter or outlaw the word *tóruidhe* is found in a few local names, none of which appear, however, to be of any antiquity. We have two hills in Ireland called Tory Hill; and in each case the name is of modern origin, and has superseded an older name. One lies to the east of Mullinavat in Kilkenny; and it received its name from Edmund Denn, a tory, who is celebrated among the peasantry to this day. He was one of the family of Denn who owned Tory Hill; and after he was outlawed he lived in a cave on the hill, in which the people still show his bed. The old name of this hill was *Sliabh-O-gCruinn* or Slieve Igrine, the mountain of the ancient territory or barony of Igrine, in which it was situated, and which was itself so called from the old tribe of *Ui Cruinn* who formerly held it (for the presence of the *g*, see chapter VIII.). The other Tory Hill lies near Croom in Limerick, but I cannot tell who the particular tory was that gave it the name: perhaps it was so called from having been a haunt of the tories. Its ancient name was *Cnoc-droma-Assail* [Knockdromassil], the hill of the ridge of *Assal*—*Assal* being the old name of the territory lying round the hill.

Ballytory in Wexford signifies the tory's townland. Near Clogher in Tyrone is a place called Ratory, a name anglicised from *Rath-tóruidhe*, the fort of the tory or outlaw; and here no doubt, in old days, some tory made his lair in the old rath, and sheltered and defended himself within the entrenchments.

Orrery. The instrument called an orrery, for showing the various motions of the planets and satellites, took its name from the title of the family of Boyle, earls of Orrery; and the following is the commonly received account of the circumstance that brought the word into circulation. The instrument was invented about the year 1700 by George Graham, who gave it into the hands of a workman to have it packed up and sent to Prince Eugene; but before packing it, this man made a copy of it, which he sold to the earl of Orrery, without making any mention of Graham or his invention. The machine sent to Boyle came under the notice of Sir Richard Steele, who referred to it in one of his papers as a very ingenious instrument, and called it an *orrery* in honour of the earl, a name which was at once adopted, and has been since retained.

Orrery, from which the Boyles took one of their titles, is an ancient territory in Munster, represented by the modern barony of Orrery in the north of the county of Cork, lying round the town of Charleville. The old form of the name is *Orbraige*, usually spelled with both the *b* and the *g* aspirated, and pronounced *Orvery*, which was easily softened down to Orrery. It was originally a tribe name; but, in accordance with a custom very usual in Ireland (see 1st Ser. Part I., c. II.) the people gave their name to the territory. Cormac MacCullenan, in his Glossary, written in the ninth century, states that they took the name of *Orbraige* from an ancestor named *Orb* or *Orbh*; *Orbraige* meaning the descendants of *Orb* (Cor. Gl. *voce*, *Orb* : *raige*, posterity—1st Ser. Part I., c. II.). O'Donovan, in his commentary on this part of the

Glossary, tells us that "*Orbh* was the ancestor of the people called *Orbhraighe*, who were descended from Fereidhech, son of Fergus Mac Roigh, king of Ulster in the first century;" but I have not been able to find any further account of this old chieftain. Whoever he was, however, his name now forms one of the varied elements in the curious mosaic of the English language, and has thus become immortalised in a manner that would greatly astonish him if he could be made aware of it.

Shamrock. The trefoil, white clover, or *trifolium repens*, is designated by the Irish word *seamar* [shammer]. But the diminutive *seamaróg* [shammeroge: see p. 28] is the term most generally used; and it has settled down into the word *shamrock*, which is now found in English dictionaries, and is beginning to be understood wherever the English language is spoken.

We find it stated by several Anglo-Irish writers that in former times the Irish occasionally ate the shamrock. Spenser, for instance, mentions that in time of famine the poor people who were reduced to the last stage of starvation were glad to eat water-cresses and shamrocks; Fynes Morrison has a passage of much the same import; while Thomas Dinely, who made a tour through Ireland in 1675, tells us that the people ate shamroges to cause a sweet breath. This has led some persons to believe that the true shamrock is the *oxalis acetocella*, or wood sorrel. I see no reason, however, why these passages should not refer to the white trefoil, which is quite as fit to be used as a food-herb as wood sorrel; for I think we may assume that neither cress nor shamrocks were eaten in any quantity except under pressure of extreme hunger, but only used with other food just as water-cress is used at the present day.

Moreover *seamar* and *seamróg* are given in Irish dictionaries as meaning *trifolium repens*, while wood-sorrel is designated by *samhadh-coille* and *seamsóg*. And as corroborating the dictionary explanations, we find the compound *scoith-sheamrach* (translated by O'Donovan "abounding with flowers and shamrocks:" *scoth*, a flower) a favourite term among Irish writers to designate a green, open plain. The old records for instance, tell us that *Fiacha Finscothach* (*Fiacha* of the white flowers) king of Ireland before the Christian era, was so called because "every plain in Ireland was *scoith-sheamrach* in his time:" and the same term is used by the Irish poet, Ferfeasa O'Cainte, about the year 1617 (Misc. Celt. Soc. 1849, p. 355), and by the writer of the Life of St. *Scuithín* (O'Cl. Cal. p. 5). In these passages it cannot be the wood-sorrel that is meant, for it is not produced in sufficient abundance, and it does not grow in open plains, but in shady places.

It is not easy to determine the origin of the Irish custom of wearing a bunch of shamrocks in the hat on St. Patrick's day—the 17th of March. According to popular belief it commemorates an incident in the life of St. Patrick:—that on a certain occasion, when he was explaining the mystery of the Trinity to the pagan Irish, he took up a single shamrock and pointed out the three leaves growing from one stem, to illustrate the doctrine of three Persons in one God. But this story must be an invention of recent times, for we find no mention of it in any of the old Lives of the saint. Neither are we able to say that the custom itself is of any higher antiquity; for though it is now observed by the Irish race all over the world, and though it is mentioned by a few writers of the last two or three hundred years—as for instance by Thomas Dinely in 1675, who describes how the people wore crosses and shamrocks on St. Patrick's day—yet we find no allusion to it in ancient Irish writings.

There are not many local names derived from this word, and I have found none recorded in any ancient written authority. It appears in its primary form in Aghnashammer near Rosslea in Fermanagh, *Achadh-na-seamar*, the field of the trefoils; in Mohernashammer on the brink of the Shannon, near Termonbarry in Roscommon (*mothar*, either a ruin or a thicket); and in Knocknashammer in Cavan and Sligo, which in the latter county has the correct alias name of Cloverhill. The diminutive is more common: there are townlands in Cork and Limerick called Coolnashamroge, the corner of the shamrocks; Gorteenshamrogue near Fethard in Tipperary, shamrock little field; and Knocknashamroge near Hacketstown in Wicklow, the same as Knocknashammer.

Barm-brack. You will not see a confectioner's shop window in any part of Dublin, on Hallow-eve, without a handbill announcing a plentiful supply of *barm-bracks* with a ring in each. This word *barm-brack* is now applied in many parts of Ireland to a sweet cake mixed with currants and raisins; and we may safely prophesy that it will ultimately fight its way into the columns of English dictionaries. The original and correct word—written phonetically—is *barreen-brack*, which is still used among the English-speaking people of the south of Ireland; it has been changed to *barm-brack* by that process of fallacious popular etymology described in First Series (Part I., c. II.); and the altered term was all the more readily accepted inasmuch as the word *barm* seems the right word in the right place. The Irish word represented in sound by *barreen*, is *bairghín*, which signifies a cake; the old Irish form is *bairgen*, which glosses *panis* in the Zeuss manuscripts; *brack*—Irish *breac*—means speckled; and a *barreen-brack* is literally "a speckled cake"—speckled with raisins and currants.

A piece of land approaching a circular shape is sometimes called *bairghín;* and in this manner the word has found its way into local nomenclature. The complete word is exhibited in Barreen, in the parish of Balraheen in Kildare. If the shape approach a semicircle, the place is sometimes designated by the compound *leath-bhairghín* [lavarreen] meaning half a cake—*leath*, half; which is pretty common as a name for fields and small denominations; and this is the origin of the names of the townlands of Lavareen and Lawarreen in Leitrim, Clare, and Mayo. As for the word *breac*, it will be treated of in chapter XVII., and need not be further noticed here.

So far regarding Irish words adopted into English. Our local nomenclature also exhibits a number of words borrowed from English into Irish; and the remainder of this chapter will be devoted to the illustration of a few words of this kind.

Parson. Of the two English words *person* and *parson*, we know that the first is derived from the Latin *persona*, and according to some, the second is derived from the same word. We have in Irish two corresponding words. One, *perso* or *persu*, genitive *persan*, meaning a *person* or an individual, is merely the Latin *persona*, borrowed; but it was borrowed at a very early age, for we find it in the very oldest manuscripts, such as those quoted by Zeuss, *Lebor na hUidhre*, &c. The other, *pearsún* [parsoon], corresponding with the English *parson*, is used in the colloquial language to signify the priest of a parish, a clergyman who has the care of souls. Some would perhaps consider that *pearsún* is the representative of the ancient loan word *perso;* but I think it has been borrowed direct from the English *parson* in its special sense. The termination *ún* is indeed presumptive evidence of this, for when it occurs in Irish, it generally marks a word taken straight from the English. We know that in Ireland the English word *parson* has lately been restricted to the rectors of the Established Church; but *pearsún* was applied to a Roman Catholic parish priest, showing that it was borrowed before *parson* began to be used in its special Irish sense; though in later times, it has begun, like *parson*, to be restricted to Protestant clergymen.

There is a parish in Limerick four miles east of the city, taking its name from a townland called Carrigparson, the rock of the parish priest, probably marking the spot where a priest lived, or perhaps where Mass used to be celebrated in times gone by. This name has been in use for more than 300 years; and the rock is to be seen close by the ruin of the old church, not far from the present chapel. Ballyfarsoon near Monasterevin in Kildare—*Baile-an-phearsúin*, the town of the parson—probably got its name from being tenanted by a parish priest; there is a place called Monaparson, the parson's bog, on the Clyda river, just by the railway, four miles south of Mallow; and Knockapharsoon (*knock*, a hill) lies four miles north of Fethard in Tipperary.

Earl. Iarla [eerla] an earl, is a word that was borrowed into Irish at the time of the Anglo-Norman invasion; it is in constant use in the annals, for the old historians, in recording events in which the great Anglo-Norman lords were concerned, did not translate the word *earl*, but simply transferred it with a slight change of form.

The Irish pronunciation is well preserved in Syerla near Dungannon in Tyrone, *Suidhe-iarla*, the earl's seat or residence. So also Kilmacanearla near Ballingarry in Limerick, the church of the earl's son; Annaghearly, the name of a lake and townland four miles north-east of Carrick-on-Shannon, the earl's *annagh* or marsh; and with the same meaning, Curraghanearla near Mallow in Cork; Tominearly in Wexford, the earl's tomb. The word returns to the English form in Coolanearl in the parish of Redcross in Wicklow, the hill-back of the earl; and in Knockearl near the village of Cloghjordan in Tipperary, the earl's hill.

Forest. The word *foraois* [furreesh], which O'Reilly and Peter O'Connell explain a forest, a fox cover, the haunt of wild beasts, is I believe a simple transfer of the English word *forest.* It occurs in the name of a little river flowing through the hamlet of Bellanagare in Roscommon, now called Owen-naforeesha, the river of the forest; and in Cornafurrish, in the parish of Lemanaghan in King's County, the round hill of the forest.

Stake, *Stack*, *Stag.* We have in Irish the word *stácadh* [stawka], which is used in two distinct senses to signify both a stake and a stack, and which I believe to be borrowed from these words, or perhaps from the northern word which is the origin of both. The former signification is exhibited in Stackarnagh, the name of a townland west of Letterkenny in Donegal, which signifies a place full of stakes or stumps of trees; a name which exactly resembles Smutternagh both in formation and meaning (compound suffix *rnach*: page 16).

In a great many places all round the coast, tall, towerlike rocks, standing isolated in the sea, which are designated by the words *cruach*, *ben*, &c., in Irish, are called *stacks* in English; but by a curious custom this is generally changed to the word *stags*. The Stags which form so prominent a feature of Ireland's Eye as seen from Howth, are an excellent example; and other illustrations will be found at various points of the coast. Similar rocks are also called stacks on parts of the coast of Scotland, especially round the Shetland islands; and in noticing these, Worsae traces the word to the Old Norse *stackr*.

Park. *Pairc* [park] means a field or enclosure, and it is of course the same as the English and German word *park*. It exists also in Welsh, but it is probable that both the Welsh and the Irish borrowed it from the Teutonic dialects. In Irish it generally means merely a field, having nothing of the modern restricted application of the English word *park*; and in this sense it is a very usual component of local names. This word forms or begins the names of about 170 townlands. As examples may be taken—Parknaglantane near the city of Cork, *Pairc-na-ngleanntán*, the field of the small glens; Parkatleva in Galway and Mayo, *Pairc-a'-tsleibhe*, the field of the *sliabh* or mountain; Parknagappul near Dungarvan, the field of the *cappuls* or horses; Tinnapark in Kilkenny and Wicklow, *Tigh-na-pairce*, the house of the field. As this is a word not liable to be disguised by corrupt changes of form, and is therefore easily recognised, it will be unnecessary to give further illustrations.

Camp. The Irish *campa* is nothing more than the English word *camp*, with a vowel sound added on to the end. The Four Masters use the word at A. D. 1548, when they record the erection of a large court then called *Campa* in Leix, which was the germ round which grew the town afterwards called Maryborough.

Several sites of former encampments still retain as their name the English word *camp*, which in most cases first passed from English into Irish, and was afterwards restored to the correct English spelling. In other cases the word retains an Irish form, as in Bawnacowma, six miles south of Limerick city, the *bawn* or green field of the camp. Camplagh near Kesh in Fermanagh exhibits the word with the suffix *lach* (p. 5), the name meaning the same as the original root—an encampment.

Spur. I am not aware of any evidence to show that the ancient Irish used spurs; indeed Giraldus Cambrensis expressly states that they did not:—"Also in riding they do not use either saddles, boots, or spurs; but only carry a rod in their hand having a crook at the upper end, with which they urge on and guide their horses." (Top. Hib. Dist. III., c. 10). This is to some extent corroborated by the writer of the Irish account of the battle of Clontarf, who states that when *Maelmordha*, king of Leinster, left Brian Boru's palace of Kincora, in anger, soon before the battle of Clontarf, he drove his horse with a yew rod. And several other passages might be cited from the Brehon Laws and other Irish writings, in which horse-rods are mentioned.

We have however the word *spor*, a spur, in Irish: it is used for instance in the Annals of Lough Key, Vol. II., p. 52, where it is recorded that a certain chieftain died from a wound by his own *spor;* and it is still heard in the colloquial language. But as it is probable that the use of the spur was introduced from England, so I think it equally likely that the word was borrowed from the English language.

This word *spor* occurs in a few local names; but it is not easy to account for its presence: probably places are called from spurs on account of some peculiarity of shape. I suppose some pointed rock gave name to Knockaspur near Cloghjordan in Tipperary. Goulaspurra is a well known suburb of Cork, the name of which signifies the fork (*góbhal*) of the spur; and there is a townland near Castle-lyons in Cork called Spurree, which is merely the plural *sporaidhe*, spurs or pointed rocks.

CHAPTER IV.

POETICAL AND FANCY NAMES.

In an early stage of society, the people are in general very close observers of external nature. The sights and sounds by which they are surrounded—the shapes and colours of hills, glens, lakes, and streams, the solemn voices of winds, waves, and waterfalls, the babbling of streams, the singing, chirping, and chattering of birds, the cries of various animals—all these attract the observation and catch the fancy of a simple and primitive people. The Irish peasantry were, and are still, full of imagination to a degree perhaps beyond those of most other countries. Many think, indeed, that this faculty is rather too highly developed, to the exclusion of other qualities less fascinating but more solid and useful. But be this as it may, it is certain that an examination of our local name system will show that the people who built it up were highly imaginative and sensitively alive to the natural phenomena passing around them. In the present chapter I will give some specimens of names exhibiting this tendency; but many others, equally appropriate and striking, will be found scattered through this volume and the former one.

When we find that the various Irish words which signify beautiful, lovely, fine, pretty, &c., are in constant use in the formation of local names, the obvious inference is that the people had a vivid perception of natural beauty, and dwelt with admiration and pleasure on the loveliness of the various objects among which they lived and moved. And they manifested this delight in a most natural and unaffected way, by bestowing a name that expressed exactly what they felt. This is the more remarkable, inasmuch as the appreciation of landscape, particularly of the landscape of mountains, woods, rocks, and precipices, seems to be very much of late growth among the people of Europe. A new sense has been gradually developed, which, however, judging from local names, appears to have been possessed in a remarkable degree, and at a comparatively early period, by the simple peasantry of this country.

One of these Irish words is *caein* [keen], which signifies, in its application to natural objects, pleasant, delightful, or lovely; it is very frequently met with, and generally assumes the anglicised form *keen*. Killykeen is the name of some places in the county Cavan, which is modernised from *Coill-chaein*, pleasant or delightful wood; Keenrath—pleasant fort—is a place by the Bandon river, four miles above Dunmanway. There is a parish in the north of Tipperary now called Loughkeen, which is a very deceptive name, seeming to indicate the presence of a pretty lake. But the Four Masters mention it as one of the resting places of O'Sullivan Bear in his celebrated retreat from Dunboy to the north in 1602; and here we find the true name, *Baile-achaidh-chaein*, the town of the beautiful field, which is pronounced by the old people, who still retain the name, Balloughkeen, and is now always called by the shorter and very incorrect name Loughkeen. Sometimes this word assumes other forms, as in the case of Drumquin in Tyrone, the correct name of which, as written by the Four Masters, is *Druim-chaein*, pleasant hill-ridge. Elsewhere this Irish name is anglicised more correctly Drumkeen and Dromkeen, which are the names of fifteen townlands in various counties; Aghadrumkeen in Monaghan, the field (*achadh*) of the beautiful ridge. There are two townlands in Clare called Drumquin; but here the Irish form is *Druim-Chuinn*, Conn's ridge. The term is very much disguised in Balleeghan, the name of a townland on the shore of Lough Swilly in Donegal, near Manor Cunningham, containing the ruins of an ancient church, the name of which is written by the Four Masters *Baile-aighidh-chaein* [Balleeheen], the town of the beautiful face or surface. There are other places of the same name in Donegal, which probably come from the same original.

Another word of similar import, which is still more frequently met with in names, is *aeibhinn* [eevin], signifying joyous, delightful, or beautiful. It is written *aimin* by Cormac Mac Cullenan, in his Glossary, and is correctly compared by him with Lat. *amœnum*. It usually occurs in the end of names in some such form as *evin* or *eevan;* and it is well illustrated in Knockeevan in the parish of Newchapel near Clonmel in Tipperary, the delightful hill; Rathevin in Queen's County, beautiful fort; Derryevin near Ballyjamesduff in Cavan (*derry*, an oak wood); and Drumeevin in the parish of Kiltoraght in Clare, beautiful hill-ridge.

Alainn [awlin] signifies bright or lovely; old Irish form, as found in the St. Gall manuscript quoted by Zeuss, *alind*. It assumes several forms in anglicised names, none of them difficult to recognise. There is a townland near the village of Gilford in Down, called Moyallen, i. e. *Magh-álainn*, beautiful plain; and near Dromore in the same county is another place called Kinallen, beautiful head or hill (*ceann*). The sound of the word is better preserved in Derraulin in the parish of Corcomohide in Limerick, *Doire-álainn*, pretty oak wood; and still better in the name of the little river flowing through Fethard in Tipperary—Glashawling, beautiful streamlet. Another form (*áillè*, beauty) of the word is seen in Rossalia in the parish of Killaha in Kerry (*ros*, a wood); but Rossalia near the abbey of Corcomroe in the north of Clare is the wood of the brine (*sáile*: see chap. XVI.).

Many of the names of this class have been translated. But Bonnyglen near Inver in Donegal is not a case in point, and is very deceptive; for it is a modification of *Bun-a'-ghleanna* [Bunaglanna], the *bun* or end of the glen, so called from its situation at the lower end of the glen through which flows the stream that falls a little farther on into the Eany.

One of the pleasantest sounds in the world is the babbling of a brook over rocks or pebbles; and it does not require a great deal of imagination to invest the restless water with life, and to hear voices in its murmurs. Donogh Macnamara, in his song "*Bán-chnoic Eireann ogh*" (The fair hills of holy Ireland), has the following line:—

> "*Na srotha 'san tsamhra ag labhairt ar neoin*":—
> "The streams in the summer-time speaking in the evening."

And another Irish poet, in an elegiac poem on the death of certain warriors who had fallen in battle, makes all inanimate nature join in a lament; and among the rest the cataracts raise their melancholy voices:—"The shores, the waves, the moon and stars, are in sorrow for the death of the heroes, and the sound (*glór*) of cataracts is becoming louder." (See Misc. Celt. Soc., 1849, pp. 378–9).

The peasants who lived and wandered on the margins of our pleasant streams, were as much alive to these impressions as the poets; and in many instances they gave names expressing what they imagined they heard in the busy waters. *Glórach*, derived from *glór* [glore], is the word usually employed in the formation of names of this kind. *Glór* is sometimes used to signify voice, and sometimes noise; but I believe the former is the original meaning. In one of the dialogues of the *Tain bo Chuailnge* (in *Lebor na hUidhre*) the hero Ferdia uses the expression "*árd glór*" (of the majestic voice), to designate Meave, queen of Connaught. (See O'Curry, Lect., III., 418). O'Clery (quoted by Dr. Stokes—Cor. Gl., *voce, babloir*) explains *babloir* by *fear morghlorach* (a man with a great voice); and in the same passage he makes *glor* equivalent to *guth*, voice or speech. The word *glor* is used in this sense also in the last quotation; and many other passages to the same effect might be cited. We may then, I think, conclude that the term *glórach* was applied to streams in the sense of voiceful, babbling, or prattling.

There are several small streams in various parts of the country called Glashagloragh, the voiceful or babbling brook. One of these is in the parish of Inch, three miles south of Borrisoleigh in Tipperary; another joins the Arigideen river, west of Clonakilty in Cork; there is still another near Kenmare; and the word is joined with *sruthán* (a little stream) in Sruhangloragh, in the parish of Kilnoe in Clare. It might be expected that a rugged ford, where streams spread widely, and murmur and wind among the rocks and pebbles, would be often designated by this word *glórach;* and we find this to be the case. In the parish of Annagh in Mayo, south of the village of Ballyhaunis, is a townland called Ahgloragh; there is another townland near Tuam, of the same name, and each was so called from a ford on the adjacent stream, the Irish form of the name being *Ath-glórach*, the babbling or purling ford. There is a little hamlet called Gloryford, three miles west of the village of Ballymoe in Galway, the name of which has the same origin as the preceding, for it is an attempted translation of *Ath-glórach.* One mile to the west of Abbeyleix in Queen's County, we cross Gloreen Bridge; the name—which is a diminutive form—was originally applied to the ford before the erection of the bridge, and has the same meaning as the last. The word Gloragh itself is the name of a townland three miles north-west of the village of Sneem in Kerry, which was evidently so called from a small stream flowing southwards through the place into the Sneem river; and there is a stream called Glory joining the King's River near Kells in Kilkenny: these two names signify "babbling river."

It seems very natural that names of rivers should be occasionally formed from roots signifying to speak.

Silius Italicus, a Roman poet of the first century of the Christian era, mentions a Gaulish river named Labarus; and Zeuss, quoting this, adds from certain mediæval charts, Labara, the ancient name of three small rivers, now called Laber, falling into the Danube near Reginum, the present Ratisbon. He suggests that these names are derived either from *labar*, speaking (modern Irish *labhair*, speak: *labhairt*, speaking); or from *labar*, proud (Gram. Celt., p. 3, note **); but from what is said in the present article, the former will perhaps be considered preferable.*

According to the Irish annalists, three rivers sprang forth in the reign of *Fiacha-Labhrainne*, one of the pre-Christian kings:—the *Fleasc* (now the Flesk in Kerry), the *Mang* (now the Maine, near the Flesk), and the Labrann, which must be one of the rivers in the barony of Corkaguiny, though the name is now obsolete (see O'Curry, Lect., II., 82). This last name corresponds with the old Gaulish names above-mentioned, and has obviously the same origin.

In the Tripartite Life of St. Patrick, it is related that when he came to *Magh Slecht* in the present county of Cavan, to destroy the great idol *Crom Cruach*, he first caught sight of the idol from a stream called *Guth-árd*, which means loud voice; but the old writer is careful to explain that it got

* At the same time it must be observed that rivers sometimes get names meaning proud. The little river that flows into the sea through Glengarriff in Cork, is called *Uallach*, though this name is not preserved on the Ordnance maps. *Uaill* signifies pride; *Uallach*, proud; and so well is this understood that the peasantry are now beginning to call the river by the English name Proudly. I suppose rivers with such names are subject to sudden and impetuous floods, as the Glengarriff river is.

this name because St. Patrick raised his voice on seeing the idol. Whether this be the true explanation or not, it is curious that we have to this day a townland (now divided into two) in the north of Kerry, three or four miles east of Ballybunnion, called by this same name, in the modern form Guhard. Whether this name was originally applied to a stream I cannot say: perhaps the place was so called on account of a remarkable echo. In connexion with this it may be worth remarking that there is a little stream in the parish of Whitechurch in Waterford, five miles south-east of Cappoquin, called the Roaring Water.

There is another Irish word, *gleoir* [glore], which not unfrequently goes to form the names of rivers, and as it is somewhat like *glór* in sound, the two are liable to be confounded when they become anglicised. *Gleoir* means brightness or clearness. The river *Gleoir* in Sligo is very often mentioned in old records (Four M., HyF., &c.). According to O'Donovan (HyF. 109) this is the river now called the Leaffony, flowing into Killala bay five miles north-east of the mouth of the Moy; but the old name is quite forgotten. There was also a river *Gleoir* in the ancient district of *Cuailnge*, the peninsula between Carlingford and Dundalk.

This old name is retained, however, by other streams in various parts of the country. There is a river Glore near Castlepollard in Westmeath, rising in Lough Glore, and joining the Inny; another near the village of Kiltamagh in Mayo; and near Glenarm in Antrim is a townland called Glore, which must have taken its name from a stream (v. Reeves: Eccl. Ant. 338). The name of the townland of Glear near Clones in Monaghan, has a like origin, for it is written *Gleeore* in the Down Survey; and its appearance, abounding in sparkling waters, justifies the name.

There is still another word somewhat like this last, namely *gluair* [gloor], meaning pure or clear; from which comes *gluaire* [glooria], purity, clearness, brightness; but I suppose *gleoir* and *gluair* are radically the same. In the Tripartite Life it is stated that St. Patrick founded a church at a place called *Gluaire* in the neighbourhood of the present town of Larne (see Reeves: Eccl. Ant. 87, note k). This word gives name to the two townlands of Glooria near Lough Key in the north of Roscommon, and to Glouria in the parish of Galey in the north of Kerry.

Before leaving this part of the subject, I must direct attention to another way of designating the sparkling brightness of streams, by comparing it with the brilliancy of silver; a comparison which is extremely common, not only in modern poetry, but in the language of every day life. This was the origin of the name of the Arigideen, literally "little silver"—the silvery little river, a considerable stream which flows into the sea at Courtmacsherry in the south of the county Cork (*airgead*, silver; diminutive *airgidín*). Near Castleisland in Kerry there is a small stream which dashes over rocks, called Glasheenanargid, the little streamlet (*glaisín*) of the silver.

In their observation of the beauties of nature, the people did not pass unnoticed the singing of birds. It would not be easy to find a prettier name than Coolkellure, which is that of a place near Dunmanway in Cork, signifying the recess of the warbling of birds:—*Cuil-ceileabhair*. The word *ceileabhar* [kellure], which enters into this name, is now commonly applied to the singing, chirping, or warbling of a bird :—

> "*Do bhél is binne*
> *Na'n chúach air bile.*
> *S'ná ceilebhar caein nan eunlaidh.*"

"Thy mouth which is sweeter than the cuckoo on the tree—sweeter than the melodious warbling of the birds." But it originally signified the same as the Latin *celebratio*, which the early ecclesiastical writers transferred into the Irish language. Cormac Mac Cullenan (Gloss. 9th cent.) mentions the word, and derives it from *celebro*. It is probable that the name Drumbinnis, which we find in Cavan, Fermanagh, and Leitrim, and Drumbinnisk in Fermanagh alone, have a similar origin :—*Druim-binnis*, the hill-ridge of melody (*binneas*, melody).

The fragrance of the fields and flowers arrested the attention, and drew forth the admiration of, these observant people, as well as the visible beauties of the landscape. And they expressed their perception and enjoyment of the perfume of any particular spot, fragrant from its abundance of sweet smelling herbs, by imposing names formed from the word *cumhra* or *cubhra* [coora], which signifies sweet scented. The word is used in this sense by Giolla Iosa Mór Mac Firbis in a poem written by him in the beginning of the fifteenth century, when he calls *O'Murchadha's* house "Habitation of the sweet-scented branches" (*Aitreb na craeb cúbraidi:* see Hy F., p. 265). Irish writers were fond of using this term *craebh cúmhra ;* and in love songs it is often applied to a beautiful young woman, as in the well known song, "*Rois geal dubh :*"—"*A chraebh chúmhra a dubhairt liom go raibh grádh agud dom:*" "O, sweet-scented branch, who hast told me that thou didst love me." There is a parish in Limerick which, curiously enough, has for name this very epithet, *Craebh-cumhradh* [Crave-coora], for so O'Heeren writes the name, meaning sweet-scented branch or branchy tree—but it is now anglicised Crecora. A place about three miles north-west from Eyrecourt in Galway has a name like this:—Scecoor, i. e. in Irish *Sceach-cumhra*, fragrant bush.

Clontycoora, the name of a townland in the parish of Cleenish in Fermanagh, is as suggestive of fields decked with summer flowers as any name of this class—*Cluainte-cumhraidh*, the odoriferous *cloons* or meadows; so also is Aghacoora near the village of Lixnaw in Kerry—sweet-scented field; and Clooncoorha, scented meadow, is the name of a little hamlet three miles north of Kilrush in Clare. At A. D. 1401 the Four Masters record that Mac Rannall, the chief of his race, was slain by another chief of the same name at *Druim-cubhra*, the fragrant-scented ridge; and the place, which lies in the parish of Kiltoghert in Leitim, still retains the name in the form of Drumcoora. There is another place of the same name near Mohill in the same county. We have also Tullycoora near Castleblayney in Monaghan (*Tully*, a hill); and the old church that gave name to Kilcoorha in the parish of Killeedy in Limerick, was probably surrounded with sweet-smelling bushes —most likely hawthorn—when it got the name. Five miles north-east from Birr in King's County, is a considerable lake called Lough Coura—which, no doubt, was so called from the perfume of the flowery herbage on its shores.

What a curious and pretty name—pretty at least

in its meaning—is Muggalnagrow, in the parish of Inishmacsaint in Fermanagh; *mogul*, a cluster; *cno*, a nut; *Mogul-na-gcno*, cluster of nuts (*n* changed to *r*; 1st Ser., Part I., c. III.) Just outside Sybil Point, west of Dingle in Kerry, there is a rock rising from the sea, called Maheraneig; i. e. in Irish *Mathair-an-fhiaig*, the raven's mother (*fiach*, a raven); and it got this name, I suppose, as being larger and more imposing in appearance than another sea rock in its vicinity, called the Raven. Among the innumerable inlets round Lettermore island in Connemara, there is one at the townland of Bealadangan, which at its opening is exposed to all the violence of the tempests that sweep over that desolate coast. A stormy and inhospitable shore was never more graphically pictured than in the name of that little inlet:—Crompaunvealduark: *crompán*, a small sea-inlet; *bél*, mouth; *duairc*, frowning or surly;—the little creek of the surly mouth. Among the many streams that flow into Killery bay from the north or Mayo side, there is one just opposite Leenane, called Sruhaun-more-ard (the large high streamlet), which tumbles over a rocky precipice into the dark depths below; and any one who understands a little of the Irish language can form a fair idea of the gloomy and dangerous character of this waterfall even without seeing it, for the name is quite enough:—Skirra-go-hiffirn, slipping to hell.

CHAPTER V.

DISEASES AND CURES.

Our native literature affords sufficient proof that the science of medicine was carefully cultivated in ancient Ireland. For we have in our museums several medical manuscripts containing elaborate treatises on the various types of diseases known in the times of the writers, with minute descriptions of symptoms, and carefully detailed directions on the methods of treatment. The office of physician was hereditary, like many other offices in this country; and these manuscripts were compiled by the several leech families, and handed down from father to son, each adding to the volume the most recent discoveries in the science, or the results of his own experience.

Several great physicians are celebrated in the pagan records of the country; and many legends are extant which show that they were believed to possess powers of cure bordering on the miraculous. The most celebrated of all was *Diancecht*, the physician of the *Tuatha de Dananns*. When this race invaded Ireland they found it already in possession of the *Firbolgs;* and a battle was fought between the two armies on the plain of Moytura, near Cong in the county Mayo, in the year of the world 3303, in which the *Firbolgs* were defeated, and their king, *Eochy*, slain. The ancient account of this battle states that *Nuada*, the king of the *Tuatha de Dananns*, had his arm lopped off with a blow of a heavy sword, by *Sreng*, one of the *Firbolg* warriors. *Credne*, the king's artificer, fashioned an arm of silver; and *Diancecht* fixed it on by his surgical skill, while his son, *Miach*, endued it with life and motion, so that the king was able to use it like the hand and arm he had lost; and he was ever after known by the name of Nuada of the silver hand.

The second battle of Moytura was fought twenty-seven years after, by the Tuatha de Dananns against the Fomorians, in which the former were again victorious; but their king, Nuada of the silver hand, was slain by the great Fomorian chieftain, Balor of the mighty blows. In this battle also, the wonderful medical skill of *Diancecht* was brought into play; for with the aid of his daughter and his two sons, he prepared a medicinal bath in the rear of the army, and endued it with such sanative virtue, that the wounded warriors who retired and plunged into it, came out restored to strength, "smooth and whole from their wounds." The bath derived its healing qualities from herbs which were gathered by *Diancecht* chiefly in a district situated near Birr in the present King's County, which, because it produced these medicinal herbs in such abundance, was called Lusmagh, the plain of the herbs (*lus*, an herb; *magh*, a plain), a name which it retains to this day.

We read also in the *Tain bo Chuailnge*, of a warrior named *Cethern* who was desperately wounded, and who was cured by the physician *Fingin*, by means of a bath medicated with the marrow of a great number of cows (O'Curry, Lect., II., 101).

If we are inclined to laugh at the simple people who believed in those marvellous cures, let us not forget that they were in no degree more credulous than myriads of our own day, who are caught by quack advertisements, and who believe in cures quite as wonderful as those performed by *Diancecht*.

The frequent notices of physicians in Irish writings, the great consideration in which they were held, and the numerous regulations regarding them found in the Brehon Laws, show that medicine was a well recognised profession from the most remote periods of history. After the introduction of Christianity we find no mention of any particular physician, so far as I am aware, till A. D. 860, in which year the Four Masters and the Annals of Ulster record the death of "Moylohar O'Tinnri, the most learned physician of Ireland." From this time forward we have information—increasing as we advance—regarding medical science and its professors. Each of the great Irish families had attached to it a physician whose office was hereditary, and who usually held a tract of land in return for service. These physicians ranked with the judges and poets; many of them resided in stately castles, and lived in fact altogether like princes.

Among these may be mentioned the O'Cassidys, who were physicians to the Maguires of Fermanagh, of whom several individual practitioners of great eminence are commemorated in the annals. This family possessed a tract in the county Fermanagh, which retains their name to this day—Farrancassidy, the land of the O'Cassidys. The O'Sheils were another very distinguished family of physicians, who were attached to the Mac Coghlans of Delvin in the King's County, and to the Mac Mahons of Oriel; and their medical manuscript—"The Book of the O'Sheils"—is now in the Royal Irish Academy. This family possessed the lands of Ballysheil near the village of Cloghan in King's County—the town of O'Sheil. There are other places of the same name in the counties of Down and Armagh.

The very names of some of these families indicate their profession. O'Lee (the name is now always written Lee) was physician to the O'Flahertys of west Connaught; and the book belonging to this family is also preserved in the library of the Royal Irish Academy. The Irish form of the name is *O'Liaigh*, which means the descendant of the *liagh* [leea], i. e. of the *leech* or physician. So also O'Hickey: the O'Hickeys were long celebrated as physicians, and different branches of the family were attached to the O'Briens and other great southern families. This name is in Irish *O'hIcidhe*, which signifies the descendant of the healer, from the root *ic* to heal (*ic*, *salus*, Zeuss, 49).

The two ancestors from whom these families respectively took their names must have sprung into sudden celebrity on account of their skill in medicine; so much so that their usual names were changed to *Icidhe* [eeky], the healer, and *Liagh* [leea], the physician; and their profession was transmitted from father to son for hundreds of years, till it finally died out in times comparatively recent—a good example of the extraordinary tenacity with which the several families clung to hereditary offices in Ireland.

It is almost unnecessary to observe that it is not my object to give here a history of disease in Ireland, but only to illustrate by a few remarks those local names that preserve in their etymology a memory of disease either general or special.

Plague. We have in Irish several words to denote a plague in general. The most usual term in use in Pagan times was *tamh* [thauv], of which I have already treated (see Tallaght, First Series). Another word in use was *teidhm* [thame], which however I do not find reproduced in names. In Christian times the word *plaigh* [plaw]—a mere adaptation of the Latin *plaga*—came into general use to denote any great pestilence or violent epidemic. This word enters into the formation of several names; and when we find a place with such a name we may draw the conclusion either that it was at some time long past depopulated by one of those dreadful pestilential visitations which are so frequently recorded in our annals, and which, as it swept over the country, concentrated its virulence on that particular spot; or that the place was selected, during the prevalence of the mortality, as an asylum for the sick; and probably in some instances names of this kind mark the spots where the victims of some sort of plague were interred in one great sepulchre (see Tallaght, First Series). Just by the chapel of Shanbally near Monkstown below Cork, there is a large rock with some ancient remains on its top; it is called on the Ordnance map Carrigaplau, representing the Irish *Carraig-a'-phlaigh*, the rock of the plague; but the popular anglicised name is Carrigafly, which is more correct, the *p* being aspirated as it ought. There is a place near Clonmel called Templeaplau—the plague church; in the parish of Donaghmore in Cork we have Commeenaplau (*commeen*, a little *com* or valley); and three miles north-west from Shrule in Mayo, is a place called Knockanaplawy, the little hill of the plague.

Leprosy. In our native records there is abundant evidence to prove that some form of leprosy existed in Ireland from a very early date. It would seem to have been a recognised disease in the time of St. Patrick;

for we are told in one of his Lives, that at one time he maintained a leper in his house, and ministered to him with his own hands. After his time our literature, especially that portion devoted to the Lives and Acts of the Irish Saints, abounds with notices of the disease; and even some of the early saints themselves are believed to have been afflicted with it, as for instance St. Finan, the founder of the monastery of Innisfallen at Killarney, in the seventh century, who was surnamed *lobur* or the leper, because, as is commonly believed, he was for thirty years afflicted with some cutaneous disease.

There are several notices of individual deaths by leprosy in the annals, and on more occasions than one it broke out in the form of an epidemic, and carried off great numbers of people. From the time of St. Patrick till the 17th century, the country appears never to have been free from it. Boate states that in his time (1645) it had disappeared; but says that formerly it was very common, and he attributes its prevalence to the practice of eating salmon out of season.

So general was the disease in former times, that leper hospitals were established in various parts of Ireland, many of them in connexion with monastic institutions; for example at Dublin, Waterford, Wexford, &c.; and Boate states that they were specially numerous in Munster, where the disease was very prevalent. This last statement appears to receive some confirmation from the epithet applied in the Book of Rights (p. 49) to Slieve Lougher near Castleisland in Kerry, namely *Luachair na lubhair*, Lougher of the lepers; which would also go to show that this characteristic, as regards at least a part of Munster, was of long standing. We find recorded in the "Monasticon Hibernicum" that an hospital for lepers was founded in 1467 at the village of Hospital in Limerick and another at Dungannon, the former of which still retains the name. The names of Spittle, Spiddle, and Spital, which are only shortened forms of Hospital, are very common in various parts of Ireland; and they mark the sites of hospitals of some kind, some of them no doubt leper hospitals.

There are several terms in Irish for cutaneous diseases of the nature of leprosy. Of these *samh-thrusc* [sauvrusk] is applied to a great epidemic which broke out in the middle of the sixth century, and which is understood to have been a sort of mange or scaly leprosy. *Clamh* [clauv] is another word in common use for some form of the same disease, as well as for a person afflicted with it; and we have this commemorated in Drumclamph near Ardstraw in Tyrone, the ridge of the lepers. But it is with the word *lobhar* [lower] we have chiefly to do here. It is generally believed that this is merely the Latin word *lepra* borrowed by the Irish. But *lobar* is used in the oldest Irish writings in the sense of *infirmus*, and is not confined in its application to leprosy; it occurs for instance, many times in the MSS. quoted by Zeuss (8th cent.) in the old form *lobor*, and always glosses *infirmus* or *debilis*. In the Book of Leinster and also in the Book of Lismore, the expression "*na lobor ocus na clam*" occurs, and in both cases, Dr. Reeves translates *clam* by "lepers" and *lobor* by "sick," which latter exactly corresponds with the *infirmus* and *debilis* of the ancient glossographer (Reeves on the Culdees, Trans. R. I. A., Vol. XXIV., p. 196). From this it would appear that *lobor* is not borrowed from *lepra*, but is merely cognate with it. If we bear in mind the sense in which this word was used in old Irish, it will not perhaps be necessary to believe that those early saints—of whom there were several—who are surnamed *lobhar*, were afflicted with leprosy; but that they were simply *infirmus* or feeble in health.

In whatever sense *lobhar* may have been used, however, in very early ages, in later times it came to be applied, not in a general manner to a person infirm or sick, but in a special sense to one afflicted with leprosy. And in this sense it is found in the local nomenclature of the country, which thus corroborates the accounts preserved in the national records, of the former prevalence of the disease. The usual anglicised forms of the word is *lour*, *lower*, *loura*, and *lure* (this last representing the Irish modified form *lubhar*, which very often occurs); and I suppose that wherever we find a name containing this word, we may generally infer that some kind of hospital or asylum for lepers was formerly established there.

Such a place is Knockaunalour in the parish of Ardnageehy, south of the Nagles Mountains in Cork—*Cnocán-na-lobhar*, the little hill of the lepers; and Knocknalower, which has a similar meaning, is the name of a small hill with a few houses at its base, in the midst of a moory tract, east of Belmullet in Mayo. There are places in Cork, Tipperary, and Galway, called Gortnalour, Gortnalower, and Gortnaloura, the field of the lepers; and in Rathnalour in the parish of Newchapel near Clonmel, the diseased must have been sheltered within the enclosure of the old fort. About five miles north of Corrofin in Clare, there is a place called Poulnalour, the lepers' pool or hole, which was probably so called from a pool supposed to possess some virtue in curing lepers who washed themselves in it. Ballynalour, the town of the lepers, is a townland near St. Mullins in Carlow; and this was the original name of Leperstown between Dublin and Bray, which is now corruptly called Leopardstown.

But no doubt, several of the places with names of this kind were so called because persons afflicted with leprosy resided in, or had them in possession; and this may be presumed to have been the case when the name commemorates only a single leper. There is a place near Kanturk in Cork, called Dromalour, and another in Cavan, half way between Butler's Bridge and Belturbet, called Drumalure, both from *Druim-a'-lobhair*, the ridge of the leper; Cloonalour, near Tralee, the leper's meadow. There is a place in the parish of Cloonoghil in Sligo, called Flowerhill, which is a strange transformation of the proper Irish name, *Cnoc-a'-lobhair*, hill of the leper. This change, which was made by translating *cnoc* to *hill*, and by turning *lobhair* (lour) to *flower*, totally hides the meaning. It is to be observed that the fact of *lobhar* being singular in a name does not exclude the supposition of a leper hospital.

Jaundice. Those who are afflicted with jaundice may be restored to health and colour by drinking the water of Toberboyoga (well of the jaundice) near Kells in Meath:—*buidheóg* [boyoge], jaundice. Wells of this kind are sometimes called *Buidheachán* [Boyaghan], a term which, like *buidheóg*, is a diminutive from *buidhe* [boy], yellow; and one of these wells has given name to the townland of Boyaghan near Irvinestown in Fermanagh. But I must observe that some of them may have been so called from the yellow colour of the clay or mud. Gortnasoolboy in the parish of Cam in Roscommon, would seem to be connected in some way with this disease, as its most expressive name appears to indicate—the field of the yellow eyes (*suil*, eye). Another name of exactly the same kind is applied to a fort, and also to a townland, in the parish of Ardcrony, three miles south of Borrisokane in Tipperary—Lisnasoolmoy, the fort of the yellow eyes. Here the *b* of *buidhe* or *boy* is eclipsed by *m* as it ought to be; but I cannot imagine why the fort got this name.

Warts. If a person's hands are disfigured by warts, he has generally not far to travel to find a well, in which if he wash them day after day for some time, the warts will disappear. Sometimes the rain-water that collects in the hollows of certain monumental stones, such as crosses, tombs, &c.—and occasionally in rocks of any kind—is believed to possess this virtue. Two miles west of Macroom in Cork, near the south bank of the river Sullane, and in the townland of Inchibrackane, is a holy well called Tobernawanny, which is the pronunciation of *Tobar-na-bhfaithnidhe*, the well of the warts:—*faithnidh* [fauny], a wart. There is another well of the same name in the townland of Derrygarriv, two miles south of Kenmare; and still another—Tobernavaunia, in the parish of Kilcummin in Galway. Fahnia lake, a small pool three miles north-east of the town of Donegal, must have been believed to possess some virtue of this kind, for the name is the English representative of the Irish *Loch-na-bhfaithnidhe* [Lough Navaunee], the lake of the warts.

Well Cures. The memory of diseases is preserved more generally in connexion with wells than with any other physical feature. For wells were very often dedicated to the early saints, after whose death they continued to be held in reverence for ages by the people; and many of them were believed to possess the power of curing diseases. Jocelin records the legend that St. Patrick caused a well to spring miraculously from the earth in the neighbourhood of Saul near Downpatrick, and this well was called *Slán* [slawn], but the Ultonians, we are told, filled it up on account of the annoyance they suffered from the great crowds that frequented it. For it was believed to possess wonderful efficacy, and the old scholiast, in explaining the name *slán* by *sanus* or health-giving, adds that it was called *slán* because all who came to it returned from it whole and sound.

A reverence for wells, and a popular belief in their sanative virtues, existed among the Pagan population of the country before the fifth century; for we find it recorded in one of the earliest narratives of the Life of St. Patrick, that he came on a certain occasion to a well called *Slan* which the druids worshipped as a god; and other passages might be cited to the same effect.

This word *slán*, which we have seen was a name for certain fountains in pagan times, and was adopted also by the early Christians, continued in use after the spread of Christianity as a kind of generic term for holy wells; and we have many examples of wells so called—all in the same sense—indicating the prevalence of a belief in their healing qualities. It must be remarked that *slán*, healthy, and the derivative *sláinte* [slauntia] health, are living words in common use at the present day. There is a Toberslane—the well of health or the healing well—which gives name to a townland in the parish of Killea a little south-west of the city of Derry; there is another well now called Toberslaun in the townland of Balleeghan near Lough Swilly in Donegal, which

O'Donovan believes, and with good reason, to be the same well mentioned in the Four Masters at 1557, by the name of *Cabharthach* [Cowrha], which has much the same meaning as *slán*, viz., helping. Tober-slauntia—well of health—is the name of a well in the townland of Knightswood, two miles south-west of the village of Multyfarnham in Westmeath; and there is a small circular lake called Lough Slaun near the east margin of Lough Ree, south of Lanesboro.

The word *slán* enters also into other names. There is an old fort in the parish of St. John's in Roscommon, which would appear by its name to have been used at one time as a kind of sanatorium:—Lisaslaun, the fort of the sick people (*eas*, a negative particle; *easlán*, a sick person). The common plantain or rib-grass is called in Irish *slánlus*, heal-herb; from which again the townland of Muingatlaunlush in the parish of O'Brennan, about six miles north-east of Tralee, has its name:—*Muing-a'-tslánluis*, the *muing* or sedgy place of the rib-grass.

While great numbers of wells are, like the preceding, celebrated for curing all sorts of diseases, many, on the other hand, were resorted to for particular disorders; and the names of not a few attest this speciality. We may with great probability conclude that wells of this kind very often derived their reputation from being dedicated to patrons who were noted for curing special diseases. As a good example of a special reputation of this kind, I will instance a curious legend in the life of one of our most celebrated early saints.

Aedh mac Bric (*Aedh* or Hugh the son of *Brec*), bishop, was the tutelar saint of the Kinelea, that is, of the people who inhabited the territory now represented by the barony of Moycashel, in Westmeath. He was one of the tribe himself, his father, Brec, being descended in the fourth generation from Niall of the Nine Hostages; he was born early in the sixth century, and he died in the year 589. The chief of a district in his native territory presented him with one of the native circular forts to be turned to Christian uses; and the saint erected a church within its fosses; whence, according to his Life, the place came to be called *Rath-Aedha*, *Castellum Aidi*, *i.e. Aedh's* or Hugh's fort, now anglicised Rahugh, the name of the parish in which he is still venerated. And the old fort still remains there. This saint is reverenced in several other places. With that taste for extreme and impressive solitude so prevalent among the early ecclesiastics, he built a little oratory, whose ruins are still to be seen, on the top of Slieve League in Donegal, where he is now called bishop Hugh Breaky; and near it is his holy well, where there were stations within the last two or three generations.

It is related in his Life that a man once came to him who was afflicted with a violent headache, and begged the saint to pray for him. The bishop said, "I cannot cure you in any way except by causing the pain to pass from you to me; but you will have a great reward if you bear it patiently." The man persisted, stating that the pain was more than he could bear; whereupon the bishop prayed, and the sufferer was immediately relieved, but the pain was transferred to the head of the holy man. Hence it came to pass, as the legend goes on to say, that persons were in the habit of invoking this saint's name for a pain in the head. The great antiquity of this custom is proved, and very curiously illustrated, by the following short poem published by Mone, archive director of Carlsruhe, from a manuscript preserved in the monastery of Reichenau on an island in Lake Constance:—

O rex, o rector regminis,
o cultor cœli carminis
o persecutor murmoris
o deus alti agminis.

·l· filio ·l· pater
Aido sanctus mech brich benibula
posco puro precamina,
ut refrigerat flumina
mei capitis calida.

Curat caput cum renibus
·l· cerebre
meis, atque talibus,
cum oculis et genibus,
cum auribus et naribus.

·l· nervibus
Cum inclitis euntibus,
cum fistulis sonantibus,
cum lingua atque dentibus,
cum lachrymarum fontibus.

Sanctus Aid altus adjuvat,
meum caput ut liberat,
ut hoc totum perseverat
sanum atque vigilat.

This poem (the Latin of which is very barbarous, as Dr. Reeves remarks) was written in the eighth century by an Irishman, one of those good men who in early ages exiled themselves from home to help to spread the Faith, and it will be perceived that it is a form of prayer to obtain relief from a headache. We may assume that the writer merely transcribed it, and that its composition may be referred to a still earlier date. Mone, who had not access to Irish hagiological authorities, conjectured that the person whose intercession is invoked was *Aedh* or Mogue, first bishop of Ferns; but Dr. Reeves at once recognised him as *Aedh mac Bric.*

Dr. Reeves concludes the paper from which the preceding account has been taken,* with the following appropriate remark:—"The little composition which forms the leading subject of the paper, possesses no literary merits, but it is a well-defined trace of that

* On the Hymnus Sancti Aidi, by the Rev. W. Reeves, D.D. Proc. R. I. A., VII., 91.

early religious emigration which commenced in the sixth century, and waxed more and more vigorous till it attained its height in the ninth, taking with it not only the language and literature of the Scoti, but also their legendary associations, which they clung to in foreign climes; and not only so, but left them on record in manuscripts which have weathered a thousand years, and are now beginning, through German industry, to be reflected on the mother country, where they find their counterparts, after a separation of so many centuries."

The counterpart of this little poem is the account quoted at p. 85 from the Life of the saint. But there is another, and if possible a more interesting one, in the fact that *Aedh mac Bric* is still invoked for a headache. Near the ruins of the old monastery of Rahugh was bishop Hugh's holy well, but it is now, I regret to say, closed up, though it would be easy to restore it; and in the same place is a large stone, still called Bishop Hugh's stone—for according to local tradition, the saint was accustomed to pray on it—to which the people of the surrounding districts have been, time out of mind, in the habit of resorting for the relief of headache.* So that the custom, which probably began soon after the saint's death, has lived on without interruption for more than twelve hundred years.

Wells that were famed for curing sore eyes were often called Tobersool and Tobernasool, the well of the eyes (*suil*, the eye); there is a Tobersool for instance in the parish of Balscaddan in the north of the county Dublin, near Balbriggan, and another called Tobernasool, one mile north-east of Lisbellaw in Fermanagh, from

* See the Rev. A. Cogan's "Diocese of Meath," II. 522.

which the adjacent lake has got the name of Lough Eyes. Of the same character must be Loughannasool, two miles east of Elphin in Roscommon, Loughannasool in the parish of Cloonygormican, same county, and Loughnasool, near the north end of Lough Arrow in Sligo, all signifying the lake of the eyes. Sometimes these wells are called Toberkeagh, blind well (*caech*, blind); but this term is often also applied to a well which sometimes dries up, without any reference to eye-cure: it is *blind* when there is no water in it. There is a place called Blindwell in the parish of Kilconla in Galway, six miles north-west of Tuam; and a stream called Owenkeagh, blind river, joins the Arigideen above Timoleague in Cork.

When children are wasting away in a decline they are bathed in the little lake called Loughaneeg, three miles south of Elphin in Roscommon:—*eug*, death, but applied here to a slow, wasting disease; Loughaneeg, the lake of the decline. The general restorative qualities of Toberanleise, near the river Barrow, in the townland of Dunganstown, parish of Whitechurch, Wexford, is indicated by its name—*Tobar-an-leighis*, the well of the cure (*liagh*, a physician—*leigheas*, cure). The little lake of Loughanleagh, three miles east of Bailieboro in Cavan, has been celebrated from time immemorial for curing all kinds of cutaneous diseases: let the eruption be ever so virulent, the patient who was bathed in this little pool and afterwards treated with poultices of the mud, was sure to show a clean white skin, in a very few days. A good many years ago, unfortunately for the people of the neighbourhood, a gentleman who had a pack of mangy hounds swam them in the water, which so offended the local guardian that the lake immediately lost its virtue, and has never since regained it. But still the name remains, to tantalize the people with the memory of what they have lost—*Loch-an-liagha*, physician lake. There are many small lakes called Loughanlea in various parts of the country, but it is pretty certain that in these cases the name means merely grey lake.*

CHAPTER VI.

OFFICES AND TRADES.

IMMEDIATELY after the time of St. Patrick, Christianity spread rapidly in Ireland; religious bodies sprang up in all directions; and the country became covered with a vast number of ecclesiastical institutions of every kind. From Britain and the Continent great numbers came hither to spend their lives in study and peaceful retirement; and in every part of Europe Irish missionaries were to be found who had voluntarily left their native land to preach the Gospel: so that Ireland came to be known by the name of *Insula Sanctorum*, the Island of Saints. As one consequence of this, we find that the Irish terms by which the various orders of ecclesiastics are designated, are intimately interwoven with the local nomenclature of the country. Names formed in this way often mark the sites of monasteries, nunneries, or churches—many of them now obliterated; or they

* For a considerable part of the information in this chapter regarding diseases in Ireland, I am indebted to the Introduction to the "Table of Deaths" in the Census of 1851, by Sir William R. Wilde.

indicate places where ecclesiastics lived, or land which was once the property of neighbouring religious institutions.

Clergy. *Clérech* signifies a clergyman without any reference to rank; and like the English term *clergy*, it is a loan word from the Latin *clericus*. Two of its most common anglicised forms are seen in Farrancleary, the name of a place near Cork city, the land of the clergyman; and in Ballynagleragh, the name of several places in Clare, Tipperary, and Waterford, the town of the clergy. In this last the *c* is eclipsed by *g*, and also in Carrownaglearagh in Roscommon and Sligo, the quarter-land of the clergy.

Bishops. The word *episcopus* was borrowed early from Latin into Irish, and in the old language it took the form *epscop*; but this has been changed by metathesis to the modern form *easpog* or *easpoc*, which is now the word in universal use for a bishop. When this term occurs in names, it is almost always easy of recognition, as the following examples will show:—Monaspick, the name of a townland near Blessington in Wicklow, signifies bishop's bog; Tullinespick in the parish of Bright in Down, the *tulach* or hill of the bishop. In a very few cases the word is disguised, as in Killaspy in the parish of Dunkitt in Kilkenny, which is written in certain old documents, Killaspucke, meaning the bishop's church.

Canons. *Cananach*, which is an adaptation of the Latin *canonicus*, signifies a canon, a church dignitary. It is pretty common in local names, and the first *c* is usually changed to *g* by eclipse. There is a townland near Letterkenny, which in old times formed part of the termon lands of the monastery of Kilmacrenan; and this circumstance is still commemorated in the name Carrownaganonagh, or in Irish *Ceath-*

ramhadh-na-gcananach, the quarter land of the canons. In the great expansion of the Shannon south of Clare, there is an island now called Canon Island in English, but always by the people speaking Irish *Oilean-na-gcananach*, the island of the canons. There was a monastery for Augustinian canons founded on this island by Donald O'Brien, king of Limerick, the extensive ruins of which can be very plainly seen from the steamer as it passes the island.

Priests. *Sagart*, or in its old form, *sacart*, a priest, is merely the Latin *sacerdos*, borrowed at the very dawn of Christianity in Ireland. It is very common in local names, and like the last, is easily known; for it usually assumes the form *saggart*, or with the *s* eclipsed by *t*, *taggart* or *teggart*. These forms are exhibited in Kylenasaggart in the parish of Ballycallen, near the city of Kilkenny, *Coill-na-sagart*, the wood of the priests; and in Carrickataggart near Killybegs in Donegal, *Carraig-a'-tsagairt*, the priest's rock. Taggartsland in the parish of Donegore in Antrim, shows the *t* preserved after the article had dropped off, the Irish name being obviously *Fearann-a'-tsagairt*, *i. e.* priest-land. There is a range of hills near the village of Ballyvourney in Cork, called Derrynasaggart, the *derry* or oak-wood of the priests. In a few cases the *s* is aspirated, and then the form assumed by the word is generally such as is seen in Drumhaggart in the parish of Burt in Donegal, *Druim-shagairt*, the priest's ridge.

Another word for a priest, but much more rare than *sagart*, is *cruimhther* [criffer, cruffer]. According to Cormac Mac Cullenan (Glossary; 9th cent.), the Irish borrowed this word from the Welsh, and the latter from the Latin: he states that *presbyter* is the original, which the Welsh ecclesiastics who were in attendance on St. Patrick, changed to *premter;* and the Irish borrowing this, altered it to *cruimther*, for "*prem* in the Welsh is *cruim* in the Gaelic." In some of our oldest records, we find this word *cruimther* applied to several eminent ecclesiastics, such as *Cruimther Aedh*, *Cruimther Colum*, &c.

A very correct anglicised form of the word is exhibited in Clooncruffer in the parish of Ardcarn, in the north of Roscommon, the *cloon* or meadow of the priest; and a less correct in the name of a far more important place, Kilcrumper, a parish near Fermoy in Cork, taking its name from a celebrated old church which is frequently mentioned in the Book of Lismore, and called *Cill-cruimthir*, the church of the priest. In Kilcumreragh, the name of a parish in the south of Westmeath, the word is so much disguised by corruption as to be unrecognisable. Mr. Hennessy writes to me to say that this name is always written in old Inquisitions, Kilcrumreragh; and that in the Down Survey it is in one place Killcrumraghragh, and in another Killcrumreaghragh; all of which point plainly to *Cill-Cruimthir-Fhiachrach*, the church of Priest *Fiachra*.

Abbots. *Ab* or *abb* signifies an abbot, and is in constant use in Irish writings. It is merely the Latin word *abbas*, but it was borrowed early, for it is found in the oldest Irish documents, as for instance in the manuscripts quoted by Zeuss. It sometimes takes the form of *ap*. Its usual genitive is *abadh* or *apadh* [abba, appa], and this is the form generally commemorated in local names. Three miles from the town of Wicklow, near the entrance to the Devil's Glen, is a well-known place called Inchanappa, the *inch* or river-island of the abbot, the *inch* being the rich meadow beside the Vartry. Nearly the same form of the word is found in Kilnappy in the parish of Faughanvale in Derry, the wood of the abbot; while it is shortened to one syllable in Ballinab in the parish of Mothel in Waterford, the abbot's *bally* or townland; and in Portanab, near Kildalkey in Meath, the bank or landing place of the abbot.

Monks. The common Irish word for a monk is *manach*, which is only an adaptation of *monachus*, from which the English word *monk* is also derived. *Managh*, one of its English forms, is also the usual anglicised representative of *meadhonach*, middle; and in individual cases the inquirer should be on his guard not to mistake one of these Irish words for the other. If *managh* be preceded by *na*, the genitive plural of the article, it may be taken to mean monks, otherwise it very often stands for middle. Thus Knocknamanagh in Cork and Galway is *Cnoc-na-manach*, the hill of the monks; while Knockmanagh in Cork, Kerry, and Mayo, is *Cnoc-meadhonach*, middle hill. When the anglicised word ends in *y* the meaning is seldom doubtful, as in the case of Farranmanny near Moate, in Westmeath, the same as Farranmanagh near Milltown, in Kerry, and Farrannamanagh near Cloyne, in Cork, the monks' land.

Kilnamanagh, which is the name of several places, generally represents the Irish *Cill-na-manach*, the church of the monks; but sometimes, as in the case of Kilnamanagh in Tipperary, the *Kil* stands not for *cill*, a church, but for *coill*, a wood. Similar in formation to this is Garranamanagh, the name of a townland and parish near Freshford in Kilkenny, signifying the garden or shrubbery of the monks; and Dunnamanagh, the name of a village in Tyrone, the monks' dun or fortress. When the word occurs in the genitive singular it is often anglicised *many*, as in Drummany, the name of several townlands in Cavan, *Druim-managh*, the ridge of the monk; in this case also when the article is used, the *m* becomes aspirated to *v*, as in Drumavanagh near the town of Cavan, *Druim-a'-mhanaigh*, the ridge of the monk; and here the interpretation is supported by the name of "The friar's avenue," which extends as far as another feature—"The friar's well." With the southern peculiarity of retaining the final *g* in pronunciation, we have Rahavanig near Ballybunnion, *Rath-a'-mhanaig*, the monk's fort. Monknewtown, the name of a parish near Slane in Meath, is a sufficiently correct translation of the Irish name, which is still remembered, *Baile-nua-na-manach*, the new town of the monks.

Nuns. *Cailleach*, a nun, is one of the few Irish ecclesiastical terms not borrowed from Latin; in an old Life of St. Brigid, it is stated to be derived from *caille*, a veil:—*cailleach*, the veiled one. But as *cailleach* also signifies an old woman—spelled the same as the former, though differently derived—it is often hard to know which of the two meanings the word bears in names.

In a spot at the south side of the city of Derry, there formerly stood a nunnery; and its memory is still preserved in the name of a piece of land that belonged to it:—Ballynagalliagh, or in Irish *Baile-na-gcailleach*, the townland of the nuns. There are several other places with this name, which probably in all these cases has a similar origin. Calliaghstown is the name of several places in Dublin, Meath, and Westmeath. We know that Calliaghstown in the parish of Kilsharvan, near Drogheda, had formerly a little church dependant on the nunnery of St. Brigid at Odder, which originated the name (see "The Diocese of Meath," by the Rev. A. Cogan, I.

172); and we may be sure that the other places got their names for a like reason. Collierstown, near Skreen in Meath, is a corruption of the same name; for in the Down Survey it is written Calliaghstown; and this no doubt is the correct name of the other places now called Collierstown.

Friars. *Brathair* [brauher] which literally signifies a brother, is also the word used to denote a friar; and in this respect it exactly resembles the word *friar* itself, which is the French *frere* (Lat. *frater*) a brother. Moreover it should be remarked that all the three words, *brathair*, *frater*, and *brother*, are only modified forms of the same original. There is a place near the city of Cork called Garranabraher, which must have been formerly a possession of some friary, for the name is *Garrdha-na-ṃbrathar*, the garden of the friars.

Anchorites. *Ancoire*, an anchorite, borrowed through the Latin from the Greek *anachōrētēs*, forms part of the name of Dunancory near Virginia in Cavan, and of Ballinanchor near Lismore in Waterford, the former signifying the fortress, and the latter the townland, of the anchorite or hermit.

Ord, genitive *uird*, is the same as the Latin *ordo*, and signifies order or rank, or ecclesiastical rule. From this term is derived the name of Kilworth in Cork (adjacent to Kilcrumper), which is to this day called in Irish *Cill-uird*, the church of the order, *i. e.* of the ecclesiastical rule or discipline.

Druids. When St. Patrick arrived in Ireland to begin his Christian mission, one of the obstacles he encountered was the opposition of the druids; and we have several accounts—some historical, some legendary—of his contests with them at Tara and at other places. Druidism was the religion of the country in pagan times; that is, if the people may be said to have had any generally diffused regular form of religion or religious worship at all, which appears very doubtful. But the druids, if they did not influence to any great extent the inner religious life of the people, exercised enormous influence in another way; for they were the depositaries of all the available knowledge of the times, and they were believed to be prophets and magicians possessed of tremendous supernatural powers. In some of the old historical romances, we find the issues of battles often determined, not so much by the skill of the commanders or the valour of the combatants, as by the magical powers of the druids attached to the armies. Both the druids themselves and the popular belief in them, however, gradually sank before the influence of Christianity.

The old Celtic word for a druid is *drui* [dree] which takes a *d* in the end of its oblique cases (gen. *druad*); the Greek and Latins borrowed this word from the Celts, and through them it has found its way into English in the form *druid*. Notwithstanding the long lapse of time since the extinction of druidism, the word *drui* is still a living word in the Irish language. Even in some places where the language is lost, the word is remembered; for I have repeatedly heard the English-speaking people of the south apply the term *shoundhree* (*sean-drui*, old druid) to any crabbed, cunning, old fashioned looking fellow. This very term is perpetuated in the name of Loughnashandree—the lake of the old druids—a very small lake near the head of Ardgroom harbour, south-west of Kenmare.

And the memory of those old druidic sages is still preserved in local names, but only in a few scattered places. There is a conspicuous hill in the parish of Skreen in Sligo now called Red Hill. Its ancient name was *Mullach-Ruadha* [Mullarua] Ruada's hill, and according to Duald Mac Firbis, it was so called from Ruada, king Dathi's wife (see 1st Ser. Part II. c. II.), who was buried on it a few years before the arrival of St. Patrick, and whose carn remains near the summit to this day. This name has been anglicised Mullaroe, which is still the name of a townland near the hill; and it was from the erroneous popular belief that the latter part of the name (*Ruadha*) was the word *ruadh*, red, that the incorrect translation "Red Hill" has been perpetuated. But the hill had another name—the one which concerns us here—viz., *Cnoc-na-ndruadh* [Knocknadrooa], i. e. the hill of the druids; and this name was given to it "because," in the words of Mac Firbis, "the druids of *Dathi*, king of Erin, used to be on it obtaining knowledge [by observing the clouds, according to another account], for it was here they predicted to Dathi that he would obtain the kingdom of Erin, Alba, &c." (Hy F. pp. 97-8-9.) The name of *Cnoc-na-ndruadh* is now however totally forgotten in the place. A name nearly the same as this is *Druim-na-ndruadh*, the ridge of the druids, which was the ancient name of *Cruachan* (now Rathcroghan near Bellanagare in Roscommon), the celebrated palace of the kings of Connaught.

There is a well about two miles from the village of Freshford in Kilkenny, called Tobernadree, described in the Proc. R.I. A., Vol. IX., p. 430, by the late G. V. Du Noyer. Mr. Du Noyer writes this name *Tober-na-druad*, and attempts to show that it commemorates a *druidess*, on the grounds that *na* cannot be the genitive plural of the article, for then there should be an eclipsing *n* (*Tobar-na-ndruad*) which there is not; and that it must therefore be the genitive singular feminine—*Tobar-na-druad*, the well of the druidess. But nothing can be inferred from the absence of the *n* in the modern form of this name. For though always in Irish, and generally in anglicised words, the sound of the eclipsing letter takes the place of that of the eclipsed letter, yet where *n* eclipses a *d* followed by *r*, the *n* invariably drops out in anglicising the word, while the *d* is retained; for the very good reason that English speakers unaccustomed to Irish find it impossible either to pronounce or to represent in English letters, the proper Irish combination of these sounds. The eclipsing letter also drops out in anglicising *g* eclipsed by *n*, and often in anglicising *b* eclipsed by *m*. So the proper Irish form of the present name is obviously *Tobar-na-ndruad*, the well of the druids.

There is a lake three miles west of Lough Derg in Donegal, called Loughnadrooa, the lake of the druids, and this name exhibits the same process of anglicisation as the last; for though in the present name there is no *n*, yet when the people pronounce the Irish name, the *n* is plainly heard. In the parish of Clogherny in Tyrone is a townland called Killadroy, which represents *Coill-a'-druadh*, the druid's wood; and a point of land in Achill Island is named Gobnadruy, the druids' point. The name of Derrydruel, near Dunglow in Donegal, must be a corruption, for the people pronounce it in Irish without the final *l*, *Doire-druadh*, the druid's oak wood.

Kings; Queens. *Righ* [ree], written *ri* in old Irish, is the usual Irish word for a king, cognate with the Latin *rex*, and with Gothic *reiks*. No general statement can be made as to why places received names containing this word; for there are many different explanations in different places. We may conclude that some places so named were in former times the residence of petty kings; that some were in the king's immediate possession; while others commemorate an event or transaction in connexion with a king. Certain places were called "King's Land" in English, or were known by some corresponding name in Irish, because they were held by tenants directly from the crown. There is a place near Dingle in Kerry called Monaree, *Moin-a'-righ*, the bog of the king; which the people say was so called from the fact that in the beginning of the last century, turf was cut in this townland, which was then a bog, for the use of the barrack of Dingle, in which there was a detachment of soldiers.

This term generally takes the form of *ree* in anglicised names; but as the genitive of *fraech*, heath, assumes in some cases the very same form, the two are occasionally liable to be confounded. Thus it is impossible to tell by an inspection of the mere modern form whether Dunaree is anglicised from *Dún-a'-righ*, the fort of the king, or from *Dún-a'-fhraeigh*, the fort of the heath; and as a fact, the name is differently interpreted in different places. In Dunaree in the parish of Donaghmoyne in Monaghan, the last syllable means heath. But Dunaree in Cavan is a different name; it means the fort of the king; and the town of Kingscourt which it includes, retains the name in an English dress. The old fort of Dunaree still exists, a little to the west of the town. The form *ree* is also exhibited in Tooraree in Limerick and Mayo, the king's *toor* or bleach-field. The Four Masters record the legend that in the second year of the reign of Heremon, the nine rivers named *Righ* (King's river) burst forth in Leinster. There are, however, only four rivers in that province now known by the name, one of which is the Rye Water, which flows into the Liffey at Leixlip, and which retains the old name almost unchanged.

We have also places named after queens. The usual Irish word for a queen is *rioghan* [reean], or in old Irish *rigan;* the genitive of which is *rioghna* [reena]. We see it in the name of Bellarena, a well-known place at the mouth of the river Roe, four miles north of Limavady; a name which was first applied to a ford across the Roe:—*Bel-atha-rioghna*, the queen's ford. In the parish of Clondermot, a little south of the city of Derry, is a townland called Tagharina, the house (*teach*) of the queen.

Knights. As far back in antiquity as our history and our oldest traditions reach, there existed in Ireland an institution of knighthood. The knights of the Red Branch, who flourished about the beginning of the Christian era and had their chief residence at the palace of Emania, are the earliest mentioned in our ancient literature; and the annalist Tighernagh records that their chief, the celebrated Cuchullin, received knighthood at seven years old. It is curious that this agrees with what another historian of a much later time and of a different nationality records, namely Froissart, who tells us that when Richard II. visited Dublin in 1395, two Irish kings or chiefs of clans were presented to him; and when they were urged to allow themselves to be knighted, they replied that they had long before received knighthood from their fathers at the age of seven years, according to an ancient practice by which Irish kings were accustomed to create their sons knights. Froissart goes on to say that the following ceremony was used on these occasions:—Each youth when about being knighted, runs a course with a slender lance proportioned to his strength, against a shield set upon a stake in the middle of a field; and he receives greater or less honor according to the number of lances he breaks. And the historian states that the same custom existed among the Anglo-Saxon kings.

There are several Irish words for a knight or hero. One is *ridire* [riddera], which will be at once perceived to be the same as the German *ritter*. Whenever this term occurs in names it is very easily detected; as it generally assumes a form which fairly preserves the pronunciation. One of the best known examples of its use is in the name of Kilruddery, the seat of the earl of Meath, near Bray in Wicklow:—*Cill-ridire*, the church of the knight. The present mansion, or rather the one that preceded it, must have been built on the site of an ancient church; for besides the evidence of the name, I have heard it stated that when the workmen were sinking the foundations fifty years ago, they dug up large quantities of human bones.

The Knight of Kerry is the owner of Ballinruddery near Listowel, which possibly got its name—meaning the knight's townland—from one of his ancestors; there is another place of the same name near Borrisokane in Tipperary; while with slight change of form, we have Ballinriddera near Multyfarnham in Westmeath, and Ballinriddery near Mountmellick in Queen's County, which is also called by the correct *alias*, Knightstown. With the same meaning, only with more serious modifications of the word, are Ballyruther near the sea coast, half way between Larne and Glenarm in Antrim; and Ballyrider near Stradbally in Queen's County. A little north of Castleisland in Kerry is the Glanaruddery range of mountains, which, like several other Irish ranges, took their name—signifying the glen of the knight—from one of their numerous valleys; while the highest of all, at the southern termination of the range, just three miles from Castleisland, is now called the Knight's Mountain. When I have instanced Mullaghruttery near Clare-Galway (*mullach*, a hill-summit), and Sheelruddera in the parish of Terryglass in Tipperary (the knight's *siol* or progeny), I have enumerated all the principal varieties of form assumed by this word.

Champions; Heroes. *Laech* [pron. lay, with an aspirated *c* at end] means a hero or champion. It is very hard to distinguish this word in anglicised names from *laegh*, a calf, unless there be written authority for the original orthography. In some cases, however, even without any ancient record, the meaning cannot be doubted. Near Fortwilliam, half way between Belleek and Ballyshannon in Donegal, there is a cromlech which has a more appropriate name than these ancient structures usually get, a name which embodies the tradition that this monument was erected over some renowned champion of far distant ages; viz., Labbinlee, or in Irish *Leaba-an-laeich*, the *bed* or grave of the hero. There is a townland of the same name south of Cootehill in Cavan—but spelt by some authorities in a way that brings out the meaning more clearly—Labbyanlee; which no doubt received its name from a similar monument.

The term usually applied to the knights of the Red Branch is *curadh* [curra], which means a champion or knight. On the road from Ballylanders to Kilfinane in Limerick, is a place called Ahnagurra, which exactly represents the sound of the Irish *Ath-*

na-gcuradh, the ford of the champions; but why it got the name it is hard to say—probably it was the scene of a battle.

I question whether any of the names derived from *ridire* are very ancient; I am inclined to think they are derived from Anglo-Norman knights rather than from the knights of early Irish history. But it is not so with those derived from *laech* and *curadh*, most of which descend I believe from a very remote period.

There are several other terms for a champion or warrior, almost all of which are perpetuated in local names. *Scál* signifies a spectre or apparition, and also a hero, which is probably a secondary meaning. It was, besides, often employed as a proper name. Thus the maternal grandfather of king Felimy the Lawgiver, was named *Scál Balbh*, or *Scál* the stammerer. The best example of its use is in *Leac-an-scáil* or Lackanscaul, an unusually large cromlech in the townland of Kilmogue, about three miles from the village of Higginstown, in Kilkenny. This name is exactly like Labbinlee, and is quite as appropriate and suggestive, signifying the flag-stone of the hero; but tradition and legend have quite forgotten who the champion was—a man of no small note he must have been—over whom this immense monument was erected.

In the ancient tale called the *Tromdaimh* or Congress of the learned men, we are told that *Guaire* the Hospitable, King of Connaught in the seventh century, had a brother, an anchorite, named *Marbhan*, who lived in a hermitage in a place called *Glenn-an-scáil* the glen of the hero. One mile from the village of Oranmore in Galway there is a place of this name, now called Glennascaul; but whether it is the *Glenn-*

an-scáil of the hermit *Marbhán*, I have no means of determining. There is also a remarkable valley near Slemish Mountain in Antrim which was anciently called *Gleann-an-scáil.* Killascaul, the hero's wood, is the name of a place in the parish of Kiltullagh in Galway. A few miles east of Dingle in the wild barony of Corcaguiny in Kerry, there is a small river flowing from a lake : the lake is called Loughanscaul, the lake of the hero ; the river is Owenascaul, the hero's river ; and on it is situated the village of Anascaul. Some intelligent persons from this neighbourhood believe that *scaul* in these names signifies a shadow, and that the name originated in the deep shadows cast on the lake by the high cliffs that rise over its waters ; while others account for the names by a legend regarding a lady named *Scál* who was drowned in the lake. I do not think either account is correct, however ; partly because the analogy of the preceding names would lead to the presumption that *scaul* here means a hero ; but chiefly because the Irish name of the lake is *Loch-an-scáil*, not *Loch-na-scáile*, in the latter of which the article and noun are feminine, while in the former both are masculine, indicating that the word is *scál* a hero, not *scáile*, a shadow, which is feminine. So with Owenascaul ; but as to Anascaul I do not know how it came by its present form ; for it would seem to be the anglicised representative of *Ath-na-scál*, the ford of the *heroes*, not of the hero.

Tréun [train] signifies strong, brave, or powerful (*tren*, fortis : Zeuss, 166) ; and hence it is applied to a strong valiant man, a hero (*tréuin*, heroes : Zeuss, 230). Some great champion, or perhaps a battle in which one of the leading warriors was slain, is commemorated in Bellatrain, a place on the borders of

Cavan and Monaghan, three miles from the village of Shercock; which took its name from an old ford on the little river flowing from the lake of Shantonagh to Bellatrain lake:—*Bel-atha-tréin*, the ford-mouth of the hero.

Galloglasses.—Those Irish soldiers called by the names *galloglass* and *kern*, figure very prominently in the history of Ireland, especially in the later history, and in the pages of Anglo-Norman writers. The galloglasses were heavy armed foot soldiers; they wore an iron helmet, a coat of mail, and a long sword; and carried in one hand a broad keen-edged battle-axe. Spenser, in his "View of the state of Ireland," asserts that the Irish took the idea of the galloglasses from the English settlers; and in this he is probably right; for we do not find them mentioned in early Irish documents. Moreover the composition of the word further supports the assertion; the Irish form is *galloglach*, which is formed from *gall*, a foreigner, and *oglach*, a youth, vassal, or soldier:—*gall-oglach*, a foreign soldier.

The Irish name of the village of Millford in the north of Donegal, which the people still use when speaking Irish, is *Bél-na-ngalloglach*, the ford of the galloglasses; and in the parish of Loughgilly in Armagh, there is a townland taking its name from a rock, called Carrickgallogly; the rock of the galloglass.

Kerns. The kern were light armed foot soldiers. They wore light clothes; carried no defensive armour except a head piece; and they fought with darts or javelins to which a long string was fastened, swords, and *skians*, or knife-like daggers. The kerns are of great antiquity; they are several times mentioned in the account of the battle of Moyrath, fought in the year A.D. 637; and Cormac Mac Cullenan speaks of them in his Glossary, a document of the ninth century, and conjectures the etymology of the word:—"*Ceithern*, a band of soldiers, whence *cethernach*, a single man out of a cohort: from *cath*, a battle, and *orn*, slaughter: i. e. slaughter in battle." The Irish word is *cethern* [kehern]; which is a collective term, never applied to a single man, but always to a body. I will however, for the sake of clearness, use the English plural from *kerns* when necessary. It must be observed that *cethern* was also used in very early times as the proper name of a man (see O'Curry, Lect., II., 313).

We have a considerable number of local names which preserve the memory of these kerns; the spots no doubt having formerly been selected as places of meeting or retreat; perhaps some of them are battle fields. In Derrykearn near Mountrath in Queen's County, the *derry* or oak wood that formerly grew in the place, probably served as a shelter for these warriors. Aughnacarney near Clogher in Tyrone, the field of the kerns, was perhaps one of their exercise grounds, or the scene of a battle; a hill in the same locality has the name of Knocknacarney (the kerns' hill), which is also the name of a hill in the parish of Errigle Trough in Monaghan. There is a hill about six miles east of Donegal town called Croaghnakern, the *rick* of the kerns; and in the same county, north of Lough Eask, is a place called Cronakerny, the kern's valley (*cro*). When a single person was intended to be designated, the adjective form *cethearnach* was used, as Cormac states in the passage quoted above; and this word appears in Knockacaharna in the parish of Modeligo in Waterford, the kern's hill.

Amhas [awas] means a hired soldier, a soldier who serves for pay; this is the sense in which the word is used in the Irish annals, and this seems to be the meaning intended in Cormac's Glossary :—" *Amos*, a soldier, i. e. *amh-fos*, restless, because he is never at rest or stationary, but going from place to place, or from one lord to another." The Four Masters at A. D. 1323, record a battle fought between the O'Farrells and the Berminghams at a place called *Coill-nan-amhus*, the wood of the soldiers ; and the name of this place, which is situated near Granard in Longford, still survives in the form of Killinawas. The word assumes a different form in Ballynanoose in the parish of Killoscully in Tipperary :—*Baile-nan-amhas*, the town of the hired soldiers.

Creaghts. For a long period, while society in Ireland was in an unsettled state, the chieftains fortified themselves in strong castles, and made war or concluded peace with their neighbours, with little or no reference to the government of the province or the kingdom. Cattle raids were a usual form of this petty warfare ; and these plundering expeditions were the frequent cause of desperate feuds ; for the spoilers were often pursued and overtaken, and then there was sure to be a battle. Traditions of such incursions are still told by the peasantry in every part of the country, and records of them abound in the pages of the Four Masters and other annalists.

Caeraigheacht [Keereeaght] signifies primarily a flock of sheep, from *caera*, a sheep ; but it is used in a general sense to signify any herd of cattle. The men who took care of cattle in time of peace, or who drove the preys in time of war, were also designated by the same word, which in the anglicised form *creaght*, is constantly met with in the pages of Anglo-Irish writers of the last three or four hundred years, and used by them in both senses. The creaghts were regularly officered like the kerns and galloglasses; and they were usually armed with a club, and a *meadoge* or long knife. They led a free and wandering life, knew the haunts and habits of cattle, and were intimately acquainted with all the intricacies, the secret paths, the toghers, and passes of the mountains, bogs, and morasses.

Places frequented by these people and their herds, or where they used to conceal their preys, still often retain names formed from this word *creaght*. Near the head of Mulroy bay in Donegal, there is a little lake called Loughnacreaght, the lake of the creaghts. There are two townlands in Tyrone called Lisnacreaght, where the old fortifications of the *lis* must have been taken advantage of to shelter and defend the cattle. Sometimes the word *caeraigheacht* was applied to the mountain boolies or temporary settlements of shepherds' huts (see 1st Ser. Part II., c. VII.); and it is in this sense no doubt that it has given names to some places in Wexford, now called Kereight, which very correctly represents the original.

Thieves. In times of civil war or social disturbance, one of the most tempting and profitable occupations a man could follow is that of a highway robber or common thief; and as we have had our own share of warfare and tumult, so we have had gangs of freebooters infesting every part of the country. We know this to be the case from history and tradition; but even local names afford very plain indications of it. Places where bands of robbers fixed their lair and hid their plunder are often known by the word *bradach*, which signifies a thief or thievish. It occurs in a good number of names, and usually takes the forms *braddagh*, *brada*, and *brady*. Boherbraddagh is the name of a townland near Adare in Limerick, signifying the road of the thieves; of similar formation is Moneenbradagh near Castlebar in Mayo (*moneen*, a little bog); and Glenbradagh near Aghada below Cork, the glen of the thieves. The hill of Benbradagh over the town of Dungiven (*ben*, a peak) must have at one time afforded asylum to the plunderers that laid the surrounding district under tribute; and at some former period a police barrack must have been sadly wanted at Balbradagh, near Bective in Meath, and at Ballybrada near Cahir in Tipperary, the names of which signify thievish town or the town of the thieves.

Gadaighe [gaddy] is another word for a thief, which is commemorated in Balgaddy, the town of the thief, the name of two townlands in the county Dublin, one near Clondalkin, and the other near Balbriggan; which has the same meaning as Ballingaddy, the name of some places in Clare and Limerick; and Ballygaddy in Galway, Kildare, and King's County.

Some of these last mentioned places took their names from a legendary personage, celebrated all over Ireland and the Highlands of Scotland, about whom many popular stories are still current in both countries, *Gadaighe dubh O'Dubhâin*, or the Black thief O'Duane.

Bards; Poets. From the earliest period of history we find mention of *bards* or poets among the Celts; they are mentioned by Cæsar, by Strabo, and indeed by every ancient writer who treats of the Celtic nations. In ancient Ireland the *bard* was inferior to the *fili;* the latter was the teacher of philosophy, literature, history, rhetoric, &c.; the former was merely a versifier or rhymester. There were various classes of bards, and each class had its own special form of poetry. Attached to every great chieftain's household there was a bard, whose office it was to recite the exploits of his patron's ancestors, to compose laudatory poems on him and on the tribe over whom he ruled, to celebrate their deeds of arms in verse, &c.

We have many places named from bards; in some cases these names indicate that the lands were held by them as a reward for their professional services; and where this is not the case they point out the places where bards formerly resided. One of these is Derrybard near Fintona in Tyrone, the bard's oak grove. But the word is generally changed in form either by aspiration or eclipse of the first letter. In the former case it usually assumes the form *ward;* as in Gortaward near Inver in Donegal, *Gort-a'-bhaird*, the field of the bard; and with the same meaning, Aghaward in Roscommon, three miles south of Drumsna. So also Glenaward in the parish of Moylagh in Meath, the bard's glen; and Ballyward, the name of some places in Down, Tyrone, and Wicklow, the townland of the bard.

In case of eclipse the word becomes *mard*, as we see in Aghnamard near Newbliss in Monaghan, *Achadh-na-mbard*, the field of the bards; Latnamard in the same neighbourhood, *Leacht-na-mbard*, the bards' sepulchral monument, indicating the spot where several were buried—perhaps the burial mound of those that lived in Aghnamard.

This is the origin of the family name *Mac-an-Bhaird* [Mac-an-Ward] i. e. literally son of the bard, which is now always written Ward. The family of *Mac-an-Bhaird* were the hereditary poets of the O'Kellys of Hy Many in Connaught; and they resided at *Muine-chasain* and *Baile-mic-an-Bhaird*, the latter of which retains the name in the anglicised form Ballymacward, now applied to a parish near Castleblakeney.

Eigeas [aigas] signifies any learned man, but the term is usually applied to a poet. In the parish of Aghnamullin in Monaghan there is a lake called Lough Egish, the poet's lake; and over its western shore rises a hill called Tullynanegish, the hill of the poets, which gives name to a townland. Near the demesne of Thomastown, six miles south-west of Athlone, a little south of the railway line, there is a little lake called Lough Nanegish, the lake of the poets. It is likely that at some former time families of hereditary poets lived at these places.

Betaghs. In ancient times an Irish chieftain usually established within his territory a sort of public hostelry, over which he placed an officer called a *biadhtach* [beetagh] or food-man (from *biadh*, food). This *biadhtach* or public victualler held a tract of land rent free, on condition that he should supply food and lodging without charge to travellers, and to the chief's soldiers whenever they happened to march in that direction. The land attached to one of these houses was called a *Baile-biadhtaigh* or victualler's town, and contained 480 large Irish acres. The biataghs were held in great estimation, and their memory is still preserved in a few place-names. There are three townlands in Cork and Kilkenny called Ballynametagh, in Irish *Baile-na-mbiadhtach*, the town of the victuallers, so called probably because they formed part of the property attached to a house of entertainment. Similar in formation, and probably in origin, is Cloonametagh near Abbeydorney in Kerry, and Garraunnameetagh near the village of Tynagh in Galway, the meadow and the shrubbery of the victuallers.

Stewards. Among the various functionaries enumerated in the *familia* of Armagh, we find mention of a *maer*, i. e. a steward or keeper, who was the appointed guardian of certain sacred relics, such as the bell, book, and crozier of St. Patrick. This office was hereditary; the family kept the relics subject to certain conditions, one of which was that they should be ready at all times to produce them when required; and in payment for this duty of guardianship, they held tracts of land from the see of Armagh, free of rent. The family to whom was intrusted the custody of the celebrated Book of Armagh, were from that circumstance called *Mac Maeir* or MacMoyre—the son of the steward or keeper; and they held in free tenancy eight townlands, which are now united into one parish called Ballymyre, the townland of the keeper, situated about eight miles south-east of Armagh (Reeves: Eccl. Ant. p. 150).

This word *maer* is pretty frequent in names; and though we have not such positive information regarding them as in the last case, we may be sure that the several places so designated were formerly held in fee by families who were guardians of lands, cattle, or sacred reliquaries, for neighbouring chieftains. Ballynamire is the name of three townlands in Carlow, King's County, and Wexford, and it signifies the town of the keepers. When the word occurs in the singular the *m* is often changed to *w* by aspiration. Tinwear near Durrow in Queen's County, is shortened from *Tigh-an-mhaeir*, the house of the keeper; Lackaweer in the parish of Inishkeel in Donegal, the steward's flag stone.

Scologes. *Scológ* signifies a small farmer; the term is still in general use, but it is used in a somewhat contemptuous sense. Wherever it occurs in a local name there is no mistaking it, as will be seen from the following examples. Near Lisnaskea in Fermanagh there is a place called Farransculloge, the *fearann* or land of the petty farmers. Ballynasculloge is the name of a place near Blessington in Wicklow, and of another near Athy in Kildare; the name signifies the farmers' townland; and in another part of Kildare this same name, in the half translated form Scullogestown, designates a parish.

Shepherds. The usual word for a shepherd is *aedhaire* [aira], which is derived from *aedh*, an old word for a sheep. It enters into the formation of a considerable number of names; and it is in general not difficult of recognition in its anglicised forms. Corraneary, the name of several townlands in Cavan and Leitrim, Corranarry in Tyrone, and Cornery in Cork, are in Irish *Cor-an-aedhaire*, the round hill of the shepherd; Killyneary in Cavan, and Killyneery in Tyrone, the shepherd's wood; Cappaneary in Queen's County (*ceapach*, a tilled plot); Drumary in Fermanagh and Monaghan, and Drumaneary near Inver in Donegal (*druim*, a hill-ridge); and we have a place called Canary in Armagh, which however does not derive its name from *canes*, dogs, like the Canary islands, but from *ceann*:—*Ceann-aedhaire*, the shepherd's head or hill.

Widows. The names of many places in Ireland commemorate widows; and this is one of the numerous examples that show how fond the Irish were of designating people by an epithet expressive of some well marked peculiarity, rather than calling them directly by their own names. *Baintreabhach* [pron. bointravagh, but generally bointra] is our usual word for a widow, probably derived from *treabh* [trav] a house and *bean*, a woman:—*treabhach*, a housekeeper; *baintreabhach*, literally a female housekeeper. A very good example of its use is found in Ballynabointra, the name of a place near Carrigtohill in Cork, *Baile-na-baintreabhaighe*, the townland of the widow. When the word occurs in the genitive plural with the article, the *b* is changed to *m* by eclipse, but otherwise there is usually very little change. This is seen in Ballynamintra near Dungarvan in Waterford, and in Ballynamointragh a mile or two from the strand of Tramore in the same county, both from *Baile-na-mbaintreabhach*, the townland of the widows; in Lisnamintry near Portadown in Armagh, (*lis*, a fort); and in Mulmontry near Taghmon in Wexford, the widows' hill.

Tanners. The peasantry had formerly a rude method of tanning the hides of animals, which, in remote parts of the country, is practised to this day. They first filled the hide with lime, and immersed it in a bog-hole to loosen the hair; after ten or eleven days they took it out, cleaned off the lime, and in order to thicken the hide, put it into a cask to steep for about three weeks, with the root of a plant called *cromelly* or *neachartách*, which also gave it a brown colour. After this it was rubbed between boards with milk, to make it smooth and pliable, and then dried, when it was fit for use. There were people who practised this as a means of livelihood, the trade probably descending from father to son; and the places where the professional tanners lived may now in numerous cases be known by their names.

Súdaire [soodera] is the Irish word for a tanner. The word is exhibited with very correct pronunciation in Kilnasudry, near the village of Killeagh, west of Youghal in Cork, *Coill-na-súdairighe*, the wood of the tanners; and in Ballynasuddery near Kilbeggan in Westmeath, the town of the tanners. When the word occurs in the genitive singular, the first *s* is usually changed to *t* by eclipse; and this is seen in Edenatoodry, southwards from Fintona in Tyrone, *Eudan-a'-tsudaire*, the hill brow of the tanner; in Knockatudor near Stradone in Cavan, the tanner's hill; and in Listooder near the village of Crossgar in Down, written Listowdrie in one of the Hamilton Patents, where a tanner practised his trade in or near the old *lis* or fort.

Another word that indicates where the process of tanning was carried on is *leathar* [laher]; it has the same signification as the English word *leather*, but is not borrowed from it, for we find the word in Cormac's Glossary in the form *lethar*: Welsh *lledr*. This word is well exemplified in Curraghalaher on the Roscommon side of the Shannon, near Athlone, the marsh of the leather; and in Clashalaher, the name of two townlands in Tipperary, one near Cashel and the other near Tipperary town, where the *clash* or trench was probably the place in which the hides were steeped.

Croiceann [crucken] signifies a skin or hide (*crocenn*, tergus; Z. 69); and when it occurs in names it is probable that, like *leathar*, it indicates the former residence of tanners. Killycracken in Monaghan represents the Irish *Coill-a'-chroicinn*, the wood of the hide; and of similar formation is Cloncracken (*clon*, a meadow), near Roscrea in Tipperary.

Potters. A potter is denoted by *potaire* [puttera], which is formed on the Irish word *pota*, a pot. Near Buttevant in Cork is a townland called Clashnabuttry; here the *p* is eclipsed by *b* in the genitive plural, the Irish form being *Clais-na-bpotaireadh*, the trench of the potters; and we may conclude that the trench supplied the clay for carrying on the manufacture. A better known place is Pottlerath in the parish of Kilmanagh in Kilkenny, which was formerly one of the residences of Mac Richard Butler, a distinguished chieftain of the Butler family in the 15th century; and where there are still the ruins of a castle and a church. This place is called in Irish documents *Rath-a'-photaire*, the fort of the potter; but in the present spoken Irish it is corruptly pronounced *Rath-a'-photaile* (change of *r* to *l*; 1st Ser. Part I., c. III.), from which by an attempted translation, the name Pottlerath (instead of the correct Pottersrath) has been formed. The old rath where the potter in some remote time took up his residence, is still there.

Weavers. Mageoghegan, in his translation of the Annals of Clonmacnoise, remarks of John, the son of Mahon O'Conor, that he "was the sonne of a woman that could weave, which of all trades is of greatest reproach amongst the Irishrye, especially the sons and husbands of such tradeswomen, and therefore Shane More was nicknamed the weaving-woman's sonne." The Irish word for a weaver is *figheadoir* [feedore]. There is a small pool a mile and a half south of Cashel, giving name to a townland, called Lough Feedora, the weaver's lake; and Ballineedora is the name of a place four or five miles east of Tralee, which exactly represents the sound of *Baile-an-fhigheadóra*, (*f* aspirated and omitted), the town of the weaver.

Fullers. Thomas Dineley, who made a tour through Ireland in 1675, thus describes, as he saw it, "The manner of tucking and thickening cloth without a mill. They place the cloth doubled upon a large wicker or twiggen door called an hurle, and work it with their hands and feet, until it becomes thick by rowling;"—sprinkling it all the time with a suitable liquid. In remote districts cloth is still thickened in this rude way by being worked for a long time with the feet in a properly prepared mixture.

A fuller is designated by the word *ucaire* [ookera]; and the occurrence of this word in names indicates the places where the home-made frieze used to be fulled and napped. As the word usually retains a form easily detected, one or two examples of its use will be sufficient. There is a townland near Aghada below Cork, called Ballynookery, i. e. *Baile-an-úcaire*, the town of the fuller; and Knockanooker near the village of Hacketstown in Wicklow, signifies the fuller's hill.

Pedlars. *Ceannaighe* [cannee] signifies a merchant, a dealer of any kind. There is a ford over a stream a mile south of Oldcastle in Meath, which is mentioned by the Four Masters at A. D. 1482, as the scene of a defeat inflicted on the Plunkets by Art O'Conor; and called by them *Ath-na-gceannaigheadh* [Annaganny] the ford of the pedlars or merchants. The place is now called in Irish by the synonymous name *Bel-atha-na-gceannaigheadh* [Bellanaganny]; but this suggestive old name has been laid aside for the modern name Mill Brook. There is a place of the same name in the parish of Aghabulloge near Macroom in Cork, now called Annagannihy, which took its name from a ford on the little river Aghalode. Near Carrignavar in the same county, two roads meet at a spot now called Crossernagannee, the cross-roads of the pedlars. *Mangaire* [mong'ara] is another Irish word for a pedlar; and we find it in Ballynamongaree near Glanworth in Cork, the town of the pedlars. It is probable that pedlars formerly lived in these places or were in the habit of exhibiting their wares there to tempt the passers by, which gave rise to the names.

Gamesters. A gambler, or gamester, is designated in Irish by the word *cearrḃach* [carvagh, carroogh], which is still in common use; in the south, even among the English speaking people, they call a card-player a *carroogh*. The peasantry are fond enough of card playing at the present day; but they appear to have been still more addicted to it in former times. Campion, in his "History of Ireland," written in the year 1571, says: "There is among them a brotherhood of *carrowes* that professe to play at cards all the yeare long, and make it their onely occupation. . . . They waite for passengers in the highway, invite them to a game upon the greene, and aske no more but companions to hold them sport." Spenser also in his "View of the State of Ireland," describes the "Carrows, which is a kind of people that wander up and down to gentlemen's houses, living only upon cards and dice."

One of the best illustrations of this word is Lisnagarvy, which was the old name of Lisburn, and which is still retained as the name of a townland adjoining the town. The origin of this name is very clearly set forth in a passage quoted in the "Ulster Journal of Archæology (Vol. V., p. 159), from a pamphlet published in 1691:—"We marched towards Lisburn: this is one of the prettiest towns in the north of Ireland: the Irish name is Lisnegarvah, which they tell me signifies 'gamesters' mount;' for a little to the north-east of the town there is a mount moated about and another to the west. These were formerly surrounded with a great wood; and thither resorted all the Irish outlaws to play at cards and dice." The "mount moated about" is one of the ancient *lisses;* and it was from this that the place took the name of *Lios-na-gcearrbhach*, the fort of the gamblers. The present name Lisburn retains the first syllable; the syllable *burn*, it is said, commemorates a conflagration by which the town was at one time totally destroyed.

The *c* of this word is usually eclipsed, as in this last name; another example of which is Cloghanna-garragh in the parish of Noghaval in Westmeath, a name which I suppose indicates that the old *clochan* or stone building was turned to the same use as the fort at Lisburn. Sometimes, however, the *c* is retained; as in Meenacharvy in Glencolumkille in Donegal, *Mín-a'-chearrbhaigh*, the *meen* or mountain meadow of the gamester.

CHAPTER VII.

STRANGERS.

WHEN a foreigner came to live in Ireland, the place in which he settled often received a name indicating his nationality. The term to express a native of any particular country is usually formed by adding the adjective termination *ach* (p. 3) to the name of the country: thus *Francach*, a Frenchman, *Lochlannach*, a native of *Lochlann* or Norway.

Welshmen. *Breathnach*, which is merely the word *Briton*, modified according to the phonetic laws of the Irish language, is used to signify a Welshman. As Mayo was called Mayo of the Saxons (see Mayo in 1st Ser.) so Gallen in the King's County was for a like reason called *Gailinne na mBretann*, or Gallen of the Britons; for a monastery was erected there in the end of the fifth century for British monks by St. Canocus, a Welshman. In the later colloquial language the word *Breathnach* has been confined in its application to those who have adopted the family name of Walsh; and this is the sense in which it is generally understood in local names. Ballybrannagh, Ballynabrannagh, and Ballynabrennagh, which are all townland names in various counties, signify "the town of the Walshes," or of the families called Walsh.

Sometimes we find the word *Breatan* with the *t* fully sounded; but in this case it seems to be a personal name, of the same origin however as *Breathnach*, i. e. indicating British or Welsh origin. *Britan* we know occurs as a personal name in early Irish history; thus *Britan Mael* was one of the sons of the mythical personage Nemedius, and according to the bardic fable gave name to Britain. Kilbrittain on the south coast of Cork, at the head of Courtmacsherry Bay, took its name from some person of this name, who probably built the *cill* or church; Gartbratton (*Bretan's* field) is the name of two townlands in Cavan; and we have Ballybritain in Derry, and Ballybrittan in King's County, Bretan's town. There is a parish in Kilkenny adjoining the county Tipperary, called Tubbridbritain, which is called in the "Circuit of *Murcheartach Mac Neill*," *Tiobraide Britain buain*, the wells of long-lived *Britan*; but we do not know who this venerable personage was.

Scotchmen. A Scotchman is generally designated

in Irish by *Albanach*, a term derived from *Alba* (gen. *Alban*), the old Celtic name of Scotland. Ballyalbanagh, the Scotchman's town, is the name of a place in the parish of Ballycor in Antrim. Two miles south of the village of Milltown Malbay in Clare, is a townland called Knockanalban, shortened from *Cnoc-an-Albanaigh*, the Scotchman's hill; and there is a place in the parish of Kilgeever in Mayo, called Derreennanalbanagh, the little oak-wood of the Scotchmen.

Englishmen. We have several terms for an Englishman, one of the most common of which is *Sacsonach*, or more generally *Sassonach*, which is merely the word Saxon with the usual termination. The word was in constant use in the early ages of the Church—the sixth and seventh centuries—when many natives of Britain came to study in the schools of Ireland; and England itself is often called in Irish writings, Saxon-land. The word *Sassonach* is still used in the spoken language, but it is now generally understood to mean a Protestant, and it is commonly used in an offensive sense; but these shades of meaning are vulgar and very modern.

Near Saintfield in Down there is a place called Craignasasonagh, the rock of the Saxons or Englishmen; Bohernasassonagh (*bóthar*, a road) lies three miles south-west from Tuam in Galway. With the first *s* eclipsed (as it ought to be in the genitive singular with the article) and with the south Munster form of the genitive, we find the word in Knockatassonig near Mizen Head in Cork, *Cnoc-a'-tSassonaig*, the Englishman's hill.

Romans. I have already mentioned that among those who came in early ages to study in Ireland, numbers were from the continent (see p. 89, *supra*).

Many of these are commemorated in the Litany of *Aengus* the Culdee, a document of the end of the eighth century; and we have besides, other historical evidences in the lives of the early Irish saints. Some came even from Rome. Near the church of St. *Brecan* on the great Island of Aran, there is a headstone which appears to be as old as the sixth century, with the inscription "VII. ROMANI," "Seven Romans," who probably spent their peaceful days as pilgrims in companionship with St. Brecan himself (Petrie, R. Towers, 139). Local names give testimony to the same effect. Kilnarovanagh is the name of an old church south of Macroom in Cork, and of another between Killarney and Miltown in Kerry; signifying the church of the Romans (*Romhanach*, pron. *Rovanagh*, a Roman); both of which probably received their names from being the burial places of Roman pilgrims. There is a townland in the parish of Kilmore in the east of Roscommon, called Rathnarovanagh; the Four Masters, in recording the fact that it was presented in 1248, by Felim O'Conor the son of Cathal of the Red Hand, to the canons of Kilmore, call it *Rath-na-Romhánach;* and Duald Mac Firbis, in his translation of the Irish Annals, (Irish Misc., I., 243), writes it with a translation, "*Raith-na-Romanach*, i. e. [the fort] of the Romans."

When persons migrated from one part of Ireland to another, the places where they settled often got names indicating the provinces from which they came; and names of this kind are contributed by all the four provinces.

Leinstermen. Laighneach [Lynagh] is a Leinsterman, from *Laighean*, the Irish name of Leinster. There is a place near Kilfinane in Limerick, called Ballinlyna; another called Ballinliny, three miles from Newcastle in the same county; a third near the village of Golden in Tipperary, called Ballinlina; and there are two townlands called Ballylina also in Tipperary:—all these names signify the town of the Leinsterman.

Connaughtmen. *Connachtach*, a Connaughtman, is preserved in Ballynagonnaghtagh (first *c* eclipsed by *g*) in the parish of Dysert, Clare, the town of the Connaughtmen. In the townland of Ballygeely in the parish of Kilshanny, north of Ennistymon in Clare, there is a great monumental mound now called *Carn-Connachtach*, the carn of the Connaughtmen; which O'Donovan believes to be the *Carn-Mic-Tail* mentioned in the Annals (Four M., V., 1669, note *u*).

Munstermen. From *Mumha*, genitive *Mumhan* [Mooan], Munster, we have *Muimhneach* [Mweenagh], a Munsterman. It would appear that immigrants from across the Shannon must have settled in Cloontymweenagh (the *cloons* or meadows of the Munstermen) near the village of Scarriff in Clare, close to the shore of Lough Derg, before or about the time of the annexation of Clare to Munster. Nearly the same form as this occurs in Bawntanameenagh near Freshford in Kilkenny, the Munstermen's *bawns* or green fields; and a slightly different in Newtown Moynagh near Trim in Meath, i.e. Newtown of the Munstermen.

Ulstermen. *Uladh* [ulla] is the Irish name of Ulster, from which we have *Ultach* or *Oltach*, an Ulsterman, which assumes slightly varied forms in different local names. Cooloultha in the parish of Erke in Kilkenny, signifies the Ulsterman's corner; a better form is seen in Knockanulty near Ennistymon in Clare (*cnoc*, a hill); and in Boleynanoultagh near Kildorrery in Cork, the booley or dairy place of the Ulstermen. As the genitive form *nah* of the article is used in Cloonnahulty in the parish of Aghamore in Mayo—indicating the singular feminine—we must conclude that the name signifies the *cloon* or meadow of the Ulsterwoman.

CHAPTER VIII.

IRISH PERSONAL AND FAMILY NAMES.

In order that the reader may better understand the substance of this chapter, it is necessary to show in a general way how Irish personal and family names took their rise, and to explain and illustrate certain laws observable in the derivation of local names from both.

It may be said that we know nearly all the personal names formerly in use in this country, through the medium of our ancient literature and inscriptions; and a large proportion of them still survive in daily use, though in most cases greatly changed from their original forms. When we examine them in their most ancient orthography, we can easily perceive that all are significant; but though most of them bear their meanings plainly on their face, many are now exceedingly obscure, either because they have been handed down to us incorrectly by the old transcribers, or that the words composing them have long since become obsolete.

In very early ages individuals usually received their names from some personal peculiarity, such as colour of hair, complexion, size, figure, certain accidents of deformity, mental qualities, such as bravery, fierceness, &c., &c.; and we have only to look at the old forms of the names to remove any doubt we may entertain of the truth of this assertion.

We need not hesitate to pronounce that the man who first received the name of *Dubhán* [Duane] was so called from his dark hair and complexion; for it is a diminutive of *dubh* [duv], black; and *Dubhán* signifies as it stands, a black or dark complexioned man. Moreover it is very ancient, for we find it in the Book of Leinster and *Lebor na hUidhre* as the name of persons mixed up with our earliest traditions; and it is still in use as a family name disguised under the forms of Dwane, Dwain, Downes, &c.

Some person of this name must have lived at Dundooan near Coleraine, and another at Dundooan in the peninsula of Rosguill in the north of Donegal, for the name of both signifies *Dubhan's* fortress. The parish of Hook in Wexford—that long narrow peninsula bounding Waterford harbour on the east—came by its present name in a curious way. The old name of the place, as it is written in several charters, was Randouan or Rindown; and it was so called from St. Dowan, who, according to a Patent Roll of Henry VIII., was the patron saint of Hook. This Dowan, whose correct name was *Dubhan*, is commemorated in the Irish Calendars at the 11th of February. He was one of a family of brothers and sisters, who settled in Ireland at the end of the sixth century, children of a British king named Bracan; among whom were *Dabheog* of Lough Derg, *Paan* of *Cill-Phaain* (now Kilfane in Kilkenny), *Mochorog* of Delgany (p. 26), and others. He was called *Dubhan Ailithir* or *Dubhan* the pilgrim, and he built a cell in a place which was afterwards called from him *Rinn-Dubhain*, *Dubhan's* point. In the lapse of long ages *St. Dubhan* was forgotten; and the people of Wexford, preferring a name for the place with an English sound, attempted to translate the old native name. The word *dubhan*, in addition to the meaning already assigned to it, signifies also a fishing hook; and as this appeared a very appropriate appellation for the long peninsula under consideration, they accordingly, knowing nothing of St. *Dubhan*, rendered *Rinn-Dubhain*, Hook Point, and called the parish itself by the name of Hook. This identification we owe to the Rev. James Graves (Kilk. Arch. Jour., Vol. III., 1854–5), whom I have followed.

Persons of this name, and of others founded on it, are commemorated in several other places. In the parish of Kilkeedy in Clare, seven miles north-east of Corofin, there is an old castle in ruins, now called Cloonoan, once belonging to the O'Briens, which was stormed by Sir Richard Bingham in the year 1586: the Four Masters, recording this event, give the true name—*Cluain-Dubhain* (*Dubhan's* meadow), which lost the *d* by aspiration in the process of anglicising. The parish of Kilmacduane near Kilrush in Clare, takes its name from an old church, once belonging to the monastery of *Inis Cathaigh* or Scattery Island; it is mentioned in the life of St. Senan and in the Annals of the Four Masters, who call it *Cill-mhec-Dubhain*, the church of *Dubhan's* son. In the year 1579, Dermot O'Shaughnessy, one of the chiefs of the O'Shaughnessys of Kinelea in the south-east of Galway, laid a snare for his brother's son, William, at a place popularly called Ardmealuane, in the parish of Beagh in Galway, four miles south of Gort; he succeeded in slaying his nephew, but the young man defended himself so well, that the assassin died of his wounds an hour after the combat.

The Four Masters, in recording this event, call the place *Ard-Maoldubhain*, *Maoldubhan's* height; it contains the ruins of a castle, which is called Ardamullivan in the Ordnance maps.

Dubhan forms a part of several other personal and family names, but I will mention only one other, viz., *Ciardhubhan* [Keeruwaun], which was formed by prefixing *ciar* to *dubhan*, very probably after the latter had lost its significance; for *ciar* itself means black or very dark. This is the original form of the family name Kirwan or O'Kirwan, so well known and widely spread in the county Galway. There is a townland in the parish of Clondagad near the mouth of the Fergus in Clare, called Craggykerrivan, which took its name from a member of this family; for the Four Masters, at A. D. 1600, call it *Craig-Ui-Chiardhubhain*, O'Kirwan's rock.

It appears to me that many—perhaps the greater number of—descriptive or commemorative personal names were originally secondary or additional names, given in after-life, and subsequently retained, so as to supersede the first name. We have ample historical testimony that this custom was very general in Ireland; but these secondary names generally seem not to have been given in an offensive or opprobrious sense, but to have been accepted by the individuals as a matter of course. There are innumerable instances of this change of name in our histories, but I will mention only three.

We are told that St. Patrick's first name was *Succat*, which old writers interpret "warrior" (the latter part being *cath*, a battle); that he was afterwards called *Cothraige*, signifying "four families," from the circumstance that, while he was a slave in Ireland, he was the property of four masters, and was forced to serve them all. And finally he received the name *Patricius*, which was a title of distinction among the Romans, meaning a patrician or noble person.

The great hero, *Cuchullin*, according to our traditional history, had several names. He was first called *Setanta*, and the reason why he received the name of *Cuchullin* is the subject of a curious legend, told in several of our very old books, among others in *Lebor-na-hUidhre*. On one occasion Culand, a great artificer in metals, who had his residence and kept his forge near Slieve Gullion in Armagh, came to the palace of Emania to invite king Conor Mac Nessa and the Red Branch Knights to a feast. Setanta, who was then a little boy, was also invited, for he happened to be on a visit at the palace at this very time; but when the company set out, he remained behind to finish a game of ball with his companions, saying that he would follow very soon. He started off in the evening, and arrived late at Culand's residence; but when he attempted to enter the house, he found the way barred by an enormous dog, which was kept by the artificer to guard his premises at night. The savage animal instantly set on him; but the brave little fellow, in no degree terrified, valiantly defended himself.

When Culand and his guests heard the dreadful uproar outside, the smith started up and asked in great alarm whether any of the company had remained behind; for no one, he said, had ever approached the house at night without being torn in pieces by the dog. Then the king all at once recollected how Setanta had promised to follow him, and Fergus Mac Roigh and several others of the guests rushed out to save him; but when they came to the place, they found the great dog lying dead, and the young hero standing over him. Fergus, in great delight, snatched up the boy in triumph on his shoulder, brought him into the house, and placed him on the floor in presence of the king and the whole assembly, who received him very joyfully.

Culand, after he had first given vent to his gladness at the boy's escape, immediately fell to lamenting his dog, complaining that his house and flocks would now have to remain unprotected. But young Setanta at once said that he would procure him a puppy of the same breed, if one could be found in all Erin, from Tonn Tuath in the north to the Wave of Cleena in the south; and he offered moreover, to take upon himself the charge of guarding the house at night till the young dog should be sufficiently grown to take his place. Whereupon, the king's druid, *Cathbad*, who happened to be present, proposed that the boy's name should be changed to *Cu-Chulaind* (Culand's hound); and he declared that he should be known by this name to all future generations, and that his fame and renown would live for ever among the men of Erin and Alba (see O'Curry, Lect. II., 362).

In the ancient historical tale called "The Feast of *Dun-na-ngedh*," there is a very good example of the manner in which secondary names were given on account of personal deformities or peculiarities. The arch rebel, *Congal Claen*, in his angry speech to the king, enumerating his wrongs, tells him how, when he was one day left alone in the garden of the *lis* where he was nursed, a little bee stung him in one eye, so that the eye became awry, "from which," he says, "I have been named Congal Claen"—*claen* signifying inclined or crooked. He goes on to relate how on another occasion he slew the king of Ireland,

Sweeny Menn; "and when the king was tasting death, he flung a chess-man which was in his hand at me, so that he broke the crooked eye in my head. I was squint-eyed (*claen*) before; I have been blind-eyed (*caech*) since." Accordingly we find him called in old documents by both names, *Congal Claen*, and *Congal Caech*.

This custom of bestowing names descriptive of some qualities in the individuals, was all along crossed by another that must have existed from the earliest ages, namely, the perpetuation of hereditary personal names. It is a natural desire of parents to call their child after one of themselves, or after some distinguished ancestor; and such names were given without any reference to personal peculiarities. Moreover, a feeling of reverence for the memory of the parent or ancestor whose name was adopted, would be a powerful motive—just as it is in our own day—to resist a change of name in after-life. This manner of designation became more and more general, till it ultimately quite superseded the other; and now, even if the names were understood, no one would ever think of finding in the name a description of the person.

It appears from our historians that hereditary family names became general in Ireland about the period when Brian Boru reigned, viz. in the end of the tenth and the beginning of the eleventh century; and some authorities assert that this custom was adopted in obedience to an ordinance issued by that monarch. The manner in which these names were formed was very simple. The members of a family—each in addition to his own proper name—took as a common designation the name of their father, of their grandfather, or of some more remote ancestor; in the first case prefixing the word *mac*, which means a son, and in the two other cases *ua* or *o*, which signifies grandson; and in all cases the genitive of the progenitor's name followed the *mac* or the *o*. Thus the following were the names of seven successive kings of the Hy Neill race from A. D. 763 to 956, and each was the son as well as the successor of the next preceding:—Niall Frassach (of the showers), Hugh Oirne, Niall Cailne, Hugh Finnliath (fair-grey), Niall Glundubh (black-knee), Murkertagh of the leather cloaks, and Domnall O'Neill. This last king was the first that adopted the surname of *Ua Neill* (Niall's grandson) which he took from his grandfather, Niall Glundubh; and from that time forward every man of his race bore the surname of O'Neill.*

Great numbers of places all through the country have received their names from individuals or from families, who were formerly connected with them, either by possession or residence or some other accident. In the formation of such names certain phonetic laws were observed, which I will now proceed to explain and illustrate. It must be remarked however, that while these laws are rigidly observed in the Irish language, it often happens that in the process of anglicising, either they are disregarded, or the effect of them altogether disappears.

I. When a local name is formed by the union of a noun of any kind with a personal name, the latter follows the former, and is in the genitive case. *Seanach* [Shannagh], which signifies wise or prudent,

* See O'Donovan's admirable essay on "Ancient names of Tribes and Territories in Ireland," in the Introduction to O'Dugan's Topographical Poem.

was formerly very common as a man's name, and it continues in use in the family name O'Shanahan. Its genitive is *Seanaigh*, which is pronounced *Shanny* in every part of Ireland except south Munster, where they sound it *Shannig*. Some saint of this name is commemorated at Kilshannig near Rathcormack in Cork, the Irish name of which is *Cill-Seanaigh*, *Seanach's* church. Kilshanny near Mitchelstown in the same county, is the same name, and exhibits the more usual sound of the genitive. The small island of Inishmurray in the bay of Sligo, is called in the annals *Inis-Muireadhaigh*, and it received its name from *Muireadhach*, the first bishop of Killala, who flourished in the seventh century.

Iomhar or *Eimher* [Eever] is a man's name which was formerly very common, and which still survives as a family name in the forms of Ivor, Ivors, Evers, and even Howard. The village of Ballivor in Meath exhibits this name very nearly as it ought to be pronounced, the Irish being *Baile-Iomhair*, Iver's town. There was a celebrated chief of the O'Donovans named *Iomhar* who lived in the thirteenth century, and from whom a considerable sept of the O'Donovans were descended. He built a castle called from him *Caislean-Iomhair*, which long remained in possession of the family; it is now called Castle Eyre, and its ruins still remain near the little village of Unionhall in the parish of Myross, at the mouth of Glandore harbour in Cork. He was a great trader; and the legends of the peasantry still relate that he lives enchanted in a lake near the castle—Lough Cluhir—and that once in every seven years his ship is seen with colours flying, sailing over the surface of the water (see O'Donovan's Four M. VI., 2439). *Muireagán*, genitive *Muireagáin*, is a very old Irish personal name, signifying a mariner, from *muir*, the sea; and it is still used in the form of Morgan. There is a place near Abbeyleix in Queen's County, called Cremorgan, the Irish name of which is *Crioch-Muireagáin*, Muregan's district. In the three last names the modification in sound and spelling of the genitive disappears in the anglicised forms.

II. The initial letter of a personal name in the genitive case, following a noun, is usually aspirated, if it be one of the aspirable letters. This occurs in the Irish language, but in the anglicised forms the aspirated letters are often restored. *Múirn* or *Múirni* (signifying love or affection), was a woman's name, formerly in use in Ireland; *Finn Mac Cumhaill's* mother, for instance, was called *Múrni Muncaim* (of the beautiful neck). There is a village and parish west of Macroom in Cork, called Ballyvourney, where some woman of this name seems to be commemorated; for the Four Masters, in recording it as one of the camping places of O'Sullivan Bear in his retreat from Dunboy in 1602, call it *Baile-Mhuirne*, Murna's townland. The aspirated *m* is restored in Carrigmoorna (*Murna's* rock) in the parish of Kilrossanty in Waterford. In this townland there is a conical stony hill, having a large rock on the summit, with an old *lis* near it; and within this rock dwells the enchantress Murna. When the wind blows strongly in certain directions, a loud whistling sound comes from some crevices in the rock, which can be heard distinctly half a mile off; and the peasantry who know nothing of such learned explanations, and care less, will tell you, among many other dim legends of the lady Murna, that this sound is the humming of her spinning wheel.

III. The genitive of *ua* or *o* (a grandson) is *ui*,

which is pronounced the same as *ee* or *y* in English; and consequently when a local name consists of a noun followed by a family name with *o* (such as O'Brien) in the genitive singular, the *ui* is usually (but not always) represented in anglicised names by *y*. This is very plainly seen in Cloonykelly near Athleague in Roscommon, *Cluain-Ui-Cheallaigh*, O'Kelly's meadow; in Drumyarkin in Fermanagh (near Clones), O'Harkin's *drum* or hill-ridge. Cloonybrien, near Boyle in Roscommon, where a portion of the Annals of Loughkey was copied, is called in Irish *Cluain-I-Bhraoin*, O'Breen's meadow. Knockycosker, north of Kilbeggan in Westmeath, is written by the Four Masters *Cnoc-Ui-Choscraigh*, O'Cosgry's hill. The barony of Iraghticonor in the north of Kerry, is called in Irish *Oireacht-Ui-Chonchobhair*, O'Conor's *iraght* or inheritance.

In the parish of Moycullen in Galway there is a townland, now called Gortyloughlin; but as we find it written Gurtyloughnane in on old county map, it is obvious that here *n* has been changed to *l*—a very usual phonetic corruption (1st Ser. Part I., c. III.), and that the Irish name is *Gort-Ui-Lachtnain*, the field of O'Lachtnan or O'Loughnane—a well known family name. This townland includes the demesne and house of Danesfield, the name of which is an attempted translation of the incorrect name Gortyloughlin, the translators thinking that the latter part was identical with *Lochlannach*, one of the Irish terms for a Dane. But the Danes had nothing to do with the name, for neither Gortyloughnane nor Gortyloughlin, could bear the interpretation of Danesfield, which is one of the many instances of false translations in our local nomenclature. The family name *O'Lachtnain* is commemorated in Bally-loughnane, the name of two townlands, one in the north of Tipperary (near Birr), and the other near Croom in Limerick—O'Loughnane's town. With *gort* for the initial term we have Gortyclery near Mohill in Leitrim, Gortyleahy near Macroom in Cork, and Gortymadden in the parish of Abbeygormacan in Galway, O'Clery's, O'Leahy's, and O'Madden's field respectively.

This *y* sound of *ui* is often altogether sunk in the *y* of *Bally* and *derry*, when a family name follows these words. The parish of Ballyboggan in Meath takes its name from a celebrated abbey whose ruins are still to be seen on the Boyne, and which is called in the annals *Baile-Ui-Bhogain*, (the abbey of) O'Bogan's town. There are several places in different counties called Ballykealy; the Four Masters give the correct form of the name when they mention Ballykealy in Kerry, which they call *Baile-Ui-Chaeluighe*, O'Keely's town. Half way between Athenry and Oranmore, just by the railway at the south side, there is an old castle ruin called Derrydonnell, the Irish name of which is given in the same authority, *Doire-Ui-Dhomhnaill*, O'Donnell's oak wood.

IV. When a local name consists of a word followed by a family name with *O*, in the genitive plural (i. e. having such an interpretation as "the rock of the O'Donnells"), in this case, whilst the *O* retains its own form unchanged, the first letter of the following word is eclipsed (if it admit of eclipse) exactly the same as if the *O* were the article in the genitive plural. As this is a very important law, and influences great numbers of names, and as besides it is very generally followed in the anglicised forms, I will illustrate it by several instances.

Many examples of this usage might be quoted from

the annalists. The Four Masters record at 1559, that Calvagh O'Donnell was taken prisoner in the monastery of *Cill-O-dTomhrair*, the church of the *O'Tomhrairs*. The ruins of this monastery are situated near the shore of Lough Swilly, two miles from the village of Rathmelton in Donegal. The name ought to be pronounced *Killodorrir*, but the Irish speaking people change the last *r* to *l* (1st Ser., Part I., c. III.), and pronounce it *Killodorril;* and those who anglicised the name from this corrupted it further by changing the *rr* to *nn*, so that the old church is now always called Killodonnell, as if it took its name from the O'Donnells. The family of *O'Tomhrair*, who now call themselves Toner, took their name from an ancestor, *Tomhrar*, whose name was borrowed from the Danish *Tomrar*, or Tomar.

Torney is now a pretty common family name, the correct form of which is O'Torna. According to O'Curry (Lect., II., 59) they derive their name from the celebrated poet Torna Eigeas, who flourished in the fourth century; and they inhabited the district of O'Torna in the north of Kerry. The name of this district is still retained in that of the monastery and village of Abbeydorney; the former, which was founded in 1154, is called in Irish by the Four Masters, *Mainistir-O-dTorna* [Mannister-Odorna], the abbey of the O'Tornas. The word "abbey" is omitted in the name of the parish, which is now called O'Dorney. Another name exactly similar to this last is Ogonnelloe, which is that of a parish in Clare; here the word *tuath* is understood:—*Tuath-O-gCoingialla*, the district of the O'Conneelys. Near Croom in Limerick is a townland called Tullovin, which exactly represents the sound of *Tul'-O-bhFinn*, the hill of the O'Finns, where the *f* is eclipsed by the *bh* or *v*; and the same family name is commemorated in Graigavine near Fiddown in the south of Kilkenny, *Graig-O-bhFinn*, the O'Finns' *graigue* or village.

In the year A. D. 869, Hugh Finnliath, king of Ireland, gained a victory over the Danes at a place called by the annalists *Cill-Ua-nDoighre* [Killoneery] the church of the O'Deerys; which Dr. Todd believes to be the place now called Killineer near Drogheda. The personal name *Doighre* [Dira] from which this family name has been formed, though formerly in use, is now obsolete; but it is preserved in local nomenclature. Some man of this name is commemorated in Duniry, now a parish in Galway, where the Mac Egans, hereditary brehons to the O'Kellys of Hy-Many, long had their residence, and which in their writings, and in the Four Masters, is called *Dun-Doighre* (*D* lost by aspiration), *Doighre's* fortress.

There is a parish near the town of Antrim, called Donegore, which Colgan calls *Dun-O-gCurra*, the fortress of the O'Curras; and the old fortress still exists, and is called Donegore moat (Reeves: Eccl. Ant. 64, note d).

The Four Masters at A. D. 1393 record a conflict between two families of the Mac Dermots, fought at a place which they call *Cluain-O-gCoinnen*, the meadow of the O'Cunnanes, which is situated near Frenchpark in the north of Roscommon, and is now called Cloonnagunnane. Near Borrisokane in Tipperary there is a place called Kyleonermody; here the *n* in the middle represents a *d* which it eclipses, the whole name being *Coill-O-nDiarmada*, the wood of the O'Dermody's, a family name still common in Limerick and Tipperary. *Diarmad* as a personal name is commemorated in Dundermot

(Diarmad's fortress) a townland giving name to a parish in Antrim, which itself takes its name from a large earthen fort over the Clough Water near where it joins the river Main. Killodiernan is an old church giving name to a parish in Tipperary, one of the churches that took their names from families, where the O'Tiernans were probably *erenaghs* or hereditary wardens of the church, the Irish name being *Cill-O-dTighearnan*. A name exactly corresponding to this is Killogilleen in Galway, exhibiting the eclipse of *c* by *g*:—*Cill-O-gCillín*, the church of the O'Killeens, or as they now call themselves, Killeens.

Occasionally in constructions of this kind, the *O* disappears in the process of anglicising, while the effect of the eclipse remains. This is seen in Rathgormuck, the name of a village and parish in Waterford, which they now pronounce in Irish *Rath-a-gCormaic*, but which, thirty years ago, the old people called *Rath-O-gCormaic*, the fort of the O'Cormacs. On this it is to be remarked that in may parts of Ireland, the *O* of family names is pronounced *A* in the colloquial language:—Daniel O'Connor for instance would be made *Domhnall-A-Conchubhair*.

In a few cases both the *O* and the eclipse are obliterated, as in Rosbercon, the name of a village in the south of Kilkenny, which on account of being situated in the ancient territory of *Ui Berchon*, is called in Irish *Ros-Ua-mBerchon*, the wood of the O'Berchans.

V. The *mac* of family names is often written *mag*, even in manuscripts of authority. Among a great many examples of this I may mention the family of Magroarty, who were keepers of the celebrated reliquary called the *caah* or *cathach*, belonging to the family of O'Donnell. The Four Masters mention this family twice, and in both cases write the name *Mag Robhartaigh* (son of *Robhartach* [Roartagh]); and the *g* holds its place in the modern form, as well as in local names derived from the family. An example of this is Ballymagrorty, the name of two townlands, one near the town of Ballyshannon, and the other near the city of Derry, which Colgan writes *Baile-Meg-Rabhartaich*, Magroarty's townland. The Magroartys resided in and gave name to these places, and it is probable that they held the lands in virtue of their office.

VI. When *mac* in the genitive follows a noun, if the noun following begin with a vowel, *n* is inserted after *mac* and before the vowel. This *n* is merely an inflectional termination, and belongs to the ancient form of declension, as may be seen by reference to Zeuss, Gram. Celt., p. 221. An excellent example of this is Kilmacrenan (*Cill-Macn-Enain*), examined in 1st Ser. It is seen also in Kilmacnoran, two miles east of Ballyhaise in Cavan, *Cill-Macn-Odhrain*, the church of the sons of *Odhran* or Oran. There is a barony in the east of Galway called Clonmacnowen, or more correctly Clanmacnowen; the name divides itself this way, Clan-macn-owen; Irish, *Clann-mic-nEoghain* (Four M.), the descendants of the son of Eoghan or Owen; and this tribe were descended and took their name from Owen, the son of Donall More O'Kelly, chief of Hy Many, who flourished in the early part of the thirteenth century.

VII. When a local name consists of a noun followed by a family name beginning with *mac*, or by any surname following *mac*, the *m* of *mac* is often aspirated; as in Derryvicneill in the parish of Attymas in Mayo, *Doire-mhic-Neill*, the oak-wood of

Niall's son; Ballyvicnacally near Dromore in Down, the town of the son of the *calliagh* or hag.

VIII. The *v* of this anglicised syllable *vic* or *vick*, is often omitted both in pronunciation and writing, leaving only *ick*, and sometimes nothing more than the mere sound of *k*. This is a contraction very common in Irish family names; and in a great many that begin with *k*, *c*, or *g*, these letters represent the last letter of the *mac* or *mag*. Keon is shortened from Mac Owen; Cuolahan from *Mac Uallachain*; Cribbin, Gribbin, and Gribbon, from *Mac Roibin*, the son of Robin or little Robert.

The Irish call the Berminghams *Mac Fheorais* [Mac Orish], i. e. the son of Feoras, or Pieras, or Pierce, a name derived from an ancestor, Pierce, the son of Meyler Bermingham, who was one of the chief heads of the family. Several branches of this family have altogether dropped the English name, and adopted the Irish; but it is almost universally contracted from Mackorish to the forms Corish, Corus and Chorus, all family names common in certain parts of Ireland. Some member of this family gave name to Ballycorus in the county of Dublin, near Enniskerry, well known for its lead mines, the full name of which is *Baile-Mhic-Fheorais*, the town of Mac Orish or Bermingham. The hereditary name Pierce or Feoras, without the *mac*, is preserved in Monasteroris, the name of a ruined monastery near Edenderry in King's County, which was founded by Sir John Bermingham for Franciscans in the year 1325, and hence called *Mainister-Feorais* (Four M.), the monastery of (*Mac*) *Feorais*. (See Sir William R. Wilde's "Boyne and Blackwater").

A good example of the custom now under consideration in its application to local nomenclature, is Ballickmoyler, the name of a village in Queen's County, which signifies the town of the son of Moyler or Myler. So also Gorticmeelra in Roscommon, Mac Meelra's *gort* or field; Killickaweeny near Kilcock in Kildare, *Coill-mhic-a'-Mhuimhnigh*, the wood of the son of the *Muimhneach* [Mweenagh] or Munsterman. Near the bank of the grand canal, two miles west of Tullamore in King's County, is an old castle called Ballycowan, which gives name to the barony in which it is situated. The Four Masters at 1557 write the name *Baile-mhic-Abhainn*, the town of the son of *Abhann* or *Aibhne*, a personal name formerly in use, and still sometimes met with in the anglicised form Evenew. There is a place in King's County and another in Kildare, called Cadamstown; the Irish form of this name is preserved by the Four Masters, who write the name of Cadamstown in King's County, *Baile-mic-Adam*, the town of Adam's son; and the correct anglicised form Ballymacadam is the name of some places in Kerry and Tipperary.

IX. The *c* of *mac* is sometimes dropped. There is a parish in Tipperary called Kilmastulla, which should have been anglicised Kilmacstulla, for it is written in the Down Survey *Killm^c Stully*, and signifies Mac Stully's church. In like manner, Ballymadun, a parish in the north of the county of Dublin, is written in an ancient Latin document, quoted by Dr. Reeves (O'Dugan, Notes, V.) *Villa Macdun*, indicating that the correct anglicised name is Ballymacdun, Macdun's townland. So Ballymascanlan, a parish in Louth, ought to have been, and indeed often is, called Ballymacscanlan, the town of Scanlan's son.

I will now proceed to instance a few characteristic Irish personal and family names, and to illustrate the manner in which local names have been formed from them; and I will first resume the consideration of these names derived from *dubh*, black, all of which, like *Dubhan*, must have been originally applied to persons with dark hair and complexion.

One of these is *Dubhthach* [Duffa], which has descended to our own day in the form of Duffy and O'Duffy. I do not wish to venture on an explanation of *thach*, the latter part of the word: it may be possibly nothing more than a suffix, for it is found in other names, such as *Carthach*, *Cobhthach*, &c. *Dubhthach* is a name of great antiquity; and those who have read the history of St. Patrick's preaching in Ireland, will remember king *Laeghaire's* arch poet *Dubhthach*, whom the saint converted when he preached before the king and his court in Tara in A. D. 433. Some individual of this name must have formerly possessed Tamnadoey near Moneymore in Derry, which is called in Irish *Tamhnach-Dubhthaigh*, *Dubhthach's* field; and we have the name also in Ballyduffy in Longford, Mayo, and Roscommon, the townland of Duffy or O'Duffy.

From the same root we have *Dubhalthach*, which means a dark complexioned lofty person; though the *alt* would bear other interpretations besides lofty. This name is generally anglicised Duald or Dudley, but it is now seldom met with in any form. Lissadulta in the parish of Kilthomas in Galway, signifies Duald's fort—*Lios-a'-Dubhaltaigh*. This personal name is strangely perverted in Moneygold, the name of a place near the village of Grange in Sligo. The last syllable, *gold*, has been extracted from the long name *Dhubhaltaigh;* but the whole process is in strict accordance with phonetic laws already explained (1st Ser. Part I., c. III.):—viz., *Dhubhaltaigh* reduced to *Dhuald* by throwing off the last syllable: representing this phonetically, and substituting *g* for *dh* ; after this it required small pressure to force Money-guald to Moneygold, for *money* naturally suggested *gold*, according to the ordinary process of popular etymology:—*Muine-Dhubhaltaigh*, Duald's shrubbery.

One of the best known names derived from this root *dubh* is *Dubhda* ; it is here combined with the ancient adjectival termination, *de* or *da* ; and signifies black-complexioned. What lover of oysters has not heard of Poldoody! It is a large pool at the shore near the Red Bank of Burren in the north of Clare; and it produces oysters of excellent quality in great abundance. The name, however, has nothing to do with oysters, for it is merely *Poll-Dubhda*, Dooda's pool. We know nothing of this *Dubhda*, but he may in all likelihood get the credit of being an epicure in oysters. A chieftain of this name, who flourished in the seventh century, and was ninth in descent from the monarch Dathi, was the ancestor of the family of *Ui Dubhda*, or O'Dowd.

Dubhagán is a diminutive of *dubh*, and signifies literally a little dark man. It is well known as a family name in the phonetic form Dugan or O'Dugan; and families of the name are commemorated in the townlands of Ballydugan in Down and Tipperary, whose name signifies O'Dugan's townland.

Personal names derived from colours are very numerous in Irish, and it may be instructive to enumerate a few of the most important and usual. *Odhar* [oar] is pale, pale-brown, pale-faced; one of the chieftains of the O'Carrolls, who was slain in 1581 by the O'Conors Faly, was styled William *Odhar*, or William the pale-faced. The term in its simple form was in former days used as a personal name.

From a chieftain of this name, who was seventh in descent from *Colla Da Chrich*, and who lived in the sixth century, the Maguires took their name. For *Uidhir*, the genitive of *Odhar*, is pronounced *eer* or *ire;* and Maguire is a tolerably correct representative, so far as sound is concerned, of *Mac Uidhir*, which signifies literally the son of the pale-faced man. Ballymaguire (Maguire's town) near Lusk in Dublin, and another townland of the same name in Tyrone, were both so called from members of this family.

The diminutive *Odhran* [Oran: little pale-faced man] is far more frequent as a personal name than *Odhar*. It was moreover in use at a very early period of our history; St. Patrick's charioteer was St. *Odhran*, who gave name to a place called Desert-Oran in Offaly. It is often found forming part of local names, of which the following are examples. There is a townland called Seeoran in the parish of Knockbride in Cavan, which is called by the annalists *Suidhe-Odhrain*, Oran's seat. Mullaghoran, Oran's summit, is the name of a place in the parish of Drumlumman, Cavan; there are some places in Tyrone and Cavan called Rahoran (*rath*, a fort); Killoran, the name of several townlands in Galway, Tipperary, and Sligo, is Oran's church; Ballyoran, Oran's townland; we have Templeoran in Westmeath, Oran's church; and the name of Templeorum near Fiddown in the south of Kilkenny, has been corrupted from this, for in the Irish elegy on the Rev. Edmund Kavanagh, by the Rev. James Lalor, it is called *Teampull-Odhrain*.

The Irish word *flann*, as a noun, signifies blood; and as an adjective, red or ruddy. From a very early period it has been used as a personal name, and it must have been originally applied to a ruddy-faced man. Flann, or, as he is usually called, Flann of the monastery, was a celebrated annalist, poet, and professor, who flourished at Monasterboice, and died in A. D. 1056. The genitive form is *Flainn*, which is pronounced Flinn or Floin; and hence the family name O'Flinn. In this name the *F* is sometimes aspirated, which altogether destroys its sound; and then the name becomes O'Lynn, which is also pretty common. But the O is now usually omitted from both names, reducing them to Flinn and Lynn. *Flann* also forms a family name with *mac*, and in this case the *F* is always aspirated and omitted; thus *Mac-Fhlainn* has given us the family name Macklin, which will remind the reader of the celebrated actor (whose real name, however, was Mac Loughlin); while other branches of the same family call themselves Magloin or McGloin. Many again drop the *Mac* or *Mag*, the *g* of which gets attracted to the *l* (see p. 140); and this gives rise to the family names Glynn and Glenn.

About three-quarters of a mile west of the town of Boyle in Roscommon, near a small cataract on the river, just at the railway bridge, there is an old church which is often mentioned in the annals by the names *Eas-Dachonna* and *Eas-Mic-nEirc* (*eas*, a waterfall), from St. *Dachonna*, the son of *Erc*, who was the patron of the place. But in later ages it has been called *Eas-Ui-Fhlainn*, O'Flynn's cataract, from the family of O'Flynn, who were the erenaghs or wardens of the church; and this old name is exactly represented in sound by the present name of the church, Assylin. Near the village of Desertmartin in Derry, there is a small lake called Loughinsholin (and sometimes incorrectly Lough

Shillin), or in Irish *Loch-innse-Ui-Fhlainn*, the Lake of O'Flinn's island. This island was a *crannoge* (see this in 1st Ser.), and was a fortress of such importance that it gave name, not only to the lake, but to the barony of Loughinsholin. From the same branch of this family two other places in the same neighbourhood took their names, viz., Desertlyn (O'Lynn's hermitage), and Monasterlynn, (O'Lynn's monastery), but the latter is now always called by the seductive name of Moneysterling.

The family name with *mac* is commemorated in Ballymaglin in Derry (*bally*, a townland); and in Crossmaglen, the name of a village in Armagh, the full name of which is *Cros-meg-Fhlainn*, Maglin's cross. And we have the personal name exhibited in Attyflin near Patrickswell in Limerick, and in Attiflynn near Dunmore in Galway, both of which are called in Irish *Ait-tighe-Flainn*, the site (*ait*) of Flann's house.

With the diminutive termination *gán*, and a vowel sound inserted (pp. 31 and 3, *supra*), the name *Flannagán* has been formed—little Flann—a little ruddy-faced man; and from this again comes the family name of O'Flanagan, or Flanagan, as they now generally call themselves. The *F* of this name becomes aspirated and omitted in Ballylanigan, the name of some places in Limerick and Tipperary—*Baile-Ui-Fhlannagain*, O'Flanagan's town.

I might give many more examples of personal names derived from colours—indeed there is scarcely a colour that does not originate a name—but I will content myself with the foregoing. I will now instance a few personal and family names derived in various ways, and give examples of local names derived from them.

Aedh [ay: sounded like the *ay* in *say*], genitive *Aedha*, is interpreted by Cormac Mac Cullenan, Colgan, and other ancient writers, to mean fire. It is cognate with Gr. *aithos*, "also with Lat. *aedes*, Skr. *edhas*, firewood. Hence the Gaulish name Aedui—Welsh *aidd*, warmth" (Stokes in Cor. Gl.: see also on the name Aedui—"Die bei Caius Julius Caesar vorkommenden Keltischen Namen in ihrerechtheit festgestellt und erläutert," by C. W. Glück, p. 9). In its original application it was probably used in the sense of a fiery warrior. This name has been in use in Ireland from the most remote antiquity; and as we have seen, it was used among the Gauls in the time of Julius Cæsar. We find it among those early colonists, the Tuatha De Danann; and it was very common among the Milesians who succeeded them. It was the name of a great many of our ancient kings; and the Irish ecclesiastics named *Aedh* are almost innumerable. Those who write in Latin use the form *Aidus;* and in English it is always made Hugh, which however is a Teutonic name, with an entirely different signification.

From it are derived the two family names of *O'hAedha* and *Mac Aedha* [O'Hay, Mac-Ay], both of which have been modified into various modern forms. The most correct anglicised form of the first is O'Hea or O'Hay, which is still common, but some families call themselves Hay. In Limerick the name is very common in the form of Hayes, which in the cities is sometimes changed to Haiz, to make it appear, I suppose, of foreign origin. The usual modernised form of *Mac Aedha* is Magee, which is correct, or McGee, not so correct, or Mackay, which would be correct if it were accented on the last syllable, which it generally is not; and it is made MKay by some.

It is very common in the form of Mac Hugh, which again is often still further modernised to Hughes.

The simple name, variously modified, is found in great numbers of local names. It is represented by *ee* (as it is in Mag*ee*) in Inishee quoted farther on. There is a parish near Killybegs in Donegal called Killaghtee, which takes its name from an old church, the ruins of which are still to be seen near the hamlet of Bruckless. The name signifies the church of *Aedh's leacht* or sepulchral monument; and a large stone about six feet high, with a curious and very ancient cross inscribed on its face, which stands in the graveyard, marks the site of the old *leacht*, where *Aedh*, who was probably the original founder of the church, lies buried. *Aedh* has the same form in Rathmacnee, the name of a parish near Carnsore Point in Wexford, where the ruins of a castle still stand, probably on the site of the ancient rath which gave origin to the name:—*Rath-mac-nAedha*, the fort of the sons of *Aedh* (*n* inserted, p. 139). But it is more usually represented by *ea*, as we see in Caherea, the name of some places in Clare—*Cathair-Aedha*, Hugh's *caher* or circular stone fortress.

Not unfrequently the name is made Hugh, as in Tullyhugh in Armagh and Sligo, Hugh's hill; Rathhugh in the parish of Ahamlish in Sligo, Hugh's fort. The barony of Tirhugh in the extreme southwest of Donegal, is called in Irish authorities, *Tir-Aedha*, the territory of Aedh; and it received that name from *Aedh* or Hugh (son of Ainmire), the king of Ireland who summoned the celebrated convention of Drumceat in 573, and who was slain at the great battle of Dunbolg in A. D. 598. Before his time this territory bore the name of *Sereth*.

This name *Aedh* is often so very much disguised by contraction as to be quite undistinguishable without the aid of written authorities. A good example of this is the well-known tribe name of Clannaboy or Clandeboy, which is a short form of the old name *Clann-Aedha-buidhe* [Clan-ay-boy] as we find it in the annals; these people were so called from *Aedh-buidhe* (yellow Hugh) or Hugh Boy O'Neill, a chieftain who was slain in the year A. D. 1283. In the fourteenth century they possessed an extensive territory in the counties of Down and Antrim, and this was the ancient Clannaboy; but the name no longer exists except so far as it is preserved in Lord Dufferin's seat of Clandeboye near Bangor in Down. Lissofin is a townland in the parish of Tullagh in Clare, the Irish name of which is *Lios-Aedha-Finn* [Lissayfin] the fort of Hugh the fair, derived from *Aedh Finn*, the ancestor of the family of Mac Namara Finn.

The family name with *O* is commemorated in Clooneyhea in the parish of Drangan in Tipperary, O'Hea's meadow; also in Ballyhay, the name of a parish in Cork, and of a townland in Down near Donaghadee (Ballyhayes, Inq.—1623), as well as in Ballyhays in Kildare—all signifying O'Hea's town. We have the family name with *mac* in Ballymacue in Tipperary, and Ballymagee near Bangor in Down: so also in Kilmakee the name of two places in the parishes of Derryaghy and Templepatrick in Antrim, the church of Hugh's son.

The personal name *Aedhagán* (little *Aedh*) is formed by adding the diminutive *gán* with a vowel sound before it (pp. 31 and 3); and this again gives origin to the family name *Mac-Aedhagain* or Mac Egan, now generally Egan, descended and named from

Aedhagan, a chieftain who lived in the eleventh century. The Mac Egans were long celebrated for learning, and one branch of them, who were hereditary brehons to the M'Carthy More, resided at Bally-Mac-Egan on the Shannon, in the parish of Lorrha in Tipperary. There are several other names formed from this name *Aedh*. See p. 29, *supra*.

Eoghan [Owen] means, according to Cormac's Glossary, well born. This name is now very common in Wales, Scotland, and Ireland, in the phonetic form Owen; but it is also often changed to Eugene, which is the corresponding Greek name having the same meaning. The family name Mac-Owen is derived from it, but it is more often written M'Keon and Keon (*c* attracted: p. 140). It generally has the form Owen in local names, as in Dunowen in Cork and Galway, called in the old records *Dun-Eoghain*, Owen's fort; Ballyowen, a pretty common townland name, Owen's town; Kilballyowen in Clare, Limerick, and Wicklow, the church of Owen's townland. Derryowen, an old castle in the parish of Kilkeedy in Clare, giving name to a townland, is called by the Four Masters, *Doire-Eoghain*, Owen's oak-wood.

Art is an ancient Celtic word which, according to Cormac's Glossary, has three meanings:—"A stone," "God," and "noble." As a personal name it was I suppose originally meant to convey the idea of hardness, bravery, and power of endurance in battle. It was much used in Ireland, and that from a very early time, several of our ancient kings having borne the name; and it was equally common in Wales in the form of Arthur—a name which will remind every reader of the great Welsh mythical hero, with his knights of the round table. As a personal name it is still used in Ireland, but is now always made

Arthur; and as a family name it exists in *O'hAirt* or O'Hart, now more generally Hart; and also in Mac Art and Mac Arthur.

Local names that end in the syllable *art*, may be considered as commemorating persons of this name, unless when it is obviously connected with preceding letters, as in *scart*, *mart*, *gart*, &c. It is seen in Carrigart, Art's or Arthur's rock, a village in Donegal; and in Drumart in Armagh, Art's ridge. Some person named Mac Art gave name to the great fortress on the top of Cave Hill near Belfast, well known as Mac Art's fort; and we have Ballymagart in Down, and Ballymacart in Waterford, Mac Art's town. *Artagan* is a diminutive of Art, from which we have the family name O'Hartigan or Hartigan, still to be met with in some of the southern counties. Dunlang O'Hartagan was the name of one of the Dalcassian heroes slain at the battle of Clontarf.

Aengus is a name which has been in use in Ireland from the earliest period. One of the most celebrated of our mythical characters was the great *Tuatha De Danann* enchanter, *Aengus an Bhrogha*, i. e. Aengus of Brugh on the Boyne; and Aengus was the name of one of the three brothers—sons of Erc—who led a colony to Scotland in the year 506, and founded the Scottish monarchy. From that period it became equally common in Scotland; and in the usual anglicised form, Angus, it will be recognised as the name of one of the leading characters in Macbeth. In Ireland it is still in use as a personal name, but nearly always changed to Æneas.

The name is compounded of *aen*, one, and *gus*, strength or valour; and it is to be interpreted as meaning a unity or concentration of strength. One of its genitive forms is *Aengusa* [Eanusa], which appears in the family names *Mac Aenghusa* and *O'hAenghusa*, or Magennis and O'Hennessy or Hennessy. Some members of the latter family gave name to Ballyhennessy in Clare, Cork, and Kerry, the town of O'Hennessy. Another genitive form is *Aenghuis*, which is popularly pronounced *Eneece;* and this is represented in Killyneece near Magherafelt in Derry, and in Derryneece in Fermanagh, both signifying Aengus's wood; and with a slight change in the sound, in Taghnoose in the parish of Kilkeevin in Roscommon, Aengus's house.

Another name containing the root *gus* is Fergus, which signifies manly strength, from *fear*, a man; and it is equally ancient with the preceding. It assumes various forms in local names. Sometimes the name remains unchanged, as in Kilfergus in the parish of Loghill in Limerick, Fergus's wood; more often *g* disappears by aspiration, as we see in Tulfarris on the river Liffey near Pollaphuca waterfall, the hill (*tulach*) of Fergus. Still more frequently the word loses the initial *f* by aspiration, as in Ballyargus in Inishowen, the town of Fergus; and often both the *f* and the *g* drop out, as we see in Attyreesh in the parish of Oughaval in Mayo, *Ait-tighe-Fhearghuis*, the site (*ait*) of Fergus's house.

Great numbers of Irish personal names were taken from the names of animals; the individuals being supposed to possess in an eminent degree the characteristic qualities of the animals they were named after. Sometimes these names were taken without any change, and applied to men or women; but more often they had diminutives or other terminations, or they were compounded with other words. We have in this way borrowed *cu*, a hound, from which numerous names are derived; *colum*, a dove, whence

Columba and Columkille, and the diminutive *Columán* or *Colman* (Latinised *Columbanus*) from which again are the present family names Colman and Coleman; *laeg*, a calf; *cuach*, a cuckoo; *os*, a fawn; *fael*, a wolf, whence *Faelán* (little wolf), and the family name *O'Faeláin*, now Phelan and Whelan; *sionnach*, a fox; *broc*, a badger, and the diminutive *brocán*, whence the family name O'Brogan or Brogan; *én*, a bird; and a host of others

Cuan, probably a diminutive of *cu*, is very usual as a man's name; there were several saints named Cuan, from whose churches the townlands and parishes now called Kilquane and Kilquain were so named. The genitive of *cu* is *con*, which is the form usually found in family and local names. *Cu* forms the beginning of a great many names; such as *Cu-mara*, hound of the sea, given first I suppose to a skilful sailor or a bold leader of maritime expeditions. From a chieftain of this name, who died in 1014, and who was 23rd in descent from Olioll Olum, king of Munster, descend the family of Mac Conmara now Macnamara. There is a parish in Mayo near the village of Swineford, called Kilconduff, taking its name from an old church which the Four Masters call *Cill-Chonduibh*, the church of Cuduff (black hound), a person of whom I know nothing more.

Cumhaighe [Cooey] is another personal name, which was formerly pretty common:—*magh*, a plain—hound of the plain. This name is often anglicised Quintin. In the parish of Ardquin in the Ards in Down, there is a lake called Lough Cowey: near the shore of Tara bay in the same neighbourhood, is an old disused cemetery called Templecowey; and there are also Quintin castle, Quintin bay, and Ballyquintin townland, which gives name to the extreme southern point of the Ards. All these, according to local tradition, received their names from a saint *Cumhaighe* or Quintin, of whom however we known nothing further. (Reeves : Ecc. Ant., p. 25).

In the townland of Ballykinlettragh, parish of Kilfian, Mayo, two miles south of the village of Ballycastle, there was in old times a fort called *Lios-letreach*, the fort of the *letter* or wet hill-side. This fort was the residence of a family of the *Hy Fiachrach* called *Mac Conletreach*, who were descended and named from *Cu-letreach* (i. e. *Cu* of *Lios-letreach*), a chieftain who was fifth in descent from Awley, brother of Dathi, king of Ireland, and who must therefore have lived about the middle of the sixth century. The townland of Ballykinlettragh took its name from the family. Besides these, we have Ballyconboy in Roscommon, *Baile-mhic-Chonbuidhe* (see p. 140), i. e. the townland of Mac Conboy, a family named from an ancestor, *Cubuidhe*, yellow hound; and many others might be enumerated.

Bran is a raven, and it was formerly a favorite name for men. Few personal names can show a long history than this. It was common in Ireland from the earliest times; and it was also used among the Gauls, for I look upon it as very likely that it is identical with Brennus, the name of the great Celtic leader who sacked Rome in the fourth century before Christ.

Among many who bore the name in Ireland, the most celebrated was *Brandubh* (black raven), king of Leinster, who defeated and slew Hugh Oirnidhe, king of Ireland, at the battle of Dunbolg, in the year A. D. 598. He had his residence at Rathbran, Bran's fort, near Baltinglass in Wicklow. Another *Brandubh* gave name to Rathfran (*b* aspirated to *f*), two miles from Killala in Mayo, well known for its abbey, which Mac

Firbis writes *Rath-Branduibh.* There is a sandbank ford across the mouth of the river, just under the abbey, which is now called the Farset of Rathfran (see Farset in 1st Ser.); but it was anciently called *Fearsad-Tresi;* and according to a story in the *Dinnseanchus*, it was so named from *Tresi*, the wife of Awley, brother of king Dathi, who was drowned in it. (Hy F. 224). There is also a Rathbran in Meath; and we have Dunbrin (Bran's fortress) in Queen's County, near Athy.

From Bran, son of *Maelmordha* (king of Leinster, slain in the battle of Clontarf), are descended the family of O'Brain, who now generally call themselves O'Byrne, or more generally Byrne, sometimes more correctly O'Brin, and occasionally Burn, Byrnes, Burns, Brin, and sometimes even Byron.

From *ech*, a horse (Lat. *equus*), comes *Echegán*, a man's name meaning literally little horse. From an ancestor of this name descended the family of *Mac Echegain* or Mageoghegan, now more generally Geoghegan and Gahagan (*g* attracted: see p. 140). *Eochaidh* [Ohy], signifies a horseman; and from this again is formed the family name *Mac Eochadha* [Mac-ōha] or Mac Keogh, now usually contracted to Keogh or Kehoe; but in some places it is made M'Goey. *Eochaidh* was formerly exceedingly common as a personal name. From a chieftain named *Eochaidh Cobha*, who flourished in the third century, a tribe descended called *Uibh-Eachach* [Ivahagh], Eochaidh's descendants, who possessed a large territory in Ulster, now represented in name by the barony of Iveagh in Down. There was another territory of the same name in the south-west of the county Cork, which was so called from a tribe descended from *Eochaidh*, seventh in descent from Olioll Olum, king of Munster in the second century.

CHAPTER IX.

NICKNAMES.

No people in the world are, I believe, so given to nicknames as the Irish, unless perhaps the Scotch. Among the rural population in many parts of the country, almost every third man is known by some name besides his ordinary surname and Christian name. Sometimes these epithets are hereditary, and commemorate some family peculiarity or tradition; but more often they describe a personal characteristic of the individual. Sometimes they carry reproach, and are not used except to insult; but very often they are quite inoffensive, and are accepted as a matter of course and with perfect good humour.

In early life I knew a village where more than half the people were familiarly known by nicknames, which were always used, the proper names being hardly ever mentioned. One man, on account of his powers of endurance in faction fights, was called *Gadderagh*, which literally means a tough fellow like a *gad* or withe (affix *rach*, p. 7); another was never called by any name but *Cloosdarrag*, red-ears (which indeed is a historical nickname, for we find it stated in O'Clery's Calendar, that St. *Greallan*, who is commemorated in it, was the grandson of a man named *Cairbre-cluais-derg*); a third was *Phil-a'-gaddy*, or Phil the (son of the) thief; a fourth *Shaun-na-bointree*, John (the son) of the widow; and one man, who was a notorious schemer, was universally called, by way of derision, or "*per antiphrasim*," *Thomaus-a'-sagart*, Tom the priest. So generally had some of these been accepted, and so completely had they superseded the proper names, that to this day I remember those people well by their nicknames, though in many cases I have no idea—and never had—of what the real names were.

On this subject Sir Henry Piers wrote as follows in the year 1682, in his description of the county Westmeath:—"They take much liberty, and seem to do it with delight, in giving of nicknames; if a man have any imperfection or evil habit he is sure to hear of it in the nickname. Thus, if he be blind, lame, squint-eyed, grey-eyed, be a stammerer in speech, left-handed, to be sure he shall have one of these added to his name; so also from the colour of his hair, as black, red, yellow, brown, &c.; and from his age, as young, old: or from what he addicts himself to, or much delights in, as in draining, building, fencing, and the like; so that no man whatever can escape a nickname who lives among them, or converseth with them; and sometimes so libidinous are they in this kind of raillery, they will give nicknames *per antiphrasim*, or contrariety of speech. Thus a man of excellent parts, and beloved of all men, shall be called *grana*, that is, naughty or fit to be complained of (literally ugly or hateful); if a man have a beautiful countenance or lovely eyes, they will call him him *cuiegh*, that is, squint-eyed (*caech:* see next page); if a great housekeeper he shall be called *ackerisagh*, that is, greedy (*ocrasach*, hungry or greedy)." (Quoted by O'Donovan in O'Dugan: p. [19]).

But all this is obviously only a remnant of what was anciently the general custom. For originally, as I have already observed, personal names were descriptive; and the people who now designate a man by a nickname, do exactly as their ancestors did thousands of years ago, when they fixed on a name by which a person was to be afterwards known. The propensity of the Irish and Scotch for nicknames may, I think, be explained by the fact, that the tradition of personal names being significant and descriptive, still remains fresh on the minds of the people; and that many of the names themselves retained their significance—that is, they were living, intelligible words—as long as the people continued to speak the Celtic language.

Our annals and histories of both Pagan and Christian times, afford numerous examples of the prevalence of this custom in remote ages. Some had their proper names altogether changed to others descriptive of some personal peculiarity (see p. 127); while others retained their original names, but had a descriptive epithet appended, like *Cuimin Fada*, or *Cuimin*, the tall; *Finan Lobhar*, or Finan the leper, &c. And of nicknames, "*per antiphrasim* or contrariety of speech," I will content myself with the mention of one, viz., *Aedh* or Hugh O'Neill, a celebrated chieftain who died in 1230, and who, on account of his incessant activity in opposing the English, was nicknamed *Aedh-Toinleasc*, a sobriquet which would not bear literal translation, but which may be rendered in decent English, Hugh lazybody.

Persons are often commemorated in local names by their nicknames. One who was either purblind or squint-eyed, or who had altogether lost one eye, was usually called *caech;* which when it is anglicised is commonly represented by the syllable *kee*. Aghakee in the parish of Crosserlough in Cavan, represents the Irish *Ath-a'-chaeich*, the ford of the purblind fellow. Killakee, a well known place at the base of the mountains south of Dublin, derived its name in a similar way, the Irish word being *Coill-a'-chaeich*, the blind-man's wood.

The word *dall* is usually applied to a person altogether blind; but it is to be observed that the distinction here made between *caech* and *dall*, is not always observed. There is a place near the town of Roscommon called Ballindall, which is called in Irish *Baile-an-daill*, the town of the blind man. The southern pronunciation (dowl) is exhibited in connexion with an eclipse, in Lisnanowl near Castlemaine in Kerry, which exactly represents the sound of the Irish *Lios-na-ndall*, the fort of the blind men.

If the blind have been commemorated, we have also the lame and the halt. A cripple of any kind is designated by the word *bacach* (from *bac*, to baulk or halt), but the word is generally understood to mean a lame man; and from whatever cause it may have arisen, this term is frequently reproduced in local names. As cripples very often take up begging as a means of livelihood, a *bacach* is understood in many parts of Ireland to mean a beggar. There is a townland near the city of Derry called Termonbacca, the *termon* or sanctuary of the cripple. A different form of the word is seen in Knockavocka near Ferns in Wexford, the cripple's hill (*cnoc-a'-bhacaigh*), in which the *b* is aspirated to *v*; and the same change is seen, with the addition of the final *g* of the south Munster pronunciation, in Coolavokig near Ballyvourney in Cork, the cripple's corner. With the *b* eclipsed by *m* we have Ballynamockagh near Ballinasloe, *Baile-na-mbacach*, the townland of the cripples or beggars.

There is a townland containing the ruins of a

castle in the parish of Killaha in the north of Kerry, called Ballymacaquim; and whoever the man may have been that is commemorated in the name, he himself got a nickname on account of some deformity in his father. The Four Masters mention the castle at 1577, and they call it *Baile-mhic-an-chaim*, the town of the son of the crooked fellow; but whether it was a stooped back, a crooked leg, or a twisted eye, that earned the epithet *cam* for the father, it is now impossible to tell.

An *amadán* is a fool or simpleton; but the word is often applied in derision as a mere nickname, to one who is not exactly a downright idiot, but who has the character of being a foolish, brainless, or spoony fellow; and this application is very common at the present day in most parts of Ireland, even where the Irish language has been long disused. Fellows of this kind are often commemorated in local names; and the forms the word assumes will be seen in Ardamadane (accented on *am*) near Blarney in Cork, the fool's height; in Tiromedan near Ballybay in Monaghan, the land of the fool; in Trinamadan near the village of Gortin in Tyrone (*trian*, a third part or division of land); and in Knockanamadane, near Sneem in Kerry, the *amadan's* hill.

A *bodach* is a clown, a surly, churlish, uncivil fellow; and this opprobrious term is still constantly heard in various parts of the country. Some such ill-conditioned person must have lived at, or owned, Knockawuddy near the village of Clarinbridge in Galway, and the same may be said of Knockavuddig in the parish of Clonmult in Cork, both anglicised from *Cnoc-a'-bhodaigh*, the hill of the clown or churl. Monavoddagh in the parish of Ballynaslaney in Wexford, signifies the clown's bog. Clownstown, the name of a place near Mullingar in Westmeath, is merely a translation of Ballynamuddagh (*Baile-na-mbodach*, the town of the clowns), which is itself a very common townland name. The *b* in this word (which occurs very often in local names) is seldom preserved intact; it is almost always aspirated, as in the first two names just quoted; or eclipsed, as in Rathnamuddagh near the western shore of Lough Ennell in Westmeath, *Rath-na-mbodach*, the fort of the churls.

The word *cábóg* is very much used in different parts of Ireland, even where Irish has disappeared, to denote a clownish, boorish, ill-mannered fellow; and the Four Masters have preserved one old name containing this word, viz., *Ard-na-gcabog*, the clowns' height, which is still applied to a hill at the mouth of the Fergus in Clare, a little south of the village of Clare.

Other ways of designating individuals by nicknames will be seen in Meenirroy in the parish of Conwal in Donegal, which is *Min-an-fhir-ruaidh*, the mountain-meadow of the red-haired man; a name exactly like Fallinerlea near Cushendun in Antrim, the *fall*, i. e. the hedge or enclosure, of the grey man (*liath*, grey); also in Clooncrim near the village of Ballinlough in Westmeath, the meadow of the bent or stooped man (*crom*).

In their passion for nicknames the people did not stop at human beings; for we find that they also vented it on inanimate objects, and townlands even still retain in their names traces of this strange custom. *Spág* [spawg] is a ridiculous name for a club foot, or a long ugly foot; and the word is applied in the anglicised form Spaug, to a townland near Ennistymon in Clare, to express probably some queer elongation of shape. It must have been in some derisive or ridiculous sense that the name of Coogyulla, i. e. *Cuige-Uladh*, "the province of Ulster," was given to a townland near Lisdoonvarna in Clare; but why exactly the place was so called I have not the least idea. It is curious that there is another townland of this same name about three miles south-east of Templemore in Tipperary, only slightly varied to the form Coogulla. Lyneen, "little Leinster," is the name of a place in the parish of Moydow in Longford (*Laighen*—pron. *Lyen*, Leinster); but I suppose this is merely a fancy name.

Near the village of Inistioge in Kilkenny there is a townland called Ballycocksoost. The tradition of the neighbourhood is, that in former days the people of this townland were very unskilful threshers compared with their neighbours; in consequence of which the contemptuous name of Ballycocksoost was given to it. But this name will not bear translation into plain English, so the reader must be content with knowing that *súist* is a flail, and that the whole name signifies the town of the dirty flail. A nickname of the same opprobrious character (containing the same root, *cac*, cognate with Lat. *caco*) is Cackanode, applied to a townland in the parish of Clondrohid, near Macroom in Cork, to intimate the extreme badness of the land:—*Cac-an-fhóid*, the dirty part of the *fode*, sod, or soil; and we have Cockow in the parish of Knockane in Kerry, dirty river.

There is a little street in the Liberties of Dublin called Mullinahack. The first part of this name (*mullen*) will be recognised as the Irish word for a mill; and Mr. Gilbert (Hist. Dub. I., 351), has traced the existence of a mill there as early as the close of the twelfth century, i. e. before the city had extended quite so far. It is probable that in the good old times when the present name was invented, the mill had fallen into ruin; and I will merely give the Irish name—*Muilenn-a'-chaca*—leaving the reader to translate it for himself, and to conjecture why such a name should be given to an old mill.

CHAPTER X.

ENGLISH PERSONAL AND FAMILY NAMES.

AFTER the Anglo-Norman invasion in 1172, English settlers began to arrive and make their home in Ireland. They were for a long time almost confined to what was called the Pale, a small portion of the eastern coast, but gradually they ventured into various other parts of the country; and after the Plantations there were few districts of Ireland, where families, either English or of English descent, were not to be found. A large number of the places where they settled changed their old names, and took the names of the new proprietors; and now our topographical nomenclature shows a considerable mixture of English personal and family names.

We have also Danish names, but they are so extremely few that I do not think it necessary to devote a separate chapter to them: I will incorporate in the present chapter those I shall have to illustrate.

When the Irish speaking people came to use or to adopt English or Danish names, they made various changes in them in accordance with the phonetic laws of their own language. It would be easy to classify these alterations minutely if the subject were of any great importance; but a statement of a few of the causes of change will be sufficient here.

1. The Irish language does not admit to such an extent as the Teutonic languages, of the union of two or more consonants in pronunciation, without the intervention of a vowel sound. Where such combinations occurred in an English or Danish name, the Irish often omitted some of the consonants; or if they were committed to writing by Irish scribes, the letters were inserted, but under aspiration, which indicated their partial or total omission in pronunciation. Thus the Danish name Godfrey, which was occasionally adopted into Irish families, is written by the Four Masters *Gothfraith*, which would indicate the suppression in pronunciation of the *d* (or of *th* which replaces it in the Irish form):—*Gothfraith*, pronounced *Goffry*. But in actual use by speakers, the *f* was also generally aspirated and consequently omitted; and the name is exhibited so curtailed in Derrygorry in Monaghan (near the village of Aughnacloy), Gorry's or Godfrey's oak wood; and in Mullatigorry in the parish of Tedavnet, same county, the hill-summit (*mulla*) of Godfrey's house. So also Redmond is generally reduced to the sound Rayman; as in Kilcreman on the borders of King's County and Tipperary, near Roscrea, in which the *c* is a remnant of *mac* (see p. 140), the name when fully written being *Coill-mhic-Remoinn*, the wood of the son of Redmond.

II. There is no sound in Irish like that of the soft *g* in English (*g* in *gem*); and when this occurs in an English name, it is always replaced in Irish by slender *s*, which is equal in sound to English *sh*. Thus George is always made *Shoresha* (two syllables) in Irish. This rule comes very frequently into operation, and I will give several examples. The Irish form of Geoffrey illustrates both this principle and the last. The Four Masters write it *Seffraigh* (Sheffry); but in actual use the *f* is always aspirated and omitted, reducing the name to Sherry or Sheara.

A little to the west of Kinsale in Cork is the bay and marine village of Courtmacsherry, the court of Mac Sherry or Geoffrey's son. The person who built his residence or "court" here, and gave the place its name, was an Englishman called Hodnet, who came from Shropshire; but according to Smith (Hist. of Cork, II., 3), "The family degenerating into the Irish customs, assumed the name of Mac Sherry." The original Mac Sherry is still vividly remembered in the traditions of the neighbourhood. Other forms of this name are seen in Raheensheara near Rathdowney in Queen's County, Geoffrey's little fort; and in Magherashaghry in the parish of Currin in Monaghan (Maghera, a field or plain), in which the *f* is replaced by the Irish aspirated *c*. In many cases the genitive is made Shearoon or Sherron; as in Knockshearoon near Borrisoleigh in Tipperary, Geoffrey's hill; Ballymacsherron in Erris in Mayo, the town of Geoffrey's son.

John is generally made *Shaun* or *Shane* in colloquial Irish; as in Glenshane near Dungiven, John's glen; Ballymacshaneboy in Limerick, between Ardpatrick and Charleville, the town of the son of yellow John. In Ballyshonock, a name found in several counties, the last syllable, *ock*, represents the Irish *óg*, young or little (see p. 28); and the whole name means young John's town. Jordan is usually changed to *Shurdane*, as in Ballyshurdane near Kildorrery in Cork, Jordan's town; but in the anglicised forms the *j* is sometimes restored, which is seen in Cloghjordan, the name of a village in Tipperary, Jordan's stone castle; and in Clonjordan in Wexford, Jordan's meadow. The name Jennings is in Irish Mac Shoneen; and hence we have Ballymacshoneen, and without the *mac*, Ballyshoneen, which are the names of several places, signifying Jennings's town.

III. The Irish does not possess the English sound of *ch* soft (as in *chaff*); and when this sound occurred in an English name, it was represented by *t* followed by slender *s* in Irish, which is equal to *tsh* in English; thus Castletownroche in Cork is called in the Book of Fermoy *Baile-Caisleain-an-Roitsigh*, the town of Roche's castle, of which the present name is a translation; and it was so called because it was the chief residence of the Roche family, where they kept a great house of hospitality in which scholars, poets, ollaves, shanaghies, &c., were received and treated like princes.

This *ts* is a very correct representation of the English *ch;* but in the spoken language it was almost always changed by metathesis to *st* or *sht*, as we see in Clogharoasty near Loughrea in Galway, Roche's stone castle; and in Ballyristeen near Bunmahon in Waterford, and Ballyrishteen near Dingle in Kerry, the town of *Rishteen* or little Richard.

IV. If an English name presented a combination of sounds not usual in the Irish language, the Irish speakers sometimes got over the difficulty by omitting altogether a portion of the name. Of this the name David affords a good illustration, for it is universally pronounced *Dau.* Ballydaw, the name of some places in Cork, Kilkenny, and Wexford, signifies the town of David; but this name is still more common in the restored form Ballydavid; and we find it near Hollywood in Down as Ballydavy. Some of these may, however, be derived from the old Irish name *Dathi;* as in case of Ballydavis near Maryborough in Queen's County, which the Four Masters write *Baile-Daithi.* William is always made *Leeam;* and even this is generally further contracted in local names, as in Derrylemoge near Mountmellick in Queen's County, the oak wood of young William. Isabel is pronounced in Irish *Shibbeal;* and this in an anglicised form gives name to Sybil Head north-west of Dingle in Kerry.

The lady who gave name to this place was Isabel Ferriter, about whom the peasantry in the neighbourhood of Dingle still tell many legends. According to the prevailing tradition, her father was a Galway chief named Lynch. He wished her to marry an Ulster chieftain; but she loved the young lord of Ferriter's castle; and on the very day when she was to give her hand to the northern suitor, she secretly married Ferriter, and fled with him to his stronghold in Kerry. A deadly feud followed; the castle was besieged by the united forces of the old chief and the disappointed suitor; and dreading that his bride might fall into the hands of his rival if the castle were taken, Ferriter hid her on the evening before the assault, in a cave opening on the sea, just under the head, which communicated with the castle by a secret underground passage.

Early next morning he made an unexpected sally from the castle; the besieging forces, taken by surprise, were routed, and the Ulster chief slain; and the father and the young lord were reconciled on the field of battle. But meantime a fearful storm had raged during the night; and when the husband and the father hastened to the cave, they found that the sea had swept through it, and no trace of poor Isabel was ever discovered from that day to this.

V. In Irish the article is occasionally used before

a proper name, as in Killeenadeema, the name of a parish in Galway, which is locally understood to mean the little church (*Killeen*) of St. Dimma: here the middle *a* is the article. But this occurs very seldom, and so far as I am aware, only in the spoken language. This form of expression, however, is very usual where English personal names are concerned. Many examples of this peculiarity might be cited, but the following will be sufficient. Near Rathkeale in Limerick there is a place called Cloghanarold, a name which is divided in this way, *Clogh-an-Arold*, literally the stone castle of *the* Harold, i. e. Harold's castle.

In Ballinrichard near Kinsale in Cork, the *n* represents the article, and the name means Richard's town; and in like manner in Ballinunty near Killenaule in Tipperary, the last part of which represents the old Anglo-Norman name Funt, the *F* being aspirated and omitted according to grammatical rule: the whole name mean's Funt's town. Knockaunabroona near the village of Mayo, the little hill of (a man named) Brown.

We know that in local names, Irish words often simulate English forms (see 1st Ser., Part I., c. II.); and in like manner many of the personal and family names that appear in our local nomenclature, though they appear to be English, are in reality Irish. Numerous examples of this might be given, but I will content myself with two. There is a townland in the parish of Templeshanbo in Wexford, now called Ballyhamilton. But in the Down Survey it is written Ballyhumblety, and the old pronunciation, Ballyhomulty, is still remembered by the people; which plainly indicates *Baile-Ui-Thomultaigh*, the town of O'Tomulty, a family name still in use in some parts of Ireland.

Whoever has been in the neighbourhood of Kells in Meath, must have remarked the beautiful fertile hill of Lloyd, a mile from the town, with a tall pillar crowning its summit; from which also the townland in which it is situated is called the Commons of Lloyd. It is considered as a matter of course to have taken its name from a man or a family named Lloyd. But the Irish name *Mullach-Aiti* (Aiti's hill ?)—so the Four Masters write it—is in reality veiled under this more modern form. The old name is still remembered in the neighbourhood, but *mullach* is generally shortened to *mul*, as it is in many other places, and the *t* of *Aiti* is changed to *d* (for *t* of ancient Irish is usually made *d* in the modern language); so that the present Irish name is *Mul-Aidi*, which is pronounced as nearly as can be represented *Mulloyda*. This name was, according to the etymological fancy of those who anglicised it, divided in this way—*Mul-Loyda*—the *l* sound being attracted to the second part like the *c* of *mac* (see p. 140, *supra*), and like the *c* of Lough Corrib (see this in 1st Ser.); and while *mul* was correctly interpreted "hill," the whole name was believed to mean the Hill of Lloyd.

CHAPTER XI.

ARTICLES OF MANUFACTURE.

In case of some of the articles mentioned in this chapter, it is often hard to say exactly why they gave names to places. Sometimes no doubt people found them in the earth when digging or ploughing deeply; for we know that arrow-heads and swords are still often found in battle-fields, butter in bogs, and various household articles in crannoges and raths. Sometimes also when a family who followed a particular trade lived in one spot for any considerable time, the place got a name derived from the things made there. And there are other explanations which will come to the surface as I go along. Whenever there is positive information or good grounds for an opinion, I will offer an explanation; otherwise I will leave the question open.

As I have to deal in this book chiefly with names, I must remark, that of the innumerable articles connected with the past social life of the Irish people, I notice here those only that have helped to build up our local nomenclature.

Chariots and Cars. Our literature affords unquestionable evidence that chariots were used in Ireland from the most remote ages. In the ancient historical tales in the *Lebor na hUidhre* and the Book of Leinster, the great chiefs, such as *Cuchullin*, *Conall Cearnach*, *Loegaire Buadach*, &c., are constantly described as going to battle in war-chariots, each driven by an *ara* or charioteer; and at a much later period, in the great battle of Moyrath—A. D. 637—*Dubdiad* the druid, while viewing the king's army, is struck with "the snorting and neighing of their caparisoned, bridle-tamed steeds bounding under chariots, supporting and commanding the battle around them in every direction," (p. 193). We know from the Lives of the early Saints, that Patrick, Brigid, Columkille, Declan, &c., journeyed in chariots in their missionary progress through the country. And as Cuchullin's charioteer, *Loeg*, is celebrated in the ancient tales, so St. Patrick had a charioteer, *Odhran*, who is equally well-known in ecclesiastical history.

In the old romances there are several descriptions of Cuchullin's chariot, as well as of those belonging to other chiefs; which are so detailed as to afford us a very good idea of the construction of the vehicle.

The chariot of Cuchullin is described in various places as having a frame made of wood; a high wickerwork body, with its sloping sides ornamented with tin; two bright brazen (or brazen coloured) spoked wheels; a silver-white pole, veined with bronze; an arched yoke, sometimes of a rich golden colour, sometimes silvery white. The war chariots are sometimes described as furnished with sharp spikes and scythe blades like those of the old Britons; while in times of peace, kings, queens, and chieftains of high rank, rode in chariots luxuriously fitted up and ornamented with gold, silver, and feathers.*

The Irish word for a chariot is *carpat*, which is obviously cognate with the Latin *carpentum*, or as some think, borrowed from it: the modern Irish form is *carbad*. We may conclude with great probability, that some at least of the places whose names contain this word—and they are pretty numerous—were exercise grounds, where the young warriors and charioteers trained their steeds and practised driving. This was no doubt the case at *Fan-na-carbad*—the slope of the chariots—a place at Tara, mentioned in the Dinnseanchus. Several other names containing this word are recorded in old Irish documents; and it is very easy to recognise it in its modernised forms.

* See the article on the Irish chariot, by J. O'Beirne Crowe, A.B., Kilk. Arch. Jour., 1871-2, p. 413; see also O'Curry, Lect., II., 272, 276, 287; and I. (Sullivan's Introd.) cccclxxv.

The parish of Tullycorbet in Monaghan took the first part of its name from a small hill; the place is mentioned in O'Clery's Calendar at the 26th January by the name of *Tulach-carboid*, the hillock of the chariot. Keating, in the reign of Dermot the son of Fergus, mentions a certain place called *Bearná-tri-carbad*, the gap of the three chariots, but the name is now obsolete. The Four Masters record that in 1567, O'Donnell, prince of Tirconnell, crossed the Foyle, and ravaged a part of the territory of the O'Neills, from *Sliabh-gcarbadach*, or the mountain of the chariots, which is the hill now called Mullagh Carbadagh in the parish of Upper Bodoney in Tyrone, ten miles nearly east of Strabane.

There are many other names through the country formed from this word. The townland of Duncarbit in the parish of Culfeightrin near Fair Head in Antrim, took its name from a fort—the fortress of the chariots; and near the village of Malin in Inishowen, is a place called Drumcarbit (*drum*, a ridge). We have also Kilnagarbet near the village of Stradone in Cavan, and Moneygorbet in the parish of Donaghmoyne in Monaghan—the first signifying the wood (*coill*) and the second the bog (*moin*) of the chariots. Near the boundary between Tipperary and Kilkenny, two miles west of Callan, is a bridge now called Carabine Bridge; but this name is a vile corruption, for the old Irish name, according to local authority, is *Droiched-na-gcarbad*, the bridge of the chariots; so that its present name should be Chariot Bridge. In a neighbouring field were found not long ago, great numbers of sword blades; and this fact coupled with the name, would seem to point out a battle field.

The Irish word *carr* is the same as the English

car, but is not borrowed from it, for it is found in Irish manuscripts nearly a thousand years old :—for example in Cormac's Glossary. Both are probably cognate with, not borrowed from, the Latin *carrus*. In Irish it was applied to vehicles either with or without wheels. It is curious that this word often enters into the names of fords; originating such names as Athnagar, Annagar, and Aghnagar; all from the Irish *Ath-na-gcarr*, the ford of the cars. The probable explanation of each of these names is, that while there were several fords on the stream, all used by foot passengers, only one was level and smooth enough to be crossed by cars; which therefore got the name of the car-ford. Other features besides fords have been named from cars. Drumnagar is a townland near the village of Stradone in Cavan (*drum*, a hill-ridge); Lisnagar Demesne near Rathcormack in Cork, the fort of the cars.

Cars without wheels, or slide cars, were also very commonly used both in ancient and modern times. They were employed until very lately in many parts of Ireland, especially in drawing peat down the steep sides of mountains. I remember seeing one in the year 1843 laden with dried turf, drawn down by a horse from near the summit of one of the Galty mountains. The sides of Seefin mountain over Glenosheen in the county Limerick, still retain the tracks of the old dray-cars—as they were there called in English—which the grandfathers of the present generation used in bringing home their fuel from the hill tops; and one particular pathway leading from the village up the hill, is still called the Dray-road.

I have already stated that the word *carr* was applied to these as well as to wheeled vehicles; but they had another name specially appropriated to them, viz., *slaed* [slade], which I suppose is connected with the English word *slide.* Carricknaslate—the rock of the slide-cars—is the name of a place near Lifford in Donegal. There is a townland in Derry, near Coleraine, called Drumslade; and another in Mayo, near the sea side, opposite Achill Island, called Drumsleed; both signifying the ridge of the slide-cars.

Arrows and Darts. It is curious that bows and arrows are very seldom mentioned in our old writings; and the passages that are supposed to refer to them are so indistinct, that if we had no other evidence it might be difficult to prove that the use of the bow was known at all to the ancient Irish. However, the matter is placed beyond dispute by the fact that flint arrow-heads are constantly found in the ground, in various parts of the country; and there is a large collection—many of them beautifully formed—in the Museum of the Royal Irish Academy, in Dublin.

Saiget, cognate with and little different from the Lat. *sagitta*, is the usual Irish word for an arrow—modern Irish *saighead* [syed]; but it is also used for a light dart of any kind, whether projected from a bow or not. It not unfrequently forms part of names, usually in the anglicised forms *sythe* and *seed;* it is very likely that places with such names were battle fields; and that they were so called because flint arrow-heads were found in digging the ground, the relics of the fight.

There is a bridge over the river Funcheon, a mile east of Kilbehenny, on the boundary between Limerick and Tipperary, called Ahnaseed; and the name renders it almost certain that a fight took place at some remote time at the crossing of the stream:—

Ath-na-saigit, the ford of the arrows. As an instance of a ford named from a circumstance like this, I may quote an entry of the Four Masters at A. D. 1532, recording the fact that a certain ford was called *Bel-atha-na-bhfabhcún*, the ford-mouth of the *falcons* or cannons, because a battle was fought at it in that year, in which the O'Carrolls defeated the earl of Ormond, and took a number of cannons from his army.

There is a place in the parish of Kilnahue, six miles north-west from Gorey in Wexford, called Monaseed, the bog of the arrows; and a little lake two miles from Templemore in Tipperary is called Moneennascythe, which has a like meaning. The form *seed* is also seen in Knocknaseed (*knock*, a hill), the name of a place situated near the river Blackwater in the early part of its course, about four miles south of Kingwilliamstown. The word takes the other form in Gortnasythe in the parish of Cam in Roscommon, and in Coolsythe in the parish of Drummaul in Antrim, the field and the corner of the arrows. There is a place in the parish of Kilreekil in Galway, which is called in Irish *Gort-na-saighead;* but the present name is Dartfield, which is a correct translation.

Ga, *gae*, or *gath* [gah] is a light spear, a lance, or javelin. It occurs in names at least as often as *saighead;* and here also we may conclude that these names generally point out battle fields. Drumgaw in the parish of Lisnadill in Armagh, and Glenga in Tyrone, signify respectively the ridge and the glen of javelins. Slightly different forms appear in Aghagah in Longford, and Aghagaw in Monaghan; also in Clonegah in Carlow, and Clonegath near Monasterevin in Kildare—all signifying the field (*achadh* and *cluain*) of the javelins. There is a name mentioned in Hy Fiachrach (p. 153) a part of which is very like this, viz., *Glaisi-guirt-na-lainne*, the stream of the field of the lances; but only the first half has survived— *Glaisi-guirt* (the stream of the field), now Glasgort, the name of a townland in the parish of Ballintober in Mayo.

Swords. One of the Irish words for a sword is *claidheamh* [cleeve], old Irish *claidem*, obviously cognate with Lat. *gladius;* Fr. and Eng. *glaive;* which is still well known in the Scotch *claymore*, i. e. *claidheamh-mór*, great sword. Perhaps the townland of Gorticleave in the parish of Errigle Truagh in the north of the county Monaghan, was "sword-land," or land conquered by the sword; for this interpretation would be borne out by the name, *Gort-a'-chlaidhimh*, the field of the sword. *Colc* or *colg* [collog] signifies a small straight-bladed sword or dirk: it forms a part of the name of Duncollog in the parish of Drung in Cavan—the fort of the swords, a name that seems to point back to the time when the old *dun* was celebrated for its abundance of military weapons.

Axes. The hill of Knockdoe about eight miles from Galway, is historically remarkable for the sanguinary battle fought there in 1504, between the earl of Kildare and Mac William Burke of Clanricard. The name of this hill is written by the Irish annalists *Cnoc-tuadh*, which Campion correctly translates the hill of the axes. Some think that the place received this name on account of the battle; but the manner in which the Irish authorities use the name, and other considerations besides, show that it is older than 1504, and that it originated in some other way.

Four miles from Newtownbarry in Wexford, there

is a place called Clobemon, whose Irish name is *Cloch-beimeann*, the stone or stone castle of the strokes or blows; which perhaps was the scene of a battle fought long ago, or a place where fighting was habitually carried on, or a military practising ground.

Shields. The ancient Irish used shields from the very dawn of their history, and indeed very probably from a period beyond the horizon of both history and tradition. In the most ancient historical tales, such as "The Cattle spoil of Cooley," "The *Brudin Da Derga*," "The Siege of Knocklong," &c., the shields of the great heroes who took part in the several battles are described with sufficient minuteness to enable us to judge pretty accurately of their various shapes, sizes, and materials.

It is highly probable that the most ancient shields were made of wickerwork, covered over with layers of hardened hide. In Ireland we have a living illustration of the very general use of such shields in former times; for, the word *sciath* [skeea], which is the most usual word for a shield, is still applied in Munster to a shallow oblong ozier basket, used generally for carrying, holding, and washing potatoes. From a careful study of ancient authorities, O'Curry (from whom I have taken this illustration: Lectures, II., 330) shows that the ancient wickerwork shields were somewhat of this shape, the convex side being turned towards the enemy; and they were often large enough to cover the whole person of the warrior.

But there were also flat circular shields made of wood—generally yew-wood—which were smaller in size than those of wickerwork. Moreover, the shields of distinguished warriors had often a rim of bronze, and sometimes even of gold or silver, and were ornamented on the outside with various devices in colours or metal work. The smaller circular shields were occasionally made of bronze, of which there is a very beautiful specimen in the Royal Irish Academy, which was found in a bog at Lough Gur in Limerick. There is also in the Academy an ancient wooden shield found at Kiltubbrid in the county Leitrim.

Several ancient authorities show that places took their names from shields: thus in the second life of St. *Carthach* of Lismore, we are told that before his time, the spot on which Lismore now stands was called *Magh-sciath*, which the writer translates *Campus-scuti*, the plain of the shield. In the year 846 the Danes were defeated by the Irish in a battle fought at a place in the county Kildare called in the Book of Leinster *Sciath-Nechtain*, Nechtan's shield.

In the parish of Rathlynin in Tipperary about four miles north-east of Tipperary town, there is a townland now called Donaskeagh, which took its name from an ancient fort on the summit of a hill, the remains of which can still be traced. In this fort, *Carthach*, the ancestor of the family of *Mac Carthaigh* or MacCarthy lived in the 11th century. The Four Masters record that the *dun* was burnt (i. e. of course the wooden residences erected within the enclosure) by the Ossorians and the men of Ormond in the year 1043; but *Carthach* pursued and overtook them near the village of Golden on the Suir, defeated them, and recovered the spoil. In this record and another, the Four Masters write the name *Dun-na-sciath*, the fortress of the shields. There was another *Dun-na-sciath* on the shore of Lough Ennel in Westmeath, far more celebrated, for it was the residence of Malachy, king of Ireland in the time of Brien Boru; but its name has been long since forgotten in the neighbourhood.

Liskea in the parish of Templetogher in Galway, derived its name from an old fort still remaining on the top of a hill: *Lios-sciath*, the fort of the shields: and there is a place called Liskeagh in Sligo, a name that has the same meaning. We may conclude that these three names were derived from the unusual number of warlike accoutrements, especially shields, stored up in the fortresses by the kings or chiefs who built or owned them.

There are no doubt many other places deriving their names from shields; but in the absence of written authority it is difficult to distinguish *sciath*, a shield, in anglicised names, from *sceach*, a whitethorn bush.

Bells. We know from the authentic Lives of St. Patrick and of other early preachers of Christianity in Ireland, that they constantly used bells in their ministrations; which were sometimes made of bronze, and sometimes of iron. The ancient consecrated bells were generally quadrangular in shape, small in size, and open at the mouth; though there was also in use a smaller pear-shaped bell, closed up, except a small opening in the side for the escape of the sound, and rung by an enclosed metallic pellet. St. Dageus, who flourished in the early part of the sixth century, was a celebrated artificer; he fabricated croziers, crosses, shrines, chalices, &c., and among the rest, bells, some plain and some ornamented with gold, silver, and precious stones.

The bells that belonged to the primitive saints were regarded by their successors with the most intense veneration; and in order the better to preserve them, they were often furnished with covers, which were sometimes made of gold and silver and other metals, elaborately ornamented with interlaced work and precious stones. They were often, like croziers and other relics, used for swearing on; and it was customary to bring them into the presence of parties who were entering into a compact, to render it more solemn and binding.

St. Patrick had a celebrated bell, which plays an important part in many of the Patrician narratives, both legendary and authentic; it was called *Finn-faidhech*, or the fair-sounding, and it would appear that other saints called their favourite bells by the same name, in imitation of their great predecessor. Many of these venerable quadrangular bells are now preserved in the Museum of the Royal Irish Academy in Dublin, as well as in other collections; and among them, one in particular is believed, with some reason, to be the very bell—the melodious *Finn-faidhech*—of St. Patrick.

Clocc or *clog* is the usual Irish word for a bell; corresponding with the Latin *clocca*, and English *clock*; but there were other Irish terms also, which it is not necessary to notice here. It is probable that the Irish borrowed the word *clog* from the Latin through the early missionaries. We see it in Ballyclug, the name of a parish near Ballymena in Antrim, which represents the Irish *Baile-an-chluig*, the town of the bell (Reeves: Eccl. Ant. 84), and there is another parish in Tyrone called Ballyclog, which is the same name. This word more usually enters into names in the genitive plural, and with the *c* changed to *g* by eclipse. There is for example a bridge over an ancient ford on the Ahaphuca river, between Glenroe and Ballylanders in Limerick, called Annaglug, i. e. *Ath-na-gclog*, the ford of the bells; Dernaglug in Monaghan (*doire*, an oak grove); and Ardnaglug, the height of the bells, is a little hamlet near the railway line, about five miles north-east of Ballinasloe.

In the neighbourhood of many of our ecclesiastical ruins the people have a pretty legend about the church bells: that in some far distant time, when despoilers—Danes or natives—came to plunder the monastery, the bells, which some of the legends say were of silver, were hastily taken down and thrown for safety into the nearest river or lake, where they remain to this day. But at intervals—some say every seven years—they are heard to ring with a faint, muffled, melancholy tone. The silver bell that once hung in the round tower of Rattoo in Kerry, now lies at the bottom of the river Brick; its voice has often been heard, but the people have never been able to find it, though they have often searched (Petrie R. Towers, 398). The bells of the ancient church of Drumcliff near Ennis in Clare, lie beneath the waters of a lakelet in the townland, which is called Poulnaglug, the pool of the bells.

Just near the southern end of the esplanade at Bray, a little way up the Head, very near the railway line, there is a church ruin, which can be seen quite plainly from every part of the esplanade; and it is well known in and around Bray, by the name of Raheenaclig. The people say that it is the oldest church in Ireland; and the style of masonry, especially of the two end windows, shows that it can hardly be later than the eleventh century. It has long ceased to be used in any way, but within the memory of the old people, unbaptized infants were buried in it. The name is very plain, and represents almost exactly the sound of the correct Irish form,

Raithín-a'-chluig, the little fort of the bell. The story told by the name would seem to be this:—that in far distant times, before the erection of the church, Mass used to be celebrated in an old rath, which had remained there from days still more ancient—for as I have mentioned elsewhere (1st Ser. Part II. c. I.) open air Masses were anciently very usual in Ireland; and that a bell was set up in the usual way, to call the people; which originated the name. After a time, when a church came to be built, it was natural that the old site should be chosen, and the old name retained. There are some remains of embankments near the church, but I saw nothing that could be identified as a portion of a rath; which however is not to be wondered at, as the ground has been cultivated up to the very walls of the ruin.

Croziers. One of the most celebrated ecclesiastical relics of ancient Ireland was St. Patrick's crozier, commonly called the *Bachall Isa*, the staff or crozier of Jesus. A well known legend in the life of St. Patrick tells us, that he received this staff from a hermit who lived in an island in the Tyrrhene sea, to whom it had been intrusted by our Saviour, with an injunction to deliver it to Patrick when he should arrive at the island. The saint kept it and bore it constantly in his hand during his ministration in Ireland; and after his death it was preserved with the greatest veneration, and covered with gold and precious stones. It was removed from Armagh to Christ Church in Dublin in the twelfth century; but in 1538 it was burned in the streets of Dublin with many other relics.

In the Royal Irish Academy there is a collection of ancient croziers, found from time to time buried in the earth, in bogs, or under the ruins of ecclesiastical buildings. They are generally highly ornamented; and some of them are elaborately adorned with gems and complicated interlaced work in metal, which even the best artificers of the present day would find it very hard to imitate.

Bachall is the Irish word for a crozier, probably borrowed from the Latin *baculus*. Some authorities would lead us to infer that Ballyboghil near Swords in Dublin, derived its name from St. Patrick's crozier; which however is doubted by others. The name at any rate signifies the town of the crozier; and the probability is that it was derived from a crozier belonging to St. Patrick—for he appears to have left more than one—whether it be the celebrated *Bachall Isa* or not.

The word *bachall* signifies any staff, such as a shepherd's crook, &c.; and one of its diminutives, namely *bachaillin* [boghaleen] is to this day applied by the English speaking people of parts of the south of Ireland, to a staff furnished with a flat end piece, which they use in washing and mashing up potatoes. However, when we find the word in names, we may be pretty sure that it is intended for a crozier. There is a place called Moyvoughley three miles to the north of Moate in Westmeath, which the Four Masters write *Magh-bhachla*, the plain or field of the crozier. Pollnamoghill, the name of a townland near Aughrim in Roscommon, exhibits the eclipse of the *b*:—*Poll-na-mbachall*, the pool of the staffs or croziers.

Brógs or *shoes*. The ancient Irish shoe was called *brócc*, modern Irish *bróg*, which is still well known as a living word, and commonly spelled *brogue* by English writers of the present day. The most ancient kind of *brôg* was made of raw or half-tanned hide, which was roughly stitched with thongs; and this form continued in use among the lower classes of people down to very recent times. *Brógs* of this kind have been found in bogs; and several may be seen in good preservation, thongs and all, in the Royal Irish Academy. Gradually they came to be more elaborate in make, especially those used by the wealthier classes; the leather was tanned and ornamented with patterns worked into it; and of this kind some beautiful specimens are also preserved in the Royal Irish Academy.

We may be pretty certain that makers of *brógs* lived at, or perhaps owned, those places whose names are formed from the word *bróg;* such as Knocknabrogue in the parish of Latteragh, Tipperary, which is anglicised from *Cnoc-na-mbróg*, the hill of the brogues or shoes; Raheenabrogue near Ballyroan in Queen's County (*raheen*, a little fort); Eskernabrogue near Clogher in Tyrone (*esker*, a sand-ridge); Finnabrogue near Downpatrick, *Fith-na-mbróg*, the wood of the brogues; and Broguestown near the village of Kill in Kildare, the name of which is translated from the original Ballybrogue, as it is written in an Inquisition of Charles I.

This conjecture will not explain the name of the little river Brogeen near Kanturk in Cork, which means little *bróg*. Why a river should receive such a name I cannot imagine, and the old people of the neighbourhood, so far as I have made inquiry, have no tradition of the origin of the name worth listening to, and are not able to offer any rational explanation. It is curious that there is another stream a little south of Miltown in Kerry, joining the Laune, called Kealbrogeen, the *keal* or narrow marshy stream of the little *bróg*. Knockavrogeen (*knock*, a hill) is the name of a place near Dingle in Kerry.

There is a townland in the parish of Inver near Killybegs in Donegal, called Luaghnabrogue, i. e. *Luach na-broige*, the *luach* or price of the brogue; and this name would be almost as puzzling as the two river names, if we were not helped out of the difficulty by a local legend:—the place was purchased one time for a pair of brogues. It is to be feared however, that the legend was invented to suit the name; and perhaps we may conjecture that in former days a shoemaker or broguemaker tenanted this townland, and paid his rent in kind, by supplying his landlord's family with brogues.

In connexion with this last name, I will step aside for a moment to remark that the word *luach*, hire or reward, forms part of other names. Five miles north-east from Thurles in Tipperary lies the village and parish of Loughmoe, with the fine ruins of the castle of the Purcells—the barons of Loughmoe—the correct old name of which, according to the Four Masters, is *Luach-mhagh*, price-plain, or the field of the reward. The peninsula west of Ardara in Donegal is called Loughros, and gives name to the two bays of Loughros-more and Loughros-beg (great and small); this place is also mentioned by the Four Masters, who call it *Luachros*, the *ros* or peninsula of hire or reward. Why these places were so called we know not; but we may fairly conjecture that in old times some tenant held them free of direct rent, as a reward for some signal service, or on condition of fulfilling some special duties.

Culinary vessels. Several of the vessels in domestic use have given names to place. In some cases these names are explained by legends; in others we may conclude that persons lived in the places who either made the vessels as a trade, or used them in some special occupation; and lastly, perhaps some have been named from ancient vessels found buried in the earth or in bogs.

Lestar. The word *lestar* denotes a vessel of any kind, or of any shape or material, (*lester*, *vas*, Z. 166) though the term was generally applied to vessels made of wood. This word is found in the names of some places in Monaghan and Tyrone, called Drumlester—the ridge of the vessels; and in Derrinlester and Derrynalester in Cavan, the first the oak wood of the vessel, the second, of the vessels.

Mether. The mether, Irish *meadar*, was a drinking vessel commonly made of yew wood, quadrangular at top, and either round at bottom, or having the corners rounded off; and commonly furnished with two or four handles, for the convenience of passing it from hand to hand round the table. It was called *meadar* because it was used for drinking *mead*, i. e. ale or metheglin. Several ancient vessels of this kind are to be seen in the museum of the Royal Irish Academy (see Sir William R. Wilde's Catalogue, p. 214). A mether maker probably lived at Drumnamether near Markethill in Armagh, the ridge of the methers; as well as at Ballymather in the parish of Killead in Antrim, the town of the *methers;* and possibly the name of Rathmadder in the parish of Kilfree in Sligo, may preserve some dim memory of the revelry carried on in old times in the *rath* or residence of the chief.

Cuinneog, a churn, gives names to Ardnaguniog in the parish of Faughanvale in Derry, to Lisnagonoge near Holycross in Tipperary, and to Lisnagunogue near Bushmills in Antrim, the first signifying the height, and the other two the fort of the churns; the *c* being eclipsed by *g* in all three.

How names of this class may take their rise from legends—or perhaps sometimes the reverse—can be gathered from the following story, of which several different versions are found in Irish writings. Keating has one; Colgan, in his Life of St. Colman Mac Duach, has two others; and the peasantry of Clare and Galway will tell the legend as fully as either.

Guaire [Goory], king of Connaught in the seventh century, who was celebrated for his generosity and hospitality, had a brother, an ecclesiastic, a very holy man, whose name was Colman. This priest went one time to spend the Lent among the rocks and forests of Burren, in the north of the present county of Clare; he was attended by only one young man, who acted as his clerk; and they lived in a desert spot, by a well of pure water, five miles from Durlas Guary, the king's palace. They ate only one meal a day, and that consisted of a bit of barley bread, a few sprigs of cress, and a drink of water from the spring.

In this manner they passed the seven long weeks of Lent, till at last Easter Sunday came round; when the poor young clerk, feeling quite worn out, as well he might, by his long abstinence and poor fare, was seized with a longing desire for flesh meat; so he came to his master, and told him that he was about to go immediately to the palace at Durlas, to have one good meal. "Stay with me," said Colman, "and I will see whether I cannot procure a dinner for you where you are:" so he prayed that meat might be brought to the clerk.

It so happened that the king's dinner was preparing at this same time in Durlas Guary; a noble dinner, with everything in lavish profusion—so it ever was in the house of Guary the hospitable ; and among a great variety of dishes, a boar and a stag, cooked whole, were brought to table on a pair of enormous trenchers. Everything was ready, and the king and his guests were seated, just as Colman and the clerk had finished their conversation. All at once the dinner was lifted from the table by some invisible power, before the wondering eyes of his majesty ; trenchers, dishes, and methers, boar and stag and all, floated gently through the open doors and windows—not as much remained on the table as would make a meal for a wolf dog—and as soon as they had got fairly outside the palace, they set off with great expedition straight towards the little hermitage among the hills of Burren.

The monarch and his guests, after recovering a little from their astonishment, resolved to make an effort to overtake their dinner and bring it back : so after a hurried preparation, they took horse ; and the whole company, horsemen, footmen, and dogs, with the king at their head, instantly started in pursuit. They kept the dishes in view, but were not able to overtake them, and after a close chase, they arrived near the hermitage, hungry and tired, just in time to see them alighting at the feet of Colman and the clerk.

The young man was much delighted to see so fine and plentiful a dinner provided for him, as well as greatly amazed at the strange manner of its appearance ; and he was about to begin his meal, when happening to look round, he saw the rocky slope of the opposite hill covered with a tumultuous crowd, all making straight towards him. So he turned once more to his master, and addressed him, saying, that he saw not the least good in getting a dinner of meat, while there was such an angry multitude ready to dispute it with him. "Eat your dinner in peace," said Colman, "there is no danger, for it is my brother, the king, and his household, and I will take care that they shall not interrupt you."

The moment he had done speaking, the feet of the horses, men, and dogs, were fastened to the ground, and the horsemen to their seats, so that they were unable to advance one inch farther; and while the monarch and his nobles were looking on, the clerk sat down and ate a hearty meal at his leisure before their eyes. As soon as he had finished, the company were released; the king recognised his brother, who explained the whole affair; and they all seated themselves—except of course the clerk—and ate their dinner in comfort and quietness.

The road traversed by the dinner, in the latter part of its flight, is still pointed out, and it is universally known by the name of *Bóthar-na-mias* [Bohernameece], the road of the dishes. It is situated in a rocky valley in the townland of Keelhilly,* in the parish of Carran, five miles south-west from the village of Kinvarra; and it runs along the base of a precipice called Kinawlia or the head of the cliff. The flat surface of the limestone rocks on the opposite hillside is full of small holes, of various shapes and sizes, very curious and very striking to look at; a geologist would say that they were worn in the rock by the rain, in the course of ages; but they are in reality the tracks of the men, horses, and dogs—the very tracks where their feet were firmly fastened to give the clerk time to eat his dinner.

* *Cael-choille*, narrow wood.

This strange legend is a good example of the manner in which fabulous tales were interwoven with the authentic acts of the early saints. The chief person here was a man well known in the history of the early church of Ireland. He was a near relative of *Guaire Aidhne*, king of Connaught, but not his brother, as the story has it. He was called *Colman-mac-Duach*, or more usually *Mac Duach*, i. e. *Duach's* son; for his father was *Duach*, eighth in descent from Dathi, king of Ireland a little before the time of St. Patrick. In the early part of his career he lived as a hermit with only one attendant, for seven years, in the solitudes of Burren. At the end of that time the king discovered his retreat, and offered him as much land as he wished to take, for the establishment of a religious community; but Colman accepted only a small spot, not far from his little hermitage, in which he erected a monastery, where he afterwards became a bishop. He died in the middle of the seventh century.

This good saint has been greatly and deservedly revered; the monastery he founded flourished long after him; and the place, which is situated three miles from Gort, contains the remains of a round tower and of several churches. Moreover it still retains the founder's name, for it is called Kilmacduagh, the church of *Duach's* son; and it has given name both to the parish and to the diocese.

Colman-mac-Duagh is still vividly remembered and much venerated by the people, and his name lives in the topography of the whole neighbourhood. There are several wells called Tober-mac-Duagh, one of which is engraved and described in the Dublin Penny Journal (Vol. I., p. 200). The ruins of his little hermitage, Temple-mac-Duagh, still remain in the lonely valley, near Bohernameece; near it is another Tober-mac-Duagh, the identical well mentioned in the legend and in the authentic Lives of the Saint, where stations are performed to this day; and immediately over it there is a cave in the rock, called Labba-mac-Duagh, or Mac Duagh's bed, in which tradition says he slept every night during his residence in the valley. It is interesting to remark that the present name of the cliff which rises over the hermitage—Kinawlia—is the very name used in the ancient Life of the saint:—"He fixed his residence near a pleasant fountain [now Tober-mac-Duagh] in the great wood of Boireann, and in that part of it which is called *Kinn-aille*, about five miles from Durlas, the palace of Guaire." (Colgan: Acta Sanctorum, 244 *b*. cap. vi.)

Half a mile east of Kinvarra, on the sea shore, stands an ancient circular fort, one of those so common in most parts of Ireland; and this is all that remains of the hospitable palace of Durlas. Moreover it has lost the old name, and is now known by the equivalent name of *Dun-Guaire*, or as it is anglicised, Dungorey, Guary's fortress. A modern castle built by the O'Heynes—modern compared with the earthen circumvallations—stands in the middle of the fort, and occupies the very site of the house of Guary the Hospitable.*

After all, the story of the dishes may, like most other legends, rest on a foundation of fact. We may suppose that on some particular Easter Sunday during Colman's residence in Burren, the king took it

* See O'Donovan's letters on the parishes of Kinvarra and Kilmacduagh in Galway, and Carran in Clare, in the Royal Irish Academy, Dublin.

into his head to go himself, with his household, to dine with him; and that as Colman had a poor kitchen, the king sent on the dinner ready cooked, and followed after with the whole assembly. Such a transaction would impress the people with wonder and admiration, and in the long lapse of ages their imagination would be sure to shape the tradition into some such marvellous story as the legend of Bohernameece.

There is a high mountain about eight miles west of Dunmanway in Cork, whose name contains this word *mías* (which is cognate with Lat. *mensa*):—viz., Mullaghmesha, in Irish, *Mullach-méise*, the summit of the dish. But here the name is probably derived from some dish-like hollow on or near the summit of the mountain.

Sacks or *Bags*. Why it is that places took their names from sacks or bags, it is not easy to determine, unless we resort to the old explanation that sack makers lived in them; or perhaps the places may have been so called from the use of an unusual number of sacks in farming operations, in storing corn, flour, &c. In the year A. D. 598 there was a terrible battle fought at a place called in all the Irish authorities Dunbolg—the fort of the sacks—near Hollywood in Wicklow, in which the king of Ireland, Hugh the son of Ainmire, was defeated and slain by *Brandubh*, king of Leinster. This name is not now remembered in the neighbourhood, though the people have still some dim traditions of the battle; but there is a parish of the same name in Cork, now called Dunbulloge.

The word *bolg*, which forms part of these names and of those that follow, and which is still in constant use, corresponds with the old Gaulish *bulga*, meaning a little bag of leather (Stokes in Cor. Gl.) Caherbullog in the parish of Kilmoon in the north of Clare, has nearly the same signification as the last name, only with *caher*, a stone fort, instead of *dun:* and with much the same meaning still, we have Moherbullog near Corrofin in the same county—*moher*, a ruined fort. It will be perceived that these four names were originally applied to circular forts, which themselves for some reason or another took their names from sacks. I will remark here that the word *bolg* is sometimes applied to a quiver for arrows; but for several reasons I do not think that this is the sense in which the word is applied in those names.

Then we have Moybolgue, now the name of a parish, partly in Meath and partly in Cavan, which is mentioned in some of our oldest authorities by the name of *Magh-bolg*, the plain of the sacks; and Clonbulloge (*cluain*, a meadow) in King's County and Carlow. There is a parish in Galway called Killimorbologue, which signifies Killimor of the sacks; while Killimor itself means the church of the patron saint Imor, who is thought to have lived in the twelfth century.

Baskets. The word *cliabh* [cleeve] a basket, is found in the oldest documents of the language, and it is still a living word: even among the English speaking people in some parts of Ireland, you will hear talk of a *cleeve* of turf, of potatoes, &c. A considerable number of names, some of them of high antiquity, are formed from this word.

One of the best known is that of Drumcliff near the town of Sligo, where a monastery was either founded by St. Columkille, or dedicated to him soon after his death, and where there are still the remains of a round tower. As being an ecclesiastical establishment of great note it is very often mentioned in ancient Irish authorities, and always written *Druim-chliabh*, the hill ridge of baskets. There is also a Drumcliff in Clare, and another in Donegal, while we have Drumcleave in Tipperary, all meaning the same thing; and there is a townland in Monaghan called Lisdrumcleve (*lis*, a fort). The *c* becomes eclipsed by the insertion of the article in Gortnagleav in the parish of Killinan in Galway, *Gort-na-gcliabh*, the field of the baskets.

The diminutive *cliabhán* [cleevaun] is used to signify a cradle. It is hard to say with certainty why a high mountain near Sallygap in Wicklow was called Mullaghcleevaun, the summit of the cradle; probably it was from the shape of some hollow or cradle-shaped rock near the top. There is also a little hill which gives name to a small lake and a townland three miles south-east of the village of Fivemiletown in Tyrone, called Crockacleaven, cradle hill (*crock*, properly *cnoc*, a hill); and Coolaclevane, the corner or angle (*cúil*) of the cradle, is the name of a place about three miles east of Inchigeelagh in Cork.

In Meath and Cavan the people use a kind of basket for fishing which they call *scudal;* from which Lough Skuddal, a small branch of Lough Sillan near Shercock in Cavan, derives its name—the lake of the fishing basket.

Hurdles. In discussing the name of Dublin in the First Series, I had occasion to speak of the word *cliath*, a hurdle, and of the application of hurdles to the construction of wickerwork fords. There are other places which have taken their names from this word, where hurdles were applied to other purposes not so easily defined. Cliffony, a village in the north of Sligo, is called in Irish *Cliathmhuine*, meaning hurdle-shrubbery (*muine*, shrubbery)—so called I suppose because the shrubbery supplied the hurdle makers with twigs.

The simple word gives name to several townlands now called Clay in Armagh, Down, and Fermanagh; another anglicised form is seen in Cleaboy in Roscommon and Waterford, yellow hurdle; and still another in Cleaghbeg, Cleaghgarve, and Cleaghmore, in Roscommon and Galway—meaning respectively little, rough, and great hurdle. It is seen as a termination in Tullyclea in the parish of Derryvullan in Fermanagh, the little hill of the hurdle; and the diminutive gives name to Cleaheen, little hurdle, in the parish of Tumna in Roscommon. I think it probable that in some of these places the hurdles were used in the construction of fords across small streams.

Nets. There may have been several reasons why places received names from nets—from fishing, or from bird-catching, or from the manufacture of the nets themselves: but I suppose the greater number of such names originated in fishing. *Cochall* is one of the Irish words for a net, especially a small fishing net; the word, however, is more commonly applied to a hood, corresponding with the Latin *cucullus*, and English cowl. At the present day, it is generally applied in the south, to any covering for the shoulders, and in the north to a net.

There is a townland near Killashandra in Cavan—a spot situated in the midst of a lake district—called Drumcoghill, the ridge of the net; Coolcoghill (*cúl*, the back of a hill) is a place near Maguire's Bridge in Fermanagh; Lisacoghill, the fort of the net, is the name of a townland in the parish of

Inishmagrath in Leitrim. At the bridge of Ballycoghill, over the Ballybay river, near the village of Rockcorry in Monaghan, the former practice of net fishing in connexion with the name, is still remembered in tradition.

Beetles. Those who have had opportunities of observing the customs of the peasantry, must have often seen the village girls beetling clothes at a stream—beating them on a large smooth stone, while saturated with water, with a flat, heavy, wooden beetle or mallet, a part of the process of washing. This beetle is called in Irish *slis* [slish].

In former days there was a ford—evidently an important one, if we may judge from the scenes enacted at it—over the Owenure river, one mile from the town of Elphin in Roscommon, on the road to Strokestown; which must have been a favourite spot for this kind of work, as it got the name of *Ath-slisean*, the ford of the beetles—for so the Four Masters designate it when recording a battle fought there in 1288, in which Cathal O'Conor, king of Connaught, was defeated by his brother Manus. There was another battle fought there in 1342, in recording which, the annalists call the place *Bel-atha-slisean*, the ford-mouth of the beetles; and this is the present name of the bridge which now spans the old ford, anglicised to Bellaslishen. We have one example in our old records of a ford deriving its name from the custom of washing at it; viz. *Bel-atha-na-nidheadh*,—so called in Hy Fiachrach—the mouth of the ford of the washings, a ford on the Owenboy river, a mile and a half from the village of Foxford in Mayo.

It was no doubt for some reason of this kind that Cappanaslish in the parish of Killokennedy in Clare received its name—*Ceapach-na-slis*, the garden-plot of the beetle. There is a mountain called Slish rising over the south shore of Lough Gill near Sligo; possibly taking its name from its shape.

Seindile [shindilla] is another word for a beetle, from which a lake on the left of the road from Clifden to Oughterard in Galway, is called Lough Shindilla, probably from some fancied likeness between its shape and that of a beetle: or perhaps the women were formerly accustomed to beetle clothes on its shores. Another and probably the original form of this word is *seimhdile* [shevdilla] from which Shivdilla near Mohill in Leitrim takes its name; and this form also gives name to Kinatevdilla, the western point of Clare island off Mayo—the *s* being here eclipsed by *t*—*Ceann-a'-tseimhdile*, beetle head.

Anvils. About three hundred years before the Christian era, there lived, according to the *Dinnsenchus*, a celebrated artificer in metals named *Lén* of the white teeth, who was *cerd* or goldsmith to the fairy mansion of Bove Derg at Slievenamon. He was employed one time to make certain precious articles—diadems, brooches, cups, &c., for the lady *Fand*, who lived at Lough Leane, or the Lakes of Killarney. He travelled, it seems, every morning from his home near Slievenamon to the lake (about eighty English miles) to begin his day's work; and returned the same journey in the evening; but before setting out for home each day, he flung his anvil before him, with such force and precision, that it always dropped down exactly at his own residence. Hence the place has been ever since known by the name of *Inneoin* [Innone], or "The Anvil." (See O'Curry, Lect., III., 203: see also 1st Ser. Part IV., c. IV.) This place was, many ages afterwards, the chief residence of the Decies, so that it was often called in the annals, *Inneoin* of the Decies. It is now called by the modernised name Mullaghnoney, the hill summit (*Mullach*) of *Inneoin;* and it is situated in the parish of Newchapel near Clonmel.

Several townlands and natural features have got names from anvils; we may, I suppose, infer that at some former time there was a forge at each of these places; and probably not a few over-critical readers, who may have some misgivings as to the truth of the legend of *Lén* and his anvil, will be inclined to account for the name of *Inneoin* of the Decies in the same simple way.

There is a place called Ballynona near the village of Dungourney in Cork; and another called Ballynooney in the parish of Kilbeacon in Kilkenny; both of which probably once belonged to smiths, for the names signify the town of the anvil. Another form of this word is seen in Tullynahinnera in the parish of Aghnamullen in Monaghan, in which *Tully* is corrupted from *talamh*, land (land of the anvil); and in Gubnahinneora, the name of a rocky point on the north coast of the western extremity of Achill island, so called because it resembles the *cor-chip* or *horn* of an anvil. I suppose the name of Killinordan, east of Strokestown in Roscommon, originated like most of the preceding:—*Coill-an-ordain*, the wood of the little sledge-hammer. So also Rathordan near Cashel, the fort of the hammers.

Scollops. A *scolb* (scollob), commonly called a *scollop* by the English-speaking people, is a spray or twig about twenty inches long, used in fastening thatch on houses. When about being used it is doubled up in the middle in the form of a loop, and its two ends, which are pointed, are driven with the hand into the thatch. According to O'Curry (Lect. III., 32) this method of fastening thatch—whether of straw, rushes, or sedge—was used in roofing the ancient Irish circular wicker-work houses; and we know that it is still practised all over the country.

The name of Derryscollop in Armagh, near Moy, indicates that there must have been formerly a *derry* or oak wood there, in which the people were in the habit of cutting twigs for scollops. Inchinsquillib in the parish of Toem in Tipperary, is the *inch* or river-holm of the scollop—so called possibly from the looped shape of the stream. Scullaboge in the parish of Newbawn in Wexford, figures unhappily in the rebellion of 1798; but its name conveys none of this history; for it is simply *Scolbóg* (see p. 19), a place producing twigs for scollops.

Candlesticks. To any one unacquainted with the multifarious ways in which local names grew up in Ireland, the name of Ballykinler, a parish on the shore of Dundrum bay in Down, would appear eccentric and puzzling; for the latter part of the name represents the Irish *coinleoir*, or in its old form *caindloir*, a candlestick (Lat. *candelabrum*), from *coinneal* or *caindel*, a candle; and the whole name is *Baile-caindlera*, the town of the candlestick. But the name is quite natural; for Ballykinler was what is called a *luminary* to the cathedral of Christ Church in Dublin, that is, it was appropriated to supply the altar of that church with waxlights. It was granted by John De Courcy about the year 1200, and it remained in possession of the old cathedral until very recently (Reeves: Eccl. Ant., p. 210). We find the very same name applied to a tract of land between Arklow and Gorey in Wexford, now divided into three townlands; but the name is in the slightly varied form of Ballyconlore, the latter part of which exactly represents the pronunciation of the modern Irish form *coinleoir*. Whether this place received its name in the same sense as Ballykinler, or directly from the article itself, I am not able to tell. One thing we know, that the *coinleóir* was formerly a usual article of furniture, and we find it laid down in the law tract called *Crith Gabhlach*, that in the house of a *bo-aire*, or tenant farmer, there should be, among many other articles, "a candle on a candlestick without fail." (O'Curry, III., 486).

Charcoal. The making of charcoal was understood and practised at a very early period in Ireland; for according to the law tract last quoted (O'Curry: same page) the *bo-aire* was obliged to have "three sacks in his house; a sack of malt; a sack of bulrushes for dressing the wounds of his cattle; a sack of coals for [forging] the irons."

The spots where charcoal used to be manufactured in times of old are still discernible in various parts of the country; for in such places the soil is to this day quite black, and mixed with the dust and small fragments of charcoal. Places of this kind often retain names containing the word *gual*, which of course is cognate with the English *coal*, and which signifies either coal or charcoal. In names, however, the local tradition always points to charcoal, which must be correct, as the introduction of coal as fuel is comparatively recent. There is a little point of land jutting into Lough Erne, a mile from the village of Pettigo, and another just opposite on Boa island, both of which are called by the same name, Rossgole, that is, *Ros-guail*, the peninsula of the charcoal. Glengoole, charcoal glen, is the name of a place near Killenaule in

Tipperary; and there is a townland near the village of Caledon in Tyrone, called Derrygooly, where of course the *derry* or oak wood supplied the materials for making the charcoal.

Milk, butter, lard. Though these commodities can hardly be ranked under the heading of this chapter, yet the names derived from them may be treated of conveniently here.

When a place got its name from milk or butter, it may be surmised that at some former time cows sheep, or goats used to be milked, or general dairy operations carried on there—something like the *boolies* of old times described in the First Series. In some cases it is certain that names of this kind were applied to rich pasture land—land producing milk and butter in abundance.

The common word for milk is *baine* [bonnia, banny], and it occurs in names in such forms as *wanny, vanny, winny*—the *b* being aspirated to *v*. Tawnawanny, the name of a townland in the parish of Templecarn in Fermanagh, signifies the field (*tamhnach*) of the milk; Tullinwannia in Leitrim and Tullinwonny in Fermanagh, milk hill; Coolavanny near Castleisland in Kerry, the corner of the milk.

New milk is denoted by *leamhnacht* [lewnaght]; but the old form, as we find it in Cormac's Glossary, is *lemlacht*, the *l* being changed to *n* (see First Ser. Part I., c. III.) in modern Irish. In its simple form it gives name to two townlands called Lennaght, one in Monaghan and the other in Kilkenny; while the diminutive Loonaghtan is the name of a place near Ahascragh in Galway, signifying new-milk land (see p. 19). There is a townland giving name to a parish near Clonmel, called Inishlounaght, the river-holm of new milk, where O'Faelan, prince of the northern

Decies, had his stronghold; and where O'Brien, king of Limerick, and O'Faelan founded an abbey in 1187. The Irish form of the name as given by Keating, is *Inis-leamhnachta*, the river-holm of the new milk; and the place obviously got this name from the beautiful *inch* along the Suir, between Clonmel and Marlfield. The word occurs in many other names, such as Drumlaunaght in Cavan (Drum, a long hill), Fahanlunaghta near Ennistimon in Clare, and Gortlaunaght in Cavan, both signifying the field (*faithche* and *gort*) of the new milk. Near the western shore of Lough Derg, in the parish of Clonrush in Galway, there is a small lake called Lough Alewnaghta, new milk lake, which may have been so called from the softness of its water.

Keating accounts for a name of this kind by a legend about one of those medicinal baths spoken of at page 74. During the short time that the Picts resided in Ireland, before their migration to Scotland, many centuries before the Christian era, Criffan, the king of Leinster, and his subjects, were sorely annoyed by a hostile people in his neighbourhood, who used poisoned weapons, so that whoever received a wound from them, no matter how trifling, was sure to die of it. The king at last consulted a learned Pictish druid named *Trosdan*, who told him to have a bath prepared on the occasion of the next battle, with the milk of 150 white hornless cows, in which each wounded man was to be bathed. Criffan, as soon as he had procured the cows, at once sent a challenge to his adversaries; and on the eve of the battle he had the bath prepared just as the druid directed. As fast as the king's men were wounded they were plunged into the bath, from which they came out as well as ever; so that the Leinster army routed their foes with dreadful slaughter. From this event the place came to be called *Ard-lemnachta*, the height of the new milk.

The art of making and saving butter appears to have been known in Ireland from the earliest ages; for it is mentioned with milk, curds, cheese, &c., in our oldest literature. In later times it was customary to sink butter deep down in bogs, closed up in casks or baskets, to give it a flavour. Among the food of the Irish, Dineley (A. D. 1675) mentions butter "mixed with store of * * * a kind of garlick, and buried for some time in a bog to make a provision of an high taste for Lent." Sir William Petty also mentions butter made rancid by keeping in bogs; and other authorities to the same effect might be quoted. Whether this custom existed in ancient times I am unable to say; but at any rate, its prevalence even at this late period, is a sufficient explanation of the fact that butter is now very often found in vessels of various shapes and sizes, deeply embedded in bogs; sometimes in firkins not very different from those now in use (see Sir W. R. Wilde's Catal. Ant., p. 212). Several specimens of this bog butter, as it is commonly called, are to be seen in the Royal Irish Academy Museum. In all cases the butter is found to be changed by the action of the bog water, into a greyish cheese-like substance, partially hardened, not much like butter, and quite free from putrefaction.

From the word *im*, butter (*imb*, in Cor. Gl.), we have several names. There is a townland near Mallow in Cork, giving name to a parish called Monanimy (accent on *im*) which signifies the bog of the butter; and we may conjecture that the bog received its name from the quantity of butter found in it. Half a mile from Clifden in Galway is a little lake called Lough Animma, butter lake; and another of the same name lies two miles east of Ballymore in Westmeath. Derrynim is the name of a townland in the parish of Cleenish, Fermanagh; and there is another called Carriganimma, seven miles north-west from Macroom, the first signifying the wood, and the second the rock, of the butter.

Why were places named from lard? Perhaps such names indicate that pigs were fattened in the respective places. Whatever the origin may be, it is certain that we have several names from the word *blonog*, which signifies lard, fat, or suet. Such for instance is Corblonog in the parish of Tedavnet in Monaghan, the round hill of the lard; Killyblunick Glebe in Tyrone,--and Derrynablunnaga south of the lakes of Killarney, these two last signifying the wood of the lard; and there is a place called Caherblonick (*caher* a round stone fort) near the lake of Inchiquin in Clare.

The following names are derived from various articles of manufacture. There is a small lake in Donegal, two miles south-east from the village of Glenties, called Lough Nasnahida, the lake of the needle:—*snáthad*, a needle. There is a parish in Longford called Forgney, taking its name from a townland, which must have been so called from some remarkable building; for *forgnaidh* signifies an edifice or a building. *Slabhra* [slavra, sloura], is a chain. Two miles east of Ardara in Donegal, is a hill called Crockasloura, which means the hill of the chain (*crock* for *knock*, a hill); and Derrintloura is the name of a townland in the parish of Islandeady, west of Castlebar in Mayo, the *derry* or oak grove of the chain (*Doire-an-tslabhra*), the *s* of *slabhra* being here eclipsed by *t* as it ought to be. In the western extremity of the townland of Athlunkard, on the Clare side of the Shannon, near the city of Limerick, there is a small rock within a few yards of the Shannon, called Carrickatloura, the rock of the chain; and in this place there is a tradition to explain the name: that at the siege of Limerick, the English army crossed the Shannon at this spot by means of a chain which was thrown across the river and fastened on the Clare side to this rock.

CHAPTER XII.

BOUNDARIES AND FENCES.

Bru and its derivative *bruach*, both signify a border, brink, or margin; but it is commonly applied to the brink of a stream or glen. The latter of the two is the term generally found in names; and its most usual anglicised form is Brough, which is the name of a place near Doneraile in Cork. Broughshane in Antrim signifies John's border; Broughderg, red border, is the name of places in Cavan, Fermanagh, and Tyrone; and it is the same as Dergbrough in Tyrone, with the root words transposed. Broughmore in Antrim is the same as Bromore in Kerry—great border. The diminutive in *án* also occurs, giving origin to Broughan and Broughane in Armagh and Kerry (little border); and to Broughanlea, the name of a place east of Ballycastle in Antrim, grey little border.

Crioch [creea] means an end, confine, or boundary; but it is an unsatisfactory term to deal with here, for it is very hard to distinguish it in anglicised names from other words like it in sound but different in meaning. When it is found in names we may conclude that it marks the ancient boundaries of farms, townlands, or territories. Its most common modern form is Creagh, which either simply or in combination, gives names to several townlands and parishes; it sometimes drops the aspirate at the end, as in Cavan and King's County, where there are some places called Cree and Creea. In an extended sense this word has come to signify also a country or territory, exactly like the Latin *fines*. For example the country of the O'Byrnes in Wicklow is called *Crioch Branach*. The Book of Rights, O'Heeren's poem, and other authorities, mention a tribe named *Ui-Buidhe*, i. e. the tribe or family of O'Boy; who are described as seated on the west side of the Barrow. In one of these old books we are told that the church of Killabban lies in the territory of this tribe; from which we are enabled to fix the exact position. This ancient territory is commonly called in Irish writings, *Crioch Ua mBuidhe*, i. e. the country of the O'Boys; and the tribe name still exists in the name of the parish of Tullomoy, which sufficiently represents the sound of *Tul-O-mBuidhe*, the hill of the O'Boys—the *B* being eclipsed by *m* according to the law explained at page 135 (See O'Donovan in Book of Rights, 213).

The accounts left us of St. Abban, the founder of the church of Killabban, south of Athy in Queen's County, are very contradictory. It appears, however, that he was born in Leinster in the sixth century; and his mother Mella is said to have been a sister of

St. Kevin of Glendalough; he founded several churches and died in a place called *Magh-Arnaidhe* [Moyarney; plain of sloes] in Wexford, greatly revered for goodness and holiness of life. In his Life published by Colgan, it is stated that when Abban and his clergy came among the tribe of *Hy-mBairrche* (from whom the barony of Slievemargy took its name—see First Series), these people gave him a joyous welcome; and he built a great monastery there, and laid the foundation of a town; "and the monastery and the town are called in the Scotic (i. e. Irish) language by one name, *Ceall Abbain*, which in Latin is interpreted *Cella-Abbani*"—in English, Abban's Church, which name has been extended to the parish.

Teóra [tora] is a border or boundary; the regular genitive is *teórann*, as it is preserved in Ballytoran on the borders of Tipperary and King's County, near the village of Cloghjordan, and in Knocktoran near Knocklong in Limerick, the town and the hill of the boundary. A corrupt modification of the word appears in the name of a lake called Loughatorick, so called because it lies on the boundary between the counties of Galway and Clare, and the boundary line ran through it in 1604, as appears by an Inquisition of that date (Hy Many, 69).

Iorrus. O'Flaherty, at page 96 of his description of Iar Connaught, says, "Many lands here, environed for the most part by the sea, are called Irros, with an adjection to distinguish them one from another. The proper form of the word is *iorrus;* and some have thought that it signifies western promontory—*iar*, west, *ros*, a promontory—while others believe that it means nothing more than a border or limit." Hardiman, the editor of O'Flaherty, says it means a border, brink, margin, promontory, or headland. There can be no doubt that the word was applied to a peninsula; for all the *iorruses* of Galway are peninsulas; as for instance *Iorrus-beag*, the peninsula lying west of Roundstone, which still retains the name of Errisbeg; *Iorrus-ainhagh*, the old name of the peninsula between the bays of Bertraghboy and Kilkerrin; *Iorrus-mor*, the peninsula which terminates in Slyne Head; *Iorrus-Flannan*, the little point of land south-west of Clifden, between Mannin bay and Ardbear bay.

The barony of Erris in Mayo is the best known place taking its name from this word; but although the name now covers an extensive territory, it may be safely assumed that it belonged originally to the peninsula at present called the Mullet, from which it was extended to the whole district. There is a townland called Erris near Boyle in Roscommon, taking its name from a little point of land jutting into Lough Key. Erris is another name for Skirk Glebe near Borris-in-Ossory in Queen's County, which O'Donovan thinks was so called because it was on the borders of the ancient territory of Ossory. Other forms of the word are exhibited in Urros in the parish of Inishmacsaint in Fermanagh; Urrismenagh (middle *urris*) in the parish of Clonmany in Inishowen, Donegal; and Urrasaun in the parish of Tibohine in Roscommon, which is a diminutive, meaning little border or peninsula. Some of the preceding are situated inland, which would tend to show that this word was used to designate a border as well as a peninsula.

Termons. In Ireland as in other Christian countries, many of the churches had the right of sanctuary. A small piece of land was usually fenced off round the church, and the four corners were often marked by crosses or pillar-stones; this land was regarded as belonging exclusively to the church; and criminals fleeing from justice, or fugitives from their enemies, were safe from molestation for the time, once they had taken refuge either in the church itself or inside the boundary.

The word *tearmann* was originally applied to those *termini* or boundaries, and in this sense it exactly corresponds with Latin *terminus;* but it was afterwards extended in meaning till it came to signify a sanctuary or asylum; and this is the sense in which it is generally used in Irish writings. It was often popularly used in a still more general way, to denote church lands, or lands belonging to a sanctuary, so that the expression "termon lands" is quite common in Anglo-Irish writings.

This word is still retained in a good many local names, marking the precincts of sanctuaries; and in several of these the spots are almost as much venerated now as they were a thousand years ago, though they no longer afford an asylum to the fugitive. The memory of St. Fechin is preserved in the name Termonfeckin—Fechin's sanctuary, now applied to a parish near Drogheda. St. *Berach*, the founder of a church in the present county of Roscommon, who was descended from Brian, king of Connaught in the fourth century, flourished in the latter part of the sixth century, and was a pupil of St. Kevin of Glendalough. After leaving Glendalough, he crossed the Shannon and founded an establishment for himself at a place called *Cluain-coirpthe* [Clooncorpa], near the shore of the river, in the desert of Kinel Dofa, which afterwards attained to great eminence. The old name is now forgotten, and the founder, who is still greatly venerated, is commemorated in the present name of the church and parish, Termonbarry, St. *Berach's* sanctuary.

The warden or lay superintendent of church land was termed the erenagh (Irish *aircheannach*); and this office was commonly held by members of the same family for generations. In some places the termons have preserved the family names of the erenaghs instead of those of the patron saints. The church of St. *Dabeog* or *Daveog*, one of the very early Irish saints, was situated in an island in Lough Derg in Donegal; but the termon lands belonging to the church lay on the mainland, near the village of Pettigo. The hereditary wardens of this termon were the Magraths; and accordingly the place is called in the Four Masters, sometimes Termon Daveog, and sometimes Termon Magrath. The latter is the name now used, though it is usually shortened to Termon; the ruins of Termon castle, the ancient residence of the Magraths, are still standing; and the sanctuary has given name to the little river Termon, flowing through Pettigo into Lough Erne.

The parish of Termonmaguirk in Tyrone was anciently called *Tearmann-cuimnigh*, which name Dr. Reeves (Adamn. 283) conjectures may have been derived from *Cuimne*, St. Columkille's sister. It got its present name from the family of MacGuirk, who were for a long time its hereditary wardens. In like manner the O'Mongans were the wardens of Termonomongan in the west of the same county; its ancient name being Kilkerril, from St. Caireall, the founder or patron of the church (Reeves: Colt. Vis. 72). Termon and Tarmon are the names of several places, indicating in every case the former existence of a sanctuary. Sometimes the word is found combined with other terms that have no reference to either patron or warden. Thus Termoncarragh, west of Belmullet in Mayo, means merely rough termon, in reference no doubt to the ruggedness of the ground. There is a place near the village of Annascaul in the parish of Ballinacourty in Kerry, called Ballintermon, the town of the sanctuary; and Ardtermon (sanctuary height) lies in the parish of Drumcliff in Sligo.

Hedge. Fál [faul] signifies a hedge or wall; the fence that separated the lands of two adjacent occupiers: and it is used in this sense in our oldest law tracts. In local names it often designates the land enclosed by a *fál;* but this is altogether a modern application, which had no existence in the Irish language. In this latter sense it is understood by the people of Falnasoogaun, three miles north-west from Ballymote in Sligo, for the townland is also called in English, Ropefield (*súgan*, a rope).

This word is usually found in anglicised names very little changed from its original form; as we see in Falcarragh in Donegal, rough or rugged, *fál*—and here also the meaning has probably been extended to a field; Falmacbreed and Falmacrilly in Antrim, MacBride's and MacCrilly's hedge or enclosure. The word is sometimes pronounced in two syllables (*fala*), giving rise to Fallowbeg in Queen's County, south of Athy (*beg*, little); Falloward and Fallowlea, both in the parish of Faughanvale in Derry (high and grey), and Fallowvee near Cushendall in Antrim, yellow hedge (*buidhe*). There is a place in the parish of Islandeady in Mayo, which is mentioned in Hy Fiachrach by the simple name *Fál;* but it is now called Kilfaul, the wood of the hedge.

Fallagh, Faulagh, and Faltagh, are adjective forms, found in various counties, all meaning a place of hedges; and Fauleens in Mayo (little hedges) is a diminutive. One of the plural forms is *fálta*, which has given names to several places now called Faltia, Falty, and Faulties; Faltybanes in Donegal, white hedges or enclosed fields.

When it comes in the end of names in the genitive plural with the article, it is usually represented by *wall*, *val*, or *vaul;* as in Cornawall near Newbliss in Monaghan, *Cor-na-bhfál*, the little hill of the hedges; Tullynavall near Carrickmacross in Monaghan, same meaning. There is an ancient fort near the village of Kilkeel in the south of the county Down, called Dunnaval, the fortress of the walls or hedges; and a little island near Slyne head in Galway, has the same name, but in the anglicised form Doonnawaul.

In an old map of Belfast engraved in facsimile by Mr. Edmund Getty in the Ulster Journal of Archæology (Vol. III.), the district immediately south of the town, in the angle between the Blackstaff river and the Lagan, is called Tuoghe-na-fall; it is written Tuoghnafall in a grant of Car. I.; and in an Inquisition of 1605 (Reeves, Eccl. Ant. 346) it is called Tuogh of the Fall. The name of this old territory is still remembered; for it is now locally known as "The Falls," and the Falls Road is a well known outlet of Belfast, leading through this district. Both the modern and the old forms of the name, obviously point to the original Irish *Tuath-na-bhfál*, the district of the *fáls*—hedges or enclosures.

CHAPTER XIII.

VARIOUS ARTIFICIAL WORKS.

Roads. On a former occasion I enumerated several terms for a road, and gave names derived from each.* There is yet another, which, though not so common as those, is yet used in the language, and deserves mention, as it enters into local nomenclature.

Ród [road]—old Irish *rót*—is exactly the same word as the English *road;* but one is not derived from the other. For the English *road* comes from the Anglo-Saxon ; and we know that the Irish word has been used in the native language from a period long before English was known in this country. In the Glossary of Cormac Mac Cullenan, a work of the end of the ninth century, *rót* is given as one of the terms for a road; and from the way in which he mentions it, the word appears to have been used to denote a road just broad enough for the passage of a single chariot. It is also constantly used in other Irish writings, such as the Book of Rights, the Topographical Poem of O'Dugan (who, for instance, designates a certain district as "*Clann Ruainne na ród sgothach,*" the Clann Ruainne of the flowery roads: p. 133), &c.; and it still continues in use in the spoken language.

We have a good many local names into which this word enters. There are two townlands in Waterford and one in Wexford, called Ballinroad, the town of the road; Lisnarode near the village of

* First Ser. Part III., c. VI

Clonaslee in Queen's County, signifies the *lis* or fort of the roads; while the diminutive Rodeen, and the shorter form Roden—both meaning little road—are the names of several places in Cork, Roscommon, Waterford, and Tipperary.

Causeway. *Tóchar*, the usual term for a causeway, has been already dealt with; but there is another word for the same thing, which is sometimes used, namely *cobhas* or *cobhsa* [couse or cousa]: in parts of the south of Ireland it is applied to stepping-stones across a river. It gives name to Couse, about two miles south of the city of Waterford; and to Tincouse in the parish of Powerstown, south of Goresbridge in Kilkenny, *Tigh-an-chobhais*, the house of the causeway.

Mound or *dyke.* An artificial mound, dyke, or rampart of any kind, is usually designated by the word *cladh*, pronounced *cly* or *clee* in the south half of Ireland, and *clee* or *claw* in the north. The word is also applied to the raised fences so universal in Ireland, separating field from field. Wherever we find this word in the name of a place, we must conclude that it originated in some remarkable rampart, erected either for purposes of defence, or to separate two adjacent territories. Many of these old mounds are to be seen at the present day in various parts of Ireland.

Smith (Hist. Kerry, p. 219) mentions an ancient boundary of this kind called *Clee Ruadg* (*cladh ruadh*, red mound), which begins at Cahercarbery near Kerry Head, runs north-east towards the river Cashen, reappears at the other side of the river, and crosses the mountain of Knockanore into Limerick. There is a still more remarkable ancient boundary wall in the valley of the Newry river, which is now commonly called the Danes' Cast; but the Danes had no hand in its construction, for it was built to separate the ancient kingdoms of Oriel and Ulidia, many ages before the Danes came to Ireland. In case of some of these old ramparts the natives have a legend that they were rooted up by an enormous enchanted black pig.

Near the village of Ballymore in Westmeath, there is a townland called Clyglass, green mound; and we have Clybaun (whitish) in Galway, Cloyfin (white) near Coleraine, Clyroe and Clykeel in Cork (red, narrow), and Clynabroga in Limerick, the mound of the brogue or shoe (see p. 183). Portacloy—the port or landing place of the rampart—is the name of a coast-guard station, and of a little bay, near Benwee Head on the north-west point of Mayo. The word is exhibited with a different pronunciation in Gortaclee near Cushendall in Antrim, the field of the mound; and another usual form is seen in Edenclaw near the village of Ederny in the north of Fermanagh, the *edan* or hill-brow of the rampart.

The two words *sonnach* and *tonnach* both mean a wall, mound, rampart, or circular enclosure. As they are identical in meaning, and differ only in their initial letters, it seems probable that *tonnach* is merely a variety of *sonnach*, the *t* replacing *s* under the influence of the article (1st Ser., Part I., c. II.); for *sonnach* is found in our oldest manuscripts, as for example in *Lebor-na-hUidhre*.

Sonnach gives names to those places now called Sonnagh and Sunnagh, in all of which some remarkable defensive rampart must have existed. But *tonnach* is far more common in names, and assumes such anglicised forms as *tonnagh*, *tunny*, *tonny*, *tony*, &c. Derrintonny in Monaghan and Fermanagh, represents the sound of *Doire-an-tonnaigh*, the oak wood of the rampart; Ardtonnagh near Lisbellaw in Fermanagh, high mound. The names of Lissatunna, and Lissatunny (the fort of the rampart) in Clare, Galway, Tipperary, and Westmeath, indicate that at each of these places there was a *lis* or fort defended by a circumvallation of unusual magnitude. In some of the preceding names the form may be *sonnach*, with the *s* eclipsed in the usual way; but this make makes no difference as to meaning.

Trench. A trench, a deep furrow, a dry ditch, or pit, is usually designated by the word *clais* [clash], which is extremely common in the southern half of Ireland, as a component of local names, usually in the anglicised form *clash.* It is seldom met with in the north. Clash constitutes or begins the names of about 130 townlands; and enters into many combinations in other positions. Clashroe in Cork, King's County, and Waterford—red trench—must have been so called from the colour of the clay; Clashnamrock near Lismore, is *Clais-na-mbroc*, the trench of the badgers; Clashwilliam in Kilkenny, William's furrow; Clashygowan in Donegal, O'Gowan's furrow. There is a little village at the entrance to Glenmalure in Wicklow, and several townlands in other parts of Ireland, called Ballynaclash, the town of the trench.

Mill stream. Among the several Irish words beginning with *sr* which denote a stream (such as *sruth*, *srubh*, &c.) *srae* or *sraeth* is used to designate a mill stream. Four miles east of the village of Ardrahan in Galway, there is a little river that sinks into the ground, called Owenshree, the river of the mill-race. But the word almost always enters into names with the *s* elipsed by *t*, which changes it to *tray*, *trea*, &c. This syllable, in the end of words, can usually be distinguished from *tray* (*traigh*) a strand, by the form of the article; for *tray*, a strand, is feminine, and takes *na* before it, when the article is used at all; while *tray*, when it means a mill-race, is masculine, and takes one of the masculine forms of the article, *an*, *a*, *n*, or *in*, before it.

This is illustrated by the two names Gort*na*traw and Gort*a*tray; the former (in Donegal) is *Gort-na-tragha*, the field of the strand; the latter (in Cork and Tyrone) *Gort-a'-tsrae*, the field of the mill race. Inchintrea near Cahersiveen in Kerry, is the river-holm of the mill-race; and Derrintray (*Doire-an-tsrae*, mill-race wood) is the name of a place near the village of Clonaslee in Queen's County. There is a townland near the city of Armagh, and another in the parish of Donaghmoyne in Monaghan, called Tray, in which *t* displaces *s* under the influence of the article—*an tsrae*, the mill race.

Plank bridges. Among the various contrivances adopted for crossing rivers before stone bridges were introduced into this country, or before they came into general use, plank bridges deserve to be mentioned:—timber planks were laid across the stream from bank to bank, if it were narrow enough, or supported on rests of natural rock or on artificial piers, if the river were wide. We know that bridges of this kind are occasionally found in use at the present day in various remote parts of the country—I know a place in the county Wicklow, where one is now in course of construction—and we have sufficient testimony both in history and in the names of places, that they were much used in old times. There was a plank bridge across the Shannon in the time of Brian Boru, near his palace of Kincora, that is, either at the very place where the bridge of Killaloe now stands, or near it. For we read in the "Wars of the Irish with the Danes," that, soon before the battle of Clontarf, when *Maelmordha*, king of Leinster, retired in anger from Kincora, a messenger from Brian followed him, and "overtook him at the end of the plank-bridge of Killaloe on the east side" ("*I cind clair Cilli Dalua:*" p. 145).

This ancient bridge is designated in the preceding passage by the word *clár*, which means literally "a plank;" its name and meaning are still preserved in the name of the bishop's house at Killaloe—Clarisford; and there is no better example of how an old Irish name may be newly varnished up so as to efface every vestige of its age and origin. For Clarisford is only a pretty way of saying the ford of the *clar* or plank; though I suppose there are few persons who suspect in the least how the name originated.

It is probable indeed that many of these structures scarcely deserved the name of bridges, but should be rather designated plank fords or plank crossings, which is the very name they commonly go by in the Irish language; for many of them even still retain names partly formed from the word *clar*, a board; while the other part of the name often consists of one of the Irish words for a ford. Moreover the people in several of those places have a tradition that the names were derived from a plank bridge; which we find to be the case for instance in the village of Clare on the river Fergus, and also in Clare Galway (see these places in First Series).

A very good illustration of this class of names is Athclare near Dunleer in Louth—the ford of the plank; which takes the form of Aghclare near Graiguenamanagh in Kilkenny; and still another form, Aclare, in Meath and Carlow. Another equally characteristic name is Belclare (for which see First Series); Bealaclare, now the name of a bridge over the Leamawaddra river, at the head of Roaring Water bay in Cork, two miles from the village of Ballydehob, shows how the river was crossed before the bridge was built—*Bél-a'-chlair*, the ford of the board.

There is a little village near Oranmore in Galway, now called Clarinbridge, but formerly *Ath-cliath-Meadhraidhe* [Aclee-Maaree], i. e. the *Ath-cliath* or hurdle ford of Maaree—this last being the name of the peninsula running into Galway bay west of the village. This was in old times a place of note, for it was the western terminus of the Esker Riada, which separated the northern from the southern half of Ireland, the eastern terminus being the great *Ath-cliath*, or Dublin (see Esker Riada in First Ser.) It is very probable that the original ford of hurdles gave place, in course of time, to a better crossing made of planks; for while the old name is lost among the people, the village has been long called in Irish *Droichead-a'-chlairín* [Drehid-a-clareen], the bridge of the *clareen* or little board, of which "Clarinbridge" is a sort of half translation.

The existence of such a bridge at some remote time over the river Bride, half a mile above the little village of Ovens, west of Cork city, is proved by the name of the present bridge—Drehidnaglaragh, the bridge of the planks. "Clare Bridge" over the Clare river in the parish of Abington in Limerick, near the village of Newport, is now a good stone structure; but both the present name, and the Irish, *Droichead-a'-chlair*, of which it is a translation, show that the original bridge was made of planks; and from this old bridge the river itself derives its name. Aughnaglaur is the name of a bridge crossing a small stream flowing from the Blackstairs Mountains, in the parish of Killann in Wexford—*Ath-na-gclár*, the ford of the planks.

Fold. The word *cro* has several meanings, one of which is a hut, hovel, or small house; and this is its most general sense when it is found in names, i. e. a hut, fold, or pen for cattle. The little building in Glendalough, now called St. Kevin's kitchen, is called in the annals *Cro-Kevin*, St. Kevin's hut. The most usual anglicised form of this word is seen in Culcrow in the parish of Agivey in Derry, near the Bann, the angle or corner of the cattle sheds; and in Clashacrow, the name of a parish in Kilkenny, *Clais-a'-chro*, the trench of the shed. In Curraghacronacon near Abbeyleix in Queen's County, the first part *curragha*, is the plural of *curragh*, a moor; and the whole name fully written, is *Curracha-cro-na-gcon*, the moors of the hut of the hounds.

Near Roscrea in Tipperary, there are two adjacent townlands called Barnagree and Pintown; the former is understood to be *Barr-na-gcroithe*, the summit of the cattle-pens; while the latter, Pintown, is a translation, which is incorrect, however, in both members (*pin* for *pen;* and *town* for *top*), and should have been made Pentop, or something bearing the same signification. There is a little islet in the south-west part of Lough Ennel in Westmeath, now called Croincha, and often Cormorant Island; where Malachy II., king of Ireland, died in the year 1022, surrounded by the chief ecclesiastical dignitaries of the country. In the annals it is called *Cro-inis*, which means the island of the hut or pen; and I suppose that the name Cormorant Island took its rise from the belief that *cro* was English *crow*, a bird—" Cormorant Island" being intended as a sort of ornamental translation of *Cro-inis.*

Ovens. *Bácús* [baucoose] means an oven. It is given by O'Reilly (in the form *bácudhas*) on the authority of Shaw's Gaelic Dictionary; but that it has been in use in Ireland we may consider as certain, even though we had no other reason for concluding so than its existence in local names. It is obviously connected with the English word *bake;* but whether it is an old Irish word, or is merely borrowed from English, I will not now undertake to determine. It is seldom much disguised in names, except only that the *b* is commonly changed to *v* by aspiration. Its usual anglicised forms are seen in Gortavacoosh in the parish of Abington in Limerick; *Gort-a'-bhácúis*, the field of the oven; in Coolavacoose in the north of Kildare, near Edenderry (*cúil*, a corner); and in Parkavacoosh (*páirc*, a field), now the name of an old fort near Lixnaw in Kerry.

Near the village of Kilmacow, in the parish of Dunkitt in Kilkenny, there is a townland called Tinvacoosh, i. e. *Tigh-an-bhácúis*, the house of the oven, or simply baking-house. In this place there lived one time, according to a local legend, a rich baker, who employed himself in cultivating a small garden round his house, whenever he was able to withdraw from the cares of his oven. One day, after placing a batch of loaves in the heated oven, he left them to bake, and went as usual to his garden. The day was very sultry, and the summer had been unusally dry; so he filled a vessel with water from a clear well hard by, and began to sprinkle his flowers and vegetables, which were drooping for want of a little moisture. He had not been long employed in this manner, when a stranger, a man of grave and dignified appearance, walked up to him, and told him that his conduct was highly improper; that he should not presume to interfere with the ordinary course of nature; but that he should leave it entirely in the hands of Providence to regulate the distribution of drought and moisture. After administering this rebuke, he walked slowly away, and disappeared among the trees of a neighbouring wood.

While the baker stood pondering on the stranger's words, he bethought him that it was time to look after his loaves; so he went to the oven and drew them forth; but found them, not baked as he expected, but covered all over with ears of wheat, which had sprouted out in the oven, and appeared as green and flourishing as if they had grown naturally in the richest soil. This wonderful occurrence convinced him that the mysterious stranger was quite right; and he resolved that he would never again venture to water his garden.

The legend of the rich baker of Tinvacoosh shows the folly of the common practice of watering plants, which is plain enough indeed to many people without a miracle at all; for is it not far pleasanter and wiser to sit at your ease on a hot summer day, and let the plants take their chance, than to go toiling in a garden with a heavy watering can in your hand?

Kilns. Sorn means a furnace, kiln, or oven. The word is often applied to a lime kiln; and its presence in names indicates the spots where kilns were once in use. The anglicised forms are easily recognised; for they are generally identical, or nearly so, with the Irish; as in Drumnasorn in the parish of Killaghtee in Donegal, and Aghnasurn on the north side of Lough Key in Roscommon, the ridge, and the field, of the kilns or furnaces. The word stands alone in the name of Soran near the village of Drumlish in Longford, and in Sorne, the name of a hill, four miles from Buncrana in Donegal; and the *s* becomes aspirated in Drumhurrin, the name of a lake and townland in the parish of Templeport, in the north-west corner of Cavan, which means the ridge of the furnace.

From *teine* [tinna] fire, and *ael*, lime, is derived *teine-aeil* [tinneel], the usual name for a lime-kiln, signifying literally "fire of lime." The word is used by the Four Masters when they record that Flaherty O'Brollaghan, abbot of the great monastery of Derry, and his clergy, erected a *teine-aeil* measuring seventy feet every way, in the year 1163. Tinneel near Ross Carbery in Cork, and Tinneel near the village of Rosenallis in Queen's County, took their names from lime-kilns; and we find the word also in Knocknatinnyweel near Newport Mayo, and in Garrynatinneel in Tipperary, near Killaloe, the hill and the garden of the lime-kiln.

Prison. *Carcair* signifies a prison: it is of course the same as the Latin *carcer*, and is probably derived from it. This word has given names to various places throughout the four provinces, now called Carker and Corker; but what kind of prisons they were, that have left their names on these places, or what their history, we have now no means of determining. In some parts of Ireland, especially in Clare, the term is applied to a narrow pass between hills, which is only an extension of the original meaning—a narrow or confined pass like a prison; and this may be its meaning in some of the preceding places.

It was certainly understood in this sense in "The Corker Road," a steep and narrow pass, leading to the abbey of Corcomroe in the north of Clare, which is mentioned by the Four Masters, and called by them *Carcair-na-gcleireach* [Carkernagleragh], the narrow pass of the clergy, a name by which it is still known. The clergy from whom the latter part of the name was derived were, no doubt, the monks of the great abbey of Corcomroe. The word *carcair* must have been applied in its original sense to Inishcorker, one of the numerous islands at the mouth of the river Fergus in Clare, whose name signifies the island of the prison.

Sepulchre. *Sabaltair* is given in Cormac's Glossary as meaning "a graveyard of a plague, i. e. a great field in which the pagans used to bury;" and Cormac derives it from the Latin *sepultura.* There is just one place in Ireland taking its name from this word, viz., the parish of Subulter near Kanturk in Cork.

Port. The Irish word *port* has several meanings; but of these there are only two which it is necessary to notice here, namely, 1. A bank or landing place, a harbour, port, or haven; 2. A fortress or military station, a royal fort; a chieftain's residence. The word is used in these two senses in both the ancient and modern language; and I will give one example of each application from old authorities. It stands for "landing-place" in a passage in *Lebor-na-hUidhre* (see Kilk. Arch. Jour., 1870-1, p. 390), in which *Cuchullin* relates:—"It was in that manner I swam the ocean until I was in the (*purt*) harbour;" while in an ancient poem on the death of Malachy (king of Ireland), quoted by the Four Masters, at A. D. 1022, it is used as synonymous with *dun*, a fortress:—

"Three hundred *ports* had the king in which flesh and food were given;
Guests from the king of the elements were in each *dun* of these."

The compounds *ceannphort* and *bailephort* (canfort, ballyfort), were also used to denote either a chief city or a chief residence.

The word always bears one or the other of these two meanings in local names; but it is often not easy to distinguish between them. It may be stated generally, however, that when the spot whose name is wholly or partly formed from this term, is situated on the sea-shore or on a river or lake, the word has the former meaning; otherwise the latter.

Port forms or begins the names of about 140 townlands, parishes, and villages. Portadown must have taken its name from an earthen *dun* on the shore of the Bann:—*Port-a'-dúin*, the landing place of the fortress. There was once a remarkable castle belonging to the O'Maddens, on the bank of the Shannon, in the parish of Lorrha in Tipperary, north of Lough Derg, which is called by the Four Masters *Port-an-tolchain*, the bank or landing-place of the little *tulach* or hill. In the Down Survey the name is written Portolohane; and it still survives in the much disguised form of Portland—now the name of a townland and residence. There is a place called Portcrusha on the Shannon, near Castleconnell, which the Four Masters, when recording the erection there, in 1506, of a wooden bridge, by one of the O'Briens, call *Port-croisi*, the landing place of the cross.

In the eastern part of the county Clare, *port* is pronounced as if written *páirt* [part], and this pronunciation is reflected in the names of some places on the Shannon, from Limerick to Killaloe, which are now called Parteen, a diminutive form signifying little landing-place.

Fairy palace. *Palas* or *pailis* signifies a palace or royal residence, a loan word from the Latin (*palatium*). We have it pretty often reproduced in names, and it is always applied to a circular fort or *lis*; but as modern stone castles sometimes came to be erected on or near the sites of the forts, the name naturally descended to them, though this is not the original application of the word. Moreover in later times, after the abandonment of the old *lisses* as residences by their human inhabitants, and since the fairies have taken possession of them, the word *pailis* is generally understood to mean a fairy palace or residence.

There are between twenty and thirty townlands called Pallas, Palace, and Pallis, three anglicised forms of this word; and all these places took their names from fairy forts or *lisses*. Pallaskenry in Limerick was so called as being situated in the old territory of Kenry or *Caonraighe*. In Sligo, the term is found in the form of Phaleesh, which is the name of a townland; and in the end of names the *p* is occasionally changed to *f* by aspiration, as in Cappafaulish in Kilkenny, the garden-plot of the fairy fort.

Monasteries. The Irish word, *mainister*, which signifies a monastery or abbey, is merely the Latin *monasterium*, borrowed, like several other ecclesiastical terms. Many of the old abbeys to which the word was originally applied, still retain it in their names, and it is generally very little disguised by letter changes.

Saint *Eimhin* or Evin founded a monastery on

the brink of the river Barrow, on a spot which before his time had been called *Ros-glas*, green *ros* or wood; but which took from him the name of *Mainister-Eimhin*—so written in all ancient authorities—Evin's monastery, now Monasterevin. He was a native of Munster, and was one of four brothers, all ecclesiastics, sons of Eoghan, who was eighth in descent from Olioll Olum, king of Munster in the third century. He lived in the beginning of the sixth century; and he is believed to have been the writer of a Life of St. Patrick in a mixture of Irish and Latin, which is still extant, and which on account of its being divided into three parts, each having a proper introduction of its own, is now well known as the "Tripartite Life."

Monasterboice in the county Louth, near Drogheda, now so celebrated for its abbey ruins, its round tower, and its magnificent stone crosses, was founded by Buite or Boethius, bishop and abbot, who is believed to have been one of St. Patrick's disciples, and who died, according to the Annals of Ulster, in A. D. 522. This great establishment continued to flourish for many ages afterwards; and among its many remarkable men, was the celebrated historian and poet, Flann, or as he is commonly called, Flann of the Monastery, who died in 1056. The place is called in Irish authorities *Mainister-Buithe;* but the *th* of the founder's name has been changed to *c* in the modern form, Monasterboice.

In that part of the parish of Athleague lying west of the Shannon, in the county Galway, there is a townland called "Monasternalea or Abbeygrey," of which the second name professes to be a translation of the first, which it is not; for the full Irish name is *Mainister-na-liatha*, the abbey of the grey (friars). This terms occurs in several other names, and the forms are slighty varied:—Aghmanister is the name of a place in the parish of Abbeymahon, in the south of Cork, meaning the field (*achadh*) of the monastery; Tullyminister in Cavan (*tulach*, a hill); Ballyministragh in the parish of Kilmood in Down, which in certain old documents is written Ballymonesteragh (Reeves: Eccl. Ant. 198), the town of the monastery; and Ballyminstra in Antrim, which is the same name.

Head Residence. The word *ceanannus*, which has been long in use, is very satisfactorily explained by the Four Masters, in a passage recording the foundation of *Ceanannus*, now Kells in Meath, in A.M. 3991. They state:—"It was by *Fiacha Finnailches* [king of Ireland] that *Dun-chuile-Sibrinne*, that is, *Ceanannus*, was erected;" and they go on to say that, wherever this king erected a habitation for himself, he called it by the name *Ceanannus*, which means head abode. From this it is obvious that the structure designated in the first instance by the name *Ceanannus*, was a *dun* or circular earthen fort in which the king resided.

The *Ceanannus* now under notice continued to be a royal residence down to the sixth century, when king Dermot Mac Kerval granted it to St. Columkille; after which time it lost its pagan associations, and soon became a great ecclesiastical centre. The old pagan name *Ceanannus* was however retained as long as the Irish language was used: but by those who spoke English it was modified to Kenlis, which was considered an equivalent name, Kenlis meaning head *lis* or fort. The literal translation of this has given name to the demesne and mansion of Headfort, from which again the Marquis of Headfort has taken his title. Kenlis was afterwards shortened to the present name, Kells. There is still an ancient earthen fort in the demesne of Headfort, which is believed to be the original royal residence that gave name to the place.

From the passage of the Four Masters quoted above, we may infer that there were several places called *Ceanannus ;* but I am aware of only one other place of the name in Ireland, and it has been similarly anglicised, namely, *Ceanannus*, now Kells, in the county Kilkenny. There are other places called Kells in Antrim, Clare, Kerry, and Limerick; but these are all probably the anglicised plural of *cill*, namely, *cealla* [kella], signifying churches.

There is a townland near Killarney called Headfort, giving name to a railway station; and another called Headford in the county of Leitrim; but in both these cases the original Irish name is *Lis-na-gceann*, the fort of the heads; leading to the presumption that the places were once used for executing criminals. The name of Headford in Galway has still a different origin. In the "Circuit of Murkertagh Mac Neill," it is called *Ath-mac-Cing*, and in another ancient authority, quoted by Hardiman in his edition of O'Flaherty's "Iar Connaught" (p. 371) *Ath-mic-Cing*, which signifies the ford of the son of *Cing* or *Kinn*. The present Irish name is a shortened form of this, viz., *Ath-cinn ;* and as *cinn* is the genitive of *ceann*, the head, the name was erroneously believed to signify the ford of the head, and translated accordingly, Headford.

CHAPTER XIV.

THE SUN.

OUR ancient annals relate that when the monarch Hugony the Great, who reigned three centuries before the Christian era, divided Ireland into twenty-five parts among his twenty-five children, "he exacted oaths [from his subjects] by the sun and moon, the sea, the dew, and colours, and by all the elements visible and invisible, and by every element which is in heaven and on earth, that the sovereignty of Erin should be invested in his descendants for ever." And Tuathal the Acceptable, king of Ireland in the second century of the Christian era, exacted a similar oath in imitation of his ancestor Hugony.

The monarch *Laeghaire* [Leary], in whose time St. Patrick came to Ireland, reigned from A. D. 428 to 458. In the ancient account of his death given in *Leabhar na hUidhre* (the Book of the brown cow) it is related that there existed from old times a prophecy, that he would meet his death somewhere between *Eire* and *Alba* (Ireland and Scotland); and accordingly, although his father, Nial of the Nine Hostages, Dathi, and others of his predecessors, were celebrated for their naval expeditions, *Laeghaire* quite avoided the sea, and carried on his wars within the limits of the island.

In the year 457 he invaded Leinster, in order to exact the oppressive tribute called the *borumha* [boru], claimed from that province by the kings of Ireland; and the Leinstermen defeated him in a battle fought at a place called *Ath-dara* (oak ford` on the river Barrow, and took him prisoner. The old account goes on to state, that they released him after he had sworn by the sun and moon, the water and air, day and night, sea and land, that he would never again demand the *borumha.* The very next year, however, he made an incursion into Leinster to enforce the tribute, and on his march from Tara, seized a prey of cows at *Sidh-Neachtan* [Shee-Nectan—the hill of Carbery at the source of the Boyne]; but as soon as he had arrived at a place called *Grellach Daphill* (the marsh of the two steeds), by the side of *Cassi, situated between two hills called Eire and Alba,* he was struck dead by the sun and wind for having violated his oath; and in this manner the prophecy was fulfilled.

These accounts show that the Irish, like most other ancient nations, observed natural objects and natural phenomena with attention, and regarded them with a certain degree of admiration and awe; but they do not prove what some have asserted, that the people worshipped the elements. And in regard to sun worship in particular, which attracted so many enthusiastic advocates in the last century, and which has not even yet quite lost its fascination, it is to be observed, that this ancient form of oath affords no more grounds for concluding that the Irish worshipped the sun, than that they worshipped the dew, the wind, or any other element.

We have in fact no reason whatever to believe that the sun was ever worshipped in Ireland: it has been often asserted indeed, and supported with enthusiastic earnestness; but nothing deserving the name of an argument has been ever brought forward to prove it. The round towers, which were held to be the temples of the sun, are after all Christian buildings; the cromlechs, "the altars on which the druids offered sacrifices to the great luminary," have turned out to be nothing more than tombs. We have a native literature, chiefly in manuscript, most ancient and most extensive—a vast collection of history, genealogy, legend, and romance—in which the manners, customs, religious observances, and superstitions of the Irish both in Pagan and in early Christian times are minutely delineated; we have numerous biographies—some in Irish, some in Latin—coming down to us from very ancient times, of the first preachers of Christianity in Ireland, in which we find descriptions of various pagan rites and superstitions, which these good men encountered in their progress through the country; but no one has ever yet been able to find in all these writings, one sentence asserting that the people worshipped the sun, or an expression that could in the least justify any one in believing that sun worship ever prevailed in the country.

There is yet another argument—the one which I am immediately concerned with here—viz. that many places throughout the country derive their names from the sun; and this is supposed to indicate that the sun was worshipped at these spots. But this is as baseless an argument as the others. There is nothing remarkable or mysterious in a place being named from the sun any more than from any other natural object. There is scarcely a class of objects, an element, or a phenomenon, in physical nature, as I have, I think, fully proved in this and the preceding volume, from which places have not derived names, and that in a manner, and for reasons, perfectly natural and intelligible.* We have names containing the word *uisce*, because the places were unusually watery; high or exposed spots got names formed from *gaeth*, wind; elevated mountain peaks or gorges, subject to thick mists, are described by the word *ceó*, a fog—and so on through all nature. Just in the same natural way, sunny spots, places on the south or south-west sides of hills, sheltered from cold winds and warmed by the sun's rays, were named from the sun. I know many spots of this kind, so named, all over the country: this is the explanation universally given by the most intelligent of the peasantry; and it is fully borne out by the physical aspect of the localities.

Whoever concludes on such testimony as this, that the sun was adored at a particular place, might with equal force of reasoning, infer that almost all objects, natural and artificial, were deified and worshipped. Besides, there is no more significance in such a name as Corrignagrena (sun-rock) than in Sunville, Sunlawn, Sunnybank, Sunnyside, and many other like English names; unless we are to believe that while English speaking people often gave descriptive names to sunny spots, those speaking Irish, for some strange reason, never did any such thing; or that there is some mystery hidden away in the dim recesses of the Irish language that is not to be found in such a plain language as English.

Grian [green] is the Irish word for the sun, and like the German *sonne*, it is a feminine noun. Its genitive is *greine* [greana], and this is the form that

* See 1st Ser. Part IV.; and Chaps. XIV. to XXII. of this volume.

most commonly appears in names. In the parish of Monamolin in Wexford, there are two adjacent townlands called Monagreany, which represents the Irish *Moin-na-greine*, the bog of the sun or sunny bog; Edenagrena near Inishkeen, a little to the west of Dundalk, is the *eudan* or hill-brow of the sun; and Inchagreana in the parish of Kilfeacle near the town of Tipperary, is sunny island or river holm.

In many anglicised names of this class, the word is shortened to one syllable; as in Tullagreen near Carrigtohill in Cork, *Tulach-greine*, the hill of the sun, and Curragrean near Oranmore in Galway, with a like meaning (*cor*, a round hill). Sometimes the formation of the word indicates directly that the place received its name on account of its aspect with regard to the sun; as we see in Coollegrean, the name of some places in Kerry, Leitrim, and Mayo—*Cul-le-grein*, literally "back to the sun."

In the year 1785 Mr. Theophilus O'Flanagan published (in the Trans. R.I.A.) an account of a remarkable monument—a sort of cromlech—situated on Callan mountain in Clare; with a copy and translation of an Ogham inscription on it, setting forth that a chieftain named Conan lay buried beneath the great flag. This monument is still to be seen, and Dr. Samuel Ferguson has, I think, shown conclusively that the inscription is genuine.* But O'Flanagan went further than this: he forged an Irish quatrain and cited it as a part of an ancient poem called "The battle of Gabhra," to the effect that Conan (the well known Conan Mael of Irish romance) had gone before the battle to worship

* See Proc. R. I. A. Vol. I., Ser II., p. 160.

the sun at Mount Callan, and that he was slain and buried on the side of the mountain under a flag, in which his name was inscribed in Ogham.*

Just under the brow of the mountain on which the monument is placed, there is a small lake in a hollow, called Lough Boolynagreana—the *booly* or dairy place of the sun; and it received this name from two circumstances; 1. that at some former time, the people of the surrounding neighbourhood used to pasture their herds and flocks, and milk their cows and goats on its banks; 2. that the whole valley in which it lies has a sunny southern aspect. It was, no doubt, the existence of this name that started in O'Flanagan's fertile brain the idea of inventing the stanza about Conan's sacrifice and death; and for some years after the publication of his paper, it was generally considered that the Callan monument afforded conclusive proof of the prevalence of sun worship in ancient Ireland.

The name *Buaile-na-greine* is not confined to Callan mountain; we find it in the parish of Kilcumreragh in Westmeath, where, however, the *booly* is corrupted to *bally*, and the full name is represented by Ballynagrenia. There are names similar to this last in other parts of Ireland, but they are somewhat differently derived. Ballynagrena near Dunleer in Louth, signifies the sunny *bally* or townland, and it is correctly translated Suntown in the name of a residence: Ballygreany in the parish of Duneany, about three miles from the town of Kildare, has the same meaning; but in Ballygreany in the parish of Clontibret in Monaghan, the *bally* represents *bealach*, a pass:—the sunny pass or road.

* See O'Donovan's Irish Gram., Introd. xlvii.

The word *grian* in local names sometimes commemorates, not the sun, but a woman; for though primarily meaning the sun, it was anciently (being a feminine noun; p. 233) a favourite female name, applied of course in the sense of brightness and beauty. Kilgreana near Galbally in Limerick, is understood by the people to mean Grian's church; but there are other places in Carlow, Mayo, and Waterford, with this name, in the slightly varying forms of Kilgreany and Kilgraney in which probably the first syllable represents *coill;* the whole meaning sunny wood.

The most interesting example of the occurrence of this word in local nomenclature as a woman's name, is Knockgrean, a hill rising over the village of Pallas-Grean in the county Limerick. The lady "Grian of the bright cheeks," from whom this place was named, was an enchantress; and the hill, which before her time was called *Cnoc-na-gcuradh* [Knocknagurra], the hill of the champions (see p. 102), was her favourite haunt.

Five young champions, the sons of Conall, came one time to attack the *sidh* [shee] or fairy mansion of Grian's father, Firae; and they destroyed the *sidh*, and slew besides, one of Grian's young handmaids. But they paid dearly for this cruel deed; for the vengeful sorceress overtook them on their return, and transformed them all into badgers.

When Conall heard of the fate of his five sons, he set out immediately, bent on vengeance, to seek for the enchantress; and when he arrived at Knocknagurra, he found her asleep on the hill. She started up as he approached, and a contest took place between them, in which Conall nearly succeeded in killing her. When she found herself worsted in the fight, she planned a stratagem to bring him within the power of her sorcery; and she said, pretending to recognise him then for the first time, "Is it thou, O Conall?" Conall answered "It is I." "Come near me," said she, "that I may give thee a blessing." So Conall came close to her, and she immediately shook ashes on him. He retired at once from her presence, but the withering spell of the ashes overcame him; and when he had come to a certain mound he died there, so that the mound was named from him, Carn Conaill.

Grian had no better fortune; for no sooner had Conall left her than she lay down and died of her wounds. And ever since, the hill has borne the name of *Cnoc-Greine* or Knockgrean, in memory of the enchantress, Grian of the bright cheeks. About a quarter of a mile from the village of Pallas-Grean, which lies at the foot of the hill, there is a large fort, now called the moat of Pallas; this is the original *sidh* or fairy mansion of Firae and his daughter: and from it the village took its name:—Pallas-Grean, i. e. the fairy-palace of the lady Grian (see page 226). There is also an ancient fort on the top of the hill, which now goes by the name of Seefin (see 1st Ser. Part II., c. I.); and this was no doubt Grian's own residence.

The enchantress Grian has been long forgotten in the neighbourhood; and the name of the place is now supposed to be derived directly from the sun. Accordingly the townland lying adjacent to the village on the west side, is called Sunglen; and near the village of "Pallas-Grean New," at the Pallas station of the Waterford and Limerick railway, is the townland and residence of Sunville; both named under the erroneous impression that Knockgrean meant the hill of the sun.

But to return to the badgers. After their transformation, they betook themselves to the nearest badger warren, and lived in all respects just like the general run of badgers. Many years after this, it happened that Cormac, who was afterwards called Cormac Gaileng, made a great feast for his father *Tadg* [Teig], at a place called Breslech; and he succeeded in procuring one hundred of every four-footed beast for this feast, except badgers only. Now the want of badgers seems to have sorely troubled the heart of his father; for we read in the ancient legend, that he called his son into his presence, and commanded him to go forth and procure a supply of these animals for the feast.

Cormac set out in obedience to his father's directions; and before he had gone far, he met Odran the druid, the son of the charioteer Laidir. "What dost thou seek?" said Odran. "I am seeking for badgers for my father's feast," answered Cormac; "tell me, I pray thee, are there any to be procured." "It has been foretold," answered Odran, "that I should procure badgers for thee, and I know that now the time is come when the prophecy is to be fulfilled. In former days," he continued, "the sorceress, Grian of the bright cheeks, threw her magic spells on the young warriors who had destroyed her father's mansion, and transformed them into badgers; and these I will procure for thee to bring to thy father's feast."

So Cormac and the druid went to the fortress of the badgers, and called on them to come forth at once; but the badgers, who still retained some vestiges of their human intelligence, flatly refused to do any such thing.

The wily druid, however, devised a cunning stratagem to draw them forth; and he said to Cormac, "They will never come out on thy protection, for they distrust thee; but give them the guarantee of thy father's spear, and they will no longer hesitate." Cormac then went back, and brought the spear without his father's knowledge; and he came to the mouth of the badger-fortress, and solemnly guaranteed their safety on the honour of the spear. Now the badgers knew quite well that no one had ever dared to question the honour of Tadg's spear; so they foolishly came out in a body without further parley; and no sooner did they show themselves, than Cormac and the druid fell on them and made short work of them.

When the feast came on, Tadg felt in his heart an unaccountable loathing at sight of the badgers; and no wonder indeed, seeing that these same badgers were his own near cousins; for both he and they were the great-grandchildren of Owen More, that renowned king of Munster, who forced Conn of the hundred battles to divide Ireland with him. And when he heard in what a treacherous manner Cormac had slain the badgers, and how he had violated the honour of his spear, he was filled with anger and indignation, and he immediately expelled the young man from his house. Cormac fled to Connaught, where he obtained a large territory for himself and his descendants; but after this event he was known by the reproachful name of Cormac Gaileng, or Cormac of the dishonoured spear.*

* *Gae*, a spear; *lang*, deceit. An abstract of this ancient legend is given in Cormac's Glossary, *voce, Gaileng*. It is given fully in the MS. H. 3, 18, T. C. D.; from which it has been published with a translation, by Dr. Whitley Stokes, in his "Three Irish Glosses," p. XLII. The barony of Gallen in Mayo derived

CHAPTER XV.

THE ATMOSPHERE.

Wind. Places in a high or bleak situation, or otherwise exposed to the wind, are often designated by the word *gaeth* [gwee, or gee] which is the Irish word for wind. It occurs in the end of names in the genitive *gaeithe* [geeha] which is correctly represented by the anglicised forms *geeha*, *geehy*, though it is often reduced to the single syllable *gee*—all easily distinguished.

Dungeeha is the name of a place near Newcastle in Limerick, which took the name from an old fort:—*Dun-gaeithe*, the fortress of the wind; Drumnagee in the parish of Ballintoy in Antrim, east of Bushmills, the hill-ridge of the wind; Tullynagee in Down and Derry, windy hill; Latgee in the parish of Errigle Trough, Monaghan, the *laght* or sepulchral mound of the wind. Elevated bleak mountain passes very often get the name of Barnageehy or Barnanageehy the *barna* or gap of the wind; which is frequently translated into the English names Windgap and Windgate. I know of only one place in all Ireland where a windmill is expressly commemorated in a name, viz., Mullingee near Granard in Longford:—*Muileann-gaeithe*, the mill of the wind, i. e. windmill.

In Meath and some of the adjoining counties, the

its name from Cormac *Gaileng*, and for this, and for a historical account of the various personages mentioned in the legend, see 1st Ser. Part II., c. II. For other place-names derived from Grian, as a woman's name, see Lough Graney and Granny's bed in 1st Series.

final *th* is often retained in the modernized names, and fully pronounced; as in Mulgeeth, two miles south of Johnstown in the north of Kildare, the hill (*mul*) of the wind.

The diminutive *gaethán* [geehan, geehaun] is used to denote a breeze: we find it in Ardgeehan near Portaferry in Down, and in Ardgehane, which occurs twice near the south coast of Cork, the height of the breeze.

Gaeth is sometimes applied to an arm of the sea; of which examples will be found in the next chapter.

Seideán [shedawn] signifies puffing or blowing (a diminutive of *séid*, to blow); as in the term *sneachta-seideain* [snaghtashedawn, snow of the wind] applied in some parts of Ireland to dry snow raised from the ground, and blown about by gusts of wind. It occurs in local names to designate breezy places, or places which are considered subject to violent windy puffs or gusts. In the parish of Taghsheenod in Longford, three miles from Ardagh, there is a townland taking its name from a little lake called Loughsheedan, the lake of the blowing or blasts; Sedenrath near Kells in Meath, gusty rath or fort, an attempted translation of *Rath-seideain;* Knocksedan, two miles west of Swords in Dublin, where there is a very beautiful ancient flat-topped fort, the hill of the blast.

This word, however, more commonly begins with a *t* in anglicised names, the *s* being eclipsed by the intervention of the article (1st Ser. Part I., c. II.) as in Lough Atedaun, a lake near Corofin in Clare, *Loch-a'-tseideán*, the lake of the breeze; Lackantedane near the town of Tipperary (*leac*, a flag-stone); Ardatedaun in the parish of Kiltallagh, about three miles from Miltown in Kerry, the height of the blowing.

On some parts of the sea coast, the term is used to designate rocks or caves or holes that shoot up jets or columns of water in time of storm; as in case of the well-known puffing holes on the coast of Clare, which are called in Irish Poulatedaun (i. e. *Poll-a'-tseideáin*), the hole of the puffing.

The diminutive in *og* is also frequently met with; as in Carrickashedoge in the parish of Magheracloone in Monaghan, the rock of the breeze; Rashedoge near Letterkenny in Donegal, the *rath* of the blast or gust. And sometimes we meet with the word *séid* with only an adjectival termination; as in Aghnasedagh, the name of a little lake, and also of a townland, near the town of Monaghan, the field (*achadh*) of the wind gusts.

The word *bolg* or *builg* [bullig] in the sense of "bellows," is applied much in the same way as the last term, to designate gusts or blasts or gusty spots; of which an excellent example is the townland of Bulligs between Killashandra and Ballyconnell in Cavan, i. e. a bellows or a gusty spot. But this word occurs generally on the coast, where it is applied like *seideán*, to puffing holes, to rocks or points, that break and spout up water during storms; and it is commonly anglicised Bullig, which is a name constantly met with all along the western coast from Donegal to Cork. The little peninsula lying on the west side of the bay of Adrigole, west of Glengarriff in Cork, is called Reenabulliga, the *rea* or mountain flat (or perhaps the *reen* or point) of the bellows or breakers.

Storm. *Gamh* [gov] denotes winter; it is also applied to a cold wintry storm; and thence to places exposed to bleak cold winds. Drumguff near Newbliss in Monaghan, signifies the *drum* or hill-ridge of the storm; the same name as Drumguiff and Drumgamph in Fermanagh, and Drumgoff over Glenmalure in Wicklow.

The word *sín* [sheen] also denotes a storm, and is applied topographically, like the last word, to high stormy places. Drumsheen, the ridge of storms, is the name of a place in the parish of Kilgarvan, Mayo; Cloonsheen in the parish of Kilconla in Galway, exposed or stormy meadow. Another word for a storm is *ainbhtheth* or *anfuth*, which often occurs in Irish writings. The name of the peninsula lying between the bays of Bertraghboy and Kilkieran in Connemara, is Irrus-ainhagh, i. e. the stormy *irrus* or peninsula; and the same term has given name to Leckanvy—the flag-stone of the storm—a little hamlet in a wild exposed situation, on the shore of Clew bay, near the base of Croagh Patrick, two miles west of Murrisk abbey.

Shelter. As places have been designated from their exposed or stormy situations, so also we find that some spots have received names indicating the very reverse—a position sheltered by trees, rocks, or hills. About half a mile south of Ardpatrick in Limerick, there is a narrow road shut in by a high fence on each side, protecting it from the west wind, which is called by the expressive name of Bohereenacluher, the *bohereen* or little road of the shelter. This word *cluthar* [cluhar], shelter, is found in other names; for example Dromcluher in the parish of Tuogh in Limerick, sheltered ridge; and Derryclure near Geashill in King's County, sheltered *derry* or oak grove. In the peninsula between Glandore harbour and Castlehaven in the south of Cork, there is a small lake called Lough Cluhir, sheltered lake.

Kilcloher (*kil*, church or wood) is the name of a townland four miles east of Cappoquin in Waterford; there is another place of the same name four miles south-west from Ennis in Clare, from which Snugville, the name of a residence has been derived.

In some cases the word *cluthar* comes in where you would least expect to find it, namely, in extremely exposed situations; of which a good example is Kilcloher on the shore of the Shannon mouth, near Loop Head in Clare; but in cases of this kind, I suppose that an artificial shelter was constructed, or a rock, or an abrupt elevation was taken advantage of, to counteract the bleakness of the situation. Perhaps in the present instance the *kil* was a wood, which received a name to express the shelter it afforded in so bleak a situation.

Snow. In most mountainous countries there are particular peaks that receive their names from the circumstance that they retain snow on their summits during the whole or a considerable part of the year. In such a country as Ireland, with a mild climate and no very high mountains, names of this kind could scarcely be expected. Yet we have a few hills whose names are partly formed from the word *sneaght* [snaght] snow, a word cognate with Latin *nix*, and with English *snow;* and although some of them are not distinguished for height, they must in some way retain snow in winter so much longer than the surrounding elevations, as to attract the attention of the people.

There are two mountains in Donegal, called Slieve Snaght, one near Carndonagh in the peninsula of Inishowen, and the other a little south of Errigle mountain; the Irish form of the name is *Sliabh-snechta*, which Colgan translates *mons-nivium*, the mountain of the snows. The people say that the snow usually remains on the summit of the Inishowen Slieve Snaght, up to the May fair of the neighbouring village of Carndonagh. The Book of *Druim-snechta* (the hill-ridge of the snow) was one of the ancient historical books of Ireland, often quoted by Irish historians, but it is not now known to exist. The only place now bearing this name is Drumsnat in Monaghan (which has dropped the guttural); and as an ancient monastery existed there, founded by St. Molua of Clonfert-Molua, it is probable that this is the place where the book was compiled.

Near Fivemiletown in Fermanagh, there is a townland called Moysnaght, the plain of the snow; and there is another place of the same name in the parish of Clontibret in Monaghan. Cloonsnaghta (snow-meadow) is the name of a townland containing a lake of the same name, two miles west of Killadysert in Clare, and of another in the parish of Moygawnagh in Mayo.

When the article is used, the *s* is commonly eclipsed by *t*, and this is followed by a further change of *n* to *r*, to facilitate the pronunciation. Altatraght in the parish of Kilteevoge in Donegal, a little west of Stranorlar, represents the Irish *Alt-a'-tsneaghta*, the height of the snow—Altatraght for Altatnaght, like crock for knock, Ardatrave for Ardatnave (see these in 1st Ser.) Precisely the same change occurs in Legatraghta in the parish of Templeport in Cavan, south-west of Swanlinbar, the snowy *lug* or hollow—the *lug* lying on the northern slope of a hill; the same name as Lugasnaghta in the parish of Cloonclare in the north of Leitrim. The additional change of the suppression of the guttural, is seen in Tullintrat near Castleblaney in Monaghan, the hill (*tul*) of the snow.

Cold. *Fuar* or *uar*, signifying cold, is found as part of a great many names: the places so designated having probably an exposed or northern aspect, or perhaps a marshy cold soil; and it is often applied to the water of springs, rivers, or lakes, which are considered to be unusually cold (see Oranmore, 1st Ser.) About a mile south of Elphin in Roscommon, there is a stream called Owenure (*Abhainn-fhuar*, cold river), which is mentioned in *Hy Many* by the equivalent name, *Glaisi-uair*, cold stream. The station next beyond Killarney towards Tralee, on the Southern and Western railway, is called Farranfore, *Fearann-fuar*, cold land; there is a lake in the parish of Annaghdown in Galway, a little east of Lough Corrib, called Lough Afoor, i. e. cold lake.

When the back of a hill had a northern aspect, it was often called Coolfore, cold back, which is the name of places in the counties of Louth, Meath, Monaghan, and Dublin. This element *fore* either as it stands, or with slight variations of spelling, is very often found in names, and may almost always be interpreted in the sense here given. Slievefoore, cold mountain, is the name of a hill in the parish of Killahurler in Wicklow, about two miles from the Wooden Bridge hotel; and there is a townland called Derryfore, cold *derry* or oak-grove, near Ballyroan in Queen's County.

The word often precedes the noun that it qualifies, as in Fourknocks in the parish of Stamullin in Meath, west of Balbriggan, which means cold *knocks* or hills; Forelacka near Kinnitty in King's County, cold flags or hill-slope. The compound *Fuar-choill*, cold wood, is of frequent occurrence: it is made Foorkill in Galway, Forekill near Urlingford in Kilkenny, Fourcuil in Cork, and Forkill in Meath and Armagh. In the parish of Clooney in Clare is the village of Spancelhill, well known for its fairs. The correct Irish name is *Cnoc-fuarchoilli* [Knock-foorkilla], the hill of the cold wood, for so the Four Masters call it, when recording a battle fought there in 1559, between the rival earls of Ormond and Desmond. In the colloquial language however, the *f* is aspirated and omitted, which reduces it to *Cnoc-urchaill* [Knockoorkill]; and as *urchall* or *aurchomhal* is a spancel, the name came to be erroneously translated Spancelhill instead Coldwoodhill.

Shower. The word *ceath* or *ceatha* [cah, caha] signifies a shower. The Caha mountains in the peninsula between the bays of Kenmare and Bantry, must have been considered specially liable to rain when they got the name, which is reduced from the present popular Irish name, *Cnoc-na-ceathain* [Knocknacahin], the showery mountain. This word probably gives name also to Dromcahan near Kenmare, *Druim-ceathain*, the ridge of the shower.

Fog. A fog or mist is denoted by the word *ceo* [keo: the *o* long; the *e* hardly pronounced], which enters into some names, chiefly in the south of Ireland. According to a passage in the life of bishop Mel, there was an ancient nunnery called *Druim-cheo*, immediately to the west of Slieve Golry near Ardagh in Longford; but both the nunnery and its name are now forgotten. The name *Druim-cheo* (the ridge of the fog) must have been originally applied to the hill west of Slieve Golry, whence it was transferred to the nunnery. Why this hill received such a name is obvious; for as it is an isolated elevation the midst of a plain, it catches the vapour and is often capped with fog, when the surrounding level country is clear; and some such explanation applies to every name containing the word *ceó*. Knockacheo, the foggy hill, is the name of a place in the parish of Ballynoe in Cork; Loughakeo, the lake of the mist, near Stradbally in Queen's County; Croncheo, four miles north-west of Killybegs in Donegal, the *cro* or valley of the fog; and Coomakeoge in the parish of Killemlagh, near Valentia in Kerry, the *coom* or valley of the mist; in which name the genitive is made *ceoig*, and the final *g* pronounced, as is usual in Cork and Kerry.

CHAPTER XVI.

THE SEA.

I NOW come to a class of names, which are generally speaking to be looked for only round the coast; though in consequence of secondary applications, or extensions of meaning, they are sometimes found inland.

The most common Irish word for the sea is *muir*, genitive *mara*; and this name for the sea exists, with slight modifications, in every Aryan language of Europe except Greek:—Lat. *mare;* Goth. *marei;* A. Sax. *mere;* Welsh *myr;* Corn. *môr*, &c.; while it is represented in Sanscrit by *mîra* (Pictet, Orig.) The word has already incidentally come under notice, as forming part of several names which have been dealt with in the First Series (see Kenmare, Connemara, &c.) As a part of compound words, it also enters pretty extensively into names, of which the following may be taken as examples. A small bay is often called *murbholg* [murvullog, murlog], i. e. sea-belly, from *bolg*, a sack or belly; and this word is generally anglicised Murlough, which is the name of several inlets mostly round the coast; among others, of the little bay lying east of Fair Head in Antrim; and of two in Donegal, one in Lough Swilly, and the other near Lifford. The bay extending eastwards from Bengore Head till it terminates in White Park bay, was anciently called *Murbholg;* but the people have lost this name. Lough Murree, a small lake in a peninsula, two miles north-east of Ballyvaghan in Clare, signifies marine lake, so called from being on the very verge of the sea.

Five miles west from Ballysadare in Sligo, on one of the inlets of Ballysadare bay, is Tanrego, a name which is exactly similar in formation to Tonregee (First Series), and exhibits another term (*go*), but one very seldom used, for the sea :—Irish *Toin-re-go*, backside to the sea.

Sál, *sáil*, or *sáile* [saul, saulia], which is a term in somewhat more common use than *muir*, signifies brine, salt water, or brackish water; cognate with Latin *sal*, English *salt.* The pretty hamlet and vale of Salrock, near the mouth of the Killeries in Connemara, takes its name from the little inlet, now called Little Killery bay, at the head of which it is situated; the name signifies St. Roc's briny inlet; but we have no written account of this saint, though he is vividly remembered in the traditions of the place, and the ruins of his church and his holy well are situated near the hamlet. The word in its simple form gives name to Salia, a little hamlet on the eastern side of Achill Island, from which the inlet called Salia bay takes its name.

Kylesalia, west of Kilkieran bay in Connemara, signifies the wood of the sea-water. There is a small river running into Wexford Haven, at the hamlet of Killinick, five miles south of Wexford town, over which there was anciently a ford, now bridged, just where the tide and river met ; from which it got the name of *Ath-saile*, the ford of the brine, now modernised to Assaly. In the parish of Kilcummin, Galway, south-west of Oughterard, there is a place with the long name, Muckanaghederdauhalia, which is a concise description of both the position of the place, and of its former use :—*Muckanagh*, a place where *mucs* or pigs used to sleep or feed ; *eder*, between ; *dau*, two ; *haile*, the same as *saile*, with the *s* aspirated :—the piggery between two briny inlets.

The diminutive Saleen was applied to any small estuary or creek, and in this sense it is still the name of several places. The word has other meanings, however ; but on the coast there can be no difficulty in determining when it signifies an inlet.

The original term often occurs with the *s* eclipsed by *t*. Just before the train from Dublin reaches the Galway station, it crosses over the narrow neck of an inlet called Lough Atalia, in Irish *Loch-a'-tsaile*, the lake of the brine : there is another brackish lake of the same name in the peninsula north of Omey Island, off the coast of Galway ; and still another—a small pool near Midleton in Cork, just where the Ballynacorra river enters the tideway of the Lee. The same change is seen in Bellataleen, a townland lying adjacent to Murrisk Abbey at the foot of Croagh Patrick in Mayo, *Bel-a'-tsailin*, the ford of the little briny inlet, which obviously took its name from the little salt water strand on the right of the road as you approach the old abbey from Westport.

In Irish writings many references are made to what are called the three *Tonns* or waves of Ireland; and they are much celebrated in ancient tales and romances. These were *Tonn Cleena* in Glandore harbour (for which see 1st Ser., Part II., c. v.); *Tonn Tuaithe* (Tooha) near the mouth of the Bann; and *Tonn Rudhraidhe* [Rury] in Dundrum bay off the county of Down. In stormy weather, when the wind blows in certain directions, the sea at these places, as it tumbles over the sandbanks, or among the caves and fissures of the rocks, utters an unusually loud and solemn roar, which excited the imagination of our ancestors; and they believed that these sounds had a supernatural origin, and foreboded the approaching death of kings or chieftains.

These names have been long since forgotten by the people; but many local denominations still survive, which contain the word *tonn*. Outside the mouth of Lough Foyle, there is a large and dangerous sandbank called the Tuns, on which many vessels have been wrecked:—"Before the mouth of this lough lyeth a great sand called the Touns, upon which it burneth greatly when the wind bloweth from the sea." (Boate's Nat. Hist. of Ireland.) This is the most characteristic application in all Ireland of the word *tonn*, for here the "Tuns" most truly means the waves or billows. This term gives names to places by rivers and lakes as well as by the sea: and in many cases the *t* is changed to *d* by eclipse. There is a lake in the parish of Moyrus in Connemara, called Loughannadown, i. e. *Lochan-na-dtonn*, the little lake of the waves; so called, I suppose, from being very much exposed to the wind, and subject therefore to high waves. Near Knocklong in Limerick, there are four adjoining townlands called Mitchelstowndown of which the proper Irish name is *Baile-Mhistealaigh-na-dtonn* [Ballyvistela-na-down]; the first part signifies the town of Mitchell, and this has been translated, while the last part has been left untouched. The whole name means "the town of Mitchell of the waves." The epithet *na-dtonn*, "of the waves," may belong to the place, as it is situated on the Morning Star river; and in this case the inference would be that it was so called to distinguish it from Mitchelstown in the county Cork, not very far off: but I think this unlikely. Or it may be that the person who left his name on the place was called "Mitchell of the waves," because he was a sailor or a voyager.

On the western shore of Lough Swilly in the parish of Clondavaddog, Donegal, there is a little hamlet called Bunnaton, the *bun* or end of the wave—a name which probably was originally applied to the highest point reached by the surge in the little bay. A varied form of the genitive is seen in Derrintin, the name of a small lake and townland near the Erriff river, four miles above Leenane at the head of the Killeries; *Doire-an-tuinn*, the oak-wood of the wave.

In the last name the word is used in the masculine. But it is more generally feminine, with the genitive *tuinne*, a form which is found in one very interesting name. According to our fabulous histories and romances, Fintan, one of the three men who came to Ireland with the lady Casara, *forty days before the flood*, died just before the beginning of the great catastrophe, and was buried in *Fert-Fintain* (Fintan's grave), otherwise called *Tultuinne* [Tultinna]. But it seems that he only pretended to die, or that he merely fell into a trance; for according to a legend in the *Lebor na hUidhre*, he survived the deluge, and lived for many generations afterwards. He was transformed from time to time into the shapes of various animals, till at length he became a salmon; and finally made his appearance as a man in the reign of Fergus MacKerval, king of Ireland in the sixth century. Most people who undergo transmigration lose all memory of previous states of existence; but it was not so with Fintan; for he remembered clearly every important event that had taken place in Ireland for two thousand years, since the time of the lady Casara; so that he was considered—no wonder he should be—the greatest sage that ever appeared in the country. Before he died for the last time, he gave a long account of the history of Ireland to St. Finnian of Movilla.

The place where he took his long sleep while the deluge was tumbling over his head, is still well known; and the name *Tultuinne* survives, but slightly altered to Tountinna (change of *l* to *n*). Tountinna is a hill near Derrycastle, rising over Lough Derg, two miles north-east of Killaloe, on the top of which was Fintan's grave; and it is well described by the name *Tultuinne:—tul*, a hill—*Tul-tuinne*, the hill of the wave—the hill rising over the wave of Lough Derg.*

There is a townland containing the ruins of a castle, called Townlough, on the verge of the lake, near the base of the hill; and it seems likely that the name has some indirect connexion with that of the hill; for the Irish form is *Tonnlocha*, the wave of the lake, though by a local extension of meaning, the word *tonn* is, in this instance, understood by the people to mean, not exactly a wave, but a watery place or a quagmire.

* See O'Donovan; Four Mast. I. 4, note .

Though there are other Irish words for the sea, none of them enter into names except in a few solitary unimportant cases. But we have many terms for all the various kinds of sea inlets; and the rest of this chapter will be devoted to them and to the names derived from them.

The most general word for a harbour or haven is *cuan*, and it is still employed everywhere round the coast. The old name of Strangford Lough, which was used till very lately, was Lough Cuan, harbour lake; and "Castlehaven," the name of a well known harbour on the south coast of Cork, is a translation of the Irish name, as the Four Masters write it—*Cuan-an-chaislein*. There is a remarkable sea cave a little west of the Giant's Causeway, called Portcoon, which signifies the *port* or landing place of the harbour.

The word *cuan* is also used in an extended sense to signify any curve or winding; and whether in any particular case it is so used, or bears the meaning of harbour, is easily determined. Accordingly the diminutives Cooneen and Coonoge are found inland as well as on shore, in rivers and lakes as well as at the sea; Coonane, another diminutive, is the name of a townland about a mile and a half north of Glengarriff in Cork. There are two townlands, one in Tipperary, and the other in Wicklow, called Coonmore, great winding. The simple word gives name to some places in Wicklow and Kilkenny, now called Coan, and also to a townland in Queen's County, near Clonaslee, called Cones. Tincone and Tincoon are two townlands in Wexford, one occupying the point of land opposite Wexford town at the other side of the river, the other on the shore of the Slaney, opposite King's Island, five miles below Enniscorthy;

both names being anglicised from the Irish *Tigh-an-chuain*, the house of the harbour or winding.

Crompán signifies a little creek, an inlet at the mouth of a small stream, or branching off from a river, lake, or sea. It is very much used in Kilkenny, and is also found in the southern and western counties. Crumpaun is the name of a little river flowing at the base of Nephin mountain in Mayo into Lough Beltra; and of another river near Limerick, joining the Shannon about three miles below the city. There is a townland called Crumpaun in the parish of Rossinver in Leitrim, two miles west of Glenade Lough, which takes its name from a little stream, one of the sources of the Black river, which joins the river Duff; and another in the parish of Kilcatherine in Cork, near the village of Eyeries.

The word *pill* has much the same meaning as *crompán*—a small river inlet; on the Wexford and Waterford coasts, where it is much used, it is applied to a deep cutting or channel made in the sea-mud by a small tidal river as it enters the sea.* It appears evident that it is merely an oblique form of *poll*, a hole :—nominative *poll*, genitive *poill* [pile]. A very apt illustration of the word is Canpill, the name of a little hamlet at a bridge, just at the head (*ceann*) of a small inlet or *pill* branching off from the river Barrow near Dunbrody abbey in Wexford.

The ancient and present Irish name of Pilltown in the south of Kilkenny, is *Baile-an-phoill* [Ballinfile], the town of the *poll*, or *pill;* and it appears to

* On this, and on several other local matters, I have got much information from George Henry Kinahan, Esq., M. R. I. A., F. R. G. S. I., who turns his journeys through various parts of Ireland to good account in obtaining a knowledge of the legends and antiquities of the country.

have taken its name from the Pill river which joins the Suir after flowing through the village. There is also a Pilltown two miles from Drogheda on the road to Laytown; and another in the parish of Kinsalebeg in Waterford, about three miles from Ardmore. Rosspile in the parish of Ballylannan in Wexford, near the head of Bannow bay, is the *ross* or wood of the inlet. Pill Lane near Church-street in Dublin, took its name from a little *pill* that branched off from the Liffey in former days, long before the river was confined by quay walls.

I have already remarked (1st Ser., Part IV., c. II.), that the word *cuas* (properly a cave) is applied along the coast of Cork and Kerry to a little cove; and that it usually takes the form of coos. It is also sometimes made *cus*, as in Cuskenny, a place about a mile below Queenstown; the name was originally applied to the adjacent little semicircular inlet, and it signifies Kenny's cove.

In the south of Ireland, the word *goilín* [goleen] is used to signify a small sea or river inlet. In the parish of Kilmore, near Mizen head in Cork, there is a little creek, which gives name to the townland of Goleen. Burnham near Dingle, the seat of Lord Ventry, is called in Irish to this day, Goleen, a name which was originally applied to the little creek into which a tiny stream flows at the western end of Dingle Harbour. There is an old castle ruin on the shore of the creek which still retains the name of Ballingoleen, the townland of the inlet. One part of the modern name was probably intended to be a translation of *goilín*—Burnham, the home of the burn or stream—formed exactly like Rockingham (see this in 1st Ser.) But it is to be remarked that the name may be an importation—a mere imitation of the English Burnham.

In the west, especially in Galway, *caisle* [cashla] is used to signify a sea inlet; of which the best known example is Cashla bay, west of Galway, which is also the name of the river flowing into it. Though this is the sense in which the word is now understood, I am inclined to think that it was originally applied to a river; and the Irish name of Cashla bay to some extent favours this opinion, viz., *Cuan Caisle*, the bay of Cashla, which looks as if the bay got its name from the river. There is a very little lake one mile east of Clifden, an enlargement of a small stream, flowing from Lough Nabrackkeagh into the Owenglin river; and the name of this lake is also a sort of confirmation of the same opinion—Lough Cashleen (diminutive of Cashla), the lake of the little Cashla. Here Cashleen must mean a stream, for both lake and stream are inland, and there is no inlet of any kind. The same observation applies to the townland of Cashleen in the parish of Ballynakill in Galway near Rinvyle Point, which evidently takes its name from the little stream on whose banks it is situated, flowing into the sea just near the Point.

It may be added that the root of the word is obviously the Irish *cas*, twisted or crooked; so that its application to a river would be generally very appropriate. In Donegal the word *caslach*, another derivative from *cas* (postfix *lach*, p. 5), is understood to mean a creek; and it appears in this sense in Kincaslough, a townland on the mainland opposite Cruit island, which gives name to a lake, and which was itself so called from its situation at the head (*ceann*) of the little inlet called "Cruit Strand."

Bléan means the groin; but in a secondary sense it is applied to a creek, branching off either from the sea or from a lake, or formed by the mouth of a river; sometimes it means any hollow or curved place. It is much used in local names, and it is found all over Ireland, especially in the northern half. Blean and Blane are the names of some places in Wicklow, Clare, Galway, and Tipperary. Blaney, the plural form of *blean*, is the name of a little bay on the southern side of lower Lough Erne, near Derrygonnelly, so called because it is formed of several smaller bays:—Blaney, literally creeks. At the extreme western end of the same lake, there is an inlet called Bleanalung, the creek of the boat. In upper Lough Erne there is an island called Bleanish, properly Bleaninish, creek island, so called from the little inlet between it and Crom Castle on the mainland; Bunnablaneybane in the parish of Clones, Fermanagh, the end (*bun*) of the white blean or curve; and Killyblane in the parish of Killesher, same county, the wood (*coill*) of the curved spot. Blainroe, red creek or curve, in the parish of Kilpool, a little south of Wicklow town.

In Galway we have Bleanoran, Odhran's or Oran's creek or curve; and Bleannagloos, a singular name, signifying the creek or curve of the ears (*cluas*), so called no doubt from some peculiarity of shape: in the parish of Annaduff in Leitrim, Bleankillew, the *blean* of the wood; which takes its name from being on the shore of that arm of Lough Bofin which is now called Lough Scannel.

I have already stated (page 241) that *gaeth* is sometimes applied to the sea; it is used in this sense, and in the old form *gaot*, in Cormac's Glossary, under *bircli*. This term occurs on the northern half of the western coast, and it is there restricted in its application to "a shallow stream into which the tide flows, and which is fordable at low water (O'Donovan, Appendix to O'Reilly's Dict., under *gaeth*). There is a townland called Gweesalia in the parish of Kilcommon in Erris, Mayo, which takes its name from its position on the shore of a tidal creek branching off from Blacksod bay; the name being *Gaeth-saile*, i. e. salt-water tide-inlet. The best known names exhibiting this word are Gweedore and Gweebarra, applied to two bays on the west coast of Donegal, into which flow two tidal streams of the same names. In A. D. 619, according to the Four Masters, Dóir, the son of Hugh Allan, king of Ireland, was slain by a chieftain named Flann Fiadhbhadh [Feeva]; but Flann himself was soon afterwards killed in revenge for this deed by the friends of Dóir, on the little island of Inishkeel in Gweebarra bay. O'Donovan (Four M. I. 242, note *t*) believes that the river and bay of Gweedore took its name from this prince:—*Gaeth-Dóir*, Doir's inlet. I think we may conclude that Gweebarra also derived its name from a man; but I do not know of any authority, written or otherwise, bearing on the point.

CHAPTER XVII.

COLOURS.

AMONG the various circumstances that determine the names of places, colour holds in all countries a prominent position; and accordingly we find the words denoting the different colours widely spread among the local names of our own country. The colours that attracted the observation of the people who imposed the names, whether applied to the surface of the land, to rocks, rivers, or lakes, are characteristic of most of these places and objects at the present day; but on the other hand, there are many instances in which all traces of the original colour have disappeared; and this is especially the case where the prevailing hue was given by trees, shrubs, bogs, or marshes, which have been removed by cultivation.

As colours are infinitely varied, and run one into another by imperceptible gradations, it is not to be expected that the colours and shades which one nation or people designates by distinct names, will be in all cases the same as those distinguished by corresponding names among other nations. And indeed in the same language, the words for colours vary greatly in their signification; the English words *green* and *grey* for instance, are applied to shades very different among themselves. So in regard to some of the Irish names for colours, it is not always easy to determine the exact hues or shades intended, or to give the precise equivalents of the terms in English.

Black. Dubh [duv], black, blackish, very dark coloured. This word is found in vast numbers of names throughout all Ireland; a fact which results in a great measure from the prevalence of bogs and boggy lands. Its most usual English forms are *duff*, *doo*, and *du*, the first of which is seen in Duffcarrick and in Carrickduff, both of which mean black rock. The little river Duff flows on the boundary of the counties of Sligo and Leitrim, and falls into Donegal bay four miles west of Bundoran. It is called *Dubh* in the annals, which in the Book of Armagh, is translated *Niger*, i. e. black. At its mouth is the townland of Bunduff, the *bun* or mouth of the river Duff. There are two townlands in Galway called Ballinduff, a name which is preserved in its correct form by the Four Masters :—*Baile-an-duibh*, the town of the black or dark-complexioned man.

Many of our lakes whose waters look inky black, partly from the infusion of bog, partly on account of the reflection of the dark sides of the surrounding hills, get the names of Loughduff, Loughdoo, and Doolough, all meaning black lake; which again gives names to several townlands, villages, and residences.

The prevalence of bogs also accounts for the great number of Irish rivers having names which signify black or dark. Douglas has already been mentioned. The diminutive Duog or Duvog—black streamlet—is the name of many small streams, corresponding in formation with Brenoge and Glanog (which see). And besides these there are the several rivers now called Blackwater.

Sometimes whole districts were designated by this word *dubh*, if their surfaces were boggy or clothed in a dark covering of heather. There is a well-known district in the barony of Scarawalsh in Wexford, now called the Duffry; but the correct Irish name, as we find it in our old authorities, is *Duibhthir* [Duffir], which signifies black territory (*tir*, land or country). The name is very correctly anglicised *Duffyr* in Clyn's annals; but the present form Duffry seems to be derived from the genitive, *Duibh-thire*, which it correctly represents in sound (1st Ser., Part I., c. II.)

The *Dinnseanchas* records a legend,* that this territory was once open and fertile—"a broad, delightful region;" and it was possessed by two brothers, Guaire and Daire. But Guaire treacherously slew his brother and seized upon his part of the territory; after which a curse fell upon the land as a punishment for the crime, and the whole district became overgrown with brushwood and heath; whence it was called *Duibh-thir*. One inference we may draw from this legend, that at the time when it was written, the land was covered with heather and scrubwood, from which, and not from bogs, it got its name. The "Faes of Athlone," a woody district in the county Roscommon, was also called *Duibhthir* (Four Masters), for the very same reason. And the word exists in the name of Drumdiffer in the parish of Drumreilly in Leitrim, the *drum* or ridge of the black district.

Dooally and Doocatteens are the names of two townlands near Newcastle in Limerick, which are the anglicised forms of *Dubh-aille*, black cliff, and *Dubh-choitchinidhe*, black *cotteens* or commonages. Dooros and Doorus signify black wood in the south, and black promontory in the north. Four miles above Listowel in Kerry, the river Feale divides and encloses an island; on one of the branches there was in old times a ford, which was called *Dubh-ath*, black ford; the old church built near it took the same name, and in its turn gave name to the village and parish, which are now called Duagh.

The word is softened down in various ways, which will be illustrated in the following names. Dinish is the name of a little island well known to Killarney tourists, situated near the Old Weir Bridge; and

* Translated by Bryan O'Looney, Esq., M. R. I. A., in Proc. R. I. A., MS. Ser., p. 184.

there are several islands in other counties called Dinis, Dinish, and Deenish; all which are shortened from *Duibh-inis*, black island. Deelis and Deelish, which are names of common occurrence, have been similarly reduced from *Duibh-lios*, black fort; which is also the Irish form of Dufless in Tyrone, of Doolis in Tipperary, and of Devleash in Mayo. It occurs as a compound in Cordevlis, the name of some places in Cavan and Monaghan, the round hill of the black fort.

The well-known mountain, Divis, near Belfast, is called in Irish *Dubh-ais*, which simply means black hill; and this old name seems to find an echo in English, for there are two other hills very near it, now called Black Hill and Black Mountain. There is another place of the same name in Mayo, slightly altered to Divish; while in Donegal it takes the form of Dooish. Diviny and Divanagh, which are the names of some townlands in Tyrone, Armagh, and Fermanagh, are anglicised forms of *Duibh-eanaigh*, black marshes. At A. D. 1146, the Annals of Innisfallen record the erection of *Caislen-Easa-duibhe* (the castle of the black cataract: pron. Cashlen-Asdee). The latter part of this long designation is still retained as the name of a little hamlet three miles west of Ballylongford in Kerry, now called Astee. The boggy little river, in time of flood, rushes over ledges of rock near the village, and this is the feature that gave it the name of the black cataract. The form *dee* is also exhibited in Clashnamonadee near Lismore in Waterford — *Clais-na-mona-duibhe*, the trench of the black bog.

At the bottom of some deep bogs there is found a half liquid stuff, as black as jet, which was formerly used by the peasantry all over Ireland for dyeing black; and is still so used in remote districts. It served its purpose admirably well, giving frieze and other woollens an excellent dye, and it was usually known by the name of *dubhadh* [dooa], which answers to the English word *blacking* (old form *dubad;* Cor. Gl.). Many of the places where this dye stuff was found are still indicated by their names; such as Carrickadooey in the parish of Maghcross in Monaghan, *Carraig-a'-dubhaidh*, the rock of the black dye-stuff: Pollandoo in Donegal, Polladooey in Galway and Longford, and Polladoohy near Crossmolina in Mayo, all take their names from the deep hole (poll) out of which the colouring matter was taken; Derrynadooey in Roscommon, and Eskeradooey in Tyrone, the oak wood and the sand-ridge of the black dye stuff.

Ciar [keer] is commonly understood to mean jet black. The ordinary name among the peasantry for a beetle or chafer is *ciaróg* [keeroge], a diminutive of *ciar*, meaning black little fellow; the other diminutive, *Ciaran*, was formerly extremely common as a man's name, meaning a dark complexioned person; and it still exists in the family name Kieran. The word is also used to signify a dull or brownish black; and this is, I suppose, the sense in which we are to understand it in local names. There is a small river called Keerglen in the parish of Kilfian in Mayo, giving name to a townland, and taking its own name from the glen through which it flows:—*Ciar-gleann*, dark coloured glen.

White. *Finn* or *fionn*, white, is a word of most ancient and extensive use in the Celtic languages. It glosses *albus* in the St. Gall manuscript of Zeuss; and still more ancient is its use in forming part of personal names, both Irish and Gaulish. *Vindus*, the termination of many Gaulish names, is another form of this word; and *Finn* has been used as a personal name in our own country, from the time of the great hero, Finn the son of Cumhal—and long before him indeed—down to our own day.

In local nomenclature the word is used to designate places either absolutely white, or whitish, fair or bright coloured; as for instance the side of a hill covered with whitish grass; and its usual anglicised forms are *finn* or *fin*. The Four Masters record a fight between the O'Neills and the O'Boyles in A. D. 1502, at a place in Donegal, which they call *Tulach-finn*, the white little hill; it is situated near Inver, and is still known by the name of Tullaghfin. Finvoy, the name of a parish in Antrim, and of a townland in Louth, is the modern way of writing the old name, as we find it in the annals—*Finnmhagh*, white or bright plain; which again takes the form Finaway near Crosserlough in Cavan. Carrickfin in Donegal and Westmeath, signifies white rock.

In the south of Ireland *finn* is commonly pronounced *feoun* or *fune*, which originates the anglicised forms *foun* and *fune*, occasionally met with. Thus Knockfune in Tipperary is the same as Knockfin in other counties; and the Four Masters give the correct form of both, *Cnoc-Fionn*, white hill. So also Coolfune is the same as Coolfin, white corner. Inchafune near Dunmanway in Cork, white *inch* or river meadow. In the King's County this word is sometimes pronounced *fan*, which is reflected in the name of Fancroft near Roscrea, a name which is greatly corrupted. In the Red Book of Ossory it is written in one place Fynchor, and in another place Fyncora; from which it is obvious that the original name is *Finn-choradh*, white weir.

Although *finn* strictly means a colour, it is used to designate water that is clear or transparent. In this way is formed the name Finglas from *glais*, a little stream:—*Finn-glais* (so written in many old authorities), crystal rivulet. The village of Finglas near Dublin takes its name from the little stream which flows through it, and joins the Tolka at Finglas Bridge; there are several streams of the same name in different parts of Ireland; and it is also modified to Finglush, Finglash, and Finglasha. Compounded with *ros*, a wood, it gives name to the village of Rosenallis in Queen's County, a name which is very much corrupted from the original. There was an ancient church here, dedicated to St. Brigid; and Colgan in enumerating it among the churches of this saint, gives the true form of the name, *Rosfinglas*, which signifies the wood of the bright stream. I may here observe that this name, Finglas, is the counterpart of another name still better known, Douglas, dark stream—which has been noticed in First Series.

Many other examples might be given of the application of this word to water, but I will mention only one more, namely, the sparkling little river Finnihy at Kenmare, which deserves its name as well as any stream in Ireland. The termination in this name is of frequent occurrence in the Munster counties, especially in Cork and Kerry; and it appears to be the same as the participial termination in verbs:—*Finnithe*, corresponding exactly with *clártha* from *clár* (*Lebor na h-Uidhre*: O'Curry Lect., II., 315); and with *odhartha* in *Cluain-odhartha*, now Clonoura in the parish of Fennor in Tipperary, pale-grey meadow, and in *Cnoc-odhartha*, pale-grey hill, now Knockoura in Cork and Galway, both from *odhar* (p. 278 : see Phœnix Park in 1st Ser.).

The compound *Finnabhair*, old form *Findabair*, was formerly common as the name of a person, generally of a woman, but sometimes of a man; and it was also used as a place-name. As the name of a place, some of the old Irish-Latin writers have translated it *campus-albus*, white-coloured field (Jocelin, Vit. Patr. c. 94); but I suppose that this is intended to express the fact that *Finnabhair* meant a whitish place, for I do not think that *abhair* can be in any case, the equivalent of *campus*. O'Curry (Lect., III., 10), translates *Finnabhair* as a personal name by "fair-browed," which would also answer very well in its application to a place—a whitish coloured brow of a field—a hill-brow. But it may be doubted whether *abair* here can mean a brow; for as Mr. Crowe remarks (Proc. R. I. A., MS. Ser. 159), the genitive of *abair* a brow, is *abrat* (thus *Eochaidh Abrat-ruaidh*, Eochaidh of the red brow—a king of Leinster); while the genitive of *Find-abair*, as a personal or local name is *Find-abrach*. It appears in fact that there are two different words, both spelled *abair* in the nominative :—*abair*, gen. *abrat*, a brow or eye-lash; *abair*, gen. *abrach* (meaning?); and that it is the latter word that appears in *Findabair*. Mr. Crowe, in the same place, translates *Find-abair* "bright-beam," comparing *abair* with Lat. *apricum;* but I do not know on what authority he bases this interpretation.

Whatever may be the exact meaning of *abair* here, we may take it that *Finnabhair* was locally applied to a whitish spot. It has several modern forms, in most of which the *b* is altogether suppressed, on account of aspiration. The most usual is Fennor, which is the name of nine townlands in the Leinster and Munster counties. Fennor on the Boyne in Meath—a place of great antiquity—is called by the annalists, *Finnabhair-abha*, i. e., Fennor of the river (Boyne), to distinguish it from other Fennors; and *Finnabhair* or Fennor in Westmeath is mentioned by the Four Masters as the scene of two battles in the years 794 and 822. This term takes several other anglicised forms; in Donegal and Fermanagh it is made Finner; in Roscommon and Clare, Finnor; Finver is found once in Donegal; while in Galway and Sligo it becomes Finnure.

The genitive, *fionnabhrach* [finnoura] appears in the name of Kilfenora in Clare, an ancient bishop's see, called by the annalists *Cill-Fionnabhrach;* and the same form occurs in Knockfenora near Bruree in Limerick. It is probable that the second part of each of these is the name of a person—man or woman:—the church and the hill of *Finnabair*. With the *f* eclipsed in the genitive plural, we find it in Ballynavenooragh near Brandon Hill in Kerry, which very correctly represents the sound of the Irish *Baile-na-bhfionnabhrach*, the town of the white coloured spots, or of the persons named *Finnabair*.

The word *ceinnfhionn* [cannon] which literally means white head (*ceann*, head), is now applied to a cow with a white spot on the middle of her forehead. The term is used by the Four Masters at A. M. 3972, when they record the legend that during the reign of king *Fiacha Finailches*, all the cows were *ceindfhiond*, white headed. The meaning of this compound is sometimes extended however, so that it is used to designate anything speckled with white spots. In this sense it is used to give name to Foilcannon, a great cliff with a smooth face of rock, under the Eagle's Nest near Glengarriff: i. e.

speckled cliff. So also Clooncannon in Galway, speckled meadow; Carrigcannon in Cork and Kerry, speckled rock; Drumcannon and Drumcanon in the northern counties, speckled ridge; Lettercannon in Kerry, speckled hill-side. Some of the preceding may have taken their names from a legendary cow (like Loughnaheery, p. 280); and this is certainly the case with Foilnacanony in the parish of Upperchurch in Tipperary, and with Glennacannon near Baltinglass in Wicklow, the cliff, and the glen, of the white-headed cow.

Bán signifies white or whitish. There is a beautiful lake in Westmeath, near the village of Fore, called Loughbane or Loughbawn, white lake; and another of the same name in Monaghan, three miles north of the village of Shercock: connected with the former is the small Lough Glass (green lake); and with the latter, Black Lake; each pair receiving their names from some real or fancied contrast of colour. Carrickbaun and Carrigbaun, white rock, are the names of places in Cork and Leitrim; Clashbane near Caherconlish in Limerick, white trench.

The promontory of Kenbane near Ballycastle in Antrim, with its castle ruins, is a characteristic example of the application of this word; the cliff is composed of white limestone, and the name, *Ceann-bán*, white head, exactly describes its appearance. Sometimes the people give the name of *gearrán-bán*, white *garron* or horse, to conspicuous white rocks, in which they fancy they can trace some resemblance to the shape of a horse. There is a hill about a mile from the village of Clarinbridge in Galway, which the Four Masters call *Cnoc-an-ghearráin-bháin*, the hill of the white horse, and which is now called Knockagarranbaun.

In very many cases the *b* of this word becomes *v* or *w* by aspiration. There is a river in Cork, called the Owvane, white river, flowing through a fine valley into the head of Bantry bay, so called, I suppose, to distinguish it from some other river whose waters are very dark from bog; and there are several other rivers of the same name in other parts of Ireland. Many little bays round the sea coast and round the shores of the larger lakes, are called Trawane, Trabane, and Trawbawn, white strand, which derive their names from the whitish colour of the sand.

Geal [gal] means white, fair-coloured, or bright. There is a place near the city of Limerick called Galvone, white bog (*Geal-mhóin*), which probably received its name either from the white sedge grass, commonly called *finane*, or from the *canavaun* or bog-down. Loughgal, white lake, is a little lake three miles south of Elphin in Roscommon; Galcussagh, literally white-footed, is the name of a townland in the parish of Desertcreat in Tyrone; and it was, I suppose, applied to low lying land covered with white flowers, or whitish grass.

Gile [gilla] is an abstract noun derived from *geal*, and signifies brightness or whiteness; it is often heard in the colloquial language, as in the common epithet of endearment, *Gillamachree*, brightness of my heart; and it is found quite as often as *geal* in local names. Lough Gill in Sligo, is always called in the annals, *Loch-gile*, the lake of brightness, or bright lake; and there is a small lake in the parish of Aghagower in Mayo, called Loughannagilla, the little lake of the brightness. This word also appears in Legilly in the parish of Clonfeacle in Tyrone, the bright *lug* or hollow.

Red. *Dearg* signifies a deep scarlet, or very decided red (*derc, rubes ;* Z. 61) ; and in the formation of names it usually takes the forms *derg*, *derrig*, and *darrig*. There are several fords and bridges all over the country called Belderg, Bellahaderg, Ballaghaderg, and Bellanaderg, all meaning red ford (*bel* and *bel-atha*, a ford : 1st Ser., Part III. c. v.), which were so called from the colour of the water, which again took its colour from the soil or mud. There is a parish in Tipperary, half-way between Caher and Clonmel, now called Derrygrath, near where Lewy Mac Con was killed (see Gortanore, in Chapter XX.) ; it took its name from a conspicuous fort, still in existence, which is called in Irish *Dearg-rath*, red rath. The same name is found in Roscommon in the more correct form Dergraw ; and there is a townland in Queen's County called Ratherrig, whose Irish name is *Rath-dhearg*, same meaning. In this last the *d* drops out by aspiration, as it does in Lickerrig near Athenry in Galway, whose Irish name, *Lic-dhearg*, red surface-flag, most truly describes the place.

Ruadh [roo], red, reddish, or fox-coloured, is equivalent to, and cognate with, the Latin *ruber*, and English *red* and *ruddy*. This word is very extensively used in the formation of Irish local names ; and though it is variously modified, its most usual anglicised form is *roe*.

There are two places in Donegal—one near the village of Convoy and the other near Kilmacrenan —called Cloghroe, red stone or stone castle ; and there is another place of the same name two miles from Ballincollig in Cork. The Owenroe or red river, a tributary of the Blackwater, flows through the village of Moynalty in Meath. Moyroe near Dungannon in Tyrone, is *Magh-ruadh*, reddish plain; which is also the Irish form of Moroe, the name of a little village in the parish of Abington in Limerick. At the little hamlet of Roevehagh in the parish of Killeely, near Clarinbridge in Galway, grew the inauguration tree of the *Hy-Fiachrach Aidhne* (see 1st Ser., Part IV., c. VIII.), from which the hamlet took its name. At A. D. 1143, according to the Four Masters, Turlough O'Brien led a hostile expedition into Connaught, and cut down this tree, which the old authority calls *Ruadh-bheitheach*, i. e. the red birch, the pronunciation of which is well represented by Roevehagh. The word takes another form in Mulroy, the name of a long bay in the north of Donegal, which must have been so called from a hill, the Irish name being *Maol-ruadh*, red bald-hill.

By means of various postfixes, several derivatives are formed from this word, which are, or were, all applied to reddish-coloured spots. With the diminutive *án*, we have Ruan in Limerick and Clare; Ruanes in Cork; Ruaunmore in Wexford (great red place); Rowan and Rowans in Armagh, Meath, and Dublin; and Rooaun in several counties. With *cán* or *chán*, Roughan and Rooghaun, the names of several townlands; with *lach* (p. 5) Roolagh in Tipperary, Rolagh in Meath, and Rowlagh in Dublin; and with *tach* (p. 8) we have Rootiagh and Routagh in Limerick, and Rootagh in Tipperary.

Yellow. *Buidhe* [bwee or boy] yellow, is evidently cognate with Latin *badius*, Fr. *bai*, Eng. *bay* (colour). The usual form in anglicised names is *boy*, though it is sometimes made *by*, *ree*, *way*, *wee*, &c., the last three by the aspiration of the *b*.

This term, like *dearg*, was often applied to fords, from the colour of the water, caused by yellow mud. The village of Athboy in Meath got its name from a ford on the river which flows through it; it is very frequently mentioned in the annals by the name of *Ath-buidhe-Tlachtga*, the yellow ford of *Tlachtga*, from the celebrated hill of *Tlachtga*, now called the Hill of Ward, in its neighbourhood. The name *Ath-buidhe* often compounds with *bél*, ford-mouth, forming *Bél-an-atha-buidhe*, the mouth of the yellow ford, which was the name of a ford on the river Callan, a little north of Armagh, where O'Neill defeated Bagenal's army in 1598. The anglicised form of this—Bellanaboy—is the name of some places in Leitrim, Mayo, Sligo, and Donegal; and it is corrupted to Ballinaboy in Cork, Galway, and Roscommon.

There are two places in Donegal called Straboy, one of which (near Glenties) is mentioned by the Four Masters, who call it *Srath-buidhe*, the yellow *srath* or river holm. Other modern forms of this word are seen in Ballybinaby near Roche Castle, four miles from Dundalk, the town of the yellow *bin* or peak; Drumbanaway in Tyrone, the ridge of the yellow peak; and Benwee itself—yellow peak—is the name of some hills in Mayo and elsewhere. Fallowvee near Cushendall in Antrim, yellow hedge or enclosure (see p. 211). The little stream Owenwee—yellow river—flows under the base of Slieve League in Donegal; and there are other streams called Owenboy giving names to townlands in Donegal and Mayo.

Brown. *Donn* is brown, dark brown; much the same in meaning as the English word *dun: donn*, fuscus, Z. 225. When the word occurs in names, which is not often, it is generally anglicised *down;* as in Barnadown, the name of some places in Kilkenny and Wexford, signifying brown gap.

Crón [crone] signifies brown, dark-brown, or swarthy; and in this sense it is still a living word. Ardcrone, brown height, is the name of a place in the parish of Currans in Kerry; Curkacrone near Callan in Kilkenny, brown oats (*coirce*) or oats-land; Cronkill in Armagh and Tipperary, and Crunkill in Roscommon, brown wood; Cruninish, brown island, the name of an islet in lower Lough Erne. There is a large lake called Lough Croan, dark brown lake, in Roscommon, four miles from Mount Talbot. The syllable *crón* has other meanings however, which it is sometimes hard to distinguish from the present in anglicised names.

Green. Glas is commonly translated green; and this is its usual acceptation, for we find it often applied to express the green of grass and foliage. But the word was also used to designate a greyish or bluish green, or rather a greyish blue, a shade of colour having in it little or none of what we should call green. For instance *glas* was often applied to a greyish blue eye; and also to the colour of the water-wagtail. In its topographical application however, it must be generally understood to mean grass-green.

The Four Masters record the erection of a fort called *Rath-Lochaid*, in the reign of *Irial Faidh*, one of the pre-Christian kings, at a place called *Glas-charn*, green carn or monument, which O'Donovan identifies with Glascarn near Mullingar; and there is another Glascarn near Ratoath in Meath. Glascarrig, green rock, is the name of a place on the coast of Wexford, remarkable for its abbey ruins. In

1493 a bloody battle was fought between two clans of the O'Neills at a place in the parish of Aghanloo in Tyrone, which the annalists call *Glas-dromainn*, green ridge, but which is now called Glasdrummond; this is also the name of other townlands in Armagh and Monaghan; and there are more than twenty in the northern and western counties called more correctly Glasdrumman. Glaslough, a small town in Monaghan, takes its name, which means green lake, from the small lake near the town; Glassillan, green island, is the name of several small islands off the coasts, and in the lakes of Mayo and Galway.

The word assumes other forms, chiefly by grammatical inflection, as may be seen in the following names. There is a place in the parish of Donaghmoyne in Monaghan, called Corcullionglish, which is anglicised from *Cor-cuillinn-glais*, the round hill of the green holly; Kilmaglush in Carlow, and Kilmaglish in Westmeath, both signify the church of the green *magh* or plain.

Blue. *Gorm* signifies blue. It is often applied to mountains, and of course in this case designates their blue colour when seen from a distance. There is a range of hills north of Donegal town, called Croaghgorm, which has also the correct *alias* name of Bluestack. Bengorm, blue peak, is a high mountain rising over the Killeries in Connemara; there is another fine mountain of the same name over Lough Feeagh, north-west of Newport in Mayo, and we have Bingorms near Slievesnaght in the parish of Gartan in Donegal—*Beanna-gorma*, blue peaks: Slievegorm, blue mountain, in the parish of Killererin in Galway.

The word *gorm* was also used to designate the colours of various natural objects, such as the soil, rocks, water, &c.; and it was applied to several shades of blue. Poulgorm, blue pool, is the name of some small lakes in Clare, Cork, and other counties; there is a little island in Lough Melvin in Fermanagh, called Gorminish, blue island; Gormagh bridge crosses the silver river, two miles north of Tullamore in King's County—*Gorm-achadh*, blue field; and there is a place called Gormlee in the parish of Dunbulloge, north of Cork city—*Gormliath*, bluish grey, a name derived from the colour of the soil.

Grey. *Riabhach* signifies greyish, brindled, swarthy, or tan-coloured—for I find it translated by all these terms: some Latin writers render it *fuscus*. The shades of colour designated by this word must have been usual in the surface of the land, for it is very general in local names; and it is commonly anglicised in the forms of *reagh*, *rea*, and *revagh*.

The Four Masters, at A. D. 1476, mention a castle called *Rath-riabhach*, grey rath, in Longford, which is now called Rathreagh, and gives name to a church and parish, where the ruins of both castle and church still remain. In Mayo there is another parish of the same name; and this is also the name of some townlands in Kilkenny and Limerick. There is a townland near Downpatrick called Ringreagh, i. e. *Rinn-riabhach*, grey point.

The simple anglicised form, Reagh, locally understood to mean grey lands, is the name of some places in Cork, Roscommon, and Down; it is softened to Ree in the parish of Agivey in Derry; while several other places in Galway and Tyrone are designated by the diminutive Reaghan, a name which signifies a small grey spot of land; and there are numerous hills in the south of Ireland, called Slievereagh, grey mountain.

In the west and north-west, the *bh* of *riabhach* generally gets its full *v* sound; and in this case, the word is usually represented by *revagh*:—Gortrevagh in Galway, grey field, is the same as Gortreagh in Tyrone and in some of the Munster counties; the same word appears in Derrygortrevy in Tyrone, the oak-wood of the grey field; Carrickreagh, grey rock, in Fermanagh, takes the form of Carrickrevagh in Leitrim. This term designates a man in Attithomasrevagh near Salthill, a suburb of Galway, which means the site of swarthy Thomas's house (*ait*, site; *teach*, house: see 1st Ser., Part III., c. I.).

Liath [leea] answers exactly to the English word grey: and in anglicised names it generally assumes the forms of *lea* and *leagh*. Leagh itself, in the sense of grey land, gives name to a number of townlands in various counties; and the word takes the form of Léa as the name of a parish in Queen's County, and of several places in other counties. The plural *Liatha*, grey spots, is represented by Leaha in Galway and Kerry, Leaghs in Tyrone, and Leahys in Limerick. As a diminutive we find it in Leaghan in Fermanagh and Tyrone, Leighin in Cavan, Leaheen in Clare, Leighan in Fermanagh, Leighon, the name of a little island near Lettermore island in Connemara—all which were originally applied to grey spots of land.

There is a village in Fermanagh, situated on the Finn, called Rosslea, whose name was obviously derived from the piece of land half enclosed by a bend of the river:—*Ros-liath*, grey peninsula. Carriglea, Carrigleagh, Carrigleigh, and Carrickleagh, are the names of townlands in Waterford, Cork, and Louth, all signifying grey rock; and there are several places in Leitrim, Monaghan, and Roscommon, called Creevelea, grey branch or branchy tree. In the parish of Two-mile-Borris, east of Thurles in Tipperary, there is a very ancient church, which is called in the annals *Liath-Mór* (great grey spot), and also *Liath-Mochaemhog*, *Mochaemhog's* grey land; and it still retains this latter name in the anglicised form of Leamokevoge, which transmits the sound truly enough. St. *Mochaemhog*, who founded this church, was the son of the sister of the celebrated St. Ita of Killeedy in Limerick (see 1st Ser., Part II., c. III.); he is sometimes called *Pulcherius*, which is merely a translation of his Irish name; for *Mochaemhog* signifies "my beautiful youth." He was a very eminent man, and died in A. D. 655. There is another church, founded by, or dedicated to, this saint, in the south of the county Kilkenny, called *Cill Mochaemhog*, and now Kilmakevoge, which gives name to a parish; but the people are beginning to call it Killivory from a notion that *caemhóg* means *ivory* (see O'Donovan in Four Masters, I., 266, note b).

Pale Grey. The word *odhar* [oar, our] signifies a dun colour, a pale-grey, or light brown. It is found in our oldest writings (*odar;* Cor. Gl.), and it continues in use as a living word. It usually occurs in names in the anglicised forms of *ore*, *ower*, or *our;* as in Ardore in Fermanagh, and Ardour in Galway, grey height; Corrower in Mayo, pale-grey hill; Moanour, the name of a hill near Galbally in Limerick, grey bog. There are two townlands in Galway called Ower, which is nothing but the simple word, and signifies dun coloured land; and Ouragh near Tullow in Carlow is an adjective form with the same meaning. The *d* becomes restored (see 1st Ser., Part I., c. II.) in the name of Odder near Tara in Meath, which is called in the annals, *Odhra*, the plural of *odhar*, signifying pale-grey spots of land.

The word *odhar* was sometimes used to designate streams, to express probably the brown colour of water that flowed through bogs. In our most ancient authority, the account of the cattle spoil of Cooley in the *Lebor na h-Uidhre*, a river is mentioned called Odras, which is an abstract noun:—*odar*, pale-grey; *odras*, pale-greyness (see p. 12 for the termination *s*). This river is stated to be at Slieve Baune in the east of the county Roscommon; and as the name would be pronounced *Oris*, the Odras is probably the same as the river now called the Feorish, which flows from the slopes of Slieve Baune, and joins the Shannon opposite Cloondara in Longford; *f* being prefixed to the name as is done so often in other cases (1st Ser., Part I., c. II.).

We have another example of this application in the name of the river Nier in Waterford, which rises from a group of lakes in the Comeragh mountains, and flows into the Suir below Clonmel. The *n* is merely the article, attracted to the name in the manner already explained (N'ier, the grey [river]: 1st Ser., Part I., c. II.); and the people carefully separate them when speaking Irish, and give each its proper declension. It appears clear that this name is an oblique form of *odhar* (which they pronounce, nom. *our*, gen. *iera*, dat. *ier*); for as I have shown (1st Ser., Part I., c. II.), the custom of using oblique forms as nominatives has grown into a sort of law in the Irish as well as in other European languages; and hence we call *Ara*, Aran; *Teamhuir*, Tara, &c. That this is the true interpretation of the name is further shown by the fact that Camalough or Cumalough, one of the group of small lakes from which the Nier flows, is sometimes called Cumalough *odhar*, grey lake, by the natives ("*Cumaloch odhar a's Com-na-gcapall;*" old song).*

The fine valley through which the river flows is called *Gleann-na-h-Uidhre* [Glanahiery], the glen of the *Odhar* or Nier; which has given name to the barony of Glenahiry. And this is a further proof of the correctness of the preceding etymology; for *na-huidhre* is exactly the genitive of *an-odhar*. There is a Glannaheera in the parish of Ballinvoher, east of Dingle in Kerry, which the people correctly interpret, the glen of the brown stream.

The word *odhar*, with the same oblique pronunciation, but without the attracted article, gives name to the little stream, now called the Ire, which flows eastwards from the well-known mountain lake of Coumshingaun (two miles from the source of the Nier), and joins the Clodiagh river.

This word *odhar* is often applied to a cow; and several places have derived their names from legendary cows with this designation. Names of this kind may be known by their terminations; for they almost always end in *naheery*, *naheera*, or *nahoora*; as in Kilnaheery near Clogher in Tyrone, and Kilnahera near Dromdaleague in Cork, *Coill-na-huidhre*, the wood of the dun cow. Under the eastern face of Slieve Beagh on the boundary of Tyrone and Monaghan, there is a small lake called Loughnaheery, with the mountain of Essnaheery rising over it, which took its name from an *ess* or waterfall; and the hill of Monahoora lies on the north side of Slieve

* Here I am drawing on information supplied by Mr. John Fleming of Rathgormuck, of whom I have spoken in the Preface to the second edition of 1st Series.

Croob in Down, *Moin-na-huidhre*, the bog of the dun cow. This is also the origin of the name of the ancient book so often quoted in these pages, called *Lebor na h-Uidhre*, [Lower-na-heera], the book of the brown cow; for according to the legendary account, it was written by St. Kieran of Clonmacnoise, and the vellum of which it was composed was made from the hide of his favourite dark grey cow.

Speckled. *Breac* [brack] signifies speckled or parti-coloured. As land, especially hill-sides or dry upland, often presents a speckled or spotted appearance, caused by different kinds of vegetation, or by the varying colours of the soil or of rocks, this word is of very frequent occurrence in local names; and it usually takes the anglicised form *brack*. At A. D. 1601, the Four Masters mention a place in Galway called *Coill-bhreac*, speckled wood—speckled, I suppose, from a mixture of various coloured trees; it is now called Kylebrack, and is situated in the parish of Leitrim. With a slight difference of form we have Kilbrack in Cork and Waterford, and Kilbracks, (speckled woods or churches) in Armagh. There is a townland near Oola in Limerick, called Brackyle, which is the same name with the root-words reversed.

The Brackbawn is a fine mountain stream flowing down the side of the Galty Mountains near Kilbehenny, and joining the Funshion; or rather it is itself the head water of the Funshion. The name properly belongs to a townland through which the river flows; and it signifies speckled whitish land (*bán*, p. 269). The word *brack* is often applied in this way, as a noun, meaning speckled land:—Bracknahevla in the parish of Killare in Westmeath, speckled land of the orchard (*abhal*); Bracknamuckley near Portglenone in Antrim, speckled land of the *muclach* or piggery. Many other places taking their names from the word *breac* have been noticed in this and the former volume.

There is another word for speckled, viz., *brit*, *briot*, or *breat*, which is also often used in the formation of names. Mullybrit, speckled summit, is the name of a townland near Lisbellaw in Fermanagh, the same as Mullybrack, Mullabrack, and Mullaghbrack, elsewhere. Brittas, which has been already noticed (p.14), is corrupted to British in the parish of Killead in Antrim, and forms part of the name of Ballybrittas in Queen's County and Wexford, the town of the speckled land.

CHAPTER XVIII.

THE ANIMAL KINGDOM.

When a place is named from some particular kind of animal, the name of the animal usually comes in at the end of the local designation, in the genitive plural. Sometimes the article is omitted, as in case of Slieve-Buck, the name of a mountain south of Enniskerry in Wicklow, of another giving name to a townland near Raphoe in Donegal, and of a few elsewhere. The Irish form of the name is *Sliabh-boc*, the mountain of the bucks or stags. But more generally the article is inserted, which eclipses the first consonant, if it can be eclipsed: this is seen in Carricknagat and Carrignagat, which occur in many places all over the country, the Irish form of which is *Carraig-na-gcat*, the rock of the (wild) cats. Occasionally the name of the animal comes first; as in Roaninish, a little island off Donegal, outside Gweebarra bay,

Rón-inis, seal island; Roancarrick, the name of several small rocks and rocky islets round the coast, resorts for seals—*Ron-charraig*, seal rock. This is the same name as Carrignarone, which is also occasionally met with. This name too has a literary and romantic interest. When the four children of Lir, who had been turned into swans by their wicked stepmother, were driven about by tempests on the rough sea of Moyle (the narrow sea between Antrim and the *Mull* of Cantire), they appointed Carrignarone as their meeting place, in case they should be separated by the storm; and when Finola, the eldest, came to the rock, and found her brothers absent, she uttered a lament which Moore has echoed in his beautiful song "Silent, O Moyle, be the roar of thy water."

There is yet another way of forming names of this kind, to which I have to direct special attention, viz., the name of the animal is brought in at the end, in the genitive singular instead of the genitive plural. And names of this class are intended to express the fact that the places were the haunts of the animals in question (the same as if the genitive plural were used), a single animal being made to stand for the whole species. An excellent example of this is Poulanishery or Poulnasherry, a well-known inlet of the Shannon near which you pass in going from Kilrush to Kilkee. It has always produced abundance of oysters; and there is still an oyster bed at its western side. This fact is expressed by the name—*Poll-an-oisire*, the hole, pool, or inlet, of the oyster (not of the oysters). It is to be observed, however, that in some names of this kind, one animal is really meant; and then the name is often connected with a legend. Whether this is the case or not in any particular place, can only be ascertained from local knowledge.

Ants and *Midges*. *Miol* [meel] denotes any kind of animal; different species being designated by means of qualifying terms. We find it standing alone in Bellaveel near Ballyhaunis in Mayo, the *bel* or ford of the beast (*b* aspirated to *v*). When this simple form is used collectively, it is sometimes intended to denote pismires; as in Drumnameel near Enniskillen, which is understood there to mean the ridge of the ants; and occasionally it stands for midges, as in Croaghnameal, a mountain six miles east of Donegal town, the hill of the midges.

The diminutive *mioltóg* [meelthoge] is the usual word for a midge; and this term is pretty general in names, always indicating a place where, in favorable weather, there are swarms of midges. There is a townland called Meeltoge near Belturbet in Cavan, and another, Meeltogues, in the parish of Kilskeery in Tyrone, both meaning a midgy place. Bohernameeltoge in the parish of Killoe in Longford, is the road of the midges; and there is a little lake called Loughnameeltoge, among the Croaghgorm hills, north of Donegal. Other derivatives of the word *miol* are applied to the same little animal:—as examples take Curraghmeelagh—midge-marsh—the name of a townland and of a little lake in the parish of Killoughy in King's County; Cornameelta near Boyle in Roscommon, and Cormeeltan in Leitrim, both meaning the round hill of the midges.

The general Irish word for a pismire or ant is *seangán* [shangaun]; which is a diminutive from *seang*, slender, and means slender little fellow. There is a small low hill near the village of Louth, where an abbey, which afterwards became much celebrated, was founded in 1148, and consecrated by the great St. Malachy O'Morgair, archbishop of Armagh. It is mentioned often in Irish records by the name of *Cnoc-na-seangán*, the hill of the ants; and it is now generally called in English, Pismire Hill; while the abbey is called Knock Abbey. There are townlands of this name in Donegal and Fermanagh, which are now correctly anglicised Knocknashangan; and near Lurgan in Armagh, is a place called Knocknashane and sometimes Knocknaseggane, both of which are varied forms of the same name.

Near the lake of Gartan in Donegal, there is a place called Maghernashangan, the plain (*machaire*) of the pismires; Coolshangan near Inver in the same county, and Coolshingaun in the parish of Inagh, Clare (*cuil*, a corner); Lisheennashingane three miles from Miltown in Kerry, on the road to Killarney (*lisín*, a little fort); Garranashingaun in the parish of Castletownarra in Tipperary (*garran*, a shrubbery); Aghnashingan in Longford, the field (*achadh*) of the ants. There is a little river near Bantry called Owennashingaun—pismire river—joining the Ilen near Dromdaleague.

With the termination *ach* (p. 3) is formed *seangánach*, which signifies a place abounding in pismires; and this term, in various anglicised forms, is the name of a great many places in different parts of the country. The best known is Shanganagh in Dublin, between Killiney and Bray, which Denis Florence M'Carthy has commemorated in his poem, "The Vale of Shanganagh." The pronunciation adopted in the poem, which is that universally used by the educated people of the city and county of Dublin [Shan-gan'na, to rhyme with *manna*] would point to the erroneous etymology, *sean-gaineamh*, old sand. But the traditional pronunciation of the native peasantry [Shang'ănă: accent on *Shang*; the other two syllables very short] shows that the name is an anglicised form of *Seangánach*. Even to this day these insects are specially abundant along the banks of the little river that runs through the townland. There is also a Shanganagh in Clare, and another about three miles from Athy in Queen's County. In Kilkenny, this name takes the form of Shanganny. In Cork it is Shananagh; in Mayo, Tipperary, and Waterford, Shinganagh; in Galway, Shinnanagh; and in Clare Shingaunagh. Shingaun, the simple word, without the termination *ach*, is the name of a place in Wexford, and has the same meaning as all the preceding—a place full of ants or pismires.

Mouse. This little animal is called *luch* in Irish (*luch*, mus: Z. 71); but the diminutive *luchóg* is the term most generally employed. It is seen in Inchalughoge, the name of a little stream and of a townland in the parish of Kilnoe in the east of Clare, the *inch* or river-meadow of the mice. Gortnalughoge, mouse field, is a place in the parish of Mevagh in the north of Donegal; there is a townland called Mullynalughoge near Clones, the summit of the mice; and Esknaloughoge is a hill, four miles west of Sneem in Kerry, which must have taken its name from an *esk* or water-channel.

Wren. In old times, this little bird was regarded as a great prophet; for by listening attentively to its chirping, those who were skilled in the language of birds were enabled to predict future events. Hence the writer of an old Life of St. Moling translates *drean*, which is one name for the bird, by "magus avium," the "druid of birds," implying that *drean* was derived from *drui-én* (*drui*, a druid; *én*, of birds), and says that it was so called on account of the excellence of its augury. Although I fear this will be regarded as a very fanciful etymology, yet it shows in what estimation the wren was held in the time of the writer. Our well-known rhyme "The wren, the wren, the king of all birds," is a remnant, no doubt, of this ancient superstition.

The wren has several names. Two of them, *dreólán* and *dreoilín* [drolaun, droleen] are different diminutives of the same root; of which the former is exhibited in Gorteenadrolane east of Inchigeelagh in Cork, the little field of the wren; and the latter in Mulladrillen near Ardee in Louth, the wren's hill-summit. The other term, *drean*, we find in Drumdran, the name of two townlands in Fermanagh and Tyrone, which means the ridge of the wrens.

Wagtail. The water-wagtail has received a name in Irish which is derived from the colour of the bird, viz., *glasóg*, a diminutive of *glas*, green or greyish-green :—*glasóg*, grey-green little fellow. This is moreover an old name, for it is the one used in the ancient Irish poetical list of animals published by Sir William R. Wilde in Proc. R. I. A., vol. VII. Lisglassock near Ballymahon in Longford, took its name from a fort, which must have been frequented by these little birds—the *lis* of the water-wagtails; and the townland of Terryglassog near Dungannon in Tyrone, should have been called Derryglassog, the *derry* or oak-grove of the wagtails.

Robin Redbreast. There is no difficulty in detecting the name of this bird in local denominations; for it is called in Irish *spideóg*, which is pronounced and usually anglicised *spiddoge*. There is a place near Stradbally in Queen's County called Kylespiddoge, the wood (*coill*) of the redbreasts; Turnaspidogy near Inchigeelagh in Cork, must have got its name from a bush from which the robin's song was constantly heard, as the name signifies the redbreast's bush. There is a townland about five miles south-west of Tullow in Carlow, containing the ruins of a castle, called Graignaspiddoge, the *graig* or village of the robins.

Sparrow. *Gealbhán* or *Gealún* [galvan, galloon] is the word usually employed to denote a sparrow; though with various qualifying terms it is also applied to the linnet, the bulfinch, the yellow-hammer, and other little birds. Sranagalloon in the parish of Inchicronan in Clare, exhibits the word with its usual southern pronunciation—*Srath-na-ngealbhún*, the srath or river-holm of the sparrows. So also Derrygalun, two miles from Kanturk in Cork, sparrow-grove; and Cloonagalloon in the parish of Meelick in Mayo (*cluain*, a meadow). The northern varieties of pronunciation are seen in Drumagelvin in Monaghan, the sparrow's ridge; and in Lisnagelvin near the city of Derry, the *lis* or fort of the sparrows. There is a small lake at the east side of Slieve Beagh in Monaghan, called Lough Galluane; another just on the boundary of Donegal and Tyrone, east of Lough Derg, called Lough Ayelvin; and a third, three miles north-west of Pettigo in Donegal, with the name of Lough Ayellowin—all from the Irish *Loch-a'-ghealbhain* the lake of the sparrow.

Snipe. A snipe is denoted by the word *naosga* or *naosgach* [naisga], which is generally easy to recognise in names. Tullyneasky, the name of a place near Clonakilty in Cork, is not much changed from the

Irish *Tulaigh-naosgaidh*, the little hill of the snipes; Garrynaneaskagh near Ardfert in Kerry, and Toornaneaskagh in the same county, the garden and the bleach-field of the snipes.

Another word for a snipe, though not commonly used, is *meantán*. Ballinaminton, three miles from the village of Clara in King's County, is written in the Down Survey, Bellanamantan, which shows that it took its name from a ford, and that the Irish form is *Bel-atha-na-meantán*, the ford-mouth of the snipes.

Grouse. We call a grouse in Irish either *cearc-fraeigh* or *coileach-fraeigh* [cark-free, colliagh-free]. The former is applied to the female, signifying literally, heath-hen—(*cearc*, a hen; *fraech*, heath); the latter to the male (*coileach*, a cock); but in common use they are applied indiscriminately to male and female. Places named from this bird are almost all wild mountain or moory districts, and any that are not so now, have been reclaimed since the time the places got the names. There is a townland nearly east of Glenties in Donegal, called Cronacarkfree, a name which is slightly corrupted from *Cro-na-gcearc-fraeigh*, the *cro* or valley of the grouse.

The full name of the bird seldom appears in names however; the word *cearc* being generally used alone; and although this word means the hen of any bird, yet in its topographical application it is commonly intended for grouse. It is easily recognised in names, as it always takes some such anglicised form as *cark*, *kirky*, *kirk*, or *gark*—the *c* being eclipsed by *g* in the last. Derrycark near Belturbet in Cavan, bears its meaning on its face—the oak-wood of (the heath-) hens or grouse; Coolkirky two miles from Ballinhassig in Cork, the grouse-hen's angle or corner (*cuil*); Glennagark in the parish of Kilcormack in Wexford, and Slievenagark two miles west of Ballina in Mayo, the glen and the mountain of the grouse-hens.

There is a well-known castle, now in ruins, on a little island in the western arm of Lough Corrib, called in the Four Masters, *Caislen-na-circe*, the hen's castle; but now anglicised Castlekirk. History tells us that this castle was erected in the twelfth century by the sons of Roderick O'Conor, the last king of Ireland; but local tradition will have it that it was built in one night by two grouse, a cock and a hen, who had been an Irish prince and princess.

The other term for a grouse, *coileach-fraeigh* or *coileach* simply, i. e. cock, is equally common. The word usually occurs with the first *c* eclipsed, as it appears in the following names:—Cornaguillagh, in Leitrim, Longford, and Monaghan, represents the Irish *Cor-na-gcoilleach*, the round hill of the (grouse-) cocks; Coumnagillagh on the side of Mauherslieve or "mother-mountain," south of Silvermines in Tipperary (*com*, a mountain glen); Knocknagulliagh near Carrickfergus, grouse hill, which same name is applied to a hill near Blessington in Wicklow, in the incorrect form of Crocknaglugh. We often find the word without eclipse; as for instance in Bencullagh, one of the Twelve Pins in Connemara, the name of which signifies the peak of the grouse; Knockakilly near Thurles in Tipperary, in which the genitive singular form appears, the name meaning the grouse's hill; and with the final *g* pronounced, we have Derreenacullig in the parish of Killaha in Kerry, the little oak wood of the grouse-cock.

Bittern. The lonely boom of the bittern is heard more seldom year after year, as the marshes are becoming drained and reclaimed. But we have names that point out the former haunts of the bird, and some of them indicate the wild moory character of the places when the names were imposed. *Bunnán* is the Irish name of the bird; it is seen in Tievebunnan in the parish of Boho in Mayo, the hill-side of the bitterns; and in Curraghbonaun near Tobercurry in Sligo, where the old people have still some memory of hearing the bittern booming from the *currach* or marsh. About four miles from the suspension bridge at Kenmare, on the road to Glengarriff, you cross the Feabunaun rivulet—the *feith* or marshy stream of the bitterns. Near the northern shore of Clew bay, about five miles west of Westport, there is a small island called Inishbobunnan: Inishbo, signifies the island of the cows; and Inishbobunnan, cow-island of the bitterns.

Pigeon or dove. *Colum* signifies a dove. In several parts of the country, holes or caves in rocks, frequented by these birds, are called Pollnagolum, in Irish, *Poll-na-gcolum*, the hole or cave of the doves. In the present spoken language *colúr* [colure] is the more usual term for the same bird; and it is found more often in names. There is a little river joining the Finow near Millstreet in Cork, called Owennagloor, i. e. *Abhainn-na-gcolúr*, the river of the pigeons; Annagloor is a townland in the parish of Drishane in the same county (pigeon-ford: *ath*, a ford); and on the top of one of the Ballyhoura mountains, on the borders of Cork and Limerick, is a large rock, called *Carraig-na-gcolúr*, which now usually goes by the name of Pigeon Rock, a correct translation of the Irish.

Cormorant. The common cormorant, a large black sea bird, well known round our coasts, has got several Irish names, most or all of which are reproduced in local names. One, *duibhén* [divean] I do not find in the dictionaries, though it is in general use among Irish-speaking people of the coasts. And it will describes this fine bird, as it means literally *black-bird; dubh*, black; *én* a bird. There is a little island in the upper end of Lower Lough Erne, called Inishdivann, cormorant island; and a townland in the parish of Killeeneen in Galway, south-west of Athenry, is called Carheenadiveane, the little *caher* or stone fort of the cormorants.

Hedgehog. The common hedgehog is called in Irish, *graineóg*, which is no doubt derived from *gráin*, signifying ugliness or abhorrence: *grainéog* ugly or hateful little fellow. If this be the case, the name embodies to some extent the idle popular prejudices against this harmless little animal; for the people formerly believed it was a witch in disguise, and that it used to suck cows, rob orchards, &c. These stories are spread over all Europe, and are probably as old as the Indo-European race. Pliny states that the hedgehog catches up apples with its prickles; and the witches in Macbeth find that it is time to begin their incantations, for

> "Thrice the brinded cat hath mewed,
> And once the hedge pig whined."

The names that commemorate the haunts of this animal are not numerous. There is a townland in the parish of Inver in Donegal, called Meenagranoge, the *meen* or mountain field of the hedgehog; another in the parish of Robertstown in Limerick, near Foynes, called Inchagreenoge, the hedgehogs' *inch* or river-meadow; and a small hill in the parish of Caheragh in the south of Cork, is called Knocknagranogy, the hill of the hedgehog.

Hare. In another place I had occasion to remark that the word *fiadh* [feea] was originally applied to any wild animal, though latterly restricted to deer (1st. Ser., Part IV., c. VII). The hare would appear to be the smallest animal to which the term was applied, if we may judge by the composition of the name *gearr-fhiadh* [gerreé]; i. e. short or small *fiadh*, from *gearr*, short or deficient. The usual plural form is *geirr-fhiadhacha*, which is pronounced something like *girriha;* and this is exhibited in Ballygirriha in the parish of Donaghmore in Cork, the townland of the hares; and in Dromgurrihy, one mile from Monkstown in the same county, the hares' ridge.

Lamb. A lamb is designated by the word *uan*, which is still a living word, and cognate with Latin *agnus;* old Welsh *oen* (*uan*, agnus: Z. 166). It usually occurs in the end of names in the genitive plural with the article, forming the easily recognised termination *nanoon*. There is a place called Strananoon west of the southern extremity of Lough Allen in Leitrim, *Srath-na-nuan*, the river-holm of the lambs; and with the same meaning Inchnanoon in the parish of Kilmacabea in Cork. Loughnanoon (lamb lake) is the name of a small lake five miles south of Killorglin in Kerry; and there is a townland called Gortnanoon, the field of the lambs, near Crosshaven, at the mouth of the Lee.

There is another word for a lamb, not in such common use as *uan*, namely *luan;* from which Maloon near Cookstown derives its name—*Magh-luan*, the plain of the lambs. There is a place called Malone immediately south of Belfast, which in the old documents quoted at page 212, is mentioned as an alias name for *Tuath-ne-fall*, and there called

Mylone; and this no doubt is the same as Maloon. The name occurs in combination in Gortmaloon in the parish of Knockane in Kerry; the field of the plain of the lambs.

Kid. The word *meann* and its diminutive *meannan* [man, manaun] both signify a kid; the latter is more commonly used than the former, and it enters pretty extensively into the names of places under several modern forms. The southern pronunciation is well exhibited in Caherminnaun, now an old castle ruin giving name to a townland near Kilfenora in Clare—the *caher* or stone-fort of the kids. Near Newrath Bridge in Wicklow, is a place called Clonmannan, the kids' meadow. Carrickmannan, now the name of a lake and townland near Saintfield in Down, and Carrigmannon on the Slaney about five miles above Wexford, both signify the kids' rock; and there is a place in the parish of Faughanvale in Derry called Legavannon, the *lug* or hollow of the kid. It is possible that the latter part of some of these denominations may be a man's name.

Wether. *Molt* signifies a wether (*molt*, vervex: Z. 67). It is well represented in Annamult, three miles from Thomastown in Kilkenny, which obviously took its name from a ford on the King's River, where sheep were in the habit of crossing: *Ath-na-molt*, the ford of the wethers. Ballynamult (*Bally*, a town) is the name of a place on the summit level of the road from Clonmel to Dungarvan; Rosmult in the parish of Moyaliff in Tipperary, the wethers' wood.

Heifer. The word *dairt* signifies a young heifer or bull, from one to two years old. This term is used in the very oldest of our manuscripts; for the *dairt*, like the *séd* (p. 310), was anciently one of the measures of value; and the dried hide of a *dairt* was used by warriors to cover their bodies and their shields going to battle. It enters into local names; but here it must be taken as meaning nothing more than this—that people were formerly in the habit of sending yearling heifers to graze in the places named.

There is a hill three miles from Dunmore in the north of Galway, called Slieve Dart; a high mountain of the same name, now called simply Dart, is situated west of Sawel mountain, just on the boundary between Derry and Tyrone; and there are others still elsewhere: — the name signifies the mountain of the yearling heifers. In Cork we have Glandart and Glandarta, the heifer's glen. The diminutive *dartan* sometimes occurs, as in Drumdartan near Ballinamore in Leitrim, the ridge of the heifer, which has the same meaning as Drumdart in the same county and in Monaghan.

A *colpa* or *colpthach* is a three year old heifer. The word is perpetually met with in old law tracts as a measure of value, and it is still in constant use in the spoken language. At the present day however, in some parts of the country at least, it is commonly used in connexion with grazing on commons; and in this sense it is often applied to various grazing animals. Six sheep are called a *collop* (this is the usual anglicised term), because they are estimated to eat as much grass as one full grown cow. However, in local names, we must understand the word in its original sense of a heifer.

Mocollop on the Blackwater above Lismore, with its castle ruins, one of the old seats of the Desmonds, is called in Irish *Magh-colpa*, the plain of the *collops* or heifers. In the parish of Racavan in Antrim, four miles north-east from Broughshane, is a place called Kilnacolpagh; and near Castletownsend in the south of the county Cork, is Bawnnagollopy, the former signifying the wood, and the latter the green-field, of the collops. At Killycolpy, in the parish of Arboe, on the western shore of Lough Neagh, a considerable portion of the old "steer's wood," as it was correctly called in English, still remains.

The word *mart* designates an ox or a full grown cow—a *beef;* and hence the compound, *mairt-fheoil*, for beef, literally ox-flesh. Stranamart is the name of a townland in the parish of Killinagh in Cavan, signifying the *srath* or river-holm of the beeves; and the term also appears in the old name of Westport in Mayo, which is still well-known:—Cahernamart, the stone-fort of the beeves.

Eel. A good many names of small places through the country are derived from the word *easgan*, an eel; and the form the word generally assumes is exhibited in Pollanaskan near Castlebar in Mayo, *Poll-an-easgainn*, the hole or pool of the eel.

The word *geallóg* [galloge], a diminutive of *geal*, white, is understood in many parts of the country to mean a white-bellied eel, though it is occasionally applied to other fish. It appears in the name of Sranayalloge east of Lough Sheelin in Cavan, which the people call in Irish, *Sruthan-na-ngeallog*, the streamlet of the white-bellied eels.

Trout. Breac [brack] signifies a trout, a name which it derives from its speckled skin (*breac*, speckled; page 281). The river Bealanabrack, flowing into Lough Corrib at its extreme western end, must have taken its name from one of its fords—probably that at Maum, now spanned by a handsome bridge—which afforded amusement to anglers;

for its Irish name is *Bel-atha-na-mbreac*, the ford-mouth of the trouts. There are numberless small lakes in all parts of the country called Loughnabrack, trout lake.

A well is sometimes met with containing one lone inhabitant—a single trout, which is always to be seen swimming about in its tiny dominion. These little animals are usually tame; and the people hold them in great respect, and tell many wonderful legends about them. It was probably a fish of this kind that gave name to a little lake in the parish of Drumlease in Leitrim, two miles north-east of Drumahaire, called Lough Aneanvrick, *Loch-an-aen-bhric*, the lake of the one trout. There is another little lake of the same name in the townland of Stranamart, parish of Killinagh, Cavan, from which a stream flows into the Shannon before it enters Lough Allen; but here the name is accounted for by a sort of legend, that when you fish in the lake you can catch only one trout at a time; if you go away and come again you will catch another, and so on; but no sacred character is attributed to the fish.

While the word *breac* is commonly used to designate a trout, it is often applied to any small fish, the different species being distinguished by various qualifying words. I have met with a great many compound terms formed in this way on the word *breac;* and in several cases it is now difficult to find out what particular kinds of fish were meant. Some were no doubt different varieties of real trout; while others were certainly not trout at all. Many of these terms enter into the names of small lakes, in which the several kinds of fish were found; and these lakes are scattered over Munster, Connaught, and west Ulster, but they are especially numerous in Donegal.

There is a species of trout, found only in the lakes of the west of Ireland, and well-known to anglers, called the gillaroo (Irish *giolla-ruadh*, red fellow), because they are distinguished by an unusual number of red spots. Great numbers of small lakes, in the counties from Donegal to Kerry, are called Lough Nabrackderg, Lough Nabrackdarrig, and Lough Nambrackdarrig, all signifying the lake of the red trouts; and it is probable that some or all of these were so named from the gillaroo. But we have also many small lakes called Lough Nabrackboy, the lake of the yellow trouts (*buidhe*, yellow): what these are I cannot venture to conjecture.

There is another curious lake-name which occurs very often in the west, all the way from Inishowen to Killarney—Lough Nabrackkeagh, the lake of the blind trouts (*caech*, blind); but why these fishes were called *breac-caech*, or of what particular kind they were, I am unable to explain. We know that the fish inhabiting the gloomy waters of the great Mammoth cave of Kentucky, and those also found in some Carinthian subterranean lakes, are blind; for their eyes have gradually degenerated from long disuse, till at last after a series of generations, they have become merely rudimentary, and totally insensible to light. Can it be that our *breac-caech* have become blind by living for ages in those subterranean waters so common in the limestone districts of the west, from which they occasionally come to the surface, where they are caught? Whatever may be the cause, one thing is certain, that the *breac-caech* is a little fish either wholly blind, or having eyes so small or so imperfectly developed, as to be hardly perceptible.

There are several small lakes in Donegal called Lough Nabrackbady; one for example, about half way between Lough Nacung and the Gweedore river, and another in the valley between the mountains of Aghla More and Aghla Beg, four miles north-west from Lough Beagh. The word *beadaidhe* (represented in the name by *bady*) is still used in the colloquial language, especially in Donegal, and signifies fond of dainties, fastidious, or saucy. This name signifies the lake of the saucy or dainty trouts; and the fish are so called I suppose from their shyness in taking a bait.*

If the angler should be scared away by the name of Lough Nabrackbady, or by that of Lough Nabrackbeg (the lake of the small trouts) near Dunglow, let him proceed straight to Lough Nabrackrawer about two miles north of Belleek, from which, if there be anything in a name, he is likely to return with a heavy basket—*Loch-na-mbreac-reamhar*, the lake of the fat trouts; or to Lough Nabrackalan, the lake of the beautiful trouts (*álainn*, beautiful); or to Lough Nabrackmore near Dunglow, where if he get a bite at all, it is likely to be worth something (*breac-mor*, a great trout).

One would think that there never was such a thing as a *drowned* trout; yet there is a small lake

* These lakes have been brought under my notice by the writer of the review of my First Series of Irish Names of Places, in the "Athenæum" of Aug. 21, 1869; and from him I have borrowed the explanation of the epithet given to these little fishes. My orthography and interpretation differ somewhat from those of the reviewer; but I believe that it is the same lake-name that is meant in both cases.

eight miles north of the town of Donegal, called Lough Nabrackbautia, the lake of the drowned trouts (*baidhte*, drowned—see c. XXII.). Perhaps the same explanation will apply to this as to Lough Nabrackdeelion, which is the name of several of the Donegal lakelets—of one, for instance, in a chain of lakes, four miles south-east of Glenties. This name signifies the lake of the flood-trouts (*dílean*, a flood); and the little fishes are so called because they always appear in those lakes after floods, which probably sweep them down from higher waters.

The diminutive, *bricín*, has given name to Glenbrickeen, north-west from Clifden in Galway, the glen of the little trout; and to another place far better known, Brickeen Bridge at Killarney, the name of which means "little-trout bridge:" for the Irish form is *Droichead-a'-bhricín* [Drehid-a-vrickeen], of which the present name is a correct translation.

CHAPTER XIX.

THE VEGETABLE KINGDOM.

Corn. The word *arbhar* [arwar, arroor] signifies corn of any kind, "particularly so called when standing, or before it is threshed" (O'Brien: Irish Dict.). It may be supposed that those places whose names are partly formed from this word, were originally isolated corn-producing spots, surrounded by uncultivated or unproductive land. It appears in Knockanarroor near Killarney, *Cnoc-an-arbhair*, the hill of the corn; and in Lissanarroor near Galbally in Limerick, which probably got its name from a *lis* or fort in which corn used to be stacked up.

Another form is *arbha* [arwa, arroo] from which *arbhar* appears to have been formed by the addition of *r* (p. 12); and it enters into names as often at least as *arbhar*. Meenanarwa in the parish of Inishkeel in Donegal, near Lough Finn, signifies the *meen* or mountain flat of the corn; Coolanarroo in the parish of Tuosist in Kerry, south-west of Kenmare (*cuil*, a corner); Clonarrow near Philipstown in King's County, corn meadow; Derryarrow near Mountrath in Queen's County, the *derry* or oak-grove of the corn.

Wheat. We know for a certainty that wheat has been cultivated in this country from the most remote ages; for we find it constantly mentioned in our ancient literature. Many illustrations of this might be given, but one will be sufficient. In A. D. 651, Donogh and Conall, the two sons of *Blathmac* [Blawmac], afterwards king of Ireland, were slain by the Leinstermen at "the mill of Maeloran the son of Dima Cron." This event is recorded in the Annals of *Tighernach* (who died in 1088), in the Annals of Ulster, and in the Annals of the Four Masters. A contemporary bard composed a poem on the event, in which he apostrophises the mill in the following stanza:—

> "O mill, what hast thou ground? Precious thy wheat!
> It is not oats thou hast ground, but the offspring of Cearbhall (i. e. the two princes).
> The grain which the mill has ground is not oats but blood-red wheat;
> With the scions of the great tree (Cearbhall) Maeloran's mill was fed."

Mageoghegan, in his translation of the Annals of Clonmacnoise, says that "Donogh and Connell were killed by the Lynstermen near Mollingare, in the mill of Oran [or Maeloran] called Mollenoran." This mill was situated on the little river that runs from Lough Owel to Lough Iron, near the point where the river is now crossed by a bridge; and the place still retains the name of Mullenoran. It is curious that a mill existed there from the time of the death of the princes—and no one can tell how long before—down to the end of the last century; and there are some old people still living there whose fathers saw it in full work.*

There are two native Irish words for wheat, *tuireann* and *cruithneacht* [crunnat]; but I will notice only the latter, for I do not find the other commemorated in names. Cormac Mac Cullenan, in his Glossary (ninth century), derives *cruithneacht* from *cruith* [cruh] blood-coloured or red, and *necht* clean: the first part of this derivation is probably correct, but I fear modern philologists will be inclined to believe *necht* a mere termination (see page 2). Be that as it may however, the etymology sufficiently proves the interesting fact, that the wheat cultivated in the time of the venerable king-bishop Cormac—1000 years ago—was the very same as the Irish wheat of the present day; for every farmer knows that the old Irish wheat—now fast dying out—is distinguished by its red colour.

It is worthy of remark that in several other languages, wheat—as Pictet shows (Les Origines, I. 261)—has been named from its colour, not indeed from its redness as in Ireland, but from its whiteness as compared with other kinds of corn. As one in-

* See O'Donovan in Four Masters at A. D. 647.

stance may be mentioned the English word *wheat*, which he shows is only another form of *white*.

Near Castleblaney in Monaghan there are three adjoining townlands called Tullanacrunat, modernised from *Talamh-na-cruithneachta*, signifying the land of the wheat; Portnacrinnaght in the parish of Kilnamanagh, Roscommon, the port or landing place of wheat; Tullycreenaght near the town of Antrim, wheat hill.

The simple word gives name to Crunagh in the parish of Loughgilly, and to Crunaght near Markethill, both in Armagh; and the diminutive (see p. 19), to Crinnaghtane near Kilworth in Cork, and to Crinnaghtaun near Cappoquin in Waterford; all these four names meaning wheat, or wheat bearing land.

Oats. The observations made about the early cultivation of wheat apply equally to oats; numerous references to its cultivation and use are found in our most ancient literature. In recent times, before the potato became very general, oats formed one of the principal articles of food of the people; and even as late as the beginning of the present century, a quern or hand-mill, chiefly for grinding oats, was a very usual article in the houses of the peasantry.

The Irish word for oats is *coirce* [curkia]; Welsh *ceirch*, Armoric *kerch;* and it appears with its full pronunciation in Lissacurkia, the name of two places in Roscommon, one near Tulsk, and the other in the parish of Tibohine, near Frenchpark—the fort of the oats, a name of like origin to Lissanarroor (p. 300); while another form of the word appears in Farranacurky near Lisnaskea in Fermanagh, oats-bearing land (*fearann*).

This word is very often shortened to one syllable; but whether shortened or not, it is easily recognised: the examples given here include almost all its anglicised forms. Gortachurk is the name of a townland near Bellananagh in Cavan; and there is a place called Coolacork in the parish of Dungans-town, south of Wicklow; the former signifying the field (*gort*), and the latter the angle or corner (*cuil*) of the oats.

Barley. The Irish word for barley is *eórna* [ōrna], which is very correctly represented in Coolnahorna, the name of places in Wexford and Waterford, the angle (*cuil*) of the barley; and in Tavnaghorna, now the name of a little stream near Cushendall in Antrim, whose proper meaning is barley-field. The word seldom gets its full pronunciation however, in modernised names, the final vowel sound being generally omitted. In the north of Derry, near Portrush, there is a townland called Craignahorn, the rock of the barley; Mulnahorn, barley hill (*mul*), is the name of two townlands in Fermanagh and Tyrone; Glennyhorn in the parish of Clontibret in Monaghan, is a corrupt form of the correct name, Cloonnahorn, the *cloon* or meadow of the barley; Cappaghnahoran west of Mountrath in Queen's County, barley-field (*ceapach*).

There is a little lake near Newry, giving name a townland, called Loughorne, barley lake; another of the same name, in the slightly different form Lough Ourna, four miles north of Nenagh in Tip-perary; and still another among the hills over Glen-garriff, which is conspicuously visible on the left hand side of the road to Kenmare, as you approach the tunnel: but this is now always called Barley Lake. It is not improbable that these lakes may have received their names from the circumstance that barley used to be steeped and malted on their margins in ages gone by.

Rye : Irish *seagal* [shaggal]: corresponding with the Latin *secale*, and French *seigle*. In modern names it appears almost always in the forms of *taggle* and *teggle*, the *s* being changed to *t* by eclipse. Lissataggle in the parish of Currans, near Castleisland in Kerry, is in the original *Lios-a'-tseagail*, the fort of the rye (see Lissanarroor, p. 300); Coolataggle near Borrisoleigh in Tipperary (*cuil*, a corner); Pollataggle near Gort in Galway, the hole or pool of the rye.

Beans. The bean is designated in Irish by the word *pónaire* [pónara]; which corresponds with the Welsh *ponar*, and English *bean;* whence we have Ardnaponra near Moate in Westmeath, corrupted from *Ard-na-bponaire*, the height of the beans. In the south and west, the *n* is commonly omitted in pronunciation [pōria]; and this contraction is also carried into local names—Coolpowra near Portumna in Galway, the hill-back (*cúl*) of the beans. In the greater number of cases the *p* is aspirated; as in Gorteenaphoria in the parish of Moyaliff in Tipperary, and Gortaphoria near Dingle bay, west of Drung hill—both meaning bean-field.

Pea. Pis [pish], genitive *pise* [pisha], signifies pease of all kinds, and is of course cognate with Eng. *pease;* Lat. *pisum*. It is almost always anglicised *pish* and *pisha* ; as in Coolnapish and Coolnapisha in Carlow, Kilkenny, and Limerick, the angle or hill-back (*cúil* or *cúl*) of the pease. From the diminutive *piseán* [pishane] is formed (by the addition of *ach*—p. 3) Pishanagh, the name of two townlands in Westmeath, signifying a place producing pease.

X

Berries. A berry of any kind is denoted by *caer* [keare]. It is sometimes represented in names by *keare*, as in Dromkeare on the shore of Lough Currane, or Waterville lake, in Kerry, the ridge of berries; and Knockcoolkeare in the parish of Killeedy in Limerick, the hill of the angle (*cuil*) of the berries. In far the greater number of cases the *c* is eclipsed by *g*, and then the word is represented by *geer* or some such anglicised form. Glennageare in Cork and Clare, is in Irish *Gleann-na-gcaer*, the glen of the berries; Croaghnageer, a remarkable hill near the gap of Barnesmore in Donegal (*croagh*, a round hill): so also Kilnageer in Mayo and Monaghan (*coill*, a wood); Gortnagier in Galway (*gort*, a field); and Monagear in Wexford, the bog (*moin*) of the berries.

Gooseberry. *Spionán* [speenaun] is a gooseberry or a gooseberry bush, a diminutive from *spín* a thorn, which is of course the same as the Latin *spina*. Spinans in the parish of Donaghmore in Wicklow, signifies a place (or rather places, for the word is plural) abounding in gooseberry bushes; and with another diminutive we have Speenoge in Donegal, north-west of Derry—same meaning: Killaspeenan near Newtown Butler in Fermanagh, the wood (*coill*) of the gooseberries. In some cases an *r* is corruptly inserted after the *p*, an example of which is Carrickspringan near Moynalty in Meath, the rock of the gooseberries. And in some parts of Munster the *i* is replaced in pronunciation by *u*; which is exemplified in Lisnasprunane, the name of a fort in the townland of Garranroe, near Adare in Limerick, gooseberry fort.

Blackberry. *Sméar* [smare] is the word for the common blackberry, and it gives name to a considerable number of places. It is seen unchanged in Smear in the parish of Columkille in Longford, signifying a place producing blackberries: indeed the word almost always preserves its original Irish form in anglicised names. Cappanasmear near Borrisokane in Tipperary, the plot (*ceapach*) of the blackberries; Creenasmear at the base of Muckish mountain in Donegal (*crioch*, a district); Coolnasmear near Dungarvan, blackberry corner; Drumnasmear in the parish of Layd in Antrim, the ridge of the blackberries. With the affix *lach* (p. 5) this word gives name to the little river Smearlagh which flows into the Feale near Listowel in Kerry, the blackberry-producing river.

Nut. A nut of any kind is denoted by *cnó* [kno: both *k* and *n* sounded]. The old form, as given in Cormac's Glossary, is *cnu*, cognate with Lat. *nux*, and Eng. *nut*, both of which have lost the initial *c*. The word has several plural forms, one of which, *cnaoi*, gives name to a parish in Tipperary, now called Knigh—a name signifying a place producing nuts. Derrycnaw in the parish of Feakle in Clare, signifies the *derry* or oak-wood of the nuts—a name with the same general meaning as Derreennacno near Dromdaleague in Cork. There is a little lake in the parish of Kilgarvan in Kerry, near the river Roughty, called Coolknoohill, which represents the Irish *cúil-cnochoill*, the corner of the nut-hazels (*coll*, hazel).

In the preceding names the *n* has kept its place; but it is generally changed to *r* in anglicised names, by a usual phonetic process explained in 1st. Ser., Part I., c. III.; and this is always the case when *g* replaces *c* by eclipse. Both changes are exhibited in Cloonnagro near Lough Graney in Clare, not far from Derrycnaw, mentioned above, in Irish *Cluain-*

na-gcnó, the meadow of the nuts; and in Cavanagrow, two miles from Markethill in Armagh, nut hill.

Flower or *blossom*. There are several Irish words for a flower, of which I find only one reproduced to any extent in names, viz., *bláth* [blaw]. It is connected with Sanscrit *phull*, to blossom; with Latin *flos;* O. H. Germ. *blôt;* A. Sax. *blosma;* English *blossom*, *bloom*, and *blow*. We have names formed from this word that not only speak of flowery fields, but testify to our ancestors' perception and appreciation of this sort of quiet natural beauty. The popular admiration for flowers seems to have been developed among the people of Ireland at a very early period, if we are to judge by the cognomen of one of our ancient kings, and the circumstance said to have given rise to it. A little earlier than the time of Ollav Fōla—ever so many centuries before the Christian era—reigned *Fiacha Finscothach* [Feeha Finscoha]; and the legendary records tell us that he received this name because "every plain in Ireland abounded with flowers and shamrocks in his reign" (see p. 54, supra). Some of the old authorities interpret *fin* in this name to mean wine (*scoth*, a flower; *finscotha*, wine flowers)—for "these flowers moreover were found full of wine, so that the wine was pressed into bright vessels" (Four Masters)—a bardic way of saying that wine was made from them. Others again believe—and this is O'Donovan's opinion (Four M., A.M. 3867)—that *fin* here means white—this king "was surnamed Ffinsgohagh of the abundance of white flowers that were in his time" (Mageoghegan, Ann. Clon.).

The names derived from this word are not numerous. Cloneblaugh near Clogher in Tyrone is one of the most characteristic, *Cluain-bláthach*, flowery meadow; Ballyblagh is the name of places in Armagh, Down, and Tyrone; and there is a Ballybla in Wicklow, all signifying the townland of the flowers or blossoms. We have in Inishowen, Donegal, Carrowblagh, and on the western shore of Lough Swilly in the same county, Carryblagh, both in Irish, *Ceathramh-bláthoch*, flowery quarterland. About five miles east of Donegal town, there is a place called Blabreenagh, which the old people still understand to be *Blath-bruighneach*, the *bruighean* [breen] or fairy-fort of the blossoms. Near Coleraine there is a place called Blagh, which represents the adjective form *Blathach*, flowery—a flowery place.

Scoth [skoh], another word for a flower, is very slenderly represented in local names. In the parish of Crossboyne in Mayo, there is a townland called Kilscohagh, a name which is anglicised from *Coill-scothach*, flowery wood; and we have Kilscohanagh near the village of Dromdaleague in Cork, which probably has the same meaning; but here the diminutive syllable *án* is inserted.

Flax. One of the names of this plant is still preserved in a great number of the European languages, the forms slightly varying, but all derived from the root *lin*. The Greek word is *linon*; Latin *linum* (whence Eng. *linen* and *linseed*); A. Sax. *lîn*; Russ. *lenû*: Bohem. *len*, &c. This shows that it was cultivated by the western Aryan people since before the time of their separation into the various nationalities of Europe. The investigations of Dr. Oswald Heer of Munich have led him to believe that the original home of cultivated flax was on the shores of the Mediterranean; it was cultivated in Egypt more than 4000 years ago; and it has been found in the oldest of the lake dwellings of Switzerland.

The Celtic tribes who first set foot on our shores, brought the plant and a knowledge of its cultivation with them; and corresponding to all the names given above, is the Irish *lín* [leen], which is still the word in universal use for flax. Besides the evidence of philology, our own records show that linen was manufactured in Ireland from the earliest historic times. It was a favourite article of dress, and was worked up and dyed in a great variety of forms and colours, and exported besides in large quantities to foreign nations. So that the manufacture for which one portion of Ireland is famous at the present day, is merely an energetic development of an industry, whose history is lost in the twilight of antiquity.

We have a great number of places to which this plant has given names, and the word *lín* generally appears in the modernised forms *leen*, *lin*, and *line*—most commonly the first. Coolaleen in the parish of Killeedy in Limerick, near the village of Broadford, is in Irish *Cúil-a'-lín*, the corner of the flax; Crockaleen near Enniskillen, flax-hill; Gortaleen in Cork and Kerry, the field of the flax.

From the nature of some of the names we may infer that the species they commemorate was the wild or fairy flax, or as they call it in some places, *lín-na-mnasighe* [leenamnaw-shee]. This was probably the case in Killaleen near Drumahaire in Leitrim, and in Killyleen near the town of Monaghan, both signifying the wood (*coill*) of the flax.

Other places seem to have received their names, not from producing flax, but because they were selected as drying places for it, after steeping; such as Lisheenaleen in Cork, Galway, and Tipperary, and Rathleen near Inistioge in Kilkenny, where, probably, the flax was spread out on the green area of the *lisheen*, *rath*, or fort. And the peasantry were, no doubt, long accustomed to put their flax to steep after pulling, in the pools of Monaleen (*moin*, a bog) near Newtown Mountkennedy, in Wicklow; and of Curraghaleen (*curragh*, a marsh) near the railway line, four miles west of Athlone.

Foxglove. The common foxglove, fairy-finger, or fairy-thimble—for it is known by all these names—the *digitalis purpurea* of botanists—is in Ireland a most potent herb; for it is a great fairy plant; and those who seek the aid of the *good people* in the cure of diseases, or in incantations of any kind, often make use of it to add to the power of their spells. It is known by several names in Irish, one of the most common being *lusmore*, great herb; but I do not find this appellation reproduced in local nomenclature. It is also called *sian* or *sian-sleibhe* (sheansleva) i. e., *sian* of the mountain, because it grows plentifully in upland or hilly districts.

As the foxglove is a showy and conspicuous plant, and one besides of such mysterious repute, it is not a matter of surprise that it enters pretty extensively into names. The initial *s* of *sian* is in every case that has come under my notice, changed to *t* in anglicised names, by eclipse; and the word generally presents itself in such forms as *teean*, *teane*, *tain*, *tine*, &c. But as the word *sidhean*, a fairy mount (see 1st Ser.) often also takes the same forms, it is sometimes hard to distinguish the correct meaning of these syllables. It often happens indeed, here as in other cases, that our only guide to the true meaning is the tradition of the old people of the neighbourhood.

Near Cushendall in Antrim is the townland of Gortateean, which would be called in Irish *Gort-a'-tsiain*, the field of the foxglove. Mullantain is the name of a place near Stewartstown in Tyrone; and there is a townland in Kildare and another in Armagh, called Mullantine:—all meaning the hill (*mul*) of the fairy finger; Drumantine, foxglove ridge, is the name of a place five miles north of Newry; Carrickateane and Carrickatane, the names of some places in and around Cavan—the rock of the foxglove.

The word *mearacán*, which properly means a thimble (a diminutive in *cán*, from *mear*, a finger, just like *thimble* from *thumb*), is also applied to this plant, and corresponds with the English name of fairy thimble. In the parish of Inchicronan in Clare, there is a townland called Gortnamearacaun, the field (*gort*) of the fairy thimbles; at the western extremity of which is a little hamlet called Thimbletown, an attempt at translating the name of the townland.

Fern. As many of the common kinds of fern grow in this country in great abundance and luxuriance, they have, as might be expected, given names to many places. The simplest form of the Irish word for the fern is *raith*, which is used in some very old documents; but this form is wholly forgotten in the modern language, and I cannot find that it has been perpetuated in names. The nearest derivative is *Rathain* [rahen] which is the Irish name (as we find it in many old documents) of the parish of Rahan in King's County, well known in ecclesiastical history as the place where St. Carthach was settled before he founded his great establishment at Lismore. This name, which signifies a ferny spot, occurs in several other parts of Ireland. The Mac Sweenys had a castle at a place called Rahan near Dunkineely in Donegal, which the Four Masters call *Rathain;* there is a parish in Cork, near Mallow, with the same name, and several places in different counties have the names Rahin and Rahans—all meaning the same thing.

The common word for the fern is *raithne* or *raithneach* [rahna] which latter form is found in Cormac's Glossary, and is used by the Irish speaking peasantry all over the country at the present day. One of its diminutives, *Raithneachán*, in the anglicised form Ranaghan (a fern-growing spot) is the name of places in each of the four provinces. All the preceding forms are further illustrated in the following names.

Ardrahan, a small village in the county Galway, containing an old castle and a small portion of the ruins of a round tower, is often mentioned in the annals by the name of *Ard-rathain*, ferny height; and this also is the name of two townlands in Kerry, and of one near Galbally in Limerick. There are several places in different counties called Drumrahan, Drumraine, Drumrane, Drumrainy, and Drumrahnee, all signifying the ridge of the ferns.

Tavnaghranny (*tavnagh*, a field) is a place in the parish of the Grange of Layd in Antrim; Lisrenny, ferny fort, is situated three miles north of Ardee in Louth. In Westport bay, just outside the town, there is a small island now called Inishraher; this name is corrupted from *Inishrahen* (change of *n* to *r*: see 1st Ser. Part I. c. III.), for the annalists, who mention it more than once as the scene of skirmishes, always call it *Inis-raithni* or *Inis-rathain*, i. e. ferny island. There is another small island near the western shore of Strangford Lough in Down, called Rainey, which is merely the phonetic representative of *Raithnighe*, i. e. ferns.

Thistle. This plant is denoted in Irish by either

fofannán or *fothannán* [fohanaun], both which are obviously the same word, varied by dialectical corruption —for in Irish there is occasionally an interchange between *th* (which sounds the same as *h*) and *f* (see 1st Ser. Part I. c. III.) Although these are the words now employed, it is obvious that the forms *fothan* and *fofan*, of which they are diminutives, were in use at an earlier period; for we find the adjective form Foffanagh (a place full of thistles) as the name of a townland a little north of Buncrana in Donegal; which is the same as *fofanny* in the two townland names, Fofannybane and Fofannyreagh (white and grey) in the parish of Kilcoo, at the northern base of the Mourne mountains. The little river of Glen Fofanny (thistle glen) flows down from Slieve Donard into the sea, a little south of the town of Newcastle. The other form gives name to Fohanagh, a parish in Galway, and to the townland of Foghanagh in Roscommon, near the village of Ballymoe, both having the same signification as the preceding.

As a termination, the word is found in Tonyfohanan in Monaghan, and Barrafohona in Cork, the mound (*tonnagh*) and hill-top (*barr*) of the thistles.

Nettle. The simple word for the common nettle is *neanta* [nanta]. The forms assumed by this word in the end of names are easily detected, for they are generally *nanta*, *nanty*, or the single syllable *nant*. Cappananty is the name of a place in the parish of Corcomohide in Limerick; and about three miles south-east of Limerick city is a place called Knockananty, the first signifying the plot, and the second the hill, of the nettles. Near Kesh in Fermanagh, there is a townland called Ballynant, which has the same meaning as Ballynanty in Limerick, and

Ballinanty in Wicklow, viz., the townland of the nettles.

Rush. The most common word for a rush is *luachair*, which is the term now always used in the spoken language; but the form generally found in local names is the genitive and plural, *luachra*. Near Cahir in Tipperary, there is a townland containing a castle in ruins and a modern residence, all bearing the very descriptive name of Loughlohery—*Loch-luachra*, the lake of the rushes, from a small lake within the demesne; Greaghnaloughry, north-east of Ballinamore in Leitrim, the *greagh* or mountain flat of the rushes; Letterlougher in the parish of Upper Cumber in Derry, the rushy *letter* or wet hill-side. The simple word gives name to Loughry, i. e. rushes, or a rushy spot, the name of some places in Tyrone; and to Lougher in Kerry and Meath: Loughermore in Antrim, Derry, and Tyrone, great rushy place.

The bullrush is denoted by *sibhin* or *simhin* [shiveen]; the latter being the older form, for we find it in Cormac's Glossary: plural *simhne* [shivna]. This word occurs frequently in local names. There is a river flowing near Mountbellew in Galway, and joining the Suck a little south of Mount Talbot, called the Shiven—Irish *Simhne*, the river of bullrushes. Another little stream with the same Irish name runs through Tollymore Park, south of Newcastle in Down; but in this case the aspirated *m* is restored (1st Ser., Part I., c. II), making the name Shimna. Cloonshivna in Galway, and Tawnanasheffin in Mayo, the meadow and the field of the bullrushes.

Another term for a bullrush is *feadh* [fā]: in the north it is used to denote any strong rush, from which they make lights. It is not so common as the others; but it gives name to Loughfea, a lake near Carrickmacross in Monaghan, the lake of the bullrushes; and to Loughaunnavaag, with the same meaning, two miles from the village of Kilconnell in Galway. In this name the final *dh* is changed to *g* unaspirated, as is done in many other cases.

Flagger. The common marsh or river flag or flagger is called *felestar* or *felestrom;* or without the *f*, *elestar* or *elestrom.* This last form gives name to several places called Ellistrom; but sometimes the *m* in the end is replaced by *n* (1st Ser., Part I., c. III.), as we find in Ellistrin near Letterkenny in Donegal, and Ellistron near Ballinrobe in Mayo:—all these names meaning a place producing flaggers. In the northern counties the word usually takes an *s* in the beginning instead of the southern *f;* and the resulting form gives name to Mullanshellistragh in the parish of Cleenish in Fermanagh, the little hill (*mullan*) of the flaggers; and to Lisatilister near Carrickmacross in Monaghan, in which the *s* is eclipsed by *t* — *Lios-a'-tsiolastair*, the fort of the flaggers.

Reed—Broom. The word *giolc* or *giolcach* [gilk, gilka: *g* hard] is used differently in different parts of Ireland. In the north and west it is generally applied to a reed, in the south and east to the common broom; but this assertion is liable to exceptions. In the townland of Guilcagh, which gives name to a parish in Waterford, there is even yet a lively tradition of the luxuriant growth of broom in former days. There is also a place called Guilkagh in the parish of Listerlin in Kilkenny; Gilkagh is the name of a townland in the parish of Moylough in Galway, and of another place near Ballymoe in the same county; and there is a townland called Gilykhill in the parish of Upper Cumber in Derry; but in some of these cases the word points to a growth of reeds. The genitive form of this word is seen in Kilgilky near Cecilstown, west of Mallow in Cork, broom-wood (*coill*, wood).

Sometimes this word is made in Irish *cuilc* or *cuilceach*, and these forms are also represented in anglicised names; as in Garranakilka in Tipperary, the broom garden. In Ulster the word is often made *gioltach*, which gives name to two townlands called Giltagh in Fermanagh, one of which is called in the Grand Jury map of Devenish, "Giltagh or Broom-hill."

Herb. The word *luibh* [luv, liv] is applied to any herb; the old form is *lub*, which is found in the Zeuss MSS., glossing *frutex;* and it is cognate with the A. Saxon *leáf*. When the word occurs in names—as it often does—we may conjecture that it was applied originally to designate places which were particularly rich in the smaller vegetable productions. It is usually anglicised *liff*, but it often assumes other forms. Drumliff is the name of three townlands in Cavan and Fermanagh, in Irish *Druim-luibh*, the ridge of the herbs; while another form of the genitive (*luibhean*) is seen in Drumliffin near Carrick-on-Shannon in Leitrim, which has the same meaning as the preceding. Clonliff—herb-meadow—is a place very near Dublin city; and there is a townland of the same name in the parish of Kinawly in Fermanagh.

This word combined with *gort* (an enclosed field) forms the compound *lubh-ghort* [looart: loovart], a garden—literally herb-plot: the old form is *lubgort*, as we find it in the Book of Armagh; and *lubgartóir* glosses *olitor* in Zeuss (Gram. Celt. 37). The Cornish representative of this compound is *luvort.* It forms part of the name Knockalohert in the parish of Kilbrin, five miles west of Doneraile in Cork—*Cnoc-a'-lubhghuirt*, the hill of the garden; and of Faslowart in Leitrim, near Lough Gill (*fás*, a wilderness); while in its simple form it gives name to Lohort near Cecilstown, west of Mallow, where there is an ancient castle of the MacCarthys, restored and still used as a residence.

The diminutive of this compound is, however, in more common use than the original, viz., *lubhghortán* [loortaun], which undergoes a great variety of changes in modern names. This is often incorrectly written *lughbhortán*, even in good authorities, and the corruption must have been introduced very early, for Cormac states in his Glossary, that this was the form in use in his time. The Four Masters mention one place of this name, and use the corrupt form *Lughbhurdán;* this is now the name of a townland in the parish of Ballintober, Mayo; and it is known by the anglicised name of Luffertaun. There is another townland called Luffertan a little west of Sligo.

A shorter form of the term is Lorton, which is the name of a hill within the demesne of Rockingham, near Boyle, from which Lord Lorton takes his title. In King's County the same name is made Lowerton; and it puts on a complete English dress in Lowertown, which is the name of four townlands in the counties of Cork, Mayo, Tyrone, and Westmeath.

Moss. Caonach [keenagh] is the Irish term for moss. Keenagh, one of its anglicised forms, which is applied to mossy land, is the name of several villages, townlands, and rivers, in Leinster, Connaught, and Ulster: there is a village of this name five miles north west from Ballymahon in Longford; and Mosstown, the name of the adjacent demesne and residence, is intended to be a translation of the Irish. The diminutive Keenaghan, with the same application, is a townland name of frequent occurrence; and another diminutive Keenoge is met with pretty often in some of the Ulster and Leinster counties. It is seen as a termination in Drumkeenagh in the parish of Cleenish, Fermanagh, and in Caherakeeny, five miles west of Tuam in Galway, the ridge and the *caher* or stone fort of the moss; also in Carrivekeeny in Armagh, near Newry, and in Carrowkeeny in the parish of Kiltown in Roscommon, north west of Athlone, mossy quarter.

Grass. The usual word for grass is *fér* or *féur;* and while topographically it was sometimes used in its simple signification, it was also, in an extended sense, often applied to a meadow, a grassy place, or lea land. One usual anglicised form is *fear*, which is seen in Fearglass in Leitrim; in Ferbane the name of a village in King's County; and in Fearboy in the same county; of which the first means green, the second whitish, and the third yellowish, grass-land. The adjective form Fearagh or Feragh, signifies a grassy spot, which is also the signification of the diminutive Fearaun, in the parish of Kilrush in Kildare.

Sometimes the initial *f* disappears by aspiration, as we find in Lissanair in the parish of Kilmihil in Clare; *Lios-an-fhéir*, the fort of the grass. This is the case in the word *moinfhéur* [monair], a mountain meadow; literally bog-grass (*móin*, bog); which is sometimes found forming a part of names; such as

Monairmore and Monearmore, the names of several townlands in Munster and Connaught, great meadow; Ballinvonear near Doneraile in Cork, *Baile-an-mhóinfhéir*, the town of the mountain meadow.

In Donegal and Derry and some of the neighbouring counties, they use the word *eibhis* [evish] to designate coarse mountain pasture, synonymous with *monair* in the south; and the word has become incorporated in many place names; such as Evish, two miles from Strabane; Avish in Derry; Evish hill over Glenariff in Antrim; Evishacrow in the same neighbourhood, the mountain pasture of the *cro* or hut—the latter built no doubt to shelter the cattle; Evishbreedy in Donegal, Brigid's pasture.

Gruag means the hair of the head. Hence the word *gruagach*, a name applied to a giant; this term being selected as marking a most noticeable feature of a giant, as he existed in the imagination of the people—viz. hairiness. This word, as well as the diminutive form *gruagan*, is also applied to a sort of fairy. In the county Antrim the fairy called *grogan* is a hairy fellow, low in stature, with broad shoulders, and "desperately strong." This is much the same as the popular idea of the "drudging goblin" that prevailed in England in the time of Milton, as he expresses it in L'Allegro:—

> "Then lies him down the lubber fiend,
> And stretched out all the chimney's length,
> Basks at the fire his *hairy strength*."

This word *gruag*, by a natural extension of meaning, is applied to long *hair-like* grass growing in a marshy or sedgy place; and in this sense it often occurs in local names. Hence we have in various parts of the country Grogagh, Grogey, Grogan, Groggan, Grogeen and Gruig, all signifying sedge—a place producing long sedgy grass.

Urla [oorla] signifying the hair of the head, is applied topographically in exactly the same secondary sense as the preceding; and gives name to Oorla near Foynes in Limerick, to Urlee in the parish of Lisselton in the north of Kerry—a place of long grass; and to Lissurland, three miles from Newcastle in Limerick, corrupted from Lissurlan, the fort of the long marshy grass.

Céabh or *céibh* [keeve, cave] means a lock of hair; it is given in Cor. Gl. as the equivalent of *urla*. Like the preceding words, it is applied to long grass that grows in morasses. There are townlands in Galway and Mayo called Cave, apparently an English word, but in reality the phonetic representative of *Ceibh*: near Ahascragh in Galway, it takes the form of Keave. The adjective forms *ciabhach* and *ciabhaigh*, with the same general meaning—a marshy place producing long grass—gives name to Keevagh in Clare; to Cavey in that part of the parish of Errigle Keeroge that lies in Tyrone; and to Kivvy in Cavan and Leitrim. Culcavy near Hillsborough in Down, the hill-back (*cúl*) of the long grass; Cloghnakeava near Gort in Galway, and Roscavey near the village of Beragh in Tyrone, the stone and the point of the long grass. Sometimes the word is pronounced *cíb*, genitive *cibe* [keeb, keeba: restoration of aspirated *b*: see 1st Ser.; Part I. c. II.]; whence we have Monakeeba near Thurles in Tipperary, the grassy bog.

Mong also signifies the hair of the head, or a mane (Welsh *mwng*, a mane); and like the three last terms, it is applied to long coarse grass, or to a sedgy place. From this we have Mong, Mongagh, Munga, Mongan, Mongaun, Mungan, Mungaun, in various counties, all meaning a morass, a wet place producing long, coarse, sedgy grass. There is a river called Mongagh, i. e. the sedgy river, flowing through the parishes of Castlelost and Castlejordan in Westmeath; and one of the mountains near Nephin in Mayo, is called Glennamong, the glen of the sedge, a name which was extended to the mountain from a glen.

Dandelion. The Irish designated the dandelion by its most prominent quality, bitterness of taste; for they commonly called it *searbhán* or *searbhóg* [sharavaun, sharavoge] two diminutives from *searbh*, bitter. In some places they call the plant *cais-tsearbhán* [cosh'tharvaun]—prefixing *cas*, twisted or curled, in reference to the form of the leaf, which causes the *s* to be eclipsed by *t*; but I do not find this term in any local names.

There is a place called Moneysharvan two miles north of Maghera in Derry, which is in Irish, *Moin-na-searbhan*, the bog of the dandelions; and the word is used with an eclipse in the genitive singular, in Toberataravan, in the parish of Tumna, east of Boyle in Roscommon, *Tobar-a'-tsearbháin*, dandelion well. The word *searbhog* has been already examined (p. 29). It is found compounded in Pollsharvoge, in the parish of Meelick in Mayo, about four miles south-east of Foxford; and in Gortnasharvoge in Roscommon, near Ballinasloe, the hole (*poll*) and the field (*gort*), of the dandelions.

Sorrel. The common sorrel is produced plentifully everywhere in Ireland, and it has given names to great numbers of places. Its Irish name is *samhadh*, pronounced *saua*, *sawva*, *sow*, according to locality; the word undergoes a variety of changes, but it is easily recognised in all its forms. As it stands it gives name to the river Sow—the sorrel-producing river—which falls into the estuary of the Slaney at Castlebridge, a little above Wexford; Sooey in the parish of Ballynakill in Sligo, near the village of Riverstown, means sorrel-bearing land; Garshooey, three miles west of Derry, *Garrdha-samhaidh*, sorrel garden; Kilsough near Skerries in Dublin, *Coill-samhach*, sorrel wood.

In the greater number of cases however, the *s* disappears, giving place to *t* by eclipse; and the various forms it then assumes—none of them difficult of recognition—are illustrated in the following names. Curraghatawy in the parish of Drumreilly in Leitrim, near Ballinamore, *Currach-a'-tsamhaidh*, the marsh of the sorrel; and similarly Derrintawy in the same county, and Derreenatawy in Roscommon (*derry* and *derreen*, oak wood); Carrowntawa and Carrowntawy in Sligo (*carrow*, a quarter-land); and Currantavy in Mayo (*cor*, a round hill). In the parish of Kilmihil in Clare, there is a place called Illaunatoo, which is correctly translated by the *alias* name, Sorrel Island, while a residence in the townland has got the name of Sorrel House; Knockatoo in Galway, sorrel hill; Carrigathou near Macroom in Cork, the rock of the sorrel. In the northern half of Ireland the *v* sound of the *mh* often comes out clearly; as in Knockatavy in Louth, sorrel hill; and in Ulster the *m* is often fully restored (see 1st Ser., Part I. c. II.), as in Aghintamy near the town of Monaghan, *Achadh-an-tsamhaidh*, the field of the sorrel.

Rue. The herb rue is denoted in Irish by what is in sound the same as the English word, namely *ru* or *rubha* [rooa]. The word has nearly the same sound as *ruadh*, red; and it is often difficult to determine to which of these two terms we are to refer a name. In a great many cases however, the old people make a clear distinction, and we may, with the usual cautions (see 1st Ser. Part I. c. I.) follow their guidance. Moreover, the names on the Ordnance maps commonly tell their own story; for those who determined the modern forms, generally distinguished between the two words by anglicising *ruadh*, *roe*, and *rubha*, *roo* or *rue*.

The Four Masters at the year 1599 mention a place near the abbey of Corcomroe in the north of Clare, called *Rubha* (rue or rue-land); it lies two miles west of the village of Kinvarra in Galway, and it is now called Roo. Very near Roo House is the little hamlet of Corranroo, so called from an old *carra* or weir; from this again the head of Aughinish bay, on whose shore the village is situated, is called Corranroo Bay; and adjacent to the hamlet is the peninsula of Inishroo—rue island. There are several other places scattered over the country called Roo, Rue, Rowe, and Roos (the English plural form), which have taken their names, not from their red colour, but from producing a plentiful growth of this herb.

Rowe in the parish of Killare in Westmeath, is mentioned in the Annals by the name *Rubha*. The Calendars mention a saint Tiu of *Rubha* in the Ards, in the county of Down; this old name is still preserved in the name of the townland of Rowreagh (*reagh*, grey: grey rue-land); and in that of "Rubane House" adjoining it (*bán*, whitish)—both situated near the village of Kircubbin. Rubha-Chonaill (Conall's rue-land) is mentioned by the Four Masters as the scene of several battles—one in A.D. 798; another in 1159. This place is situated two miles east of Mullingar; its Irish name is pronounced Ru-

connell, which sound is still retained by some of the old people; but it is corruptly anglicised Rathconnell, which is now the name of a townland and parish. There is another place called Rathconnell in Kildare; but here the name means Connell's rath or fort. Gortaroo, the name of a place three miles from Youghal, on the left of the road to Cork, and Gortarowey in the parish of Drumcliff, north of Sligo town, both signify the field of the rue.

Wall fern. The *polypodium vulgare* or wall fern is denoted by *sgeamh* [scav]. The simple word gives name to Drumnascamph in the parish of Clonduff in Down, *Druim-na-sceamh*, the ridge of the wall ferns. Its diminutive is seen in Carrigskeewaun in the parish of Kilgeever in Mayo; and in Meenscovane in the parish of Duagh, Kerry, the former meaning the rock, and the latter the smooth plain, of the wall-ferns.

Watercress. The ancient Irish used the watercress for food--probably much in the same way as it is used at the present day; for among the prerogatives of the king of Ireland, mentioned in the Book of Rights, are the cresses of the river Brosna in Westmeath. *Biorar* [birrer] is the word for watercress, and it is obviously derived from *bior*, water, by the addition of the collective termination *r* (p. 12). In the colloquial language the middle *r* of this word is always changed to *l* by a common phonetic law, and it is consequently pronounced *biller*.

In Cork and Kerry there are several townlands called Billeragh—Irish *Biolarach*, a place producing cresses; in Donegal, Monaghan, and Tyrone, it takes the form Billary, and in Wexford, Bellary, both of which represent the oblique case *biolaraigh*. In the end of names the *b* is commonly aspirated, and the word is then anglicised *viller*. There is a townland in the parish of Killann in Wexford, taking its name from a little stream running down the eastern slope of the Blackstairs mountains, called Askinvillar—Irish *Easc-an-bhiolair*, the wet land, or the water-course of the cresses; Toberaviller near the town of Wicklow, watercress well.

Marsh mallows. The simple form of the word denoting marsh mallows is *leamh* [lav], or in old Irish *lem*, as we find it in the St. Gall MS. of Zeuss (Gram. Celt. p. 274). It is curious that the very same word is applied to the elm, and it is often therefore difficult to say which of the two plants is meant, when we find the term in names. It is probable that the words for marsh mallows and for elm are radically different, and have accidentally assumed the same form (see Max Müller: Lectures on the Science of Language, 2nd. Ser. p. 287). In modern Irish a difference in sound is made between the two words, which helps us to distinguish them one from another, *when we hear them pronounced*. There is a peculiar nasal sound in the latter part of *leamh*, when it means marsh mallows, which it is impossible to indicate on paper; but the pronunciation is not very different from *lew*; and besides this, the term usually employed (for this plant) is not the simple form, but the derivative *leamhach*, which is pronounced something like *lewagh*.

Whatever amount of uncertainty there may be in the word, the following names may be referred, without much danger of error, to this plant, and not to the elm. In Kilkenny and Tipperary there are places called Leugh; Lewagh is a townland near Thurles; Leo is near Ballyhaunis in Mayo; Leoh in the parish of Donaghmore in Wicklow; Luogh, the name of a small lake and two townlands, near the cliffs of Moher in Clare:—all these names were originally applied to a place producing marsh mallows—and all show, in their modernised orthography, an attempt to represent the peculiar sound of the Irish. The word appears compounded in Rathnaleugh near the village of Rathdowney in Queen's County, the fort of the marsh mallows.

Dock-leaf. The diminutive *copóg* [cuppoge] is the word now always used for the common dock-leaf; but judging from some of the derivatives that follow, it would appear that the primitive *cop* and another diminutive *copán* must have been in use at some former time. The usual form (with the adjective suffix *ach*) is seen in Glencoppogagh in the parish of Upper Bodoney in Tyrone, the glen of the dock-leaves; and with the *c* eclipsed to *g* in Lagnagoppoge (*lag*, a hollow), a little south of Strangford in Down, and in Cloonnagoppoge in Mayo, dock-leaf meadow. This termination, *goppoge* or *gappoge*, is extremely common all over the country. From the root *cop* is formed *copánach* (by the addition of the diminutive and the adjective terminations), signifying a place abounding in dock-leaves, which, with very little change, is anglicised Coppanagh, the name of some places in Ulster, Connaught, and Leinster; while the oblique form gives name to several townlands called Copney and Copany, in Tyrone, Armagh, and Donegal.

Garlic. The common wild garlic is denoted—among other words—by *creamh* [crav: craw], which in anglicised names appears as *craff*, *crave*, *crew*, *cramph*, &c. Clooncraff, now a parish in Roscommon, and once a place of some ecclesiastical note, is often mentioned in the annals by the name of *Cluain-creamha*, the meadow of wild garlic. There is a townland of the same name not far from the town of Roscommon; near Killucan in Westmeath, the name is varied to Clooncrave, and in Limerick to Cloncrew, which is the name of a parish. There is a little island in Lough Corrib opposite the castle of Cargins, now called Inishcraff, which is often mentioned by the annalists, and called by them *Inis-creamha*. O'Flaherty, in his account of Iar Connaught, speaks of it in these words:—"Iniscreawa, or wild garlic isle . . . . where the walls and high ditch of a well fortified place are still extant and encompass almost the whole island. Of this isle, Macamh Insicreawa (the youth of Inishcraff), a memorable ancient magician, as they say, had his denomination." The walls mentioned by O'Flaherty, which are cyclopean in their character, still remain; and the people say they are the remains of the fortress of Orbsen who gave name to Lough Corrib (see this in 1st Series).

In the northern counties, the word is often anglicised *cramph* (like the change of *damh* to *damph*, &c.—see 1st Ser. Part I. c. III.), as in Derrycramph near the town of Cavan, the oak wood of the wild garlic, the same name as Derrycraff in Mayo, and Derrycrave in Westmeath. This change, with the eclipse of the *c* by *g*, is exhibited in Drumgramph in Fermanagh, Monaghan, and Tyrone, *Druim-gcreamh*, garlic ridge.

Creamh combined with *coill*, wood, forms the compound *creamhchoill* [cravwhill: wild garlic wood], which undergoes many curious transformations in anglicised names, closely corresponding with the various forms of *leamhchoill* (see Longfield in 1st Ser.). One modification is Craffield, which is the name of a townland in Wicklow; and we have Clooncraffield (the meadow of the wild-garlic wood) near Castlerea in Roscommon. There is a parish in Antrim called Cranfield, which exhibits another form: Colgan calls it by its correct Irish name, *Creamh-choill*, but in a lease of 1683 it is written "Croghill alias Cranfield," showing that at that period the name was in process of change from an old and correct anglicised form, to what it is now. The townland of Cranfield also, which occupies the southern extremity of the barony of Mourne, and gives name to Cranfield Point at the entrance of Carlingford Lough, was formerly called Craughill (see Reeves: Eccl. Ant. p. 87). In Sligo this name becomes Crawhill, and in the parish of Ahoghill in Antrim, Crankill.

It appears probable that the correct form of this word is *cneamh* [*knav*: *k* and *n* both pronounced], and that this has been corrupted to *creamh* like *cnoc* to *crock*; for we find *cneamh* preserved in several names. Knavagh is the name of a townland in the parish of Tiranascragh, near the Shannon, north of Portumna in Galway, which is the adjective form *Cneamhach*, a place producing wild garlic. In the parish of Inchicronan in Clare, one mile from the village of Crusheen, there is a townland called Drumminacknew, which took the first part of its name from a low ridge or *drumman*. But this little hill—as in many other cases—after giving name to the townland, got a new name itself, which however is a correct translation of the old name; and it is now called Garlic Hill. There is a place near Lismore in Waterford called Curraghacnav, the garlic-producing marsh.

Parsnip. The word *meacan* [mackan] is used to denote the taprooted plants; and the several kinds are designated by means of distinguishing terms;

such as *meacan-ragam*, horse-radish; *meacan-buidhe-an-tsleibhe*, the common spurge, &c. Taken without any qualifying term, however, the word is commonly understood to mean a parsnip, and I will translate it in this sense in the few names mentioned under the present heading.

From this word are derived the names of all those places now called Mackan, Macknan, Mackanagh, Macknagh, and Mackney—the second the diminutive in *an*, the three last the adjective form *meacanach;* all so called from producing in abundance parsnips or some other sort of tap-rooted plant—wild no doubt;—Cloonmackan and Clonmackan, parsnip meadow; Gortnamackan and Gortnamackanee, the field of the parsnips.

Wood; forest. The word *fothar* [fohar] is given by Peter O'Connell in his dictionary, as meaning a forest; and he also gives the plural form *foithre*. It is a term often met with in Irish writings, though it is not given in the dictionaries of O'Brien and O'Reilly. In ancient times there was a woody district to the north-west of Birr in King's County, which is called in the annals, *Fothar-Dealbhnach*, i. e. the forest of Delvin, from the old district in which it was situated; and though this great wood has long since disappeared, its name and memory are preserved in the townland of Ballaghanoher, halfway between Birr and Banagher, which correctly represents the sound of the old name, as the Four Masters write it, *Bealach-an-fhothair*, the road of the forest.

The word more commonly occurs, however, in the plural form *foithre* [fihra, fira, fweera], which is often understood to mean underwood, or copse, or forest land, and is anglicised in several ways. Gortnafira, in the parish of Mogeely in Cork, not far from the village of Tallow, signifies the field of the underwood. There is a townland near the village of Ferbane in King's County, which gives name to a parish, now called Wheery, but locally pronounced *Fweehra*, which is a correct anglicised representation of *Foithre*, woods; and from this also is named the townland of Curraghwheery, the marsh of Wheery. In the parish of Kilbelfad in Mayo, south-west of Ballina, on the shore of Lough Conn, this name is found in the form of Wherrew; and in Kerry the idea of plurality is conveyed by the addition of the *s* of the English inflection, forming Fieries, the name of two places, one in the parish of Molahiffe, four miles from Miltown, and the other near Castleisland.

Fire-wood. *Conadh* [conna] signifies firewood: old form as given in Cor. Gl. *condud:* Welsh *cynnud*. The word has been used in this sense from very early times, for we find *connadh*, "fire-bote," mentioned in the Book of Rights as a portion of the tribute of the unfree tribes of Leinster to the king of that province. It occurs very often in names; and it was no doubt applied to places where there was abundance of withered trees and bushes, the remains of a decayed wood or shrubbery.

The word takes several modern forms, which will be understood from the following examples. In the Four Masters, and also in the "Annals of Ireland," translated for Sir James Ware by Duald Mac Firbis, it is recorded at the year 1445, that Lynagh Mageogheghan was slain at a place called *Coill-an-chonaidh*, the wood of the "fire-bote:" the place is situated in the parish of Kilcumreragh in Westmeath, and it is now called Killyconny. There is another place of the same name in Cavan, and a village called

Kilconny, also in Cavan—this last having the same signification. Other forms are seen in Drumminacunna near Cappaghwhite in Tipperary (*drummin*, a low hill); also in Moneyconey west of Draperstown in Derry, and in Monachunna in the parish of Dunnamaggan in Kilkenny, the former signifying the shrubbery, and the latter, the bog, of the firewood. In Cork and Kerry, the final *dh* is often changed to *g* (as in many other cases), which is fully pronounced; as we see in Clooncunnig in Cork, the same as Clooncunna, Clooncunny, and Clooncomy in other counties, all meaning fire-wood meadow. And lastly by the aspiration of the *c* to *h*, the word is frequently anglicised *honey*, which is a pretty common termination, especially in the north; as in Drumhoney near Irvinestown in Fermanagh, fire-wood ridge.

Stump or stake. The word *smut*, and its diminutive *smután*, are used to denote a log, a stake, a stump of a tree. This is a pretty common element in names; and I suppose it was applied to places where some of the branchless stumps of an old wood, or some one remarkable trunk, still remained standing. Some thing like this last must have been the case in Smuttanagh near Balla in Mayo, which is called in Hy Fiachrach, *Baile-an-smotáin*, the town of the stock or trunk; but the modern form, Smuttanagh, means a place full of trunks. The word appears in its simple form in Clashnasmut a little north of Carrick-on-Suir, the *clash* or trench of the trunks. But the diminutive is more common. There is a townland in Mayo, and another in Tipperary, called Gortnasmuttaun, the field of the stakes. Ballysmuttan (town of the tree-trunks) is a well-known place on the river Liffey, near Blessington; Toorsmuttaun in Galway (*tuar*, a bleachfield); Coolasmuttane near Charleville in Cork, and Lissasmuttaun near Portlaw in Waterford, the angle (*cuil*) and the *lis* or fort, of the trunk.

Another word for a tree-stock, stake or block, is *ceap* [cap], which is often used and applied in much the same sense as *smut*: cognate with Lat. *cippus*, a sharp stake, and with Welsh *cyff*, a trunk. It generally appears in the anglicised form *kip*, which represents the genitive *cip*. In 1573, a battle was fought between two parties of the O'Briens of Thomond, at a place which the Four Masters call *Bel-an-chip*, the (ford-)mouth of the tree-trunk; the name is now Knockakip, which is applied to a hill on the seashore near Lahinch in the County Clare. There was an old ford over the Shannon, near Carrick-on-Shannon, which is mentioned several times in the annals, by the name of *Ath-an-chip*, a name having the same meaning as *Bel-an-chip*. It is probable that a large trunk of a tree stood near each of these fords, and served as a mark to direct travellers to the exact crossing. What gave name to Kippure mountain, from the slopes of which the rivers Liffey and Dodder run down to the Dublin plain, it is now hard to say with certainty; but probably it was so called from the remains of some large old yew, for the name exactly represents *Cip-iubhair*, the trunk of the yew tree. Coolkip near Holycross in Tipperary, and Coolakip in Wexford, both mean the corner of the trunk.

The *c* is often changed to *g* by eclipse, and then the word becomes *gap* in anglicised names. Gortnagap is the name of a townland near Tullaroan in Kilkenny; and there is another called Askanagap in the parish of Moyne in Wicklow—the former meaning the field (*gort*) and the latter the wet land (*easga*) of the trunks. *Kippeen* (*cipín*, little stick), one of the diminutives of this word, is well-known by all people having any knowledge of Ireland, as a popular term for a *shillelagh* or cudgel: it gives name (though not exactly in this sense) to Kippin in Westmeath; also to Kippinduff in the same county, and Kippeenduff (black little trunk) near the village of Clara in King's County.

Thorn. *Dealg* [dallog] means literally a thorn; but in a secondary sense it is applied to a pin or brooch. It occurs in names in the forms *dallig*, *dellig*, *dollig*, &c., but always in the primary sense of a thorn or a thorn bush. There is a townland called Moneydollog near Ahoghill in Antrim, the Irish name of which is *Muine-dealg*, the thorny shrubbery; and Kildellig (church of the thorns) is the name of a parish in Queen's County.

When this word comes in as a termination, the *d* often becomes eclipsed by *n*, as in Reennanallagane in the parish of Glanbehy in Kerry, which also exhibits a diminutive of the word under consideration, *Rinn-na-ndealgán*, the point of the little thorn-bushes. The plural form is seen in Delliga, near the village of Milford, in the parish of Kilbolane in Cork, which the Four Masters write *Delge*, i.e. thorns; and in Delligabaun in the parish of Aghaboe in Queen's County, whitish thorn-bushes.

Brier or *bramble.* The word *dreas* or *dris* [drass, drish] is used in very old documents to signify a brier or bramble of any kind; but the diminutive *driseóg* [drishoge] is the term now commonly employed, and it is usually applied to a brier, or a blackberry bush, or any bramble. Our local nomenclature exhibits a great variety of derivatives from the word *dris*. Three diminutives as well as the primitive, give names to places; but they are applied topographically, not to a single bramble, but rather to a brake of briars or a brambly place.

The river Drish (brambly river) joins the Suir near Thurles. Drishane on the Blackwater near Mill-street in Cork, is well known as one of the former seats of the M'Carthys, where the ruin of their castle still remains, from which the parish has its name; and there are several other places of the same name in Cork and Tipperary. Another diminutive gives name to Drisheen, a little west of Skibbereen in Cork: a third, Drishoge, is the name of several places in Dublin, Roscommon and Tipperary, which assumes in Meath and Carlow, the form Drissoge, and changes to Dressoge in Fermanagh and Tyrone.

There are several other derivatives, which are also applied in the same sense as the preceding—to a brambly place. Drishaghaun—a diminutive of the adjective form *driseach*—is the name of six townlands in Roscommon, Galway, and Mayo; while we have Dresnagh, the name of a place a mile from Castle-finn in Donegal, formed from the primitive *dreas* by the addition of the suffix *nach* (see p. 6). Dristernan and Dresternan, which occur frequently in the north-western counties, exhibit the compound termination *rnán* (p. 41); but I cannot account for the *t* except as a mere euphonic insertion. Similarly, we have with *rnach* (p. 16) Dresternagh near Ballyhaise in Cavan; which with the change of *d* to *t*, becomes Tristernagh, the name of a well known place on the shore of Lough Iron in Westmeath. Dressogagh, an adjective from one of the diminutives, is the name of two townlands in Armagh.

It is perfectly easy to recognise this word in all its

forms when it occurs as a termination. The simple form appears in Gortnadrass near Achonry in Sligo, the briar field; and in Kildress, a parish in Tyrone, the church of the brambles; so also Ardrass in Mayo and Kildare, and Ardress near Loughgall in Armagh, *Ard-dreas*, the height of the brambles.

Sallow. If the Irish distinguished, in their tongue, the different species of sallow one from another, these distinctions do not appear in that part of the language that has subsided into local names; for the word *sáil* [saul] is used to designate all the different kinds—cognate with Lat. *salix*, and with Manx *shell*, and Welsh *helyg*, willows.

Solloghod, now a parish in Tipperary, derives its name from this tree; and for this etymology we have the authority of Cormac MacCullenan. He states in his Glossary that *Salchoit*, as he writes the name, comes from *sal*, the sallow, and *coit*, a Welsh word for wood; and he further tells us that a large wood of sallows grew there; but of this there is not a trace remaining.

This word has a great variety of derivatives, and all give names to places in various parts of the country. The simple word *sáil* is seldom heard, the adjective form *sáileach* and the diminutive *saileog* being now universally used to designate the plant. The former is anglicised *sillagh*, *silla*, and *sallagh* in the end of names, and the latter *silloge* and *silloga*. Both are exemplified in Corsillagh near Newtown Mountkennedy in Wicklow, and in Corsilloga in the parish of Aghnamullen in Monaghan, each signifying the round hill of the sallows. Lisnasallagh, the fort of the sallows, is the name of two townlands in Cork, and of one near Saintfield in Down; while the same name is found in Roscommon in the form Lisnasillagh; Currasilla in Tipperary and Kilkenny, the *curragh* or marsh of the osiers.

There are several diminutives, from one of which, Sylaun (a place of sallows), the name of some places in Galway is derived. Tooreennasillane near Skibbereen in Cork, signifies the little bleach-field of the osiers; Cloonsellan is the name of some townlands in Longford and Roscommon (*cloon*, a meadow); and there is a considerable lake near Shercock in Cavan, called Lough Sillan, the osier-producing lake. Other derivatives are exhibited in Sallaghan in Cavan and Leitrim, and Sallaghy in Fermanagh, all meaning a place of sallows or osiers.

Sometimes the *s* is changed to *t* by eclipse, as in Kiltallaghan in the parish of Killamery in Kilkenny, and Kiltillahan near Carnew in Wexford, both of which would be written in Irish *Coill-tsaileacháin*, the wood of the sallows, the same as Kilsallaghan, the name of a parish near Swords in Dublin. In these three names there is a combination of the adjective termination *ach* and the diminutive *án*. The eclipse also occurs along with the diminutive in *óg* in Kyletilloge, in the parish of Aghaboe, Queen's County, which has the same signification as Kilsallaghan.

Fir. Giumhas [guse: *g* hard] denotes a fir tree. In some parts of the country the word is in constant use, even when the people are speaking English; for the pieces of old deal timber dug up from bogs, which they use for firing, and sometimes for light in place of candles, are known by the name of *gewsh*.

This tree has not given names to many places, which would appear to show that in former times it was not very abundant; and when it does occur it may be a question in any individual case, whether the place was so called from the living tree or from bog-deal. In the parish of Moore in Roscommon, there is a townland called Cappayuse — *Ceapach-ghiumhais* (*g* changed to *y* by aspiration), the garden plot of the fir. The name of Monagoush near Ardmore in Waterford, indicates that the bog (*moin*) supplied the people with winter stores of *gewsh*; in Meenaguse near Inver in Donegal (*meen*, a mountain meadow) the fir is still taken out of the bog; and we may probably account in the same way for the name of Lough Ayoosy, a little lake five miles south-west from Crossmolina in Mayo, and of another small lake—Lough Aguse—two miles from Galway.

Arbutus. The arbutus grows in most parts of Ireland, though it is generally a rare plant; it is plentiful, however, in parts of Cork and Kerry, especially about Killarney and Glengarriff, where it flourishes in great luxuriance. Some think that it was brought to Ireland from the continent by monks, in the early ages of Christianity; but it is more generally believed to be indigenous; and it appears to me a strong argument in favour of this opinion, that we have a native term for it. The Irish call it *caithne* [cahĭna]; and in the neighbourhood of the Killarney lakes, this word is known, but veiled under a thin disguise; for even the English speaking people call the berries of the arbutus *cain*-apples, though few or none of them suspect how this name took its rise. Moreover this name has been long in use; for Threlkeld, who wrote his "Synopsis Stirpium Hibernicarum" in 1727, notices it, and recognises it as an anglicised form of *caithne*.

The arbutus has not given name to many places. The wood at the back of the Eagle's Nest near Killarney, is called Cahnicaun (see p. 19) or arbutus wood; and the stream that flows from Barley lake down to Glengarriff, is named Owenacahina, the river of the arbutus. The Irish name of the village of Smerwick near Dingle in Kerry, which is still used, is *Ard-na-caithne* (now pronounced Ardnaconnia), the height of the arbutus. Isknagahiny is the name of a small lake near Lough Currane in Kerry, five miles north-east of Darrynane:—*Eisc-na-gcaithne*, the stream-track of the arbutus trees.

In Clare and the west of Ireland, the name of this tree is a little different, viz., *cuinche*, pronounced very nearly *queenha;* this form is found as the name of a village and parish in Clare, now shortened to Quin, where Sheeda Macnamara founded an abbey in 1402, the ruins of which are yet to be seen. The Four Masters, who mention it several times, call it *Cuinche*, arbutus or arbutus land; and this ancient name is correctly anglicised Quinchy in Carlisle's Topographical Dictionary, and Quinhie in the Down Survey, this last being almost identical in sound with the western name of the arbutus. In the same parish is a townland now called Feaghquin, but written in an old quit rent ledger, Feaghquinny, i. e. arbutus land. One of the many islands in Clew bay, a very small one, is called Quinsheen, a diminutive form signifying little arbutus island.

CHAPTER XX.

THE MINERAL KINGDOM.

Gold. It appears certain that gold and silver mines were worked in this country from the most remote antiquity; and that these precious metals—especially gold—were found anciently in much greater abundance than they have been in recent times. Our oldest traditions record not only the existence of the mines, but also the names of the kings who had them worked, and even those of the artificers. According to the bardic annals, the monarch Tighernmas [Tiernmas: about 1000 years B. C.], was the first that smelted gold in Ireland, and covered with it drinking goblets and brooches; the mines were situated in the *Foithre*, the woods or woody districts (see p. 330), east of the Liffey; and the artificer was *Uchadan*, who lived in *Fercualan*, that part of Wicklow lying round Powerscourt. Whatever amount of truth there may be in this old legend, it proves very clearly that the Wicklow gold mines were as well known in the far distant ages of antiquity as they were in the end of the last century, when the accidental discovery of a few pieces of gold in the bed of a stream, revived the long lost knowledge, and caused such an exciting search for several years. This stream, which is now called the Gold mine river, flows from the mountain of Croghan Kinshella, and joins the Ovoca near the Wooden Bridge hotel. On account of the abundance of gold in Wicklow in old times, the people of Leinster sometimes got the name of *Laighnigh-an-óir*, the Lagenians of the gold (O'Curry, Lect. I., 5).

Several other early kings are celebrated for having introduced certain golden ornaments, or made the custom of wearing them more general. And Irish literature abounds in allusions to golden bosses, brooches, pins, armlets, crowns, &c. In later and more authentic annals, we have records also which show that gold was every where within reach of the wealthy, and used by them in numerous works of art.

The general truthfulness of these traditions and records is fully borne out by the great quantities of manufactured gold found in various parts of the country; and whoever looks on the fine collection in the Royal Irish Academy, which, rich as it is, is only a small remnant of our ancient golden ornaments, will be scarcely prepared to discredit the ancient accounts. These ornaments moreover are not alloyed—the gold is absolutely pure, as far as the old gold workers were able to make it so. And this universal purity, and the corresponding richness of colour, gave rise to the expression *derg-ór*—red gold—which occurs so often in Irish writings, both ancient and modern.

The Irish word for gold is *ór* [ore], cognate with Latin *aurum*, and Welsh *aur*. It enters into the formation of a considerable number of names of places, in each of which we must conclude that gold in some shape or another was formerly found. In many of these places traditions are current of the former presence of gold, and in some it is found at the present day. Near the village of Cullen, on the borders of Limerick and Tipperary, there is a bog which has been long celebrated for the quantities of manufactured gold found in it. For the last 150 years, innumerable golden articles of various kinds have been dug up from the bottom of this bog, as well as many of the implements used by the old goldsmiths in their work, such as crucibles, bronze ladles, &c. ; from which it is probable, as O'Curry remarks, that this place was anciently—long before the bog was formed, and when the land was clothed with wood—inhabited by a race of goldsmiths, who carried on the manufacture there for generations. O'Curry, in a portion of a very interesting lecture, has endeavoured to identify the goldsmiths of this place with a race of artificers, who, according to their genealogy as given in the Book of Leinster, were descended immediately from Olioll Olum, king of Munster, and who followed the trade uninterruptedly for seven generations, from about A.D. 300 to 500 (Lectures, III., 205). It may be added that the bog of Cullen is proverbial all over Munster for its riches :—

> " And her wealth it far outshines,
> Cullen's bog or Silvermines."

(See " The Enchanted Lake" in Crofton Croker's " Fairy Legends").

The celebrated fort of Dunanore, in Smerwick Bay in Kerry, was correctly translated Fort-del-or (fort of the gold), by the Spaniards, who landed and fortified themselves in it in 1580. The Four Masters call it in one passage *Dun-an-óir*, and in another *Oilen-an-óir* (island of the gold), of which the former name shows that the rock must have been originally occupied by a circular *dun* or fort. As to why it was called the Fort of Gold, there are several opinions and traditions, none of which seem either sufficient to explain it, or worthy of being recorded. Another name like this is Casheloir (*caiseal*, a stone fort), applied to a fine circular fort of the most ancient cyclopean masonry, lying near the village of Ballintogher in Sligo, three miles from Drumahaire.

One of the various ways in which a place may have derived its name from gold is illustrated in the account of the death of Lewy Mac-Con, king of Ireland in the second century. It is stated that on one occasion this king was at a place called *Gort-an-óir* (near *Derg-rath* : see p. 311), standing with his back against a pillar stone, engaged in the royal occupation of distributing gold and silver to the poets and learned men of Ireland. A certain poet named Ferchas, the son of Coman, who lived at a place called *Ard-na-Gemlech* (height of the fetters), otherwise called *Cnocach* (*i.e.*, hilly place), when he heard how the king was occupied, entered with some others into the assembly, with a kind of javelin called a *rincné* in his hand, which he drove with one thrust through the king's body, so that it struck the pillar stone at the other side ; and Mac-Con died immediately. It is added that "*Gort-an-óir* (field of the gold) has been the name of that place ever since ; and it has been so called from the quantity of gold distributed there by the king to the bards and *ollamhs* of Ireland." This place, which is well known, and still retains the name of Gortanore, is situated just near the fort of Derrygrath, in the parish of the same name, four miles nearly east of Cahir in Tipperary ; and the poet's residence has left the name of Knockagh on a townland in the immediate vicinity.

In the legendary account of the origin of the name of the ancient principality of Oriel (originally comprising the territory now occupied by the counties of Monaghan, Armagh, and Louth), we have another illustration. This kingdom was founded by the three Collas in the year 332 ; and it is stated that one of their stipulations with the neighbouring kings was that whenever it should be found necessary to fetter a hostage from their newly-formed principality, chains of gold should be used for the purpose. Hence the name—used in all our authorities—*Oir-ghialla* [Oreyeela] golden hostages, which has been modernised to the form Oriel.

In every case I know of, the word *ór*, and its genitive *óir*, take the form of *ore* in anglicised names; but it must be remembered that this syllable *ore* occasionally represents other words, as for instance *uabhar*, pride.

In the parish of Feakle in Clare, near Lough Graney, there is a townland taking name from a hill, called Slieveanore—*Sliabh-an-óir*, the mountain of the gold; and there is a mountain of the same name a little west of Carrantuohill, the highest of the Reeks in Kerry; while we have Knockanore—golden hill—the name of places in Cavan, Kilkenny, and Waterford (but Knockanore near Kerry Head, at the mouth of the Shannon, is *Cnoc-an-uabhair*, the hill of pride); and Tullynore near Hillsborough in Down, the little hill (*tulach*) of the gold. At the base of the hill of Mullaghmesha between Bantry and Dunmanway in Cork, there is a small pool called Coomanore (*cúm*, a hollow among mountains); Laganore, near Clonmel in Tipperary, has much the same meaning (*lag*, a hollow); and Glananore—golden glen—is the name of a place near Castletownroche in Cork.

Silver.—As in case of gold, we have also very ancient legends about silver. Our old histories tell us that king *Enna Airgtheach*, who reigned about a century and a half after *Tighearnmas*, was the first that made silver shields in Ireland, which he distributed among his chieftain friends. The legend goes on to say that they were made at a place called *Argetros* or Silverwood, situated in the parish of Rathbeagh on the Nore in Kilkenny, which was said to derive its name from those silver shields. Rosargid, which has the same meaning, was, according to O'Dugan, the ancient name of a place near Toomyvara in Tipperary; but the name has not reached our day.

The Irish word for silver is *airgeat* [arrigit]; it is cognate with the Latin *argentum*, and with Sanscrit *ragata*, all being derived from a root *arg* or *rag*, signifying white or shining (Pictet). As silver is the standard of value, the word *airgeat* is, and has been for a long time, the common Irish word for money. It is generally easy to detect the word in local names; for its modern forms do not often depart from what would be indicated by the Irish pronunciation. Three miles from Ballycastle in Antrim, there is a place called Moyarget, the field or plain (*magh*) of silver; Cloonargid, silver meadow, is the name of a place in the parish of Tibohine, Roscommon, five miles south-west from Ballaghaderreen, which is correctly translated Silverfield in the name of a residence in the townland. There are many small lakes through the country called Lough Anargid and Lough Anargit (*Loch-an-airgit*, lake of the silver); one for instance in Galway, and another eight miles north of the town of Donegal, over which rises the "Silver Hill," which was so called from the lake. Whether these lakes took their names from a tradition of money having been buried or found in them, or from their silvery brightness, like the river Arigideen in Cork (see p. 69), it is difficult to tell.

It is certain, as I have already stated, that many of the names in the foregoing part of this chapter indicate that, at some past time, gold or silver was dug from the earth, or found in the beds of streams, at the particular places. But this is not the origin of all such names; and there is good reason to believe that a considerable number of them originated in treasure legends. There is scarcely any class of superstitions more universal, or that have taken more firm hold of the imagination of the people, than those connected with hidden treasure; and no wonder, for there are few, from a lord to a peasant, who would not be delighted to find a *crock* filled with old coins of gold and silver. Legends about hidden treasure abound in our popular literature,* and we must not wholly disbelieve them; for in all ages of the world, especially in times of turbulence or war, people have been in the habit of burying in the ground hoards of money and other valuables, on any sudden emergency or danger; and what one man hides and leaves behind him, is generally found out sooner or later by some one else.

That it has not been reserved for the people of our day to fall in for such pieces of good fortune, is shown by many old records: and as one example we find it stated in the "Tribes and Customs of Hy Many" (pp. 63-4-5) that among other emoluments, the king of Connaught ceded to the people of Hy Many "the third part of every treasure found hidden or buried in the depths of the earth."

In almost all the countries of Europe hidden treasure is popularly believed to be guarded by supernatural beings; and to circumvent them by cunning, or by some other more questionable agency, is the grand study of money seekers. In Ireland the fairies are usually the guardians; and they are extremely ingenious in devising schemes to baffle treasure seekers, or to decoy or frighten them from their pursuit. The antiquity of this superstition is proved by a curious passage in the "Wars of the

*See Crofton Croker's "Fairy Legends."

Irish with the Danes," a document as old as the eleventh century. The writer is describing the robberies perpetrated by the Danes, and their ingenuity in finding out hidden hordes of valuables, and he says:—"There was not in concealment under ground in Erin, nor in the various solitudes belonging to Fians (i.e. ancient heroes: see 1st Ser. Part II. c. I.) or to fairies, anything that was not discovered by these foreign, wonderful Denmarkians, through paganism and idol worship"—meaning "that notwithstanding the potent spells employed by the Fians and fairies for the concealment of their hidden treasures, the Danes, by their pagan magic and the diabolical power of their idols, were enabled to find them out" (Todd, in note, p. 115).

I have seen in various parts of Ireland the marks of treasure-seekers' work in old raths, castles, and abbeys, and many a fine old ruin has been sadly dilapidated by their nightly explorations.

It is probable that from legends of this kind some of the preceding names are derived, and others like them; and a similar origin may in all likelihood be assigned to the following: in most of these places indeed stories of adventurous searches after treasure are still told by the people. Lisanargid, Lisheenanargid, and Rathargid (all signifying the fort of silver or of money) are names of very frequent occurrence; Scartore—the *scart* or thicket of gold—is a place near Dungarvan in Waterford; and there is a townland called Cloghore—stone of gold—in the parish of Kilbarron in Donegal, near Belleek.

Iron. We know that among the people of Europe, weapons and instruments of stone were used in war, and in the arts of every-day life, long before the time of historical records; and that stone was superseded by bronze, and bronze by iron. It is believed that the change from one material to another was very gradual; that stone continued in use long after the introduction of bronze; and that for a period of unknown duration, bronze and iron were used contemporaneously, till the former was gradually relinquished as the latter became more plentiful.

When it was that iron mines began to be worked in this country, our annals or traditions do not inform us. It is certain that the metal was known amongst us from the earliest period to which Irish history or tradition reaches; for we find it repeatedly mentioned in our most ancient tales, romances, and historical tracts, as being the material from which were made defensive armour, and weapons of various kinds, such as clubs, spears, swords, &c. In the Book of Rights, which refers to a very early period of society, we find mentioned among the tributes due to the king of Connaught, "seven times fifty masses of iron" (p. 105). It is curious that the word used for "masses" is *coera*, i. e. sheep; a "sheep" of iron corresponding to the term "pig" used at the present day.

All this shows that some progress must have been made in very early times in the art of raising and smelting ore; but as to the particular methods employed, or to what extent the iron mines of the country were utilised by the native Irish, our literature does not, on the whole, give us much information. In the fifteenth, sixteenth, and seventeenth centuries, iron mines were extensively worked, chiefly by the Anglo-Irish lords; and the vast consumption of timber in smelting was one of the main causes of the destruction of the great forests.

The Irish word for iron is not very different from the English:—*iarann*, old Irish form *iarn* [both pronounced eeran], and the word exists in various forms in Welsh and in several of the northern languages; such as Gothic *eisarn*, old High German *isarn;* Angl.-Sax. *îren*, Welsh *heyrn*. We have numerous names formed from this word, indicating the spots where the ore was found; and some of them are mixed up with our earliest traditions. Thus the annals reckon *Loch-niairn* (the lake of iron) among the nine lakes which burst forth in the time of *Tighearnmas* (see p. 340); and this lake, which is situated in Westmeath, still retains the name, modernised to Lough Iron. According to tradition the iron mines of Slieveanierin, east of Lough Allen in the county of Leitrim (*Sliabh-an-iairn*, Four M., the mountain of iron) were worked by *Goibnen* the great *Tuatha De Danann* smith; and it is now as celebrated for its iron ore as it was when it got the name, long ages ago.

In a few cases the Irish term is simply changed to the English word *iron*; as in Derryiron (oak grove of iron) in the parish of Ballyburly, five miles from Philipstown in King's County. But it more commonly assumes other forms. Toberanierin is a place five miles from Gorey in Wexford, well known as one of the battle-fields of 1798:— *Tobar-an-iarainn*, the well of the iron. One of the hills rising over Glenmalure in Wicklow, is called Fananierin, the *fán* or slope of the iron. In the parish of Clondermot, about three miles from Londonderry, is a townland called Currynierin (*currach*, a marsh); and with a like meaning we have Annaghierin (*eanach*, a marsh), the name of a lake near Shercock in Cavan. Lisheenanierin is a townland near the village of Strokestown in Roscommon; and there is a Lissanierin in King's County, four miles north of Roscrea: both signifying the fort of the iron. Lough Anierin is a small lake about a mile from the hamlet of Kilty-clogher in Leitrim.

It may be conjectured that some of the forementioned places, as well as others, received their names, not from the actual discovery of the metal itself, but from the reddish, rusty appearance of the soil, indicating the presence of iron. However, the presence of ferruginous mud was generally indicated by a distinct term, which will form the subject of the next article.

Iron scum. When the soil is impregnated with iron, water springing from the ground or flowing along the surface deposits a reddish mud; which also sometimes floats on the top and forms a thin, shining, metalliferous looking scum. This rusty-looking mud or scum is sometimes used in colouring cloth, and it is known in most parts of Ireland—or was known when Irish was spoken—by the name of *rod* or *ruide* [ridda]. It got this name from its colour; for *rod* signifies red. This word is given in the old form *rot*, in Cormac's Glossary, where it is stated that it signifies "everything red." It is of course cognate with Eng. *red* and *ruddy*.

The word is pretty common in names, and it is easily known, for it is never much disguised by corruption. It is anglicised *rud*, *rudda*, *ruddy*, *riddia*, &c., all which forms are illustrated in the following names. Near the village of Ballyconnell in Cavan, is a lake remarkable for this kind of deposit, called Lough Rud; and there is a small pool called Lough Arudda in the county Leitrim, one mile from the north-western end of upper Lough Macnean. Moneyrod, the shrubbery (or perhaps the bog) of the iron scum, is the name of a place in the parish of Duneane in Antrim; Corrarod in Cavan (*cor*, a round hill); Boolinrudda at the northern base of Slievecallan mountain in Clare (*booly*, a dairy place). Raruddy, with its old castle ruins, near Loughrea, and Cloonriddia in the parish of Killererin, both in Galway, the *rath* or fort, and the meadow, of the scum; the latter the same as Clonrud near Abbeyleix in Queen's County. In Bunnaruddee (*bun*, the end, the mouth of a stream) near Ballylongford in Kerry, there is a spa; and all the land round it is (as a person once described it to me) "covered with shiny stuff." The final *g* belonging to the adjective form appears—after the manner of the extreme south—in Kealariddig in the parish of Kilcrohane, west of Kenmare in Kerry—the *keal* or narrow marshy stream of the iron scum.

Sulphur. The pretty little river that flows through Oughterard in Galway, deposits a sulphur scum on the stones in its bed, and along its margin, which may be seen when the water is very low. O'Flaherty (Iar C. p. 53) records that in a great drought in 1666 and 1667, "there was brimstone found on the dry stones [in the bed of the river] about the bridge of Fuogh." From these sulphury deposits he states "it was commonly called *Owan Roimhe*, or Brimstone River;" and this name is now modernised to Owenriff. This word *ruibh*, sulphur, is found in a few other names, but it does not occur often. Revlin in the parish of Killymard, near the town of Donegal, probably received its name for the same reason as the last:—*Ruibh-linn*, sulphur pool or stream. Moneenreave in the parish of Inishmagrath in Leitrim, the little bog of the sulphur.

Salt. The art of preserving provisions by means of salt is of great antiquity in Ireland; and salt itself is often mentioned as an important article of consumption in the old laws regarding allowances and tributes. The Irish word for salt is *salann*—old form *salond*, as given in Cormac's Glossary—corresponding with Welsh *halen*, Lat. *sal*, Gr. *hals*, Slav. *solĭ*, Goth. and Eng. *salt;* and the Irish dictionaries give the diminutive *salannán*, as meaning a salt pit.

A good number of places have taken their names from this word, as if marking the spots where salt was dug up, where it was manufactured from sea water, or where it simply impregnated the soil. But in every case I have met with, the *s* is eclipsed by *t;* and the word is nearly always anglicised *tallin*, *tallon*, or *tallan*, forms which are easily recognised.

Glenatallan is a townland near Loughrea in Galway, whose Irish name is *Gleann-a'-tsalainn*, the glen of the salt. Coomatallin in Cork, and Lugatallin in Mayo, both signify salt hollow; Tawnytallan in Leitrim, the salt field (*tamhnach*); and Loughatallon, a small pool two miles south west of Castletown in Westmeath, the lake of the salt.

Quarry. A quarry of any kind, whether producing stone or slate, is called *coiléir* [cullare]. The Four Masters (vol. v., p. 1261) mention a place in the county Monaghan called *Ath-an-choiléir*, the ford of the quarry. There is, or was, a quarry in the parish of Drum in Mayo, west of Balla, which has given name to the townland of Cuillare; and another near Athenry in Galway, whence the townland of Cullairbane has got its name, signifying white quarry. Pollacullaire in Galway, Poulaculleare in Tipperary, and Clashacollare near Callan in Kilkenny, all mean simply quarry-hole (*poll*, a hole; *clais*, a trench). The word is slightly disguised in Knockacoller near Mountrath in Queen's County, and in Craigahulliar (*c* changed to *h* by aspiration) near Portrush in Antrim—the hill and the rock of the quarry.

Slate. *Slinn* is a slate or any very flat stone or tile. There is a hill in the townland of Fleanmore, parish of Kilfergus in Limerick, called Knocknaslinna, signifying the hill of the slates; Derrynasling in the parish of Ardcrony in Tipperary, and Mullaghslin in a detached part of the parish of Clogherny in Tyrone, the oak wood (*doire*) and the summit (*mullach*) of the slates.

Lime. Notwithstandingt hat lime is so plentiful in Ireland, comparatively few places have taken their names from it. Our word for lime is *ael*, and it appears in at least one name preserved in the annals. The Four Masters twice mention a place called *Ael-mhagh*, i. e. lime-plain; but the name is now obsolete. O'Dugan in one place calls Kilkenny by the appropriate name, *Cill-Chainnigh na cloch n-aoil*, Kilkenny of the limestones (p. 94).

In anglicised names the word usually appears as a termination in the form of *eel*. Bawnaneel in the parish of Kilmeen, west of Kanturk in Cork, represents the Irish *Bán-an-aeil*, the lea-field of the lime. Near Trim in Meath there is a place called Cloncarneel, the *clon* or meadow of the limestone carn; Toneel in the parish of Boho in Fermanagh, the bottom-land (*tón*) of the lime; Knockananeel in the parish of Crossboyne in Mayo, *Cnocan-an-aeil*, little limestone hill.

Gravel. *Grean* [gran] is often used to signify land in general; but it is more usually restricted to mean gravel, and occasionally the gravelly bed of a stream. This word sometimes gets confounded in anglicised names with *grian*, the sun, and with *grán*, grain; but when the Irish pronunciation can be heard, it is always sufficient to distinguish them;

2 A

for *grean* is sounded short [gran], and the other two long [green, graan].

From this word a considerable number of names are derived. There is a stream flowing into the Maigue, near Adare in Limerick, called the Greanagh, which is the adjective form with the postfix *ach* (p. 3), signifying gravelly stream; and some townlands in Galway and Derry are called Grannagh and Granagh —gravelly place. With the oblique inflexion this same word gives name to Granny, which occurs in each of the three counties, Kilkenny, Derry, and Roscommon; and this name is modified to Granig, near Tracton, south of Cork harbour, in accordance with the custom of pronouncing the final *g* prevalent in Cork and Kerry. The diminutive Granaghan (on the adjective form *greanach*) is the name of many other townlands, and has the same meaning as the preceding.

The English *gravel* is sometimes transferred into the Irish; it is spelled *gairbhéal*—pronounced *gravale*— and has given name to Gravale, a high mountain near Sallygap in Wicklow.

Sand. There are several Irish words for sand, of which the one most generally used is *gaineamh* [gannav]. The simple word gives name to Ganniv in Cork, to Gannew in Donegal, and to Gannow in Galway. From the adjective *gainmheach*, sandy, are derived Gannavagh in Leitrim, Gannaway near Donaghadee in Down (Gannagh, Inq.), and Gannoughs (sandy places) in Galway; while the diminutives are seen in Gannavane in Limerick, and Gannaveen in Galway. Pollaginnive in Fermanagh signifies the sandpit (*poll*, a hole); Clonganny in Wexford, sandy *cloon* or meadow; and on the shore near Bangor in Down, is a place called Glenganagh, the glen of the sand.

Jewels, Pearls. The Irish term *séd* (shade) old form *set*—was anciently used to denote a measure of value. According to Cormac's Glossary there were several kinds of *sets*; but they were all understood to be cattle of the cow kind. The word was most commonly applied either to a three-year old heifer, or to a milch cow; but sometimes it was used to designate property or chattels of any kind.

This word had also a somewhat more specific meaning; for it denoted a pearl, a precious stone, or a gem of any kind; thus Con O'Neill who was killed in 1493, is designated by the Four Masters, in recording his death, "the bestower of *seds* and riches," and O'Donovan here translates *seds* by *jewels*. This latter is the sense in which the word is now, and has been for a long time, understood; and this is the meaning with which I am concerned here.

Several Irish rivers were formerly celebrated for their pearls; and in many the pearl muscle is found to this day. Solomon Richards, an Englishman, who wrote a description of Wexford about the year 1656, speaking of the Slaney, says, "It ought to precede all the rivers in Ireland for its pearle fishing, which though not abundant are yet excellent, for muscles are daily taken out of itt about fowre, five, and six inches long, in which are often found pearles, for lustre, magnitude, and rotundity, not inferior to oriental or any other in the world. They have lately been sold by a merchant that dined this day with me for 20s, 30s, 40s, and three pound a pearle, to goldsmiths and jewellers in London." (Kilk. Arch. Jour.—1862-3, p. 91). O'Flaherty states that in the Fuogh river or Owenriff, flowing by Oughterard in Galway, "muscles are found that breed pearles," and to this day they are often found in the same river. In Harris's Ware it is stated that pearls are found in the fresh water muscles of the Bann, and in those of several of the streams of Tyrone, Donegal, and elsewhere. He tells us that a present of an Irish pearl was made to Anselm, archbishop of Canterbury, by Gilbert, bishop of Limerick, about 1094. In Kerry also, he remarks that several other precious stones are found, namely, Kerry diamonds, amethysts, topazes, emeralds, and sapphires of good quality. Many of the streams of Donegal produce the pearl muscle in which pearls are often found (see Dub. Pen. Jour. I., 389); and the same may be said of streams in several other parts of Ireland.

The word *séd* designates all such precious stones; and from what I have already said no one will be surprised to find that this term is often found forming a part of local names. When it occurs in names it is not easy to determine in each case the precise sense in which it is used; sometimes it indicated no doubt that pearls or other gems were found in the respective places; it may have been occasionally applied to cattle; while in other cases, the names probably mark places where hordes of valuables of some kind were kept.

The old name of Baltimore on the south-coast of Cork was *Dun-na-séd* (Annals of Innisfallen), the fortress of the jewels; but the name was originally applied to a circular fort on a high rock, the site of which is now occupied by the ruins of O'Driscoll's castle, to which the name is still applied. I will not venture any conjecture as to why the old fortress got the name of *Dun-na-séd*.

With regard to the present name, we are told in the topographical Dictionaries of Seward and Lewis, that the place was called *Beal-ti-mor*, the great habitation of Beal, because it was one of the principal seats of the idolatrous worship of Baal. But for this silly statement there is not a particle of authority. The name is written in several old Anglo-Irish documents, *Balintimore*, which accords exactly with the present Irish pronunciation ; the correct Irish form is *Baile-an-tighe-mhoir*, which means merely the town of the large house ; and it derived this name no doubt from the castle of the O'Driscolls, already spoken of.

This name has got a new lease of life in the United States, where in the year 1632, George Calvert, Lord Baltimore, who derived his title from the Irish village, obtained a grant of Maryland from Charles I. and founded a town in it, to which he gave the name of Baltimore.

The word *sed* appears in Cloghnashade, the stone of the jewels, now the name of a townland and of a small lake in Roscommon, two miles east of Mount Talbot. They have a legend in Munster, that at the bottom of the lower lake of Killarney, there is a diamond of priceless value; which sometimes shines so brightly that on certain nights the light bursts forth with dazzling brilliancy through the dark waters. Perhaps some such legend gave name to Loughnashade (lake of the jewels), a small lake four miles north-east from Philipstown in King's County; to Loughnashade, a lakelet two miles west of Armagh ; and to a third lake of the same name, a mile from Drumshambo, just where the Shannon issues from Lough Allen.

In the *Leabhar Breac*, or Speckled Book of the

Mac Egans, a collection of ancient pieces compiled in the fourteenth century, there is a pretty legend to account for the name of *Loch Bél Séad*, one of the lakes on the Galty mountains. *Coerabar*, the beautiful daughter of the great Connaught fairy queen, Etal, had one hundred and fifty maidens in her train, who every alternate year were transformed into as many beautiful birds, and in the other years had their natural shapes. During the time that they lived as birds they always remained on *Loch Crotta Cliach* (*Crotta Cliach*, the ancient name of the Galty mountains); and they were chained in couples with chains of silver. One of them especially was the most beautiful bird in the whole world; and she had a necklace of red gold on her neck, with three times fifty chains suspended from it, each chain terminating in a ball of gold. So the people who saw the birds every day, called the lake *Loch Bél Séad*, the lake with the jewel mouth, from the gold and silver and gems that glittered on the birds. (O'Curry: Lect. on MS. materials, 426). This lake has long lost its old name, and it is now called Lough Muskry, from the old territory of *Muscraighe Chuirc* in which it is situated. Curiously enough, however, there is a lake of this name, now Lough Belshade, at the eastern base of the Bluestack mountains, about six miles north-east of the town of Donegal; but I have not heard of a legend in connexion with it.

CHAPTER XXI.

THE SURFACE OF THE LAND.

Talamh [tallav] signifies the earth or land, corresponding with Lat. *tellus*. It is not often found in local use, and a few names will be sufficient to illustrate it. A short distance north of Killary harbour, there is a little island near the coast, called Tallavbaun, which signifies whitish land. Tallavnamraher is the name of a townland in the parish of Kilbegnet in Galway—*Talamh-na-mbrathar*, the land of the friars. It sometimes takes the form of *tallow*, as in Tallowroe in the parish of Killeeneen in Galway, red land; Shantallow and Shantalliv, the names of several places, old land, which were probably so called because they had been long cultivated, while the surrounding district remained waste. The genitive form is *talmhan*, the pronunciation of which is exhibited in Buntalloon near Tralee, a name which exactly corresponds in meaning with Finisterre and Land's End.

Fearann, land, ground, a country. In its topographical use it is applied to a particular portion of land or territory. It is widely disseminated as a local term; and in the anglicised form Farran it constitutes or begins the names of about 180 townlands. Farranagalliagh in Roscommon must have formerly belonged to a nunnery—*Fearann-na-gcailleach*, the land of the nuns. Farrangarve near Killashandra in Cavan, rough land; Farrantemple in Kilkenny and Derry, the land of the church; Farranatouke, near Kinsale, the land of the hawk; Farrandahadore near Cork city, the land of the dyers—*dath*, a colour; *dathadoir*, a dyer.

A great many of the denominations beginning with *fearann* have the latter part formed of a personal or family name, commemorating former possessors. Thus Farranrory in Tipperary is *Rudhraidhe's* or Rory's land; Farranydaly in Cavan, O'Daly's land; Farrangarode in Sligo, and Farrangarret in Waterford, both signifying Garret's land.

When this word forms the end of a name, it often loses the *f* by aspiration, as in the common townland names Laharan and Laharran, which represent *Leath-fhearann*, half land, a name applied to one half of a townland, which for some reason had been divided in two. Raheenarran in Kilkenny, the little *rath* or fort of the land or farm.

Fód [fode] means a sod, soil, or land. In its topographical application it is commonly used to designate a spot, which, compared with the surrounding land, has a remarkably smooth, grassy surface. In many cases, however, it is understood to mean merely the grassy surface of the land.

As a part of names, this word usually comes in as a termination; but the *f* almost always disappears either by aspiration or eclipse. The aspirated form is seen in Moyode, three miles from Athenry in Galway; *Magh-fhoid*, the field of the (grassy surface or) sod; in Castlenode, a mile from Strokestown in Roscommon, the castle of the green sod; and in Bellanode, which was once the name of a ford on the Blackwater river, three miles from the town of Monaghan, a name shortened from *Bel-atha-an-fhoid*, the ford-mouth of the sod.

The termination *ode* or *node* (the *n* belongs to the article) is almost always to be interpreted as in the preceding names. The word takes other slightly different forms, as in Lisoid, near Ardglass in Down, which is the same name as Lissanode, near Ballymore in Westmeath (*lios*, a fort).

When the *f* is eclipsed it forms the termination *vode*, the use and interpretation of which is seen in Mullannavode, near St. Mullins in Carlow, *Mullán-na-bhfód*, the green field of the sods, i. e. of the remarkably grassy surface; and Slievenavode near the Wooden Bridge Hotel in Wicklow (*sliabh*, a mountain), a name given, I suppose, to indicate that the sides of the mountain were covered with green patches.

The diminutive Fodeen—little sod or sod-covered surface—is the name of a townland near Tara in Meath; and the plural, Fodeens, is found near the village of Kill in Kildare; while with the adjective termination, we have Fodagh in Wexford, a soddy place, i. e. a place with a very grassy surface.

Lea land. *Bán* [bawn] is applied in various parts of Ireland, especially in the Munster counties, to denote a green field or lea land—untilled or uncropped grass-land. It is often anglicised *bawn*, which forms or begins the names of a great many places. Bawnanattin near Thurles signifies the field of the furze (*aiteann*); Bawnluskaha near Castleisland, *Ban-loisgithe*, burnt field, i. e. the surface burned for agricultural purposes; Bawnnahow near Dromaleague in Cork, the field of the river (*abha*).

As *bawn* is also the modern form of *badhun*, the enclosure near a castle (for which see 1st Ser., Part III. c. I.), some caution is necessary before one pronounces on the signification of this word *bawn*.

Bán assumes in combination other forms, whose meanings are scarcely liable to be mistaken; for example, Ballinvana near Kilmallock in Limerick signifies the town of the field (*b* changed to *v* by aspiration); Tinvane near Carrick-on-Suir, and Tinvaun in Kilkenny, both anglicised from *Tigh-an-bhain*, the house of the field.

There are several diminutives of this word. One, *banóg* (little lea field), gives names to all those places now called Banoge, Bawnoge, and Bawnoges. The word has been disguised by corruption in Bannixtown near Fethard in Tipperary, which ought to have been anglicised Banogestown; for the Irish name is *Baile-na-mbanóg*, the town of the *banoges* or little lea fields; Barranamanoge near Lismore in Waterford, has a name with a similar formation—the *barr* or summit of the little bawns. Another diminutive is seen in Cranavaneen in Tipperary, the *crann* or tree of the field; and still another in Baunteen near Galbally in Limerick, which as it stands means little lea field.

The plural of this word is *bánta* [baunta] which is seen in Bawntameena near Thurles, smooth green fields (*mín*, smooth); and in Bawntard near Kilmallock in Limerick, *Banta-arda*, high fields; while uncompounded it gives name to several places now called Baunta.

Sward. Scrath [scraw] signifies a sod, a sward, a grassy surface. The word is still current in the south of Ireland among people who no longer speak Irish; and they apply the term *scraws*, and the diminutive *scrawhoges*, to the flat sods of the grassy and heathery surface of boggy land, cut with a spade and dried for burning. There is a hill one mile south of Newtownards, called Scrabo, the name of which signifies the sward of the cows; Scralea in Tyrone, grey sward. Ballynascraw and Ballynascragh in Longford and Galway, the town of the *scraws* or swards. The diminutive *scrathan* (little sward) is more common than the original; it takes the forms Scrahan and Scrahane, which, with the plural Scrahans, forms the whole or part of the names of several townlands in Cork, Kerry, and Waterford.

Shelf. *Fachair* [faher] shelving land ; a shelf-like level spot in a hill, or in the face of a cliff: used in this sense in Donegal and Mayo. I have heard it in Kerry and Cork, and it gives names to places in various counties. In Donegal and other counties there are several townlands called Faugher—meaning in all cases a shelf or a shelving hill side. There is a place called Fagher near Stradbally in Waterford ; a high cliff on the north side of Valentia Island is called Fogher; and Faher is the name of a mountain north west of Kenmare. Knocknafaugher near Dunfanaghy in Donegal, the hill of the shelf.

Scumhal [skool] signifies a precipice, a sharp slope, a steep hill. It gives names to several places now called Scool, Scoul, and Skool. The Four Masters mention a place in the county Clare, as the site of a battle fought between two parties of the O'Briens in 1562, called *Cnoc-an-scamhail*, which is now called in Irish *Cnoc-an-scumhail*, the hill of the precipice; it is situated about two miles south west from Corofin, and the name is anglicised Scool Hill. There is a place a little north of Knockainy in Limerick called Ballinscoola (with a different inflexion for the genitive), the town of the precipice; and another place called Drumskool near Irvinestown in Fermanagh, the ridge of the precipice.

Round hollow. *Crón* is a very uncertain term to deal with; for it has several meanings, and it is often very hard to know the exact sense in which it is applied. In Wicklow and Carlow and the adjoining districts, the people—when Irish was spoken—often applied it to a round basin-like hollow. Crone itself is the name of several places in Wicklow; Cronebane near the Wooden Bridge Hotel, is well known for its copper mines, and Cronroe near Rathnew, for the beauty of its scenery; the former signifies white, and the latter, red, hollow. Cronybyrne near Rathdrum, signifies O'Byrne's hollow (*y* representing *O*: see p. 134); and the place is still in possession of an O'Byrne.

Sandbank. *Dumhach* is used on some parts of the coast to signify a sandbank; but it is very difficult to separate the word from *dumha*, a grave mound, and from other terms approaching it in sound. A very excellent example of its application is seen in Dough Castle near Lehinch in Clare, which the Four Masters, when recording the death there in 1422 of Rory O'Connor, lord of Corcomroe, call *Caislen-na-dumhcha*, the castle of the sandbank; and it was most aptly so called, for it is built on a large mound altogether formed of sea sand. There are other places in Clare also called Dough, while another form of the name, Doagh, is common in several of the northern counties.

The word *beartrach* means a sandbank; and in a secondary sense it is often applied in the west of Ireland to an oyster bank. A very characteristic example of its use is found in the name of the little island of Bartragh at the mouth of the Moy, near Killala, which is remarkably sandy—in fact formed altogether of sand thrown up by the meeting of the tide and river currents. The point of land jutting into Clew Bay, opposite Murrisk Abbey, at the base of Croagh Patrick, is called Bartraw. There is a well known sea inlet in Connemara called Bertraghboy, which must have received its name from some point on its shore, for it means yellow sandbank.

CHAPTER XXII.

QUAGMIRES AND WATERY PLACES.

In the sixth chapter of Part IV. of the First Series, I have treated of several terms which designate marshes, and have given many names derived from them. But besides these, there are various words denoting swamps, quagmires, sloughs, puddles, and watery places of all kinds; and these I now propose to enumerate and illustrate. And here it is necessary to reiterate a remark made in the beginning of the forementioned chapter:—that while many places that derived their names in distant ages from their marshiness are still as marshy as ever, others—and perhaps the greater number—have been drained, and the names are no longer correctly descriptive of physical character.

The Four Masters, when mentioning the place now called Bellaugh near Athlone, call it *Lathach*, which signifies mud, a slough, a puddle, a miry spot; and this word gives names to a good many places. It is seen in its simple form in Lahagh, east of Templemore in Tipperary, in Laghey near Dungannon in Tyrone, and in Laghy in Donegal; while we have Laghaghglass, green slough, in Galway. As a termination it usually takes some such form as *lahy*, as in Monalahy, north of Blarney in Cork, the *moin* or bog of the puddle; Gortnalahee in the same county, and

Gortnalahagh near Castleconnell in Limerick, both signifying the field of the miry place. The diminutive, Laheen (little slough) is also the name of several places in Cavan, Donegal, and Leitrim.

Abar signifies generally a mire or puddle—sometimes a mire caused by the trampling of cattle in a wet place; and occasionally it is understood to mean a boggy or marshy piece of land. This word is interesting, inasmuch as it may be—and indeed has been—questioned whether it is not the same as the Welsh *aber*, a river mouth, corresponding with our word *inbher*. I do not believe that it is, for I think it quite improbable that we should have, running parallel in the Irish language, two different words corresponding with the Welsh *aber*, unless we got one of them by borrowing from the Welsh, which I think equally unlikely. It is found forming a part of names chiefly in Donegal, and occasionally in the adjoining counties.

There is a place near Kilmacrenan called Ballybuninabber, whose name signifies the town of the *bun* or end of the mire. A muddy little stream in the parish of Innishkeel in the same county, is called Abberachrinn, i. e. (the river of) the miry place of the *crann* or tree. Sometimes it becomes *ubber*, as in Buninubber near the north eastern shore of Lower Lough Erne, the same name as Bunnynubber near Omagh, the *bun*, end, or bottom, of the mire.

The word *salach* is applied to anything unclean or filthy, and has several shades of meaning; but topographically it is applied to a mere dirty place—a place of puddle or mire. It often takes the form of *slough* and *slagh* in anglicised names, as we see in Curraghslagh near Clogheen in Tipperary, the dirty *curragh* or marsh; a name which takes the form of

Curraghsallagh in Roscommon. So also in Crannslough in Tyrone, dirty tree, which I suppose took its name from a tree growing in a miry spot.

The meaning of the anglicised termination *sallagh* is, however, often doubtful; for the Irish word *saileach*, a place of sallows, often assumes this very form; and here, as in all such cases, we must be guided by the local pronunciation or tradition, or by the original Irish spelling if we can come at it. It would be impossible to tell what Kilsallagh means as it stands; for *kil* might be either wood or church (*coill* or *cill*), and *sallagh* either a dirty place or an osier plantation. But the Four Masters when they mention Kilsallagh near Ardagh in Longford, clear up the doubt, so far as that place is concerned, for they call it *Caill-salach*, miry wood. And it is pretty certain that this is the interpretation of all the other Kilsallaghs, of which there are eight in different parts of the country; in several of them indeed, I know that this is the popular explanation. All these places called Rathsallagh must have taken their name from a *rath* or fort surrounded by a miry ditch; for everywhere the traditional translation is dirty fort, with which the local pronunciation agrees. Ardsallagh is the name of several places, including a parish in Meath; but it would not be safe to give a general translation: all that can be said here is that it means either miry height or the height of sallows.

From the word *crith* [crigh], to shake, several terms are derived, which are applied to morasses of that kind which the peasantry call "shaking bogs." With the addition of the postfix *lach* (p. 5.) it gives name to Creelogh in Gorumna island in Galway, to Creelagh near Rathdowney in Queen's County, and to Crylough in the parish of Ballymore in

Wexford—all meaning a shaking bog. In the oblique form we have the same word in Crilly, the name of some places in Donegal and Tyrone; and in the latter county, near Dungannon, there is a small lake called Lough Nacrilly, the lake of the morass.

Another derivative of the word, with still the same meaning, is *crithleán*, which gives name to Crillan near Kesh in Fermanagh, and to Crillaun in Mayo; Loughcrillan in the parish of Inishkeel in Donegal, the lake of the shaking bog. With the diminutive termination *án*, followed by *ach* (see pp. 3, 20, *supra*) we have Crehanagh, the name of a townland near Carrick-on Suir, which, though now for the most part good dry land, was such a dangerous quagmire a little more than a century ago, that the people thought it was only a miracle that enabled a fugitive to cross it, when escaping from a troop of dragoons.

Criathar [crihar] signifies a sieve (*criathar*, cribrum, Z. 166), and it is derived from *crith*, to shake, (by the addition of *r*; see p. 12) in allusion to the manner in which a sieve is used. This word is also applied, chiefly in the north and west of Ireland, to boggy or swampy places, or to broken land intermixed with quagmires and brushwood, either on account of their being cut up with holes or pits (like a sieve) or from shaking under the foot. There is a place called Creeharmore (great sieve) on the Roscommon side of the Suck, a little below Mount Talbot. Druminacrehir in the parish of Columkille in Longford, is the little ridge of the sieve; but this was probably so called because the people used to winnow corn on it. It is generally not *criathar* itself however that is used, but a derivative from it. The Four Masters (at A. D. 1496) designate a morass by *criathrach* (suffix *ach*, p. 3); and MacFirbis (Hy F.

p. 202) mentions "the three townlands of *Criathrach;*" this name is still retained by the natives when they speak Irish, but the place, which is situated one mile from Ballinrobe, is called in English the "Demesne of Creagh." In Mayo and Tipperary there are places called Creeragh, which is a correct anglicised form of *criathrach.* The diminutive gives name to Creeran in Monaghan, and Creeraun in Galway. Macreary in the parish of Kilmurry in Tipperary, the plain of the shaking-bog.

According to Cormac's Glossary, the primary meaning of *múch* is smoke:—"*Múch*, i. e. a name proper for smoke: unde dicitur *muchud* (to smother)." From this word *múch*, in its secondary sense of "to suffocate or smother," is derived the diminutive *muchán*, which is applied to a morass, probably from some fanciful notion that in such a place men or beasts are liable to be suffocated. There is a little lake on the railway line, two miles from Newmarket-on-Fergus in Clare, called Mooghaun Lough, in which great quantities of gold antiquities were found in 1854; and this name very well represents the sound of the original Irish. The same word gives name to places now called Moohane in Kerry and Limerick. Knockamoohane near Listowel in Kerry, the hill of the quagmire; Curraghmoghaun in the parish of Clooney in Clare, the smothered *curragh* or marsh.

Gréach is a mountain flat, a level moory place, much the same as a *reidh*, explained in the First Series. It is very common as an element in townland designations in the counties of Cavan, Leitrim, Roscommon, Monaghan, and Fermanagh; and it is found also, but less frequently, in some of the counties bordering on these. Greagh, the usual anglicised form, is the name of several places; Greaghawillin in

Monaghan, the mountain flat of the mill; Greaghnagleragh in Fermanagh, of the clergy (*cleireach*); Greaghnagee in Cavan, of the wind (*gaeth*).

The word *muing* signifies, according to O'Donovan (App. to O'R. Dict. *in voce*), "a sedgy morass, a flow bog or shaking bog." I think there can be no doubt that this word is merely an oblique case of *mong*, long hair (p. 321); and this opinion is strengthened by the fact that *muing* is also used to denote a horse's mane. From this it will appear that the places whose names are derived from *muing* were so called in the first instance from the long mane-like sedgy grass they produced; exactly like those from *mong*, *gruag*, &c. (pp. 320, 321, *supra*).

This word, as a local appellative, is almost confined to the south and west of Ireland. In the beginning of names it is usually made Muing and Moyng, which are themselves the names of some townlands; Muingnaminnane east of Tralee, the sedge of the kids; Muingbaun in Galway, white sedge; Muingatogher in Mayo, the *muing* of the *togher* or causeway.

In the end of words—as a genitive—it assumes several forms, all easily recognisable. Coolmuinga near Kilrush in Clare, the *cul* or back of the morass; and with the same form, Barnamuinga near Shillelagh in the south of Wicklow, the same as Barrawinga near Rathdowney in Queen's County (*barr*, the top). The *m* becomes aspirated in this last name, as well as in Derryvung in the parish of Kiltullagh in Roscommon (*derry*, oak-grove), a well-known morass which is accessible only on one side; also in Ballinwing north-east of Carrick-on-Shannon, and Moanwing near Rathkeale in Limerick, the townland and the bog, of the sedgy morass.

Cladach or *clodach*, a word in general use along the western coast of Ireland, from Donegal to Kerry, signifies a flat stony sea-shore—stony as distinguished from a *traigh* or sandy beach. The Rev. William Kilbride, in an article on the "Antiquities of Aranmore" (Kilk. Arch. Jour. 1868, p. 108), states that the people use *traigh* to designate that part of the beach between high and low water mark; the *cladach* lies above the *traigh*, and the *duirling* higher still; and O'Donovan makes much the same statement (Appendix to O'R. Dict., *voce, cladach*)—designating *cladach* as "a flat stony shore." The best known example of the use of this word is the Claddagh, a suburb of Galway, now inhabited chiefly by fishermen. But it undergoes several modifications of pronunciation, as if written in Irish *cladhdach*, *claodach*, and *claoideach* [clydagh, claydagh, cleedagh]; and in its signification it is also varied. In one or all of these various forms it is known over Ireland; and inland it is very commonly applied to a muddy or miry place; to the muddy bank of a lake or river; and to a river with a sluggish course, and muddy, miry banks. This last is its most usual signification, but it would appear that in its application to a river, it sometimes carries with it the meaning attached to it along the western coast—a stony water margin—for I know some rivers to which it gives name, in no degree muddy or sluggish—mountain torrents rather, having their beds strewn with stones brought down from the glens in which they rise.

This two-fold meaning corresponds with the explanation of the word given in Peter O'Connell's Dictionary:—"Cladach, the sea shore or strand; dirt, filth, slime, puddle." Which of these two meanings the word bears, must be determined in each case by local knowledge.

There are numbers of rivers all over Ireland, whose names are formed from this word; and in many cases they have, in their turn, given names to townlands, villages, and parishes. The village of Clady lies on the Tyrone side of the Finn, four miles from Strabane; there are several townlands of the same name in Tyrone, Antrim, and Armagh; Clydagh is equally common in some of the western and southern counties; and there is a parish in Queen's County called Cloydagh. Clodagh occurs several times in Kerry; near Killarney, we find the word in the form of Cleedagh; and in another place an *r* is inserted, making the name Clodragh.

The little river Clody, flowing from the slopes of Mount Leinster into the Slaney, gave the name of Bunclody to the pretty village at its mouth (*bun*, a river mouth), which has been lately put aside for the new name, Newtownbarry. Cleady is the name of a small tributary joining the Roughty a little above Kenmare; the river Clodiagh runs into the Suir through Portlaw and the demesne of Curraghmore; another stream of the same name flows by Tullaghmore; and another still runs into the Nore three miles below Inistioge. The Clyda stream joins the Blackwater near Mallow; the river Claddagh falls into upper Lough Erne after flowing through the village of Swanlinbar; and Lough Nacung in Donegal pours its surplus waters into the Atlantic by the river Clady, opposite Gola island.

We have, in a few instances, the authority of ancient documents for the orthography of this name. Clady in Tyrone is called *Claideach* by the Four

Masters, when they record a battle fought there in 784, between the Kinel-Owen and the Kinel-Conall; and the Annals of Ulster, recording the same event, write the genitive of the name *Cloitigi*, which points to a nominative from *Cloiteach*.

It will be observed that all these are derived from the root *clad* or *cloed*, to which the adjectival termination *ach* has generally been added: but in one case—Clodragh, already mentioned—the termination is *rach* (see p. 7), all which implies that those who gave the names had a distinct perception that they were building on *clad* or *cloed* as a foundation.

Caedh [quay, kay] signifies a quagmire or marsh —occasionally a wet natural trench; and though not in very common use, it occurs in each of the four provinces. In Scotland and Ulster it is still retained with its proper meaning by the English speaking people, in the word *quaw*, which is used for a quagmire. Its several anglicised forms retain fairly enough the original pronunciation. One of these is exhibited in the name of Kye in the parish of Clooncraff in Roscommon. There is a little hill near Silvermines in Tipperary, called Keywee, *Caedh-bhuidhe*, yellow marsh; and in the same county, west of Nenagh, is Bawnakea, the *bawn* or green field of the *quaw*. In the north of Donegal, near the village of Millford, is a little lake called Lough Nakey; in Limerick we have Bunkey, the *bun* or end of the morass. In Dublin it forms part of the name of Coolquoy, west of Swords, the back (*cul*) of the quagmire. Keyanna about four miles east of Limerick city, is merely a plural form, and signifies quagmires.

Feith [feah] is used in some places to designate a boggy stream, a stream flowing through a marsh or a trench; in other places a soft, boggy, or marshy place: the former is its general signification. Four miles north west of Thurles is the townland and demesne of Dovea, which is mentioned by the Four Masters, and called by them *Dubh-feth*, black boggy stream or marsh. There is a place called Baurnafea in the parish of Shankhill in Kilkenny, the top of the marshy stream; and near Lismore in Waterford is Monafehadee, i. e. *Móin-na-feithe-duibhe*, the bog of the black quagmire.

Bréan, which signifies putrid, foul, fetid, or stinking, is often applied to spots that omit an offensive smell. There are various circumstances that may originate foul smelling exhalations from land. One of the indications that led Colonel Hall to the discovery of copper mines at Glandore in Cork, was the fetid smell emitted from a fire of turf cut in a neighbouring bog, which turned out to be strongly impregnated with copper; this bog was known as the "stinking bog" (*móin-bhréun*); and the people had it that neither cat nor dog could live in the house where the turf was burnt.* There is a place called Brenter in the parish of Inver, east of Killybegs in Donegal, whose name is in Irish *Bréan-tír*, stinking district; and it got this name from the strong sulphureous smell of a spa which is in the townland. There was a celebrated district of the same name lying north east of Mount Callan in Clare, which is often mentioned in the annals (always as *Brentir*), but I do not know why it was so called. In most cases places with names of this kind are swamps, pits, or bogs, which emit foul odours from decaying animal or vegetable matter.

There are ten townlands in various counties, called

* See Mrs. Hall's Ireland, I. 142.

Breandrum, stinking ridge. Breanshagh, east of Castlemaine in Kerry, and Breansha near the town of Tipperary, both mean fetid land; the latter part of each name being merely the termination *seach* (p. 9). The two diminutive terms *Glanóg* and *Brenóg* are often applied to small streams or inlets of the sea, but in opposite senses. The former, which is from *glan*, clean, is used to designate a bright clear little stream, flowing over a gravelly bed. There was a stream of this name near the castle of Cargins in Galway, which is mentioned by the Four Masters as the scene of a battle in 1469. Glan itself was sometimes given as a name to wells; for we read in O'Clery's Calendar that, before the time of St. Patrick, Donaghmore in Tyrone was called *Ros-Glanda* (wood of Glan), and that it took this name from a well called Glan. The diminutive in *an*—Glannan—which was originally applied to a clear stream, is now the name of a townland in the parish of Donagh in Monaghan. The other term *Brenog*, is, on the contrary, a foul, lazy-flowing, fetid stream. The Four Masters mention a place called *Bun-Brenoige*, the mouth of the Brenog, in the townland of Lissadill near Drumcliff in Sligo. The adjective form Breanagh (with the same meaning) gives name to a little stream in Kerry, joining the Feale in the upper part of its course; and there is a place called Breany (an oblique form of the last name) near Ardagh in Long ford.

The level, soft, meadow-land or holm—often swampy and sometimes inundated—along the banks of a river or lake, is generally called *srath*. It is a very common term in Irish local names; and it is often greatly disguised by inflection and corruption. Its most correct anglicised forms are Sra, Srah, and Sragh, which are the names of numerous places. But a *t* usually becomes inserted between the *s* and the *r*, in accordance with a euphonic law noticed in First Series (Part I. chap. III.); as in Strabane in Tyrone, which took its name from the meadow land along the river Mourne, and which the Four Masters write *Srath-bán*, the fair or whitish river-holm. Under the influence of this corruption also, the simple word becomes Straw in the names of some townlands in Derry. There is a parish in Carlow and another in Queen's County, called Straboe, a name which signifies the srath of the cows. Straness near the town of Donegal takes its name from a cataract—*Srath-an-easa*, the holm of the waterfall.

This word is exhibited as a termination in Ballinastraw, the name of several places in Carlow, Wicklow, and Wexford, and in Ballynasrah in King's County, both meaning the town of the river-holms. In the end of names, when it is in the genitive singular, the *s* is usually eclipsed by *t*, which considerably disguises the word; in this form it is seen in Mullantra near Kingscourt in Cavan, *Mul-an-tsratha*, the hill-top of the *srath*; and in Corrintra near Castleblayney in Monaghan, the round hill of the river-holm. Ballintra, the name of several places, is usually anglicised from *Baile-an-tsratha*, the town of the *srath*; but in a few cases it is differently derived (see Ballintra in 1st Ser.).

The word *mín* [meen] signifies fine or smooth, and it has several other shades of meaning which need not be noticed here. It is used in its proper sense in Clonmeen and Cloonmeen, the names of several townlands—*Cluain-mín*, smooth meadow; and in Barmeen near Cushendun in Antrim, the smooth *barr* or hill-top.

Topographically it is often applied to a green spot, comparatively smooth and fertile, producing grass and rushes, on the face of a mountain, or in the midst of coarse rugged hilly land. It is used all over Ireland, but is far more common in Donegal than in any other part of the country. There are upwards of 230 townlands whose names begin with this word, in the anglicised form of *meen*, about 150 of which appear in Donegal alone, 36 in the rest of the Ulster counties, and something over 40 in the other three provinces

Its application in this sense will be understood from the following examples. Meeniska near Kilbeggan in Westmeath signifies the *meen* of the water (*uisge*)—a wet mountain meadow; Meenbane near Stranorlar in Donegal, Meenvane near Skull in Cork, and Meenwaun near Banagher in King's County, are all anglicised from *Mín-bhán*, whitish field. There are two places in Donegal, one of them near Stranorlar, called Meenagrauv; the *r* here represents *n* (as *crock* for *cnoc*: see 1st Ser.), while the *g* eclipses *c*; and the full name is *Mín-na-gcnamh*, the mountain-meadow of the bones (*cnamh*)—a name which would appear to indicate the site of a battle. In the parish of Donaghmore in Cork is a place called Meenahony, and there is another place of the same name in Donegal, of which the Irish form is *Mín-a'-chonaidh*, the mountain-field of the fire-wood.

One of the plural forms of this term in its present application is *mínte* [meenta], which appears in Meentanakill near Inver in Donegal, and in Meentyflugh in the parish of Kilmeen in Cork, the former signifying the *meens* of the church, and the latter wet mountain fields. A diminutive form is seen in Meentoges in the parish of Kilcummin in Kerry, i. e. small green spots.

Leana means in general a wet or swampy meadow—grassy land with a soft spongy bottom. The word is in use more or less all over Ireland, but it is commoner in Ulster than in the other provinces. In Derry it is used to signify any green field, meadow, or pasture land; but its usual meaning is the one first given. In its simple form it gives name to the parish of Leny in Westmeath, as well as to the townland of Leany near Corrofin in Clare; and Lenamore, great wet-meadow, is the name of many townlands scattered through several counties. Near the town of Antrim is a townland with the half English name of Quarter Lenagh, that is, the wet-meadow quarter; and in the parish of Aghnamullen in Monaghan, we have Tievaleny, the hill-side of the meadow; Moanleana near Newcastle in Limerick, the bog of the wet meadow.

In most parts of Ireland the people understand and habitually use the word *slug* in the sense of swallowing drink—gulping it down quickly and greedily. Lever's witty Irish soldier, Maurice Quill, used to creep among his comrades in the heat of battle, holding in his hand a can of ale, and saying, while he offered each poor fellow a drink, "Here, take a *slug* before you get a *bullet*." The Irish form of this word is *slog*, and it is often applied to a swallow hole in a river or lake, that is, a deep pool with an open at bottom, from which the water escapes as fast as it enters—often with a gurgling noise. Such pools often gave names to places; and the word *slog* assumes various anglicised forms, which are, however, seldom so far removed from the original as to be difficult of recognition.

Lough Slug—the lake with the swallow—is the name of several small lakes in Donegal. A common derivative is *slogaire* [sluggera], literally a swallower, i.e. topographically a swallow-hole, which gives name to Sluggara near Cappoquin in Waterford, to Sluggary south west of Limerick city, and to several other places. The *s* is eclipsed in Parkatluggera near Dungarvan, *Pairc-a'-tslogaire*, the swallow-hole field. One mile from Mitchelstown in Cork is the townland and wood of Glenatlucky, the name of which is in Irish, *Gleann-a'-tslogaidhe*, the glen of the swallow-hole. There is a village called Creeslough, near the mouth of Sheephaven in Donegal, five miles south east of Dunfanaghy, which took its name from a little lake. In this name a different Irish word is used, viz. *craos*, gluttony :—*Craos-loch*, a lake that swallows up everything.

Dobhar [dovar, dower] is one of the many Irish terms for water, corresponding to the Sanscrit *dabhra*, the sea (Pictet). Cormac MacCullenan, in his Glossary, remarks that *dobhar*, water, is common to the Irish and the Welsh languages; and from it he derives the Irish name for an otter, viz., *dobhar-chu*, which literally signifies water-hound. One of the rivers in the south west of Donegal was anciently called *Dobhar;* for in a poem in the book of Fenagh, we are told that the old territory of Banagh extended from the river *Edhnech* (the Eany at Inver) to the "Bright *Dobhar* which flows from the rugged mountains." This name is now however obsolete.

The simplest modern form of this word is Dower, which is the name of a place one mile east of Castlemartyr in Cork, so called from a little river which runs for some distance under ground; and there is a townland of this name also in the parish of Kilnamanagh, Roscommon. Another form is seen in Dore in the parish of Tulloghobegly in Donegal. The name of Bundoran in Donegal (the *bun*, end, or mouth of the Doran) shows that the little river flowing into the sea at the village must have been anciently called the Doran; and although there is no documentary evidence that I am aware of for the original form of this river name, there is little doubt that it is a diminutive of *Dobhar*—*Dobharan*, little water—little when compared with the adjacent rivers Drowes and Erne. In Scotland this diminutive is exactly represented in the name of the river Doveran, in which the *v* sound of the *bh* is preserved, while it is lost in the Irish.

Dur is given by O'Reilly as meaning water, but I have never met it in any Irish text. Although it does not enter extensively into names, it is venerable for its antiquity as a topographical term; for Ptolemy, in his map of Ireland, has given the name of Dur to a river in the west of the island. There are several local names in various parts of the country, which must be derived from this word. In Antrim, Kerry, King's County, and Longford, we find townlands called Doory, the anglicised representative of the Irish *Dúire*—as the people still call it—which is probably an abstract-noun formation, signifying wateriness or watery land. There is a parish in Clare, now called Doora, which represents the genitive of *dúr*, the Irish name being *paráiste-dhúire*, the parish of the *Dúr* or water; and this parish was anciently, and is still, celebrated for its abundance of water, marsh, and bog. The adjective form Dooragh is the name of a place near Stewartstown in Tyrone.

A meeting of any kind would be designated by *comhrac;* and from this general signification come two of its principal secondary meanings:—first, the meeting of rivers or roads; and second, a combat, i. e. the meeting of opposing sides in battle. We have these two meanings perpetuated in local names, and it is often impossible to distinguish them without some local history or tradition to guide us. But it is certain that far the greater number of such names are derived from river confluences. The Four Masters, at the year 1473, have a record of a battle between the MacRannals and some of their neighbours, fought near the village of Carrigallen in Leitrim. The people still retain a vivid tradition of this event, and point out the townland of Clooncorick near Carrigallen as the scene of the combat. Here we have history and tradition both agreeing; and although historical names very seldom originated so late in the fifteenth century, yet we can hardly avoid the conclusion that the place got its name from the event:—*Cluain-comhraic*, the field of conflict. There is a place of the same name in Fermanagh, and another called Cloncorig in Tipperary.

About five miles north of Borrisokane in Tipperary, near the shore of Lough Derg, there is a little village called Carrigahorig, where, according to a record in the Four Masters, some battles were fought in 1548. Here however the coincidence is merely accidental, for the name is older than the sixteenth century, and was not derived from the battles mentioned by the annalists. The correct orthography is preserved in the record:—*Carraig-an-chomhraic*, the rock of the meeting; but I cannot tell whether the name originated in a battle or in a confluence of streams.

This word in its simple form gives name to several

places in Cavan, Derry, and Tyrone, now called Corick: Corick near Clogher in Tyrone, was so called because it is situated near the confluence of the two rivers Blackwater and Fury. The two great roads from Castlebar and Crossmolina to Belmullet in Mayo, meet at a bridge over the Owenmore river, about eleven miles from Crossmolina, where two small streams join the Owenmore. For ages before the bridge was built or the roads made, there was a ford at this spot across the Owenmore, which, from the meeting of the streams, was called *Bel-atha-a-chomh-raic*, the ford mouth of the confluence; and this name is now applied to the bridge, in the anglicised form Bellacorick, which very well represents the sound of the long Irish name. There is a place of the same name in Clare, near the mouth of the little river Owen-slieve, in the parish of Clondagad, for the Irish name of which we have the authority of the Four Masters, who write it *Bel-atha-an-chomhraic*; but it is now corruptly called Ballycorick.

In Cormac's Glossary the word *inesclund* is explained "*sribh luath no tren*," "a swift or strong stream." This word has long been obsolete in the language, but it still remains in the names of a good many places. The parish of Dromiskin in Louth takes its name from a very ancient ecclesiastical establishment built on a rising ground—said to have been originally founded by St. Patrick—which is often mentioned in the annals, and which still retains a round tower—a vestige of its former importance. Its old name is *Druim-ineasclainn* [Druminisklin] as we find it in many Irish documents, and this name is retained to this day by the old people who speak Irish; it signifies the *drum* or ridge of the strong stream. There are in the county Cavan two townlands, one near Ballyjamesduff, the other near Belturbet, whose names are the same as this, but more correctly anglicised Druminisclin; and in Meath, near the village of Moynalty, is another, which is incorrectly modernised Druminiskin.

This root-word is seen also in Clooninisclin near the village of Ballinlough in Roscommon, the meadow of the rapid stream. In its simple form it gives name to two townlands in Tyrone, called Inisclan, and to another called Inisclin in Fermanagh. In accordance with a well known custom (prefixing *f*: 1st Ser., Part I., c. II.) this word is often found beginning with *f*; and so we have five townlands in Galway, Roscommon, Leitrim, and Sligo, with the names of Finisclin, Finisklin, and Finnisglin. The word has its original application as the name of the little river Finisclin, which joins the Breedoge two miles north of Frenchpark in Roscommon. It must be observed that in a few of the above-mentioned places there are now either very trifling streams or no streams at all; from which we must infer, either that there has been considerable physical change in those places, or that Cormac's explanation does not apply to the whole of Ireland.

Lín [leen] means to fill; connected with Lat. *plenus*. The diminutive *líonán* [leenaun], which means filling or flowing, is used pretty often as a topographical term. Sometimes it is applied to creeks on the sea shore where the tide flows in. It is in this sense no doubt that it gives name to the well known hamlet called Leenane, near the head of Killery bay in Connemara, which is called by the Four Masters, *Líonan*, or more fully, *Líonán-chind-mara*, the *línan* or tide-filling spot at the head of the sea (*ceann-mara*, head of the sea: see Kenmare, 1st

Ser.); and to Leenane near Crookhaven, west of Cape Clear island in Cork, which is situated on a narrow tidal channel. There is a small lake called Lough Aleenaun, the lake of the filling or flowing, four miles east of Kilfenora in Clare, which in dry summers supplies the surrounding district with water.

Linn signifies a pond or pool, water, the sea; and it occurs in local names, but only as meaning a pool or pond. The English speaking people of Scotland retain the word to the present day, but they apply it to a waterfall:—

> "Whyles owre a linn the burnie plays."

> "Let me in for loud the linn
> Is roarin' o'er the warlock craggie."

Here however the word was transferred from the pool which is under every waterfall, to the waterfall itself; just as happens sometimes in Ireland in the case of the word *lug*, which properly means a basin-shaped hollow in the side of a mountain, but which is now in a few cases applied to the mountain itself (see Lugduff and Lugnaquillia, 1st Ser.).

This word is very ancient as a topographical term, and enters into names, not only in Ireland, but also in Great Britain and on the continent. It helps to form a few important names in Ireland, some of which have already been discussed in the First Series; but it is not in very general use. At the point where the two rivers Glyde and Dee in Louth meet, two miles south east of Castlebellingham, the waters expand into a sort of lake, just before they enter the sea. This little expansion was anciently called *Linn-Duachaill* or *Linduachaille;* and the mouth of the stream was called *Casan-Linne* (the path of the pool). There was here in former days a celebrated monastery which flourished for a long time, and it took the name of *Linduachaill* from the little river-lake on the shore of which it was situated. Tighernach records, at the year 700, the death of St. Colman of *Linduachaill*, and the same record is found in several other authorities. At a later period the Danes had a settlement at the same spot, and we owe to them, no doubt, the effacement of every vestige of the ancient monastic establishment. St. Colman is commemorated in the martyrology of Aengus, and the writer of the gloss quotes a legend to account for the name of *Linduachaill* (the pool of *Uachall*): that before the time of Colman, a demon named *Uachall* infested the waters of the lake, from which he often rose up and did great mischief to the people. The two parts of the name *Casan-Linne* are still preserved in two different denominations, the former in Annagassan (for which see 1st Ser.), and the latter in Linns, which is the name of a townland lying between the river Glyde and the sea.

In the parish of Clonelty, near Newcastle in Limerick, there is a townland taking its name from a ford called Aughalin, the ford (*ath*) of the *lin* or pool; and a ford on a little river in the parish of Ballybrennan in Wexford, has a name with a like signification; it is now called "The Ford of Ling," and it takes its name from a pool at the mouth of the river. Near Clogher in Tyrone, is a place called Cloghlin, the stone of the pond; Cushaling—the foot of the pond—is a small river giving name to two townlands, about half way between Rathangan and Edenderry.

Cong, *conga*, or *cunga* means a narrow neck, a strait where a river or lake contracts, the stream by which one lake empties itself into another very near it. It appears to be connected with *cuing*, which is the common word for the yoke borne by horses that are harnessed to a chariot or carriage. This term belongs chiefly to the north west of Ireland; it is common in Donegal, where indeed it is still a living word among the old natives who speak Irish; and it is found as a local appellative in this county, as well as in Mayo, Galway, and Tyrone. An admirable example of its application is seen in Lough Nacung, a pretty lake at the base of Errigle mountain in the north west of Donegal. This lake is connected with another—Dunlewy lake—by a very short and narrow strait, which is now called "The Cung," and which has given name to Lough Nacung, the lake of the "cung" or neck. Another *cung* connects this—which is called Upper Lough Nacung—with Lower Lough Nacung, from which the townland of Meenacung (*meen*, a mountain meadow) takes its name. The narrow passage between Lough Conn and Lough Cullin in Mayo, now crossed by a road and bridge, has given name to Cungmore point, lying near the crossing.

The best known example of the use of this word is Cong in Mayo, which derived its name from the river on which it is situated, connecting Lough Mask with Lough Corrib. But though this is the most remarkable place in Ireland of the name, the river is by no means a good characteristic example of a "cong," for it is somewhat scattered, and partly subterranean. The great abbey of Cong is celebrated as being the place where Roderick O'Connor, the last native king of Ireland, passed the evening of his days in religious retirement; and it still exhibits in its venerable ruins many vestiges of its former magnificence. It was either founded originally by St. Fechin in the seventh century, or was dedicated to his memory; and hence it is called in Irish documents *Cunga* or *Conga Feichin.*

Lough Cong is the name of a small lake south east of the Twelve Pins in Connemara; and there are two townlands, one near Maguire's Bridge in Fermanagh, and the other in Tyrone, with the euphonious name of Congo, all from the same word. The narrow strait connecting Ballycong lake with the lake of Carrowkeribly, in the parish of Attymas in Mayo, five miles south of Ballina, is called *Dubh-conga* by the Four Masters; and the ford over it was anciently designated *Ath-cunga* (Hy F.); this ford is now called *Bel-atha-conga*, the ford-mouth of the *cong* or strait, which has been anglicised to Ballycong, the present name of the small lake.

Buinne [bunnya—two syllables] means a wave or flood, any flow of water; and this word, or a derivative from it, is pretty often found forming a part of local names, applied to watery or spewy spots, or places liable to be inundated by the overflow of a river or lake. It is very well represented in Cloonbunny in the parish of Tibohine in Roscommon, the *cloon* or meadow of the flood or stream—a streamy, watery field; and this same name is found in Westmeath, Clare, Longford, and Roscommon, in the slightly modified form of Cloonbony; in Tipperary it is Clonbunny; while Clonbunniagh near Enniskillen exhibits the adjective form *buinneach.* Lisbunny is the name of a parish in Tipperary, and of a townland in Derry, each of which must have been so called from a circular fort whose fosse was flooded.

Watery or oozy places, soft, wet, spongy ground, or spots liable to be overflowed, are often designated by the word *fliuch* [flugh], whose simple meaning is "wet:" *fliuch*, humidus; Z. 66. It is seen in its best anglicised form in Killyflugh near Ballymena in Antrim, the wet wood; and in Glenflugh in Wicklow, near the source of the Liffey, now the name of a mountain, but originally that of a glen at its base:—*Gleann-fliuch*, wet or marshy glen.

The derivative *fliuchanach* signifies a wet or spewy place; it gives name to Flughanagh and Flughany in Leitrim and Mayo; and it comes in as a termination in Gortalughany, the name of two townlands in Fermanagh, the wet *gort* or field—the *f* in the beginning having dropped out by aspiration, under the influence of the article (see 1st. Ser., Part I., c. II.). The word is corrupted in Flegans, about three miles north west of Athlone, which we find written Flughan in an Inquisition of James I.; and this old spelling, together with the preservation of the plural form in the present name, shows that the original name is *Fliuchain*, wet places.

From *baidh* [baw], meaning to drown, also a wave, comes the adjective *baithte* [bawtha], signifying "drowned." This term is applied to places which are often submerged, or *drowned* with water. I may remark that when the annalists wish to express that the Danes destroyed the sacred books of the churches and monasteries they plundered, by throwing them into water, they often use this very word: that is, they say the books were *drowned* by the Danes; and this shows that the application is not modern.

We see the word (with the *b* aspirated) in Curra-watia near Moycullen in Galway, the *drowned* or inundated *curragh* or morass. With the adjectival termination *ach*, it gives name to Bauttagh, west of Loughrea in Galway, a marshy place. Very often it takes the diminutive termination *óg* (p. 28), as in Mullanabattog near the town of Monaghan, the *mullagh* or hill-summit of the morass. This form is well exhibited in the name of the little river Bauteoge running through Stradbally in Queen's County, which richly deserves its name, for it flows lazily through level swampy land, which it always inundates in wet weather. In parts of the west, they change the initial letter to *m*, which gives rise to the forms *máiteog* and *maiteach;* and in this way we have the name of Mauteoge, near Crossmolina in Mayo, and of Mautiagh in the parish of Rossinver in Leitrim, both signifying watery land.

Dry Spots. As many places received names from being wet or swampy, so there were spots which, either by the nature of their surface or by artificial drainage, were dry in comparison with the surrounding or adjacent marshy ground, and whose names were derived from this circumstance. The only word I will introduce here to illustrate this observation is *tirm*, which is the common Irish word for dry. With the *t* aspirated to *h*, it is seen in Tullyhirm, the name of places in Armagh and Monaghan—*Tulaigh-thirm*, dry little hill. This is also the original form of the name of the parish of Tullaherin near Gowran in Kilkenny, which has been corrupted by a change of *m* to *n* (1st Ser. Part I. c. III.), though the correct anglicised pronunciation, *Tullowheerim*, is still often heard among the people.

CHAPTER XXIII.

SIZE ; SHAPE.

Great ; small. The terms *mór* [more] and *beg*, meaning respectively large and small, are used to express size, both relative and absolute, more than any other words in the Irish language ; and they are in general easily recognised, being almost always spelled *more* and *beg* in anglicised names.

In the parish of Moviddy in Cork, near the southern bank of the river Bride, stand the ruins of Castlemore castle, once the residence of the chief of the Mac Sweenys, and afterwards of the M'Carthys ; and its name indicates that it was considered the most important fortress of the locality :—*Caislen-mor*, great castle. The parish of Castlemore in Mayo, or as it is sometimes called, Castlemore-Costello, because it is in the barony of Costello, in like manner took its name from a castle, which is called *Caislen-mór* in the annals of Lough Key. Castlemore is also the name of a townland in Carlow. Of the correlative term Castlebeg, small castle, as a townland name, one example occurs north west of Comber in Down. There is a point of land jutting into the Foyle from the Donegal side, about five miles below Derry, called Culmore, where Sir Henry Docwra erected a fort in the year 1600 ; the Four Masters call it *Cuil-mór*, great corner or angle. The townland of Downkillybegs in the parish of Drummaul in Antrim, is written by Colgan, *Dun-chille-bice*, the fortress of the little church.

Very often these terms were employed to express comparison as to size, between the feature named and some other feature of the same kind in the immediate neighbourhood. There can be no doubt that Inishbeg—small island—in the harbour of Baltimore in the south of Cork, received that name by comparison with the larger island of Ringarogy in the same harbour. So also Bunbeg on the shore of Gweedore bay in Donegal, was so called from its situation at the mouth of the little river Clady :—Bunbeg, small *bun* or river mouth—small in comparison with the adjacent estuary of the Gweedore river.

In a great many cases the application of these terms originated in the subdivision of townlands into unequal parts. Three miles south of Kanturk in Cork, in the angle formed by the rivers Allow and Blackwater, there is what was once a single townland called Dromcummer; and it took its name from its situation at the junction of the two rivers:—*Druim-comair*, the ridge of the confluence. But this townland was divided into two parts, containing respectively 373 and 249 acres; and the former is called Dromcummer-more, and the latter Dromcummer-beg. Sometimes in a case of this kind, the larger portion retained the original name without any distinguishing postfix, while the smaller kept the name with the addition of *beg;* as in the case of Derrycullinan (Cullinan's oak grove), and Derrycullinan-beg in Leitrim.

Beg is very seldom altered in form by either grammatical inflection or corruption: but the *m* of *mór* is often aspirated to *v* or *w*; as we see in Baravore near the head of Glenmalure in Wicklow, the great *barr* or summit. Occasionally—though seldom—this aspirated sound has been dropped, leaving nothing of the postfix but *ore*. This happens in Inishore, the name of an island in upper Lough Erne, three miles from the village of Lisnaskea, which the Four Masters call "*Inis-mhór* of Lough Barry," the great island of Lough Barry (this last being the local name for that part of Lough Erne). We see this change also in Seskinore the name of a little village in Tyrone, whose correct Irish name is *Sescenn-mhór*, great marsh.

Like Irish limiting terms in general, these words commonly come after the words they qualify. But not unfrequently it is the reverse. Moraghy is the name of a townland in the parish of Muckno in Monaghan, which signifies great field (*achadh*); but Aghamore, with the same meaning, is a more common name. Rathmore or Ramore, great fort, is a very usual local name; but in the parish of Drumlease in Leitrim, it is made Morerah. So also with *beg*. Rathbeg is a name of frequent occurrence, and signifies little *rath* or fort; but in the county of Louth, a little above Drogheda, is a place called Begrath, which has the same meaning. There is a small island close to the land in Wexford harbour, called Begerin or Begery, which is celebrated as the place where St. Ibar, after having preached the Gospel in various parts of Ireland, founded a monastery in the fifth century, and established a school, in which he instructed a vast number of students; and the place still retains the ruins of some of the ancient buildings. The name is written in the annals, *Beg-Eire*, which, in the Life of the saint, is translated *Parva Hibernia*, Little Ireland; but why this epithet was applied to it I cannot imagine. There is another Begerin in the same county, in the parish of Old Ross, four miles from the town of New Ross.

When these terms are translated, *mór* is generally rendered *great* or *big*, and *beg*, small or little. But occasionally we find the former translated by *much*.

Muchknock and Muchrath in the parish of Killinick in Wexford, are half translations of Knockmore and Rathmore, great hill and great fort. There is a fine rocky precipice in Howth, just over the castle, the proper name of which is Carrickmore; but it is now beginning to be generally called Muchrock, which seems to me a change for the worse.

The word *min*, among other significations, means small, and it is occasionally used in the same manner as *beg*. There is a townland on the Blackwater in Meath, three miles above Kells, called Meenlagh, i. e. small lake, which probably took its name from some enlargement of the river. A far better known place is Menlough or Menlo near Galway; this was properly the name of the small expansion of the river Corrib, on the shore of which the village is situated; and in comparison with Lough Corrib, it was called *Min-loch* or small lake, which name was transferred to the village and castle. Derrymeen, the name of places in Fermanagh and Tyrone, signifies small *derry* or oak-grove, that is, composed of small slender trees; and we have Moneymeen in Wicklow, the small-tree shrubbery.

Length. The usual words to express length and shortness of dimension are *fada* and *gearr*. As long as *fada* retains the *f*, it is easy enough to detect the word in anglicised names, for it does not undergo much corruption. Its most correct forms are seen in Knockfadda, long hill, a name of frequent occurrence; and in Killyfaddy in the northern counties, long wood. But it is very often shortened to one syllable, as in Knockfad and Killyfad, the same respectively as the two preceding names. The *f* is often omitted on account of aspiration, which somewhat obscures the word; of this a good example is

Banada in Sligo and Roscommon, which very correctly represents the sound of *Beann-fhoda*, as the Four Masters write it, meaning long *ben* or peak. The word is quite disguised in Creewood, a place about three miles north west from Slane in Meath, which in King John's charter to the abbey of Mellifont, is called Crevoda, representing the Irish *Craebh-fhoda*, the long *crave* or branchy tree.

Short. The opposite term to *fada* is *gearr* [gar] short; and this is seen in Castlegar, the name of some places in Galway and Mayo, which, in a document of 1586 called "Division of Connaught" (quoted by Hardiman, Iar C. p. 44, note g) is correctly translated "short castle"; Glengar in Tipperary, short glen. Sometimes it comes in the beginning of a name, but in this case it is liable to be confounded with *garbh*, rough; thus Garbally, which is the name of several townlands, in some places means short town, and in others rough town; as Garracloon is translated in one place short meadow, and in another, rough meadow.

Breadth. Leathan [lahan] signifies broad. The best anglicised form is *lahan*, which is seen in Ardlahan near the mouth of the river Maigue in Limerick, broad height. But it is very often shortened to *lane*, especially in the north; as in Gortlane near Cushendall in Antrim, broad field; the same name as Gortlahan in the parish of Kildacommoge in Mayo: Lislane in Derry and Tyrone, broad fort.

From the same root as the last (by the addition of *d*: p. 14) comes the noun *leithead* [lehed], which signifies breadth; and we have this term also very often used in local nomenclature. It is seen in its most correct form in Moylehid, south-west of Enniskillen, which is pronounced in Irish *Mul-leithid*, the hill of breadth, i. e. broad hill-top. But like *leathan*, it is often shortened to one syllable, as we see in Carriglead near St. Mullins in Carlow, broad rock.

Narrowness. There are corresponding terms signifying narrow, which are found in names as often as the preceding. The principal is *cael* [kale, keel], which, with its simple adjective meaning, is almost always represented in anglicised names by *keel*. Glenkeel, narrow glen, is the name of some places in Cork, Fermanagh, and Leitrim; Derrykeel, narrow oak wood.

This word is often applied to a narrow stream, a stream flowing through a long narrrow glen, or through a marsh; and it is the usual term also for a narrow strait. It is in some one of these senses that it gives name to all those places called Keel, Keal, and Keale. As applied to a strait, the word is very happily illustrated in Loughnadreegeel near Ballyjamesduff in Cavan, the name of a lake, which exactly represents the sound of the Irish *Lough-na-dtri-gcael*, the lake of the three straits, so called because it narrows in three places.

Keelaghy in Fermanagh represents *Cael-achadh*, narrow field; and Keelagh and Keilagh, which are the names of several townlands, are in some places understood to be shortened forms of the same name; while in other places they are considered nothing more than the adjective form *caelach*, i. e. something narrow.

Fat or thick. *Reamhar*, or in old Irish *remor*, is a word which is very extensively employed in the formation of names. It means literally gross or fat; and locally it is applied to objects gross or thick in shape, principally hills and rocks. It is pronounced differently in different parts of the country. In the south they sound it *rour*, and it becomes anglicised accordingly, as in Carrigrour near Glengarriff in Cork, *Carraig-reamhar*, thick rock ; Beenrour, gross or thick peak, the name of a hill over Lough Currane in Kerry ; and Reenrour, a name frequent in Cork and Kerry, thick *rinn* or point. As we go north the pronunciation changes : sometimes it becomes *rawer*, as in Dunbunrawer near the village of Gortin in Tyrone, the fort of the thick *bun* or hill-base. Elsewhere in the north, as well as in the west, we find the *mh* represented by *v*, as in Killyrover in the parish of Aghalurcher in Fermanagh, thick wood, which I suppose means a wood of thick or gross trees (see Derrymeen, p. 393, *supra*).

In the northern half of Ireland, the aspiration of the *m* is sometimes altogether neglected, and the letter becomes restored in the manner shown in 1st Ser. (Part I., c. II.) ; which is exemplified in Killyramer near Ballymoney in Antrim, and in Cullyramer near the village of Garvagh in Derry, both the same as Killyrover. The highest summit on Rathlin Island off Antrim is called Kenramer, fat or thick head; the same name as Canrawer near Oughterard in Galway. The restoration of the *m* is illustrated in a name more familiar than any of the preceding—that of Lough Ramor in the south of the county Cavan, which is an abbreviation of the full name Lough Munramer, for it is called in Irish authorities *Loch - muinreamhair*. The latter part, which signifies fat-neck (*muin*, the neck), was a man's name anciently pretty common in Ireland ; and this lake received its name from some one of the old-world heroes who bore the name.

Cas signifies twisted :—*Cas-an-tsugáin*, " the twisting of the rope." The word is exhibited in Cashlieve, the name of a place between Castlerea and Ballinlough in Roscommon, which exactly conveys the sound of the Irish *Cais-shliabh*, twisted *slieve* or mountain.

Crooked or *curved.* *Cam* signifies crooked (*cam*, curvus, Z. 64); but it has other meanings which do not concern us here. Its most frequent application is to rivers and glens; and there is an excellent illustration of its use, and of its Munster pronunciation, in Glencoum or Glencaum, a remarkable defile near Macroom in Cork, crooked or winding glen: there is a Glancam near the railway, five miles north of Blarney, and a Glencoum near Graiguenamanagh in Kilkenny. Several small streams in various parts of Ireland are called Camlin and Camline—that is crooked or curved line. The river Camowen flows through Omagh in Tyrone; and it well deserves the name:—*Cam-abhainn*, winding river. The parish of Cam or Camma in Roscommon, west of Athlone, took its name from a church dedicated to St. Brigid, which is called *Camach* by MacFirbis (Hy F. 78); while Cam, the plural Cams, and the adjective form Camagh, are the names of several townlands—names derived originally from curved objects of some kind, such as rivers, lakes, long hills, &c.

The diminutive *Camóg*, in the several forms Cammoge, Commoge, and Commock, is employed to designate various natural features, principally winding rivers. The little river Cammock or Camac, which joins the Liffey near Kilmainham, is so called because it flows through the "winding glen" of Crumlin (which see in 1st Ser.). There is a townland near Enniskillen called Camgart, curved field or garden, a name which in Galway is made Camgort; and Cangort near Shinrone in King's County, is a corruption of this last form (by the usual phonetic change of *m* to *n*), being spelled indeed by some authorities Camgort. Between Oranmore and Galway, near the ruins of a church and a round tower, a long narrow peninsula juts into Galway bay, called Roscam, a name which stands exactly as it was written in Irish authorities, and which signifies crooked peninsula.

By the addition of *s* (see p. 12 *supra*) is formed the derivative *camas*, which is applied to a bend in a river, and sometimes to a curved bay; and which in the forms of Camas and Camus gives name to many places. St. Comgall of Bangor founded a monastery in the fifth century at Camus on the Bann, two miles above Coleraine; it is called Cambas in Adamnan's Life of St. Columba, and *Camus* in the annals; and it received the name from the curve in the Bann river, near which it is situated. The monastery, which flourished for many centuries, has quite disappeared; and St. Comgall's ancient establishment is now represented merely by a graveyard. There is a spot on the Suir, two miles north west from Cashel, which is mentioned by the Four Masters at A. D. 1623, by the name of *Ath-an-chamais*, the ford of the *camus* or winding—for the river curves at one side round a little island; but a bridge now spans the Suir over the ancient ford, which still retains the name of Camus Bridge.

Bends and slopes. Crom means bent, inclined, stooped or crooked. It is a term of very common occurrence in local names, but many of those of which it forms a part, have been already examined. In anglicised names it usually takes the forms *crom* and *crum*, and occasionally *crim*. One of the peaks of the Mourne range is called Bencrom, stooped mountain. Macroom in Cork is written in the Irish authorities *Magh-cromtha* [Macromha]; the latter part is the genitive of the participial form *cromadh* ; and the whole name means the sloped or inclining field or plain; which accurately describes the spot on which the town stands, for it is a slope at the base of Sleveen hill. The name corresponds with that of Cromaghy, a place near the village of Rosslea in Fermanagh—sloping field. Cromane and Cromoge, two diminutives, signify anything sloping or bending, and give names to many places: whether they are applied to glens, hills, fields, &c., must be determined by the character of the particular spot in each case. Sometimes they are applied to streams, as in the case of the Crummoge, a rivulet a little south of Borrisoleigh in Tipperary, which, like Loobagh (p. 401) received its name from its sinuous course.

Claen [clane] has several meanings, one of which—and the only one which concerns us here—is inclining or sloping. "*Is aire is claen an lis* ;" "this is the reason why the fort slopes"—Cormac's Glossary. This quotation naturally calls up Rathcline in Longford, a townland which gave name to a parish and barony, and which itself must have taken its name from a fort situated on sloping ground; and this is the traditional interpretation of the neighbourhood. It is exactly the same, only with the terms reversed, as Cleenrah in the north of Longford, and Cleanrath the name of three townlands in Cork. This, moreover, is a very ancient name; for we are told in one of the historical tales in *Lebor na h-Uidhre*, that Caherconree, the great fortress of *Curoi mac Daire*, on Slievemish mountain in Kerry, was also called *Cathair-na-claen-ratha*, the stone fort of the *Claen-rath* or sloping rath (O'Curry, Lect. III. 82).

The word Cleen itself, signifying simply a slope,

is the name of three townlands in Fermanagh, Leitrim, and Roscommon. The English plural form Cleens is found in the parish of Devenish in Fermanagh, and the Irish plural Cleeny near Killarney, both meaning slopes; while the adjective forms Cleenagh and Clenagh, occur in Donegal, Fermanagh, and Clare. The Four Masters at A. D. 1247, mention a lake called *Claenloch*, which seems a singular name, for it means sloping lake; and although the name is forgotten in Leitrim, it still survives in the parish of Drumsnat in Monaghan, in the form of Clenlough. It is probable that these names took their rise from the configuration of the ground round the lakes, as people sometimes imagine that a stream flows against the hill. Another name of the same class is *Claenghlais* [Cleanlish]—so the Four Masters write it—which signifies sloping streamlet, the name of a district in the south west of Limerick, in the parish of Killeedy, near the borders of Cork and Kerry, which is now commonly called Clonlish.

Fán or *fánadh* [fawn, fawna] signifies a slope or declivity; and the forms it assumes in anglicised names will be seen in the following examples. In the parish of Killonaghan in the north of Clare, there are two townlands called Faunarooska, *Fán-a'-rúsca*, the slope of the fighting or quarrelling; and Faunrusk, the name of a place a little north of Ennis, has the same meaning. The simple word *fán* gives name to some places in Leitrim, now called Fawn, while *fánadh* is anglicised Fauna in Wicklow, and Fawney in Tyrone and Derry. It appears as a termination in Tobernafauna near Fiddown in Kilkenny, the well of the slope.

Loops. From the word *lúb*, signifying a loop, bend, or fold, many rivers and other curved objects take their names. The adjective form Loobagh is the name of the river that flows by Kilmallock; and meaning, as it does, full of loops, winding or serpentine, it describes exactly the character of that river. The word generally takes such forms as *loob*, *loop*, or *loopy*; thus Aughnaloopy near Kilkeel in Down, signifies the field of the loop or winding. About four miles from the village of Hollymount in Mayo, is the demesne and residence of Newbrook; the Irish name, as preserved in an ancient poem in the Book of Lecan, is *Ath-na-lúb*, which the people still retain with the addition of *bél* a mouth, *Bel-atha-na-lúb* [Bellanaloob], the ford of the *loops*, from the windings of the little river flowing through the demesne into Lough Carra. An adjective form derived from the diminutive is seen in Derrynaloobinagh near Ballybay in Monaghan, the oak wood of the windings; and also in Sheskinloobanagh, the name of a marsh in the townland of Croaghonagh, about four miles south west from Ballybofey in Donegal, which the Four Masters, at 1603, write *Seascann-lúbanach*, the marsh of the windings.

Nook. *Cluid* is a nook, a corner, an angle. It takes the anglicised forms Clood, Cluid, and Cluide, which are the names of several townlands. Cloodrevagh in Leitrim, and Cluidrevagh in Galway, both signify grey nook (p. 276); Cloodrumman in Leitrim, the corner of the *drum* or ridge.

Floor. Several of the terms which designate a level spot of land have been already examined; and the last I will instance is *urlar*, which signifies a floor, sometimes a threshing-floor. Near the village of Stranorlar in Donegal, along the little river that flows through it, there is a remarkably level holm or river meadow, which has given the village its name—

Srath-an-urlair, the holm or river bank of the floor. The simple word gives name to Urlar in Sligo, and to Urlaur in Mayo—both meaning a level place like a floor. There are several townlands in the Connaught counties called Carrownurlaur, the quarter-land of the floor, i. e. a flat piece of land, or a threshing-floor.

Nail. *Ionga* [inga] signifies a nail, talon, or hoof; and it was sometimes applied to pointed rocks, or to long pointed pieces of land. The sound is well preserved in Inga, the name of a place near the village of Killimor in the south east of Galway. Near the mouth of the river Fergus in Clare, a short distance west of Newmarket, is a little promontory jutting into the river, called Ing Point, which has given name to three townlands. Just outside Bannow Bay in Wexford, near the village of Fethard, is a long point with a cliff rising over the sea along one side; and it is called Ingard—high nail. Duninga, the name of a place on the Kilkenny shore of the Barrow, between Goresbridge and Bagnalstown, the fort of the nail or point. The correct genitive is *iongan*, which is represented in Clooningan in the parish of Achonry in Sligo (*cloon*, a meadow); and we find the plural in Drumingna in the parish of Kiltubbrid in Sligo, the hill-ridge of the talons.

Tail. The Irish word *earball* was often applied to the extremity of any natural feature, such as a long, low hill; or to any long stripe of land, which was either the extremity of a larger portion, or which was, for any reason, considered by the people to bear some resemblance to the tail of some animal. This word *earball* [commonly pronounced urbal] signifies the tail of an animal; and according to Cormac's glossary, it is derived from *iar*, hinder, and *ball*, a member. In its topographical application, it is liable to singular corruptions in pronunciation, in the several ways illustrated by the names that follow. It will be observed also that the people often imagined they saw in certain features a likeness, not merely to a tail, but to the tail of some particular animal.

Urbal, which is a correct anglicised form, is the name of several townlands in some of the northern counties. There is a place near the town of Monaghan called Urbalkirk, which signifies the tail of the *cark* or hen; Urbalshinny in Donegal is the fox's tail (*seannach*, a fox). In some of the Ulster counties it is made *warble;* as we see in Warbleshinny about three miles south of Derry, the same name as the last. In Connaught, the word is usually pronounced, by a metathesis, *rubble;* and this corruption is reproduced in the name of two townlands called Rubble in Mayo and Leitrim. The townland of Erribul near the Clare side of the Shannon, opposite Foynes, exhibits the usual Munster pronunciation.

Ear. In designating places by their shape, the ear was a favourite object of comparison. A lateral, semi-detached portion of land, or a long stripe, would often be called an ear; and this fancied likeness has given origin to some odd freaks of nomenclature. *Cluas* [cloos] is the Irish word for ear: in local names it usually takes the forms of *cloos* and *cloosh.* Near Castlegregory in Kerry is a townland called Cloosguire—*Cluas-gadhair*, the dog's ear; and there is another near Mountrath in Queen's County, called Clooscullen, with a similar signification—*Cluas-coileain*, the whelp's ear. One of the innumerable small lakes in the parish of Moyrus in Galway, is called Lough Clooshgirrea, the lake of the hare's ear (see p. 293). With the *c* eclipsed by *g* in the genitive plural, we have Lisnagloos in the parish of Killora in

Galway, south of Athenry, and Coolnagloose in the parish of Kilcavan in Wexford, the former signifying the fort, and the latter the angle, of the ears.

Tongue. The Irish word *teanga* [tanga] a tongue, is often applied to long-shaped pieces of land or water, just in the same sense as we say in English "a tongue of land." There is a place called Bryantang in the county Antrim, not far from Ballycastle, which derives the latter part of its name from a tongue of land at the meeting of two streams: the little tongue itself is now called "Bryantang Braes." The first part *bryan*, represents the Irish *bruighean* (see Bohernabreena in 1st Ser.), a fairy fort; for a remarkable ancient circular fort stood not long since near the junction of the streams, but it is now obliterated:—Bryantang, the fairy-fort of the tongue. Just before the river Inny falls into Lough Ree, it is joined by the little river Tang, two miles from Ballymahon. There are two townlands in Donegal called Tangaveane, middle tongue (*veane* from *meadhon:* p. 417): Tangincartoor in Mayo, the tongue of the *cartron* or quarter-land.

Skull. The word *claigeann* [claggan], which signifies a skull, is often applied to a round, dry, hard, or rocky hill; and in this sense it gives names to all those places now called Clagan, Claggan, and Cleggan. The adjective form *Claigeannach* is used to designate a place full of round rocky hills, from which we have such townland names as Clegnagh and Clagnagh. And the simple plural is exhibited in Clegna, the name of a place east of Boyle in Roscommon, i. e. skulls or round hills.

Breast. The front of a hill, a projection from its general body, is often designated by the word *ucht*, which signifies the breast. The most correct anglicised form is *ught*, which is seen in Ughtyneill near Moynalty in the county Meath, O'Neill's hill-breast (*y* for *O*: see p. 133, *supra*). But it more often takes the form *ought;* of which an excellent example is seen in Oughtmama, the name of a parish in Clare, meaning the breast or front of the *maam* or mountain pass—Oughtymoyle and Oughtymore in the parish of Magilligan in Derry, signifying bare breast and great breast respectively, the *y* being a corruption in both names.

There is a small island in the eastern side of Lough Mask, about four miles south west of Ballinrobe, called Inishoght, the island of the breast; and the Four Masters mention another little island of the same name, which they call *Inis-ochta*, in Lough Macnean in Fermanagh, as the scene of a fight between the O'Rourkes and the MacRannalls in A.D. 1499. But this name, though used in the last century, is now forgotten; the present name of the islet is Inishee, i. e. *Inis-Aedha*, the island of *Aedh* or Hugh; and according to the tradition quoted by O'Donovan (Four M., IV.—p. 1250 m.) it received this name from a king named *Aedh* who once lived on it. Inishee or Hugh's Island is also the name of a place in the parish of Clonfert in the east of the county Galway. There is a parish in the east of Galway, including within it the village of Eyrecourt, now called Donanaghta; but in the Inquisitions the name is written Doonanought, both of which point to the meaning, the fort of the breast, i. e. built on the breast of a hill.

Cleft. The word *gág* [gaug] means a cleft, chink, a split or chasm in a rock. It is well represented in Coolnagaug near Kinsale in Cork, in Garrygaug in the south of Kilkenny, and in Ballygauge in Queen's

County; the angle, the garden, and the town, of the cleft or chasm. Gaugin mountain, eight miles west of Stranorlar in Donegal—Gaugin, little cleft—must have taken its name from some chasm in its side.

There is another word slightly different from this in sound, used in Munster, and especially in Clare—namely *goug*, or as it would be spelled in Irish, *gobhag;* and this is applied to a split or cavern in a cliff, or to a narrow nook into which the sea enters—a long narrow sea inlet. The diminutive Gougane is the name of a townland near the village of Banteer in the north of Cork; and Gougane Barra (for which see 1st Ser.) is well known to every Irish tourist. A little stream called Gougane flows into the strait separating Valentia Island in Kerry from the mainland.

Kneading trough. In former days when families generally made their own bread, a kneading trough was an article found in almost every house. *Losaid*, or in an anglicised form, *losset*, is the Irish word for a kneading trough; and curiously enough it is in very common use, as a component in local names. Here, however, the allusion seems to be not so much to shape, as to use and production; for the word is applied to a well tilled and productive field, or to good rich land. A farmer will call such a field a *losset*, because he sees it covered with rich produce, like a kneading trough with dough. The word is used in this sense chiefly in the northern counties, but it is also found in the south; and in the form of Losset, it is the name of a dozen townlands, in various counties from Donegal to Tipperary. Cappanalosset in the parish of Lemanaghan in King's County, signifies the garden-plot of the lossets, i. e. a rich, productive plot.

The genitive and plural form is *loiste* [lusty], and this gives name to all those places now called Lustia and Lusty—both signifying simply fertile spots. There is one example of the genitive in the Four Masters, namely at A.D. 1597, where they mention a place called *Druim-na-loiste*, the ridge of the kneading trough; which is situated near Inver in Donegal, and is now called Drumnalost. Another anglicised form is seen in Loyst, the name of a place near Rockcorry in Monaghan, which also occurs in Tullaghaloyst in the parish of Currin in the same county, the hill of the *losset*: Annaloist near Portadown in Armagh, shows the word compounded with *ath* a ford. Aghalust near the village of Ardagh in Longford, is the same as Aghalustia near Ballaghaderreen in Mayo, the field *(achadh)* of the kneading trough, i. e. simply a rich fertile field.

Trough. *Amar* or *umar* signifies a trough or font; and the term is locally applied to designate a hollow place. Both the sound and sense are well preserved in Lugganammer and Leganamer, two townlands in Leitrim, the names of which mean the *lug* or hollow of the trough, i. e. a *lug* formed like a trough. So also Bohammer near Balgriffin in Dublin, written in the Inquisitions Bothomer, which comes near the Irish *Both-amuir*, the hut of the trough; Glennanummer in the parish of Kilcumreragh in the north of King's County, and Glennanammer near Athleague on the Roscommon side of the Shannon, both of which mean the glen of the troughs—a glen in which there are deep pools.

In some cases a *b* or a *p* is inserted after the *m*, in accordance with a phonetic law already examined (1st Ser., Part I., c. III.). This is the case in Killynumber in the parish of Kilcronaghan in Derry, which represents *Coill-an-umair*, the wood of the trough; as well as in Coolumber in the parish of Moore, in the south of Roscommon, and in Coolamber on the boundary of Longford and Westmeath, both having names of similar import to Culdaff, signifying the back of the trough or deep hollow; and we have a *p* in Cloondahamper five or six miles east of Tuam in Galway, the meadow of the two (*da*) hollows.

Caldron. Round deep hollows were often designated by the several Irish terms which correspond with such English words as *vat*, *keeve*, *caldron*, &c ; just as the crater of a volcano was so called from the Greek word *kratér*, a cup or chalice. *Coire* [curra, curry] signifies a caldron or boiler—such a caldron as was always kept in every public victualling house, and in every chieftain's kitchen. Locally the word was applied to a deep round hollow in a mountain, often also to the deep pool formed under a cataract, and sometimes to a whirlpool in the sea. In such applications it is very common in Scotland, but it is not so much used in Ireland. There are two townlands in Tipperary, one near the village of Toomyvara, the other near Kilsheelan, called Poulakerry; and there is a place at Glanmire near Cork city, called Poulacurry—all from *Poll-a'-choire*, the caldron-hole. In the wild district east of Achill Island in Mayo, there are two mountain lakes, one called Corryloughaphuill, the caldron of the lake of the hole—a name sufficiently expressive in all conscience; the other Corranabinnia, the caldron of the *bin* or peak—the peak being a very high mountain which rises over the lake.

In the sound betwen Rathlin Island and the coast of Antrim, there is a whirlpool caused by the violent conflict of the tides, which was in old times as celebrated among the Irish as Charybdis was among the ancient Greeks; and it was known by the name of *Coire-Breacain* [Corry-Breckan or Corryvreckan], Brecan's caldron. Cormac MacCullenan in his Glossary, written in the ninth century, gives the following spirited account of this great whirlpool:—" *Coire Brecain*, i. e. a great whirlpool which is between Ireland and Scotland to the north, in the meeting of the various seas, viz., the sea which encompasses Ireland at the north west, and the sea which encompasses Scotland at the north east, and the sea to the south between Ireland and Scotland. They whirl round like moulding compasses, each of them taking the place of the other, like the paddles of a mill-wheel, until they are sucked into the depths, so that the caldron remains with its mouth wide open; and it would suck even the whole of Ireland into its yawning gullet. It vomits that draught up again, so that its thunderous eructation and its bursting and its roaring are heard among the clouds, like the steam-boiling of a caldron on the fire."

He then goes on to say that a certain merchant named Brecan, grandson of Niall of the Nine Hostages (Niall died in A. D. 405), had fifty *currachs* or boats trading between Ireland and Scotland, and that on one occasion they were all swallowed up (with Brecan himself) in this caldron. Hence the name *Coire-Breacain*, Brecan's caldron, which Adamnan, who mentions it, Latinises *Charybdis Brecani*. The old name has been long forgotten however, and the whirlpool is now known by an equally expressive one among the people of Antrim and Rathlin, viz. *Slog-na-mara*, the swallow of the sea (v. pp. 378, 248). The name is remembered in Scotland, but it is applied to a dangerous whirlpool between the islands of Scarba and Jura, which is mentioned by Sir Walter Scott in "The Lord of the Isles"—

> "And Scarba's isle, whose tortured shore
> Still rings to Corrievreken's roar."

That the original Corry Breckan was that between Antrim and Rathlin, and that the name was borrowed by the monks of Iona for the Western Isles, is made quite evident from the authorities quoted by Dr. Reeves in his "Adamnan," p. 29, and in his "Ecclesiastical Antiquities," p. 289.*

Vat. *Dabhach* [davagh] signifies a vat, a kieve, or large tub: it occurs in Irish names much oftener than the last term; and it is generally applied to a well, a deep pit or pool, or to any deep hollow like a vat or caldron. Davagh, its most correct anglicised form, is the name of some townlands in Monaghan and Tyrone; Mullandavagh near Clones in Monaghan, the summit of the vat-like hollow; Glendavagh near Aughnacloy in Tyrone, means a glen having deep pools along its course (like Glennanummer: p. 407).

One of the genitive forms of this word is *daibhche* [divha, diha], which is variously modified in the modern forms of names. It is well represented in Gortnadihy in the parish of Kilmeen in Cork, which in the "Genealogy of *Corca Laidhe*" is called *Gort-na-daibhche*, the field of the vat or round hollow. There is another place of the same name near Skibbereen in the same county; and two called Gortnadiha in Waterford, which is still the same name. So

* In the latter there is a complete account of *Coire-Breacain*, from which I have condensed the sketch given here.

also Knocknadiha in Limerick, Drumdiha in Tipperary, and Dromdihy in Cork, all meaning the hill of the round hollow. Portdeha (port of the vat) is the name of a little bight on the eastern shore of Aranmore; but this name is now accounted for by a legend in the life of St. Endeus, which is related at length by the Rev. W. Kilbride in his description of Aranmore (Kilk. Arch. Jour. 1868, p. 106).

In these names the *bh* sound is suppressed and that of *ch* retained as an *h;* but in other names it is the reverse—such for example as Letterdife in the parish of Moyrus in Galway, the hill-side of the vat. We have a diminutive form of the word in Loughdeheen in the parish of Lisnakill near Waterford city; in Loughdiheen, one of the mountain lakes under Galtymore; and in Rindifin near Gort in Galway, the two first of which mean the lake, and the last the point, of the little vat or pool. In Donegal this word is sometimes applied to a flax-dam, which is illustrated in Culdaff (Cooledagh, Inq.), the name of a village and parish in Inishowen, signifying the *cul* or back of the flax-dam.

False or pseudo men. In various parts of Ireland, a standing stone, whether natural or artificial, placed in a conspicuous position, so as to look at a distance something like the figure of a man, is called by the name *fear-bréige* [farbreaga], literally a false man—a fantastic or *pseudo* man; or if there be two or more, together, *fir-bréige* [firbreaga], false men. The term is also applied to a scare-crow, or to any artificial object made to represent a man. In some cases such stones have given names to the townlands or hills on which they stand; as in Farbreague in the parish of Moyne in Wicklow; Farbreague, a hill lying five miles north east of Roscrea in Tipperary; and Farbreagues, east of Athleague in Roscommon. There is a Farbregagh—a tall rock in the sea—at the north side of Scarriff Island outside Kenmare Bay; and a group of standing stones on one of the Ballyhoura hills, on the borders of Cork and Limerick, is called Firbreaga.

Sometimes the word *buachaill*, a boy, is used instead of *fear*. The hill lying immediately south of Knocklayd, near Ballycastle in Antrim, is called Bohilbreaga. Near the village of Ballyneety in Limerick, there is a long stone standing on the top of a hill, which may be seen on the right of the railway as you approach Pallas from Limerick; and it is well known by the name of Boughal-breaga: there is also a Boghil Bregagh near the demesne of Seaforde in the parish of Loughinisland in Down. The word *buachaill* itself, without the other term, is often applied to a standing stone. There is a mountain called Boughil, five miles from Kenmare; and the driver of the car will point out the conspicuous standing rock—the *boughil* himself—which gave name to the mountain, on the left of the road as you go to Killarney. And several townlands in various parts of Ireland are called Boughill and Boghill, whose names originated similarly. Boughilbo is a townland near Shanagolden in Limerick, the name of which signifies "cow-boy."

The word *breug* [breague] signifies a lie; and in several senses, and in various modified forms, it is pretty commonly used in the formation of local names. There is a townland called Dromorebrague near Loughbrickland in Down, concerning which the people have a local tradition, that the founders of Dromore in the same county, at first intended the town to be here; but that they changed their minds and built it on its present site, so that the former place was called Dromorebrague, false or *pseudo* Dromore. The city of Armagh has also a similar representative—a sort of shadow, or ghost, or *fetch*, of itself, viz., Armaghbrague in the parish of Lisnadill in the same county.

The term is sometimes used to designate streams that are subject to sudden and dangerous floods, or which flow through deep quagmires; and in this case it means deceitful or treacherous. An excellent example is the little river Bregoge in Cork, which joins the Awbeg (the Mulla of Spenser) near Doneraile. Bregoge is a diminutive of *breug* (see p. 28) and signifies "little liar or deceiver." This river is formed by the junction of the principal stream which rises in a deep glen on the side of Corrinmore hill, with three others—all four of the same length, flowing down the face of the Ballyhoura hills, and meeting nearly in the same spot, whence the united stream runs on to the Awbeg. These rivulets carry very little water in dry weather; but whenever a heavy shower falls on the hills, four mountain floods rush down simultaneously, and meet together nearly at the same instant, swelling the little rivulet in a few moments to an impetuous and dangerous torrent. This little stream is celebrated by Spenser in his "Colin Clouts come home again;" he calls it "False Bregoge," which is quite a correct interpretation; and in his own fanciful way, he accounts for the name in one of the most beautiful pastorals in the English language.

There is a little stream called Breagagh about three miles south east of Thurles in Tipperary; and another of the same name flows near the city of Kilkenny; but these probably received their names from flowing through treacherous marshes. A name of similar import is Srahanbregagh in the parish of Ettagh, south of Birr in King's County—false *sruhan* or little stream. The bay of Trawbreaga at Malin in Donegal, well deserves its name, *Traigh-brege*—so Colgan writes it—treacherous strand; for the tide rises there so suddenly that it has often swept away people walking incautiously on the shore.

CHAPTER XXIV.

SITUATION.

THE relative situation of a place with regard to one or more others, is a circumstance that has been often taken advantage of in the formation of local names; so that several of the terms expressive of this sort of relation, such as those for upper, lower, middle, far, near, lateral direction, outer or beyond, &c., are quite common in every part of Ireland as forming part of our nomenclature.

Upper. Uachdar signifies the upper part. It is also the word for cream (as being on the top of the milk), but we may leave this meaning out of the question here, though in some places the people believe that this is the sense it bears in local names. It is sometimes used to designate a high place simply; but it is oftener applied in a comparative sense to indicate that the place is higher than some other in the same neighbourhood. Its usual form is *oughter*, which is easily recognised. There is a hill a mile north of the Recess hotel, on the road from Clifden to Galway, just at the eastern base of the Twelve Pins, called

Lissoughter, upper fort, probably from a *lis* or fort on its summit. Killoughter, upper church, is a place near Rathnew in Wicklow, which gives its name to a railway station; and there is a townland of the same name near Ballyhaise in Cavan. The townland of Ballyoughter in the parish of Moyaliff in Tipperary, should have been called Bella-oughter; for the name was originally applied to a ford across the Clodiagh river, over which there is now a bridge; and its Irish form is *Bel-atha-uachdair*, the mouth of the upper ford. There are places of this name in the same county and in Mayo, and some townlands in Wexford called Balloughter; but these are probably *Baile-uachdar*, upper town. Oughteranny, partly the name of a barony in Kildare, is anglicised from *Uachdar-fhine*, upper *fines* or district.

The adjective form *uachdarach* is as common as the original; it is seen in its several anglicised forms in Ballyoughteragh, Ballyoughtragh, and Ballyoughtra; all signifying upper town. The word *uachdar* is not unfrequently anglicised *water;* as in Clowater near Borris in Carlow, *Cloch-uachdar*, upper stone or stone castle; and this change operating on the adjective form has given origin to Watree near Gowran in Kilkenny, which is simply the phonetic reduction of *Uachdaraighe*, upper lands.

Lower. The opposite term to *uachdar* is *iochdar*, which signifies lower; and this and the adjective form *iochdarach*, appear in anglicised names in such forms as *eighter*, *eighteragh*, *etra*, &c., which are illustrated in Carroweighter in Roscommon, lower quarterland; in Broighter on the railway line between Magilligan and Derry, *broghiochdar*, lower *brugh* or fort; and in Moyeightragh near Killarney, lower plain. In the parish of Desertoghill in Derry, there are two adjacent townlands called Moyletra Kill and Moyletra Toy. Moyletra signifies lower *mael* or hill; *kill* is "church;" *toy* is *tuath*, a layman, or belonging to the laity; and these two distinguishing terms indicate that one of the townlands belonged to some church, and the other to a lay proprietor.

Very often when a townland was divided into two, the parts were distinguished by the terms *oughter* and *eighter*, upper and lower, or by the anglicised adjective forms *otra* and *etra*, or *otre* and *etre;* which is seen in Moy Etra and Moy Otra in the parish of Clontibret in Monaghan, lower Moy (plain) and upper Moy; as well as in many other names.

Low. *Iseal* [eeshal] means low in situation. In its most correct anglicised form it is seen in Gorteeshal near Ballyporeen in Tipperary, low field; and in Agheeshal in Monaghan, low ford. There is another much better known place of this name in Tipperary, on the river Suir, four miles from Cashel, but incorrectly anglicised Athassel, where stand the fine ruins of the priory founded in the twelfth century by William Fitz-Adelm. The annalists write the name *Ath-iseal*, and the ford was probably so called to distinguish it from the ford at Golden, a mile higher up the river. The people of the place, however, believe that it means merely "shallow ford"; for they say that even children can cross it when the river is in its ordinary state. *Magh-iseal* [Moy-eeshal] low plain or field, is the name of several places, but it is usually contracted to two syllables: in Carlow it assumes the form of Myshall, the name of a village and parish; in the parish of Magourney in Cork, is the townland of Meeshall; and near Bandon in the same county, there is a place called Mishells, low plains.

Middle. We have several words for middle, the most common of which is *eadar* [adder], old Irish form *etar*, cognate with Latin *inter:* the literal meaning of the word is "between." Names were formed from this word on account of the position of the places or objects between two others. It is seen in Gragadder near Kilcock in Kildare, central *graig* or village. Similar to this in signification are Adderville and Adderwal in Donegal, both meaning central town, the last syllable of each representing the Irish *baile.* Another form is exhibited in Ederglen in Mayo, and Edercloon in Longford, central glen and meadow. The Four Masters mention a church situated somewhere near Armagh, called *Magh-etir-di-ghlais*, the plain between the two streams; which Dr. Reeves (Adamn. p. 154, note) considers is probably Magheraglass in the parish of Kildress near Cookstown in Tyrone; for besides the similarity of the names, there are in this townland the remains of an ancient chapel.

From *eadar*, by the addition of the suffix *nach* (p. 6) is derived the adjective form *eadarnach;* from which comes Edernagh near Cookstown in Tyrone, meaning central place. The oblique inflection changes this to Ederny, which is the name of a village in the north of Fermanagh. There are two townlands in the same county called Dooederny, black central-land (*doo* from *dubh*, black). Another adjective form is *eadarach*, which gives name to Ballyaddragh near Greenore point, south of Wexford harbour; and to Dunadry three miles from the town of Antrim (pronounced by the Scotch settlers Dun-eddery), central dun or fort, in which the termination is modified by oblique inflection.

Meadhon [maan] is another term for middle, corresponding with Latin *medius.* In one of its anglicised forms it is seen in Inishmaan, the name of the middle island of Aran in Galway bay ; and there are other islands of the same name in the slightly modified forms of Inishmean and Inishmaine, in Lough Melvin and Lough Mask. Inishmaine near the eastern shore of Lough Mask, has the ruins of an abbey which is mentioned by the Four Masters at A.D. 1223, by the name of *Inis-meadhon.* The barony of Kilmaine and the parish of Kilmainemore in Mayo, both take their names from an old church situated in the parish, which the annalists call *Cill-meadhon,* middle church. The adjective form *meadhonach* [maanagh] also enters into names, usually in the forms *menagh* and *mena ;* as in Drummenagh, the name of some townlands in Armagh, Tyrone, and Fermanagh, middle ridge. But the *m* is often aspirated to *v*, an instance of which is Reevanagh in the parish of Tiscoffin in Kilkenny, middle *reidh* or mountain flat.

The word *lár* [laur], which properly signifies the ground, or a floor, is used to denote the middle ; and in this sense it often finds its way into names, usually in the forms of *lare* or *laur*. Rosslare is a long narrow peninsula near Wexford, giving name to a parish ; its name signifies middle peninsula ; and it was probably so called as being the boundary between Wexford Haven and the outer sea. Ballinlaur in the parish of Kilreekil in Galway, is *Baile-an-láir*, the town of the middle, or middle town ; Ennislare in the parish of Lisnadill in Armagh, middle island or river meadow.

Across. *Tarsna* signifies across, i. e. it is applied to anything having a transverse position with respect to something else. The word is always anglicised *tarsna*, or by metathesis, *trasna*, and cannot be mistaken, so that one or two illustrations will be sufficient. Kiltrasna is the name of a townland in Cavan, and of another in Galway, whose Irish form is *Coill-tarsna*, cross-wood; Drumtarsna near Borrisoleigh in Tipperary, cross ridge. Trasna is the name of a townland in Fermanagh, and Tarsna of another in Tipperary; there is a small island in Strangford Lough called Trasnagh; one in Upper Lough Erne, and another in Lower Lough Erne, near Enniskillen, called Trasna; all so called on account of their transverse position.

Near, *outer*. The word *gar*, near, is occasionally employed to form names. In the centre of Glengarriff bay, is a little island called Garinish, near island; it was so called by the people of Glengarriff to indicate its relative position in respect to the more distant island of Whiddy; so also Garinish near Sneem is compared with Sherky, lying further out; and there are several other islets of the same name round the coast of Cork and Kerry.

The whole district in which the village and parish of Kiltamagh in Mayo are situated, was formerly wooded, which is plainly indicated by the number of local names in the neighbourhood containing the word *coill* a word, or the plural *coillte*; such as Kyletrasna, cross wood; Kylewee, yellow wood; and "The Woods," which is the name of a little hamlet one mile from Kiltamagh. Two miles east of the village, there are two small lakes near each other; one called Cuiltybo (lake), the woods of the cow, which is also the name of places elsewhere; and the other Cuiltybobigge (lake), the woods of the little cow. The Irish name of the village and parish is *Coillte-amach*, outer woods; and the people say that these old woods were so called because they formed the western or outer extremity of the ancient forest.

CHAPTER XXV.

THE CARDINAL POINTS.

WHEN we find the term for one of the cardinal points forming part of a local name, we may infer that the object or place was so called on account of its direction, either from the people who gave it the name, or from some other place or object or territory lying near it.

The four cardinal points were designated by the Irish in the same way as by the ancient Hebrews and the Indians; for they got names which expressed their position with regard to a person standing with his face to the east.*

East. The original Irish word for the east is *oir* [ur, er]; which however, is often written *soir* and *thoir* [sur, hur]; and a derivative form *oirthear* [urher, erher], is used in the oldest Irish writings. Moreover, the first and last are often written *air* and *airthear* (*air* is everything eastern: Cor. Gl.). Our ancient literature affords ample proof that these words were used from the earliest times to signify both the front and the east, and the same double application continues in use at the present day. As one instance out of many, may be cited the two-fold translation of *airther* in the ancient druidical

* See Zeuss; Gram. Celt. page 57, note.

prophecy of the coming of St. Patrick:—"*A miasa i n-airther a tighi*" (his dishes [shall be] in the east of his house). For while Murchu, in the Book of Armagh, translates *airther* by the Latin word *anterior*, or front, on the other hand the same word in the same passage has been translated by its more usual equivalent *oriens* or *orientalis* (i. e. east) in the Scholia to Fiech's Hymn, and in several of the Lives of St. Patrick—(See Reeves's Adamnan—page 82).

Oir is usually represented in anglicised names by *er*. It commonly occurs in the end of names, and when it does, it always carries the accent, a test by which it may generally be recognised. Tullaher (accent on *her*) the name of a townland and also of a lake, four miles nearly east of Kilkee in Clare, represents the Irish *Tulach-oir*, eastern hill; Emlagher in the parish of Carn in Kildare, two miles south of Curragh Camp, and Annagher at the village of Coal Island, four miles from Dungannon in Tyrone—both signify eastern marsh (*imleach*, *eanach*, a marsh).

There is a celebrated abbey near Killarney which is now always known by the name of Mucross; but this is really the name of the peninsula on which it stands (see Mucross in 1st Ser.), and the proper name of the abbey, as we find it in many old authorities, is *Oirbhealach* [Ervallagh], the eastern *bealach* or pass; which Anglo Irish writers usually anglicise Irrelagh. The present abbey was built in the year 1340, according to the Four Masters, for Franciscan friars, by Donall MacCarthy More, prince of Desmond; but we know from the Irish annals that a church was situated there long previously. There is a tradition current in the county regarding the foundation of the abbey, that MacCarthy More was admonished in a vision to erect a monastery at a place called *Carraig-an-chiuil* [Carrigahule], the rock of the *ceól* or music; but as he knew no such rock, he sent out a number of his followers to search for a place bearing this name. They searched long in vain, and were returning home unsuccessful and downcast; when as they were passing by *Oirbhealach*, they heard a sweet strain of music issuing from a rock; and they came straight to their chieftain, and told him what had occurred. MacCarthy More hearing their story, at once concluded that this was the very rock which had been revealed to him in his vision, and he immediately began to build the monastery.* (See O'Donovan, Four M. III. 566.)

This name *Oirbhealach* is found elsewhere also; in the form of Ervallagh it designates three townlands in Galway, one in Connemara, and the other two near Ahascragh. One mile from Headford in the same county, lie the ruins of the monastery of Rosserrily, which, according to the Four Masters, was founded for Franciscans in the year 1351. In recording its foundation they call it *Ros-oirbhealaigh*, the wood of the eastern pass, the sound of which is well conveyed by its present name; but at the year 1604 they call it *Ros-Iriala*, which would mean Irial's wood. It is likely that the former is the correct ancient name.

The other form *orthear*, is also common in local nomenclature. The ancient kingdom of *Oriel*, which was founded by the three Collas in A.D. 332, com-

* The legend of music heard from rocks is very general in Ireland; and I take it that this is the origin of the name Carrigapheepera, the Piper's Rock, applied to certain rocks in many parts of the country: perhaps some were dancing places.

prised the present counties of Monaghan, Armagh, and Louth; the eastern part of it, which was the patrimony of the O'Hanlons, received the name so often met with in our annals, *Oirtheara* [Orhera]. This word is plural, and was originally applied not to the territory, but to the inhabitants; and it is translated by several of the Latin-Irish writers *Orientales*, i. e. easterns or eastern people; and it was also called *Crioch-na-nOirthear*, which carries out the same idea; for the latter part is in the genitive plural, and the whole designation has been translated by Probus in his Life of St. Patrick, *Regio Orientalium*, literally the country of the eastern people. But after a fashion very common in Ireland, the territory ultimately got the name of the people who inhabited it; and the ancient *Airtheara* still exists in the modernised form Orior, as the name of two baronies in the east of the county Armagh. The same anglicised form of *Oirthear* appears in Tullyorior, the name of a townland in the parish of Garvaghy in Down, not far from Banbridge—eastern *tulach* or hill.

The most easterly of the old forts in the ancient *Taillteann* or Teltown (see Teltown in 1st. Ser.) on the Blackwater, near Kells in Meath, was called *Rath-airthir*, (Four M.) eastern fort; but its present Irish name is *Baile-orthaidhe* [Ballyōry], a modification of the old designation; and this again has been translated into Oristown, which is now the name of a village and of two townlands, occupying the old site. The most eastern of the Aran islands is called by Cormac MacCullenan *Ara-airthir*, i. e. eastern Aran. Its present anglicised name is Inisheer, which is very puzzling; for it exactly represents the pronunciation of *Inis-siar*, *western* island; and it is hard to believe that it could have been modernised from *Inis-soir*—for I have never found *soir* represented by *sheer*, or *oir* by *eer*, in anglicised names. Perhaps we may take Inisheer as it stands, and interpret it western island, on the supposition that this was a later name given to the island by the people of the mainland about Galway.

Iar [eer] signifies the hinder part, a meaning which is illustrated in the word *iarball*, applied to the tail of an animal, i. e. the hinder *ball* or member (see p. 402). It also signifies the west; in which sense it appears in Ardaneer near Shanagolden in Limerick, the western height.

This word more usually enters into names in the adjective form *iarach* or *iarthach*. There is a mountain called Baurearagh, over Glengarriff in Cork, near the tunnel on the Kenmare road, which also gives name to the stream flowing through the deep valley which you cross going towards Kenmare after leaving the tunnel; the name is *Barr-iarach*, western summit. Cloonearagh in Kerry and Roscommon, western *cloon* or meadow. The western extremity of Little Island in the Lee below Cork, is called Inchera, which was probably the original name of the whole island, for it means western island—*Inis-iarthach*—so called on account of its position with respect to the Great Island.

As *oir* is often used with an initial *s*, so *iar* is quite common in the form of *siar* [sheer]. Clonshire, a townland giving name to a parish in Limerick, was probably so called on account of its direction from Adare—*Cluain-siar*, western meadow; and Cloonshear near Inchigeelagh in Cork, has the same meaning.

There is a derivative form, *iarthar*, corresponding

with *oirthear* (page 420), which is in very general use; but as I have not found it in any of our surviving local names, I will not notice it further.

Deas [dass] means literally the right hand side; old Irish form *des*, corresponding with Lat. *dextra*, Gr. *dexia*, *Sanscr. daksha*; and it is also the word for the south, as the right hand lies towards the south when the face is turned to the east. The word is used in both senses at the present day; and it would be easy to prove by quotations from old Irish authorities, that this was the case in the very earliest ages. It is often written *teas* [tass] of which we have a very good example in Ratass, a parish in Kerry, near Tralee, which took its name from a fort:—*Rath-teas*, southern fort.

This word as forming the names of two territories in Ireland, reminds us of an interesting event in our early history. In the time of Cormac MacArt, monarch of Ireland in the third century, there dwelt at the south side of Tara, a tribe descended from *Fiacha-Suighdhe* [Feeha See], who was brother of Conn of the Hundred Battles, and consequently Cormac's grand-uncle. As they lived south of Tara, they were called *Desi*, southerns, or southern people* (just like *Airtheara*, eastern people—p. 423); and the two baronies of Deese in Meath still retain their name.

Cormac on one occasion sent his son Kellach with a body of warriors to enforce the borumean tribute or cow tax, which Tuathal the Acceptable, king of Ireland, had imposed on Leinster about 150 years

* This is the interpretation of Dr. Todd, Proc. R. I. A., MS. Ser., p. 25; and it is confirmed by Zeuss, Gram. Celt. 57, note.

before, and which the Leinster people scarcely ever paid without compulsion. Kellach returned with the cows; but he exceeded his instructions, and insulted the Leinstermen by bringing also 150 maidens into captivity. Among these there happened to be one who belonged to the *Desi*, and not to the tribute paying tribes of Leinster. At this time the principal man of the *Desi* was Aengus, a powerful chieftain, who had proclaimed himself the defender of his tribe and the avenger of all insults offered to them; and he always carried a celebrated spear which has become inseparably connected with his name, for he was called, and is known in history as, Aengus of the poison-javelin.* This chieftain was the maiden's uncle; and as soon as he heard of the degradation of his kinswoman, he went straight to Tara, where he found her among others of the captives, fetching water for the palace from the well of Nemnach. He returned with her to his own house, repaired again to Tara,† and this time went into the king's presence. Here after an angry altercation, Aengus slew the king's son, Kellach, with one thrust of his terrible spear; and when drawing out the weapon in his fury, he accidentally struck the king's eye with the point and destroyed it; while at the same moment the end of the handle struck the house steward and killed him on the spot. In the confusion that followed Aengus escaped and reached his home in safety.

As it was unlawful for a king with a personal blemish to reign at Tara, Cormac abdicated and retired to a private residence at *Acaill*, or the hill

* Irish, *Aengus Gaei-buaibhtech.*

† Keating assigns a different cause for Aengus's hostility.

of Skreen, in the neighbourhood of Tara, where he spent the remainder of his days. Meantime he began criminal proceedings against the *Desi* to recover damages for the threefold injury; and in a great assembly convened on the hill of Usnagh (in Westmeath), it was decided that the tribe, instead of being free as heretofore, should in future pay tribute to Cormac and his descendants, and acknowledge themselves as vassals for ever. The *Desi* rejected these terms with indignation, and a long feud followed, which ended in the expulsion of the whole tribe from their original home. They wandered for many years through different parts of Leinster and Munster, till at length they settled in the latter province, in a territory given to them by the Munster king, *Olioll Olum*. This district lies in the present county of Waterford; and the two baronies of Decies still preserve the name of the tribe, though they do not include the whole of the ancient territory. It will be observed that the original word *Desi* is plural (meaning people and not territory), and by the addition of the English inflection *s*, the idea of plurality is retained in the present name Decies.*

Deisceart [deskart], a derivative from *deas*, is a term in more general use to designate the south than the original; the latter syllable is cognate with Latin *pars* (for Irish *c* often corresponds to Latin *p*):—*deisceart*, southern part or direction. From this word is derived the name of the two townlands of Deskart in Monaghan, and that of Diskirt in the parish of Ardclinis in Antrim.

* This account has been taken from Dr. Todd's translation of the original in the ancient Book of Fermoy (Proc. R.I.A., MSS. Ser. 25). Another version, differing in some particulars, is given by O'Curry, Lect. II., 326.

Deisiol [desshul] is another derivative from *deas*, and signifies towards the right hand, or southwards. The Celtic people were—and are still—accustomed to turn sunwise, i. e. from left to right, in the performance of various rites, some of them religious, some merely superstitious: and the word *deisiol* was used to designate this way of turning. Toland notices this custom (Celtic Rel. p. 143); and Martin describes it as existing in his day among the Scotic people of the Hebrides (p. 20). In Cormac's Glossary (voce *prull*) the spirit of poetry in the form of "a young man, kingly, radiant," is stated to have met *Senchán Torpeist* (chief poet of Ireland in the time of Guaire Aidhne king of Connaught in the seventh century), and "then he goes sunwise (*dessiul*) round Senchan and his people." Readers of Kenilworth will remember how the old leech made the *deasil* by walking three times in the direction of the sun round the wounded Edward, before beginning his examination of the wound. Even at this day the Irish peasantry when they are burying their dead, walk at least once—sometimes three times—round the grave yard with the coffin from left to right. From left to right is considered lucky; the opposite direction, unlucky. Tempo or Tempo-Deshill in Fermanagh, has been already quoted as deriving its name from this custom; and the word also forms part of Modeshil, the name of a parish in Tipperary; but here it is probably intended to designate simple direction:—*Magh-deisiol*, southern plain.

Tuaith [tooa] means properly the left hand; and as *deas* is applied to the south, so this word is used to signify the north. About eleven miles due north from Ratass (p. 425), there is another parish with the corresponding name of Rattoo:—*Rath-tuaidh*, northern fort. It took its name from a rath; but whether Ratass and Rattoo received their names by comparison one with another, or each with some other rath, I will not undertake to determine.

The word assumes various forms which are exemplified in the following names. There is a place called Kiltoy, one mile from Letterkenny in Donegal, whose name is a corruption of the Irish *Cul-tuaidh*, northern *cool* or back of a hill. Much the same meaning has Tievetooey in the parish of Templecarn in the same county, northern hill-side (*taebh*); Cloontooa in Galway and Mayo, northern meadow. Very often the first *t* is changed to *h* by aspiration, as in Drumhoy in the parish of Aghavea in Fermanagh—*Druim-thuaigh*, northern ridge. And in Cork and Kerry we often find a hard *g* in the end; as in Raheenyhooig near Dingle, *Raithínidhe-thuaig* northern little forts.

Corresponding with *deisceart*, we have *tuaisceart*,—northern part or direction, which enters into the names of Cloontuskert and Clontuskert, already quoted in First Series. (See for ample illustration of this word, Reeves, Eccl. Ant. p. 71.)

CHAPTER XXVI.

VARIOUS QUALITIES AND CIRCUMSTANCES.

DISPUTES about land are of common occurrence in all countries where the population is moderately dense, and where the majority of the people are engaged in agricultural pursuits. In Ireland there have been plenty of such contentions, from the earliest historical times to the present day; and I suppose they will never entirely cease. We have a singular way of recording squabbles of this kind, for the lands themselves often retain names indicating the feuds maintained by the parties who disputed their possession. We see this in plain English in "Controversy," the name of a townland in the parish of Killoscully in Tipperary; and in "Controversy Land" in the north of Queen's County; both of which are translations of some of the Irish terms that follow. It is also seen in "Clamper Land," a place in the parish of Lower Cumber in Derry, whose name means disputed land; for *clampar* is a wrangle or a dispute. The same word, and for a like reason, appears in Clamperpark near Athenry in Galway; in Coolaclamper near Cahir in Tipperary (*cúl*, a hill-back); and in Clampernow in the parish of Clondermot in Derry, "new controversy," i. e. land which had recently been the subject of dispute.

Imreas [immeras] means a controversy or dispute of any kind. There are fields in various parts of the south of Ireland, called Parkanimerish, the field of the controversy—one for instance near Mitchelstown in Cork; Boulanimerish (*ball* a spot) is a place near Killorglin in Kerry; Meenanimerish is situated four miles north east of Killybegs in Donegal (*meen* a mountain meadow); and Ummeras, which signifies simply contention, is the name of a townland in the parish of Lackagh in Kildare. A name very like these is Quintinmanus near Dungannon, the first part of which is *cointin*, controversy:—Manus's controversy or disputed land.

Several other terms are used to express contentions, disputes, and squabbles of various kinds; but it would not be safe to assert that the land bearing the name was itself, in every case, the subject of the dispute. In some at least of the following cases, we may assume that the name merely commemorates a contention; but what it was all about it would now be vain to conjecture. Near Lismore in Waterford, there is a townland with the name of Knockacomortish, the second part of which is a common Irish word, *cómórtus*, signifying emulation, comparison, or contention. Probably the inference to be drawn from this name is, that the little hill (*knock*) was the scene of peasant gatherings in former times, where the young men used to contend with each other in hurling and other athletic games and sports.

There is a townland in the parish of Templeport in Cavan, called Tullynaconspod, the hill of the controversy (*conspoid*). *Trodan* signifies a quarrel; and from this word we have the names of two places in Armagh:—Carricktroddan in the parish of Grange, and Ballytroddan in the parish of Clonfeacle, the rock, and the townland, of the quarrel or strife.

The word *togher* we know generally signifies a causeway; but in a few cases it represents the Irish word *tachar*, a battle or skirmish. The Carntogher mountains in Derry took their name from some particular hill with a carn on its summit: and that from a battle fought round it at some unknown time, all record of which is lost except the old name, which Colgan writes *Carn-tachair*, battle mound. It is not improbable that the carn may have been erected in commemoration of the battle. There is a place near the town of Roscommon now called Cloontogher; but the natives, when speaking Irish call it, not *Cluain-tóchair*, but *Cluain-tachair;* and here we may conclude with certainty that the *cloon* or meadow was the scene of some memorable fight. The village of Ballintogher in Sligo is mentioned three times by the Four Masters; at 1566 they give the name *Baile-an-tóchair*, the town of the causeway, which the present name correctly represents; but on two other occasions they call it *Bel-an-tachair*, the ford-mouth of the battle. It is very unusual for the annalists to contradict themselves in the spelling of a name; and perhaps we may suspect that in these records different places are meant.

The Miskish mountains near Castletown Bear-haven in Cork, took their name from one particular hill, called Slieve Miskish, the mountain of enmity. The word *mioscuis* (the sound of which is exactly represented by Miskish) signifies enmity, spite, or hatred (*miscuis*, odium; Z. 749); and this name would seem to indicate that the possession of the mountain was long and bitterly disputed by two neighbouring clans or proprietors.

Dunglow in Donegal took its name from a fight or contention of some kind. The present village was originally called Cloghanlea (grey *cloghan* or step-ping-stones): the real Dunglow lies a little distance off; but a good many years ago, a fair which was held there was transferred to Cloghanlea, as a more convenient place; and the name followed the fair. The latter syllable of the name—Irish *gleo*—signifies a noisy contention or tumult; and Dunglow means the fort of contention or strife.

There are two townlands in Leitrim called Conray, and one named Conrea in Mayo: in these places the disputes must have terminated in a pacific manner; for the name represents the Irish word *cunnradh*, a covenant or treaty. We have a name of this kind in the county Wicklow, which is very satisfactorily explained in some of our old books, for it originated in a historical event. The following account is taken from an ancient historical tale called "The Battle of Dunbolg."

In A. D. 598, was fought the terrible battle of Dunbolg near Hollywood in Wicklow (see p. 192, *supra*), between Bran Dubh, king of Leinster, and Hugh Mac Ainmire, monarch of Ireland, in which the latter was slain and his army routed. Some time before the battle, Bran Dubh went up on the high grounds with a strong detachment, to reconnoitre the royal army; and on Slieve Nechtan, a mountain overlooking the plain of Kildare, he fell in with a considerable band of Ulidians, who had come from their own province to the assistance of Hugh. Bran Dubh immediately took them prisoners, and ultimately persuaded them to join his own army, and fight against the king of Ireland. Whereupon both parties entered into a solemn treaty of friendship; in commemoration of which they erected a carn on the mountain, and changed its name from Slieve Nechtan to Slieve Cadaigh, the mountain of the covenant. It is a large and conspicuous mountain rising over the left of the road as you go from Hollywood to Donard, about midway between them; and it is still well known by the name, in the slightly altered form of Slive Gadoe; but it is sometimes called Church Mountain, from a little church ruin, with a holy well near it, standing on its summit.

There is a place called Drumalagagh in the county Roscommon, four miles east of Ballinasloe. The word *ealagach* signifies noble—readers of early Irish history will remember that *Inis-ealga*, noble island, was one of the ancient bardic names of Ireland; but in the neighbourhood of the place in question, the people understand the term in the sense of "just"—the ridge of justice or equity. Accordingly the chief residence in the townland is now universally called Mount Equity. Perhaps we may be permitted to conjecture that in old times some celebrated brehon (or judge) lived there; and if this were the case, the present name would be singularly appropriate.

In and near the town of Urlingford in Kilkenny, the people have a very vivid tradition of a great battle fought round the spot where the little river now crosses the road under a bridge at the town. The account states that a king of Ossory led a plundering expedition into Tipperary; and that when returning with immense herds of cattle and spoils of every kind, he was pursued by the vengeful Munster army under a leader named Finn, and overtaken at the ford, where there was then no bridge. Here a dreadful battle was fought; the Ossorians were ultimately driven back, and the Munstermen recovered the spoils; and the slaughter was so great that the stream was impeded in its course by the heaps of slain.

There can be little doubt that this tradition is founded on fact; for it is corroborated by the name of the town, which is called in Irish, *Ath-na-nurlaigh* [Ah-na-noorly], the ford of the slaughters; and the present name is a half translation of this:—Urlingford, i. e. slaughter-ford.

The word *martra*, which literally signifies martyrdom, is borrowed from Greek through Latin; but it has been long naturalised in Irish. It was sometimes applied to any place where there was a massacre or slaughter: and of this there is a very good example in an ancient poem quoted by O'Curry in his Lectures (II. 344: the poem relates that

Ninde, prince of Tirconnell, now Donegal, made a predatory incursion into Connaught, but that he was overtaken and defeated with great slaughter, at the old cataract of Eas-dara or Ballysadare):—

> "Ten hundred heads of the Conallians
> Was their loss ere they reached Eas-dara;
> The defeat of the flood we gave
> To Ninde and his shouting hosts;
> We changed the name of the cold cataract;
> From thenceforth it is called *Martra*."

But the word sometimes means "relics" (of martyrs?); and this may be its meaning in some local names.

There are a good many places scattered here and there through the country, whose names contain this word; and at several of them the people still retain dim traditions of massacres in olden times. One of the best known is Castlemartyr in Cork, whose proper name is Ballynamartra—for so it is written in the Annals of the Four Masters, and in the Depositions of 1652—signifying the town of the martyrdom or slaughter. A townland in the parish of Witter in Down has much the same name,—Ballymarter—which has a similar meaning and origin. Two miles west of Macroom in Cork is Kilnamartry, now the name of a parish, the church of the massacre, or of the relics. The simple word has given names to Martara in Kerry, to Martray in Tyrone, and to Martry in Clare, Meath, and Roscommon; and we may I suppose apply to some or all of these the explanation given of the name *Martra* in the above quotation, that each place was at some former time the scene of a massacre of some kind.

I am greatly puzzled to account for names—of

which there are several—containing the word *anam*, the soul (gen. *anma:* the Latin *anima*, borrowed); such, for instance, as Killananima in the parish of Killanummery in Leitrim, whose original form there can be no question about, for the Four Masters write it *Coill-an-anma*, the wood of the soul; and Killynanum in the parish of Denn in Cavan, which has the same meaning. Some believe that places with such names were bequeathed to some church or monastery for the soul's health of the donor or of some relative; while others again assert that the names originated in ghosts. But this is all conjecture; and I will give a few examples of such names, without being able to throw any further light on the matter.

There is a place called Knockananima in the parish of Killukin, in the north of Roscommon:—*Cnoc-an-anma*, the hill of the soul. Drummonum (*druim*, a hill-ridge) is a townland near the town of Cavan; Annaghananam (*eanach*, a marsh) in the parish of Desertcreat in Tyrone; Ballinanima near Kilfinane in Limerick, and Ballynanama in other places:—*Baile-an-anma*, the town of the soul.

When we meet with local names formed from the words for certain seasons, festivals, or days of the week, we may, I think, fairly conclude that the peasantry were formerly in the habit of meeting at these places at the times indicated, for the celebration of games or festivals. I have already enumerated many names of this kind (1st Ser. Part II. c. VI.), and I will here instance a few more, quite as interesting.

In many parts of Ireland the young people used to meet on Easter Sunday or Easter Monday, and amuse themselves with various sports and pastimes; but the custom has nearly died out. We find these meetings sometimes commemorated by the word *cáisc* [causk], signifying Easter, which is merely the Latin loan-word *pascha*, with the usual change of *p* to *c*, as in *curcur* from *purpura*. Near Abbeydorney in Kerry is a place called Knocknacaska, the hill of Easter. There is a little island in the river Shiven in Galway, two miles above its junction with the Suck, called Island Causk, which has left its name on the adjacent bridge. Laghtcausk, Easter *laght* or sepulchral mound, lies near Elphin in Roscommon; Boolanacausk in the parish of Killeely in Clare, and Mullanacask in the parish of Errigle Trough in Monaghan, the dairy place (*booley*) and the hill summit (*mullach*) of Easter. There is a townland near the village of Street in Westmeath called Cornacausk, and another in Galway, near Athleague, called Cornacask; both signify the round hill of Easter; and the latter has the *alias* name—not quite correct though—of Easterfield.

I suppose the youths and maidens used to retire on Saturdays to the shore of the lonely lake of Coomasaharn—or as it is usually and correctly called by the peasantry, Coomataharn—eight miles east of Cahersiveen in Kerry, and refresh themselves with a merry-making after the week's toil:—*Cúm-a'-tsathairn*, the valley of Saturday. So also with Aghataharn in the parish of Aghamore in the east of Mayo, *Achadh-a'-tsathairn*, Saturday field, the eclipsing *t* of this name being preserved on the Ordnance Maps, as it ought to be.

We find spring and summer often commemorated in this manner; but here we may probably conclude that the places were so called from their warm and sunny aspect, or because the leaves became green or the flowers began to bloom sooner than elsewhere in the neighbourhood. There is a place in the parish of Ardcarn near Lough Key in Roscommon, called Derreenanarry—*Doirín-an-earraigh*, the little oak-grove of spring: *earrach*, spring; Lat. *ver;* Gr. *ear*. Our word for summer is *samhradh* [sowra], corresponding with the German *sommer*, A. Saxon *sumer*, Eng. *summer*. Near Old-castle in Meath, there is a place called Drumsawry, with the *alias* name of summer bank, which is sufficiently correct (*druim*, a hill-ridge); and this was the old name of the village of Summerhill in the same county, as appears from the Down Survey map, and other old documents.

In the north of Ireland the aspirated *m* is usually restored to its primitive sound, as we find in Lurgan-tamry in the parish of Donaghcloney in Down, (*lurgan*, a long low hill); in which also the *s* is eclipsed by *t*, as commonly happens in other names. This change, and the south Munster final *g* sound, are both exemplified in Maughantoorig in the parish of Kilcummin, north east of Killarney, which very well represents the sound of the Irish *Macha-an-tsamhraig*, the farm-yard of summer; and there is a small lake with this same name, one mile south of the village of Killorglin in the same county. It is highly probable that the people used to feed their cattle, and live themselves, in these places during the summer half year, which was formerly a common practice in many parts of Ireland (see "booley" in 1st Ser.); and that this circumstance gave rise to the names.

There are several terms, besides those already enumerated in the former volume, which denote popular meetings and assemblies of various kinds; and nearly all go to form local names, indicating the places where the meetings used to be held. One of these is *drong*, which is still in common use for a crowd, party, or troop; and it was sometimes used to denote a sept or tribe or any particular people—for instance it is often found in this sense in the topographical poem of O'Dugan. It is obviously cognate with the A. Saxon and English word *throng*. There is a conspicuous hill called Drung, rising over Kenmare Bay, on the left of the road from Kenmare to Eyeries; and this is the very form of the name found in the Book of Rights. This is also the name of two townlands and of a little river in Donegal, as well as of a townland in Cavan, which gives its name to a parish. The oblique form, Dring, is the name of some places in the counties of Cavan, Fermanagh, and Longford. Perhaps these places were so called, not from meetings, but from being inhabited by some remarkable or unusually powerful sept, tribe, or people.

The diminutive Drungan is the name of a townland in the parish of Rossinver in Leitrim; and another diminutive, Dringeen, occurs near Cong in Mayo. We have the word in combination in Aghnadrung near Virginia in Cavan, *Achadh-na-ndrong*, the field of the tribes, meetings, or throngs; and in Cornadrung on the western shore of Lough Gowna in Cavan, the round hill of the septs or assemblies.

The Irish borrowed the word *synodus* from the Latin in the early ages of Christianity; and the form it assumed in the Irish language was *senad* or *senud*. One of the raths at Tara was called *Rath-seanaidh*, synod fort, from the fact that three ecclesiastical meetings were held on it at different times, by the three great saints, Patrick, Brendan, and Adamnan. There is an island in Upper Lough

Erne whose ancient name was *senad*, i. e. synod (island), but why it got this name there seems no means of finding out. It was for a long time in possession of the family of MacManus, and hence it is usually called in the annals, Senad MacManus; but this old name has been long obsolete, and the island is now called, on account of its beauty, Belle-Isle.

This island is a classical spot, for it was here the Annals of Ulster were compiled by Cathal Mac Manus, who, besides being a very learned man and a great historian, kept a house of hospitality on the island, where he died of small pox, according to the Four Masters, in A.D. 1498. It was O'Donovan who first identified Belle-Isle with Senad MacManus —a mere unit of his innumerable discoveries in Irish historical topography; and I wish very much that Mr. Porter, the present proprietor, would restore the old name.

The only place in Ireland that I am aware of, now bearing a name derived from this word, is Shanid near Shanagolden in Limerick, remarkable for its fine castle ruins, perched on the summit of a hill. This castle was one of the seats of the earls of Desmond—the powerful Fitzgeralds—and it was from this that one branch of the family adopted the war cry of Shanid-Aboo, which is still the motto of the Knight of Glin; while the Leinster branch, represented by the Duke of Leinster, retains the motto, Crom-aboo, from the castle of Croom in the same county.

The commonages, so generally met with near villages, not only in Ireland, but also in England and Scotland, are designated in this country by several terms, the most usual being *coitchionn* [cut-

teen]: *coitchen*, commune: Z. 179. The simple word gives name to several places in the south, now called Cutteen; to Cottian in Donegal; and to Cautheen in Tipperary. The plural is seen in Cutteanta in Sligo (commons); the adjective form in Cotteenagh, the name of a little island in the Shannon near Clonmacnoise; and we have the word in combination in Ardcotten near Ballysadare in Sligo, the height of the commonage.

I have already noticed the name of Benburb (proud peak—see 1st Ser.), and that of the *Uallach* or "Proud River" at Glengarriff. It is curious that the Irish terms for "proud" or "pride" often enter into local names; but whether the places got such names from their commanding position, like Benburb, or from some great and strong fortress, or from belonging to a powerful family, or from some other circumstance, it is now I fear beyond our power to discover.

The word most generally employed is *uabhar* [oover, oor], which means pride; and it is usually anglicised *over*, *ower*, or *ore*; but it requires care to distinguish the meaning of the last syllable, for it may also mean gold (see p. 341). About the original form and meaning of Donore in Meath, we can have no doubt, for the Four Masters write it *Dun-uabhair* the fort of pride. Even without the help of the annalists we could tell that *ore* here means "pride," and not "gold;" for the peasantry of the neighbourhood still call the place Donover. Other places in various parts of the country are called Donore, Donoure, Doonoor, Doonour, Doonore, and Dunover, all having the same meaning. There is a place in the parish of Killerry in Sligo, called Castleore, whose correct name, *Caislen-an-uabhair*, the castle

of pride, is also preserved by the Four Masters. We have a name corresponding to this in Galway—Cloghanower (*cloch*, a stone or stone castle). Lissanover is the name of a place in the parish of Killeany in Galway, and of another near the village of Bawnboy in Cavan, a name which corresponds with Donore. Regarding Lissanover in Cavan, the people have a tradition that the castle was in former days held by a chieftain named Magauran, who was a merciless tyrant; and they tell that on one occasion he slew a priest on the altar for beginning Mass before he had arrived. This is believed to have given origin to the name—*Lios-an-uabhair*, the fort of pride.

The word *uallach* is exhibited in Cuilleenoolagh, the proud little wood, which is applied to a hill, formerly wooded, and to a townland, in the parish of Dysart in Roscommon. *Diomas* [deemas] is another Irish word for pride. There was a celebrated chieftain of the O'Neills in the time of Elizabeth, who, on account of the lofty haughtiness of his character, was called *Shane-an-diomais*, John the proud. From this word is formed the name of *O'Diomasaigh* or Dempsy, a family deriving their name from a progenitor who was called *Diomasach*, i. e. proud. The word appears in the name of Derdimus, a townland about three miles south west of Kilkenny, *Doire-diomais*, the oak-grove of pride.

There is a townland near Derrynane Abbey in Kerry, called Coad, which has given its name to a mountain and a lake; and another townland of the same name is situated near Corrofin in the county Clare. There is some uncertainty about the original form of this name; but I believe that it is *comhfhod* [coad], a bed or grave. In a passage of the *Dinnsenchus*, translated by Mr. O'Beirne Crowe (Kilk.

Arch. Jour., 1872, p. 150), the dwarf's grave at Tara is called in one place, *cubhad*, and a little farther on, *comhfod*. Mr. Crowe thinks that both are forms of the Latin *cubitus;* but it may be doubted whether this applies to the second at least, for it is an intelligible Irish word as it stands, formed from *comh* (Lat. *con*,) and *fada*, long:—*comhfod*, "as long as" [the human body], a very natural and expressive term for a grave or tomb. Coad in Clare is called *comhad* by the Four Masters (V. p. 1365); but here they have omitted the aspirated *f*, as they appear to have been doubtful of the etymology. There is an old graveyard in the Kerry Coad, with a large stone standing on it, round which the people often pray; and the grave marked by this old monument is probably the original *comhfhod* from which the townland takes its name.

Many of the qualities by which Irish rivers have been designated, have been noticed incidentally in various parts of this and the preceding volume; and I will here add a few more. Rivers often receive names from the manner in which they flow, whether quickly or slowly, straight or curved, &c. There is a considerable stream in Wexford, joining the Bann, three miles west of Gorey, called the Lask, which is a very expressive name, for it is the Irish word *leasc*, lazy.

The word *dian*, strong or vehement, has given name to several rivers. The river Dinin in Kilkenny, which joins the Nore above the city, is subject to sweeping and destructive floods; so that it is most accurately described by its name *Deinín*, a diminutive form signifying vehement or strong river. The little river Dinin joins the Nore at Borris in Carlow; and the Deenagh—the name of which is an

adjective form with the same meaning—runs into the lower lake of Killarney near the town.

The Lingaun river in Kilkenny flows eastward from the slope of Slievenaman; it runs at all times very rapidly, a character which is exactly expressed by the name:—*ling* to spring or leap forward; Lingaun, the leaping or bounding river.

The most common term for the quality of roughness or coarseness is *garbh*, of which the usual anglicised forms are *garriff* and *garve.* The word is often applied to the surface of the ground, as in Parkgarriff and Parkgarve, rough field, which are the names of several places in Cork, Waterford, and Galway. It is also a frequent component in the names of rivers, of which Glashgarriff, Glashagarriff, and Owengarve—rough stream or river—which are the names of many streams in the south and west, may be taken as examples. It is applied to a person—to express probably roughness or rudeness of manner or character—in Toberagarriff, in the parish of Abington in Limerick, *Tobar-a'-ghairbh*, the well of the rough (man).

Other and less usual anglicised forms are seen in Garracloon in Clare, Galway and Mayo, Garryclone and Garrycloyne in Cork and Waterford, all from *Garbh-chluain*, rough meadow, which is the same as Cloongarve in Clare, only with the root words reversed. There are several places in Leinster, Munster, and Connaught, called Garbally, which is generally interpreted short-town (*gearr*, p. 394) but which sometimes means rough town. In one case, however, it has a different interpretation, viz. in Garbally in the parish of Moylough in Galway, where there was in old times a castle of the O'Kellys; in mentioning this castle the Four Masters give the true name,

Garbh-dhoire, rough oak-wood, which should have been anglicised Garderry.

The diminutive Garvoge is often used to designate coarse cloth; and it is also the name of a townland in Kildare, meaning in this case a rugged spot of land.

Carrach is rugged, rough; swarthy or scabby as applied to a person. In local names it is almost always anglicised *carragh* or *corragh*, of which Slievecorragh and Slievecarragh, rugged mountain, the names of several hills, may be taken as examples.

Aimhreidh [avrea] has several shades of meaning, all derivable from what is indicated by the composition of the word:—*aimh* a negative prefix, and *reidh* open or smooth—i. e. not clear or open—uneven, rugged, difficult, intricate, &c. O'Dugan applies the word to the territory of Kinel-connell, now the county of Donegal:—"*Aimhreidh fonn an fini sin*"—rugged is the land of that tribe.—p. 40. Perhaps the best known example of its topographical application is Lackavrea, the name of a remarkable mountain rising over Lough Corrib at its western arm, near the Hen's Castle:—*Leac-aimhreidh*, the rough or complicated flag-stone; for it is formed of quartzose rock which presents a peculiarly rough surface.* This mountain is also called Corcoge (which means a beehive) from its shape.

The word stands by itself in the name of a townland in the barony of Farney in Monaghan, two miles from the village of Shercock in Cavan; this place is now called Ouvry, but in 1655 it was called

* See G. H. Kinahan, Esq., in Sir W. R. Wilde's Lough Corrib—p. 26, note.

Eaverie, which fairly represents the pronunciation of the original.* There is a small island off the coast of Connemara, between Mac Dara's Island and Mason Island, called Avery, another form of *Aimhreidh;* for it consists wholly of rugged rocks which are washed by the waves in storms. A river flows into Blacksod Bay in Mayo, which is called Owenavrea, rough river. And in Tarrea in the parish of Killeenavarra in Galway, near the village of Kinvarra, we have an example of a *t* prefixed under the influence of the article:—*an taimhreidh* the rough land, like Tardree for Ardree (see this in 1st Series).

The word *cruadh* [croo] hard, is sometimes found forming a part of local names, and it is used in all such cases to designate hard surfaced land, a soil difficult to till on account of tough clay, surface rocks, &c. A good example is Cargacroy in the parish of Drumbo in Down, *Cairrge-cruadha*, hard rocks. Mullaghcroy near Castletowndelvin in Westmeath, signifies hard summit; Crooderry near Boyle in Roscommon, hard *derry* or oak-wood, or the hard place of the oak-wood.

No one would ever suspect the origin of the name of the village of Athea in Limerick from its present form; and the inquirer would not be much enlightened even by the popular pronunciation in Irish—*Awthay.* But there is a little old ruined church near the village, whose Irish name removes the difficulty; for the people call it *Thoumpul Awthlay* (the church of Athlea or Athea). Here there is an *l* after the *th*, which, curiously enough, is not inserted in the name of the village itself; and this *l* makes the

* See this name in Shirley's "Barony of Farney."

whole thing quite plain; for according to the southern pronunciation, *Awthlay* is the phonetic representative of *Ath-a'-tsleibhe*, the ford of the mountain, as Ballintlea is reduced from *Baile-an-tsleibhe* (see this in 1st Ser.). The ford stood where the bridge now spans the river Galey; and the mountain from which it was designated is Knockathea, or the hill of Athea, rising over the village.

Between the town of Roscommon and Lough Ree, there is a stream called the Banew. The people have a tradition that the monks of the abbey of Inchcleraun in Lough Ree were in former days in the habit of meeting those of Roscommon at this stream; and from the salutations exchanged between them at meeting and parting, the river got its name: —*beannughadh* [bannooa] i. e. blessing or salutation.

Beannacht—old form *bendacht*—a blessing, is merely the Latin *benedictio*, borrowed in the early ages of Christianity, and softened down by contraction and aspiration; from which again is derived the verb *beannaigh*, to bless, and the verbal noun *beannughadh*, just mentioned. This last is not unfrequently found in place-names; and it is probable that in the greater number of such cases there are local traditions connected with the names, something like that of the river Banew.

In the wild district south east of Cahirsiveen, there is a lonely valley shut in by hills and precipices, called Coomavanniha, a name which exactly conveys the sound of the Irish *Cúm-a'-bheannuighthe*, the valley of the blessing. Glanbannoo, with the same meaning, is the name of a secluded valley and townland near Castledonovan, west of Dunmanway in Cork. A little pool at the western base of Sugar-

loaf mountain near Glengarriff in the same county, is called Toberavanaha, the well of the blessing; but here we may look for the origin of the name in one of the innumerable legends connected with holy wells. There is an ancient and very remarkable stone in the parish of Moore in Roscommon, called Clogherbanny, the blessed or consecrated stone. A name exactly the same as this—except that *cloch*, the common word for a stone, is used instead of *clochar*—is Clobanna, three miles north of Thurles in Tipperary.

But it must be confessed that we have a far greater number of names from cursings than from blessings. The word that is commonly used in forming names of this kind is *mallacht*, signifying a curse; its old form is *maldacht*, which was derived from the Latin *maledictio*, like *bendacht* from *benedictio*. It is hard to know what gave origin to such names. Possibly they may have been the scenes of massacres, or of strife, or of bitter feuds carried on between the neighbouring hostile clans or families. Connected with some of them there are popular traditions, which, if they are worth very little—as many of them undoubtedly are—indicate at least what the people would consider a natural and sufficient explanation of names of this kind. Such is the Kerry legend about the little mountain stream, Owennamallaght, which flows into Tralee Bay near Castlegregory, which, it is to be feared indeed, was invented in late times to account for the name. The people will tell you that on a certain occasion, when St. Patrick was passing through this part of Kerry, he ran short of provisions, and requested the fishermen to give him some of the fish they had just caught in the river. But they refused him in a very churlish

and offensive manner; whereupon he pronounced a curse on the river, and predicted that no fish should be found in it for evermore. And accordingly there is no fish in it—so at least the people say.

I could enumerate more than a dozen names containing this word *mallacht;* but as it is hardly ever corrupted—except that occasionally it loses the final *t*—a few illustrations will be sufficient. There is a small village in Galway, situated on the Owendalulagh river, where it flows from the slopes of Slieve Aughty; it takes its name, Bellanamallaght, from an ancient ford, the Irish name of which was *Bel-atha-na-mallacht*, the ford-mouth of the curses. Ballynamallaght in the north of Tyrone is evidently a corruption of the same Irish name, and was so called from the old ford on the Burn Dennet, which is now spanned by the village bridge. Another name like these is Aghnamallagh near the town of Monaghan, the original form of which was *Ath-na-mallaght*, the ford of the curses. But in Aghnamallaght, three miles north of Roscommon, the first syllable (*agh*) signifies a field.

There is a townland, giving name to a lake, five miles north west of Ballyhaunis in Mayo, called Carrownamallaght, the quarter-land of the maledictions, which, as well indeed as the last name, may have been a bone of contention between two neighbouring rivals. Barnanamallaght (*bearna*, a gap between hills) is a place in the north of Clare, about four miles south east of Ballyvaghan; we have Drummallaght (*drum*, a hill-ridge) near Ballyjamesduff in Cavan; and Cloghnamallaght in the parish of Monamolin in Wexford, corresponds with Clobanna, mentioned at page 448.

It appears difficult to account for the application of the word *sean* [shan], old, to certain natural features; for so far as history or tradition is concerned, one mountain, or river, or valley, cannot be older than another. Yet we have Shanow, Shannow, and Shanowen (old river), all common river names, especially in the south; there are many places called Shandrum (old ridge) and Shanaknock (old hill), the former sometimes made Shandrim, and the latter Shancrock: Shantulla and Shantullig, old *tulach* or hill.

It is probable that *sean* in such names refers to use:—a river was called Shanowen, because the people had been from time immemorial living, fishing, or boating on it; a hill got the name of Shandrum because it was inhabited, cultivated, or grazed, long before any other in the neighbourhood. They use the word very much in this sense in the west and south: thus Shannafreaghoge in the parish of Rahoon in Galway, the old or famous place for *freaghoges*, *hurts*, or whortleberries; Shanavagoon a little south of Castlemartyr in Cork, an odd name, signifying literally "old bacon;" but the real meaning is probably the old place for pigs or bacon.

The following names and many others like them, originated in a similar way:—Shangort, old field, in Galway and Mayo; Shanmoy in Tyrone, old plain; Shanaghy in several counties, old field; all names implying that the places had been longer under cultivation than the surrounding land.

It is easy enough to account for such names as Shanafona in the parish of Duagh in Kerry, old pound;* Shanawillen in Kerry, old mill (*muilenn*);

* In connexion with this name, I may remark that the word *pōna*, a pound, is found in other names, as for instance, Ahafona near Ballybunnion in Kerry, *Ath-a'-phōna*, the ford of the pound.

Shanavoher in Cork, and Shanvoher in Galway, old *bóthar* or road;* Shaneglish in Armagh, old church (*eaglais*); and Shantraud—*Sean-tsráid*, old street or village. For the names merely express the fact that at the time these several structures were so called, they were old as compared with others in the neighbourhood more recently erected; or that they were simply old, without implying any comparison.

This word *sean*, whose old form is *sen*, is cognate with Latin *senex* and Sanscrit *sana*. It is a frequent component of local names; but I do not think it necessary to give any more illustrations of its use, as it is nearly always anglicised *shan*, except where the *s* is eclipsed by *t*, when it becomes *tan*. Bawnatanavoher in Waterford and Tipperary, the *bawn* or green field of the old road—*Bán-a'-tsean-bhóthair;* Carrowntanlis near Tuam, the quarter-land of the old *lis* or fort; Gortatanavally near Inchigeelagh in Cork, and Garryantanvally near Listowel in Kerry, the field and the garden, of the old *bally* or town.

I suppose the word *scáth* [skaw], a shadow, which is occasionally found in names, was locally used in its natural and obvious sense, to designate spots shadowed by overhanging cliffs, or by a thick growth of tall leafy trees. There is a small river four miles south east of Newcastle in Limerick, called Owenskaw, the river of the shadow; Skaw itself, i. e. shadow, is the name of a townland near Ballymore in Westmeath; and there is a place near Templemore in Tipperary called Barnalascaw, the gap of the half shadow (*la* for *leath*, half), so called probably because the gap runs in such a direction that when the sun

* Remark in several of these names, the insertion of a euphonic vowel sound:—see page 3, *supra*.

shines, one side is thrown into shadow. In the parish of Molahiffe in Kerry, near the Farranfore station of the railway to Killarney, there is a place called Skahies, which is the anglicised form of the plural *Scátha*, shades or shadows.

Land which was held free of rent or duty of any kind was sometimes designated by the word *saer*, free. There are two townlands, one near Killashandra in Cavan, the other in the parish of Macosquin near Coleraine, called Farranseer, free land (*fearann*); and another south of Ballyshannon, called Clontyseer, shortened from *Cluainte-saera*, free *cloons* or meadows. *Saeirse* [seersha], among other meanings, signifies a freehold, whence we have Seersha near Newmarket on Fergus in Clare, and Seersha north west of Killarney; which again is shortened to Serse in Armagh, not far from Newry; and modified to Seershin, three miles from the village of Barna, a little west of Galway.

On the west side of the Shannon, in that part of the county Roscommon extending between Drumsna and Lanesboro, there were anciently three districts, called respectively *Cinel Dobhtha*, *Tir Briuin na Sinna*, and *Corca Eachlann;* these, both in the annals, and among the people, were often called simply "*Na Tuatha*" [na-tooha] i. e. the *Tuathas* or territories, and though their individual names have perished, this last still survives. On the road from Rooskey to Drumsna, where it crosses an arm of the Shannon between two lakes, there was an ancient weir, very much celebrated, called *Caradh-na-dtuath* [Cara-na-doo], the *caradh* or weir of the (three) *tuaths* or districts. A bridge now spans the stream on the site of the weir, and it is well known by the name of Caranadoe Bridge.

In the county of Longford they tell a story of the origin of Lough Gowna, which forms the head of the chain of lakes traversed by the river Erne; this legend also accounts for the eruption of Lough Oughter and Lough Erne. There is a well in the townland of Rathbrackan, one mile from Granard, out of which a stream runs into Lough Gowna; from this well a magical calf sallied forth, once on a time, and the water of the well rushed after him as far as the sea at Ballyshannon, expanding in its course, first into Lough Gowna, and afterwards into the two Loughs Erne, in memory of which the well is still called Tobor Gowna, and the lake, Lough Gowna, the well and the lake of the calf.

Among the many circumstances taken advantage of by the observant Irish peasantry, to designate places, one of the most striking and poetical is solitude or loneliness. There is a district east of Kells in Meath, which, even in the earliest period of our history, was noted for its solitariness; so that persons going to reside there were considered to have retired altogether from the view of the world. When the celebrated Lewy of the Long Arms, who according to ancient tradition, was skilled in all the arts and sciences, came to reside at the court of Tara, the artists and learned men who had been up to that time in the king's service, felt themselves so overshadowed by the brilliant talents of the new professor, that they retired in shame from Tara, and betook themselves to this very spot—the *Diamhraibh* or solitudes of Bregia, as it is called in the old narrative (one of the legends in the Dinnseanchus), where they remained in obscurity ever after. The word *diamhar*, of which *diamhraibh* is a plural form, is still used in the spoken language in the sense of

mysterious, hidden, or obscure; and the district in question still retains the old name, in the slightly modified form of Diamor. In O'Clery's Calendar, a place is mentioned called *Cluain-diamhair*, solitary meadow.

The allusion to the professors who retired from Tara, occurs in the legendary history of the name of Turvey, a place situated on an inlet of the sea in the north of the county Dublin, two miles from Lusk. The old writer states that *Tuirbhi* [Turvey], the father of the great artist, Gobban Saer, who lived in the seventh century, had his residence on this strand; and that every evening after ceasing from his work, he used to throw his hatchet (as Lén of the white teeth used to throw his anvil: p. 197, *supra*) from an eminence, which was afterwards called *Tulach-an-bhiail* or the hill of the hatchet, to the farthest point reached by the tide. Hence the place was called *Traigh-Tuirbhi*, Turvey's strand, which is now shortened to Turvey. The narrative adds that it was not known to what people he belonged, unless he was one of the dark-complexioned race who fled from Tara to the solitudes of Bregia (see Petrie, R. Towers, p. 386).

We have still another word,—*uaigneas* [oognas], to express the same idea. In the parish of Tuosist in Kerry, on the left of the road from Kenmare to Eyeries, there is a hill called Knockanouganish, the hill of solitude; and we have the adjective form exhibited in Glenoognagh in the parish of Lismullen in Meath, lonely glen.

I believe I may safely assert that there is not a place-name in any part of the world, that could not be matched in Ireland. For our names are scattered broadcast in such infinite profusion and variety, that

they seem to have almost exhausted human invention. It would be easy to bring together a collection of odd and eccentric local designations, unusual in formation or strange in origin, from every part of the world, and then to produce from the abundance of our local nomenclature, names corresponding to them all. And after this, I think I could find many names in my own country that it would be hard to match anywhere else. Scotland would be a dangerous competitor, but even here I should feel very confident as to the result of the comparison; and I should have no fear at all about the rest of the world.

Will any great topographer or learned etymologist find me such a river name as "The Morning Star" anywhere outside Ireland? We have a river of this name, a fine stream rising in the Galty mountains, flowing through the town of Bruff in Limerick, and joining the Maigue below Bruree. The old name of this river, as we find it in various ancient authorities, was *Samhair* or *Samer;* and this is also well known as the ancient name of the river Erne, from which again the little island of Inis-Samer (now called Fish Island) near the Salmon-leap at Ballyshannon—an island connected with some of our oldest legends—took its name.

It is to be observed that Samer was in former times used also as a woman's name; but what the radical meaning of the word may be, I cannot venture to conjecture. As a river name, Pictet (Origines Indo-Europiennes) connects it with the old names of several rivers on the continent of Europe, and with the Persian *shamar*, a river:—for example the Samur, flowing from the Caucasus into the Caspian; the Samara, flowing into the Sea of Azov; and the ancient Celtic name, Samara, of a river in Belgium

It must be confessed that our "Morning Star" came by its fine name through a mistake, or in plain words by a false translation; but it is a mistake turned to such happy account that one would never wish to correct it:—for in the colloquial Irish of the people, the old name *Samhair* was corrupted to *Camhair;* and as this word signifies the first appearance of day light, or the break of day, so they translated it into "Morning Star."

There is a townland called Glenastar near Newcastle in Limerick; but this name has nothing to do with the stars. The correct anglicised form, divided etymologically, would be Glen-as-daar. Just where the river that traverses the glen flows by the townland, it falls over a rock into an *unfathomable* pool, forming a fine cascade; this is the *as* (Irish *eas*, a waterfall); and as the name of the river is the Daar, the glen was called *Gleann-easa-Dáire*, the glen of the cataract of the Daar.

When Washington Irving wrote his Legend of Sleepy Hollow, he imagined no doubt, that such a name was not to be found in any part of the world except on the banks of the Hudson—if indeed he did not invent it to suit his story, which I strongly suspect he did. But if he had only come over to Ireland, and travelled through certain parts of the county Cork, he would find that we had been beforehand with him; for as he passed near the little town of Inishannon, he could see from the railway carriage window, close to the line, a gentleman's residence and a townland, called Coolcullata, which corresponds exactly in meaning with his sleepy hollow. The first syllable is the Irish *cúil*, a recess or corner; while *codlata* [cullata] is a genitive form of *codla* [culla], sleep; and these two words put

together, and spelled in English letters in accordance with the sound, make Coolcullata, the recess of sleep, or sleepy hollow. Moreover, the county Cork can boast of another drowsy spot; for there is a hill at the western extremity of the Nagles Mountains, near the village of Killawillin, called Knockacullata, the hill of sleep.

But why it is that Coolcullata was so called; whether it was from the solitude of the spot; or from its drowsy accompaniments—its murmuring waters, its rustling leaves, and its humming bees, as Irving describes his somniferous valley; or from the sleepy character of the natives—but indeed I do not believe this, for the Corkonians are as wide-awake a people as can be found in any part of Ireland; whether any or all or none of these, gave name to the place, I am sorry to say I can give no satisfactory account. Perhaps Coolcullata was another Castle of Indolence,

> "A pleasing land of drowsy head,
> Of dreams that wave before the half-shut eye,"

Where

> "Was nought around but images of rest;
> Sleep-soothing groves, and quiet lawns between;
> And flowery beds that slumbrous influence kest,
> From poppies breathed; and beds of pleasant green."

But however we may be at fault in our attempts to account for the name, there it stands as a fact; and if I am right in believing that Washington Irving invented the American name, I can claim one superiority for our Coolcullata over his Sleepy Hollow, that his name "is a fiction, but mine is reality."

INDEX OF NAMES.

(N.B.—Many names that do not occur in the body of the present work or in the First Series are explained in this index).

INDEX OF ROOT WORDS.

WITH PRONUNCIATION, MEANING, AND REFERENCE.

Comhfhod [coad], a bed or grave, 442.
Comórtus, contention, 431.
Conadh [conna], fire-wood, 331.
Cong, a narrow strait, 385.
Connachtach, a Connaughtman, 123.
Coirce [curkia], oats, 303.
Coire [curry], a caldron, 408.
Copóg, a dock-leaf, 327.
Creamh [crav], wild garlic, 327.
Crioch [cree], a boundary, 206.
Criathar [crihar], a sieve, 368.
Crith [crih], to shake, 367.
Cro, a hut, 220.
Croiceann [cruckan], a hide, 115.
Crom, sloping, 398.
Crompan, a little sea-inlet, 255.
Crón, a colour, 363.
Crón, a round hollow, 274.
Cruadh [croo], hard, 446.
Cruimhther [cruffer], a priest, 91.
Cruithneacht [crinnaght], wheat, 302.
Cu, a hound, 153.
Cuas, a cove, 256.
Cubhra [coora], sweet scented, 70.
Cuilc, cuilceach [quilk, quilka], a reed, 317.
Cuinneog [cunnyoge], a churn, 186.
Cunnradh [cunraw], a treaty, 432.
Curadh [curra], a knight, 102.

D as a termination, 14.
Dabhach [davagh], a vat, 410.
Dairt [dart], a heifer, 294.
Dall, blind, 159.
Dán, a dim. termination, 35.
Dealg [dallig], a thorn, 334.
Dearg [darrig], red, 271.
Deas [dass], south, 425.
Deisceart [deskart], south, 427.
Diamhar [deevar], mysterious 453.
Deisiol [deshul], southwards, 428.
Dian [deean], strong, 443.
Diomas [deemas], pride, 442.
Dobhar [dovar], water, 379.
Donn, brown, 273.
Drean [dran], a wren, 286, 287.
Dreas [drass], a bramble, 334.
Dreolán [drolaun], a wren, 287.
Drong, a crowd, 439.
Drui [dree], a druid, 96.
Duairc [dooark], surly, 72.
Dubh [duv], black, 260.
Duibhén [duvean], a cormorant, 292.
Duille [dullia], a leaf of a tree, 10.
Duilleabhar [dillure], foliage, 10.
Dumhach [doovagh], a sand-mound, 364.
Dúr [door], water, 380.

Eadar [adder], between, 417.
Eag, death, 88.
Ealagach, noble, just, 433.
Earball, a tail, 402,
Earrach, spring, 438.
Easgan, an eel, 296.
Easpog [aspug], a bishop, 90.
Eibhis [evish], coarse pasture, 320.
Eigeas [aigas], a poet, 111.
Elestar, a flagger, 316.
En, ene, a diminutive termination, 150.
Eorna [ōrna], barley, 304.

Fachair [faher], a shelf in a cliff, 363.
Fada, long, 393.
Faithnidh [fahnee], a wart, 82.
Fál [fawl], a hedge, 211.
Fán [fawn], a slope, 400.
Feadh [fa], a rush, 315.

Fearann [farran], land, 359.
Féith [fea], a wet trench, 315.
Felestar, a flagger, 316.
Fér [fair], grass, 319.
Figheadoir [feedore], a weaver, 116.
Finn, white, 264.
Forgnaidh [forgny], a building, 204.
Fliuch [flugh], wet, 388.
Fód [fode], a sod, 360.
Fofannán, a thistle, 314.
Foraois [furreesh], a forest, 58.
Fothannan [fohanan], a thistle, 314.
Fothar [fohar], a forest, 330.
Fuar, cold, 246.

Ga, a dart, 175.
Gaeth [gee], wind, 240.
Gaeth, a sea-inlet, 258.
Gadaighe [gaddy], a thief, 109.
Gág [gaug], a cleft, 405.
Gaineamh [ganniv], sand, 354.
Gairbhéul [gravale], gravel, 354.
Galloglach, a heavy-armed foot soldier, 105.
Gamh [gauv], winter, storm, 242.
Gán, a dim. termination, 31.
Gar, near, 419.
Garbh [garrav], rough, 444.
Geal [gal], white, 270.
Gealbhún [galloon], a sparrow, 288.
Geallóg [galloge], a white-bellied eel, 296.
Gearr [gar], short, 393, 394.
Gearr-fhiadh [girree], a hare, 293.
Giolc [gilk; *g* hard], a reed, broom, 316.
Giumhas [guse], fir, 337.
Glas, green, 274.
Glasóg, a wagtail, 287.
Gleo [glo], strife, 432.
Gleoir [glore], brightness, 68.
Glór [glore], a voice, 65.
Glórach, voiceful, prattling, 65.
Gluair [gloor], purity, 69.
Goilin [goleen], a narrow little sea-inlet, 256.
Gorm, blue, 275.
Graineóg [granoge], a hedgehog, 292.
Gréach, a mountain flat, 369.
Grean [gran], gravel, 353.
Grian [greean], the sun, 233.
Gruag, hair, long grass, 320.
Gual [goole], coal, charcoal, 200.
Gus, strength, 151.

Iarla [eerla], an earl, 57.
Iarann [eeran], iron, 348.
Ic [eek], to heal, 76.
Im, butter, 203.
Imreas, a dispute, 430.
In [een], a dim termination, 30.
Ineasclann [inisclan], a strong stream, 382.
Inneoin [innone], an anvil, 197.
Iochdar [eeter], lower, 415.
Ionga [inga], a nail, 402.
Iorrus [irrus], a peninsula, 207.
Iseal [eeshal], low, 416.

Lach, a termination, 5.
Laech [lay] a champion, 102.
Laighneach [lynagh], a Leinster man, 122.
Lár, middle, 418.
Lathach [lahagh], a slough, 365.
Leamh [lav], marsh mallows, 326.
Leamhnacht [lewnaght], new milk, 201.
Leana, a wet meadow, 378.
Leasc [lask], lazy, 443.
Leathair [laher], leather, 115.
Leathan [lahan], broad, 394.
Leigheas [lease], a cure, 88.
Leithead [lehed] breadth, 394.
Lestar, a vessel, 186.
Liagh [leea], a physician, 76.
Liath [leea], grey, 277.

Lin [leen], flax, 309.
Lin [leen], to fill, 383.
Ling, to spring, 444.
Linn, a pond, 384.
Lobhar [lower], a leper, 79.
Luachair [looghar], a rush, 315.
Luan, a lamb, 293.
Lubhghort [looart], an herb garden, 317.
Lúch, a mouse, 286.
Luibh [luv, liv], an herb, 317.

Maer [mare] a steward, 112.
Mainister [mannister], a monastery, 226.
Mallacht, a curse, 448.
Manach, a monk, 93.
Mart, a bullock, 296.
Martra, martyrdom, 434.
Meacan [mackan], a parsnip, 329.
Meadar [mether], a kind of vessel, 186.
Meadhon [maan], middle, 417.
Meann, meannan [man, mannawn], a kid, 294.
Meantan [mantan], a snipe, 289.
Mearacán, foxglove, 312.
Mías [meece], a dish, 192.
Min [meen], fine or smooth, small, 376, 393.
Míol [meel], a beast of any kind, 284.
Míoltog [meeltoge], a midge, 284.
Miscuis [miscush], enmity, spite, 432.
Mogul, a cluster, 72.
Moinfheur [mōnear], a meadow, 319.
Molt, a wether, 294.
Mong, hair, long coarse grass, 321.
Mór [more], great, 390.
Múch [mooh], smoke, 369.
Múchadh [mooha], to smother.
Múchán [moohawn], a morass
Muimhneach [mweenagh], a Munsterman, 123.
Muing, a sedgy place, 370.
Muir [mur], the sea, 248.

Nach, a termination, 6.
Nan, a dim. termination, 33.
Naosga [neasga], a snipe, 288.
Nat, a dim. termination, 27.
Ne, a dim. termination, 25.
Neanta [nanta], a nettle, 314.

Odhar [ower], dark brown, 278.
Og [oge], a dim. termination, 28.
Oir [ur], east, 420.
Oirthear [urher], east, 420, 421, 422.
Oisire [ishera], an oyster, 283.
Or [ore], gold, 341.
Ord, order, ecclesiastical rank, 95.

Pairc [park], a field, 59.
Palas, pailis, a fort, a fairy palace, 226.
Pearsan, a parish priest, a parson, 56.
Pill, a small inlet, 255.
Pis [pish], pease, 305.
Plaigh [plaw], a plague, 77.
Pona, a pound, 450, note.
Ponaire [pōnara], a bean, 305.
Port, a bank, a landing place, a fortress, 224.
Potaire [puttera], a potter, 115.

Rach, a termination, 7.
Raithneach [rah'ina], ferns, 312.
Re, a termination, 11.
Reamhar [rower, rawer], fat, thick, 395.
Ri, righ [ree], a king, 98.
Riabhach [reeagh], grey, 276.
Ridire [riddera], a knight, 101.
Rioghna [reena], a queen, 100.

Rnach, a compound termination, 16.
Ród [road], a road, 213.
Rod, ruide [rud, ruddia], iron scum, 350.
Romhánach [rovanagh], a Roman, 122.
Ruadh, [rua], red, 271.
Rubha [roo], the plant rue, 323.
Ruibh [riv], sulphur, 351.

Saeirse [seersha], a freehold, 452.
Saer [sair], free, 452.
Sagart, a priest, 91.
Saighed [syed], an arrow, a dart, 174.
Sáil, sáile [saul, saulia], salt water, brine, 249.
Sail, saileach, saileóg [saul, saulia, saulioge], a sallow tree, 336.
Salann, salt, 352.
Samhadh [sowa], sorrel, 322.
Samhradh [sowra], summer, 438.
Samhthrusc [sauvrusk], leprosy, 79.
Sassonach, an Englishman, 121.
Satharn [saharn], Saturday, 437.
Scál [scaul], a hero, 103.
Scáth [skaw], a shadow, 451.
Sceamh [scav], wall fern, 325.
Sciath [skeea], a shield, 177.
Scolb, a *scollop*, 198.
Scológ [skologe], a small farmer, 112.
Scoth [skoh], a flower, 309.
Scráth [scraw], a grassy boggy surface-sod, 362.
Scudal [skuddal], a fishing-net, 194.
Scúmhal [skool], a steep, 363.
Seach [shagh], a termination, 9.
Seagal [shaggal], rye, 305.
Seamar, seamróg [shammer, shamroge], a shamrock, 53.
Sean [shan], old, 450.
Seangan [shangaun], a pismire, 284.
Searbh [sharrav], bitter, 322.
Searbhán, searbhóg [sharvaun, sharvoge], dandelion, 322.
Séd [shade], a cow, a jewel, 355.
Séid [shade], to blow, 241.
Seideán [shedawn], a breeze, a gust, 59.
Seindile [shindilla], a beetle, 197.
Senad, a synod, 439.
Sian [sheean], foxglove, 311.
Sibhín [shiveen], a rush, 315.
Sín [sheen], a storm, 243.
Slabhra [sloura, slavra], a chain, 204.
Slaed [slade], a slide-car, 174.
Slán [slaun], health, 83.
Slin, a slate, 353.
Slis [slish], a beetle, 196.
Slog [slug], to swallow, 378.
Sméar, a blackberry, 305.
Smut, a stock or trunk, 322.
Sneacht [snaght], snow, 244.
Sonnach, a mound or rampart, 215.
Sórn, a kiln, 222.
Spág [spaug], a long ugly foot, 161.
Spideóg [spiddoge], a robin redbreast, 287.
Spíonán [speenaun], a gooseberry bush, 305.
Spor [spur], a spur, 60.
Srae [sray], a mill race, 216.
Srath [srah], a holm or river-meadow, 375.
Stáca [stawka], a stake, 58.
Snáthad [snawhad], a needle, 204.
Súdaire [soodera], a tanner, 114.
Súil [sool], the eye, 87.

Tach, a termination, 8.
Tachar, a fight, 431.
Talamh [tallav], land, 359.
Tamh [tauv], a plague, 76.

THE END.

OTHER WORKS BY DR. JOYCE.

The Origin and History of Irish Names of Places.

(FIRST SERIES).

Third Edition, 592 pages. Price 7s. 6d.

CONTENTS.

PART I.

THE IRISH LOCAL NAME SYSTEM.

Chapter I.—How the Meanings have been ascertained. Chapter II.—Systematic Changes. Chapter III.—Corruptions. Chapter IV.—False Etymologies. Chapter V.—The Antiquity of Irish Local Names.

PART II.

NAMES OF HISTORICAL AND LEGENDARY ORIGIN.

Chapter I.—Historical Events. Chapter II.—Historical Personages. Chapter III.—Early Irish Saints. Chapter IV.—Legends. Chapter V.—Fairies, Demons, Goblins, and Ghosts. Chapter VI. —Customs, Amusements, and Occupations. Chapter VII.—Agriculture and Pasturage. Chapter VIII.—Subdivisions and Measures of Land. Chapter IX.—Numerical Combinations.

PART III.

NAMES COMMEMORATING ARTIFICIAL STRUCTURES.

Chapter I.—Habitations and Fortresses. Chapter II.—Ecclesiastical Edifices. Chapter III.—Monuments, Graves, and Cemeteries. Chapter IV.—Towns and Villages. Chapter V.—Fords, Weirs, and Bridges. Chapter VI.—Roads and Causeways. Chapter VII. —Mills and Kilns.

PART IV.

NAMES DESCRIPTIVE OF PHYSICAL FEATURES.

Chapter I.—Mountains, Hills, and Rocks. Chapter II.—Plains, Valleys, Hollows, and Caves. Chapter III.—Islands, Peninsulas, and Strands. Chapter IV.—Water, Lakes, and Springs. Chapter V.—Rivers, Streamlets, and Waterfalls. Chapter VI.—Marshes and Bogs. Chapter VII.—Animals. Chapter VIII.—Plants. Chapter IX.—Shape and Position.

INDEX OF NAMES. INDEX OF ROOT-WORDS.

OPINIONS OF THE PRESS.

MR. JOYCE'S work reminds us that there are two kinds of popular writers. The one knows barely enough to enable him to write his book; he has no surplus of knowledge. The other is the man of extensive scholarship, who makes clear the more abstruse parts of his knowledge for the benefit of the less learned. His work, though sometimes heavy, is always accurate. Mr. Joyce belongs to this latter class; but in his case, notwithstanding the difficulties of his subject, his arrangement is so admirable, and his explanations are so lucid, that his book never becomes dull. It will be studied with satisfaction by those who know Ireland, and may be read with interest even by those who have never seen her green hills and pleasant meadows.—*The Athenæum.*

Mr. Joyce is in everything a member of the rational school. His whole method is scientific; there is no guess work about him. To work out the local nomenclature of any country, a man must have a good stock alike of sound scholarship and of sound sense; and Mr. Joyce seems to have no lack of either. . . . . . Mr. Joyce goes most thoroughly through the various classes of names, and the various kinds of objects, persons, and events, after which places are called. . . . . We can heartily recommend Mr. Joyce's book as interesting and instructive to all who care for the study of language and nomenclature, whether they boast of any special Irish scholarship or not.—*The Saturday Review.*

Learned and curious.—*The Daily News.*

If any one wishes to have a notion how many pitfalls beset the path of the topographical etymologist, and what an amount of collateral knowledge and of curious criticism is requisite to avoid them, he cannot do better than study this book of Dr Joyce's, which, if we mistake not, will make an era in this branch of antiquarianism . . . . . . These specimens will give our readers an idea of what an instructive and entertaining commentary Dr. Joyce's book furnishes on the history and geography of Ireland.—*The Scotsman.*

The book is full of interest, and is a real contribution to Irish, as also to Scottish, topographical nomenclature.—*The North British Review.*

A work which will be welcomed by all students of Irish history and antiquities. Mr. Joyce has brought to his interesting search the highest qualifications, combined with unusual industry and indefatigable perseverance, and the result is a volume of the highest value, whether estimated from an historical, philological, or antiquarian point of view. The style is clear and fresh, and the subject in Mr. Joyce's hands never becomes dry or uninteresting.—*Public Opinion.*

No work of its size yet published furnishes so much sound and interesting information about the passed-away things of Ireland.—*The Dublin University Magazine.*

We can recommend the book to everybody. It is a learned yet popular history, a series of separate yet skilfully combined stories, and the by-ways of many an ancient narrative are here lighted up and illumined by the geniality and sympathy of an earnest student and an accurate scholar.—*The Freeman's Journal.*

Dr. Joyce devotes a chapter to this subject ("Fairies, Demons, Goblins, and Ghosts"). It is one of the most agreeable pieces of reading that has fallen in our way for many a day. The extent of fairy mythology in Ireland, the names it has given to townland and borough, to mountain peak and way-side well, are all most learnedly sought out from stores of our ancient MSS., and are very graphically narrated.—*The Nation.*

2.

Irish Local Names Explained.

Cloth, Price 2s. 0d.

In this little book the original Irish forms and the meanings of about 2,500 of the principal local names in Ireland are given. A large number of these occur many times in various parts of the country; so that in reality the names of five or six thousand different places are explained. The pronunciation of all the principal Irish words is given as they occur.

3.

Ancient Irish Music:

Comprising one hundred Irish airs not before published; many old popular songs, and several new songs.

Large paper copy, cloth, 6s. 6d.; small paper copy, wrapper, 4s.

4.

HOW TO PREPARE FOR CIVIL SERVICE COMPETITION UNDER THE NEW REGULATIONS,

Containing full directions as to the proper books to study and how to study them. This book will enable any industrious student to prepare for examination without the aid of a teacher. It contains, besides, the most recent Regulations, several sets of the Questions given at the Open Examinations, the Staff and Salaries of the Open Offices, and the Programmes, Staff and Salaries of the Offices not Open. A complete Guide to the Civil Service.

Second Edition. Price 3s. 6d.

"It is impossible to imagine a more excellent work than 'How to Prepare for Civil Service Competition.'"—*Civilian.*

5.

A HANDBOOK OF SCHOOL MANAGEMENT AND METHODS OF TEACHING.

Fourth Edition (17th Thousand), 3s.